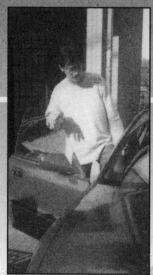

Konomi, Takeshi: Right-handed
Height: 180 cm
Blood type: O
Born: 6/26

Favorite Brands:
Shoes: Fila (Mark Philippoussis Mid)
Racket: Bridgestone (Dynabeam Grandea)

Best Move:
Jump Smash

Favorite Food:
Sashimi, crab, seafood nabe, eel, tangerines, etc.

Hobbies:
Hawaiian music, going to the gym, karaoke

(Taken from *Sadaharu Inui's Secret Data Note No. 101*)

About Takeshi Konomi

Takeshi Konomi exploded onto the manga scene with the incredible **THE PRINCE OF TENNIS**. His refined art style and sleek character designs proved popular with **Weekly Shonen Jump** readers, and **THE PRINCE OF TENNIS** became the No. 1 sports manga in Japan almost overnight. Its cast of fascinating male tennis players attracted legions of female readers, even though it was originally intended to be a boys' comic. The manga continues to be a success in Japan. A hit anime series was created, as well as several video games and mountains of merchandise.

THE PRINCE OF TENNIS
VOL. 7
The SHONEN JUMP Graphic Novel

STORY AND ART BY
TAKESHI KONOMI

English Adaptation/Gerard Jones
Translation/Joe Yamazaki
Touch-up Art & Lettering/Andy Ristaino
Cover & Interior Design/Terry Bennett
Editor/Michelle Pangilinan

Managing Editor/Elizabeth Kawasaki
Director of Production/Noboru Watanabe
Vice President of Publishing/Alvin Lu
Vice President & Editor in Chief//Yumi Hoashi
Sr. Director of Acquisitions/Rika Inouye
Vice President of Sales & Marketing/Liza Coppola
Publisher/Hyoe Narita

Printed in the U.S.A.

Published by VIZ, LLC
P.O. Box 77010
San Francisco, CA 94107

SHONEN JUMP Graphic Novel Edition
10 9 8 7 6 5 4 3 2 1
First printing, April 2005

www.viz.com

PARENTAL ADVISORY
THE PRINCE OF TENNIS is rated A for All Ages. It is recommended for any age group.

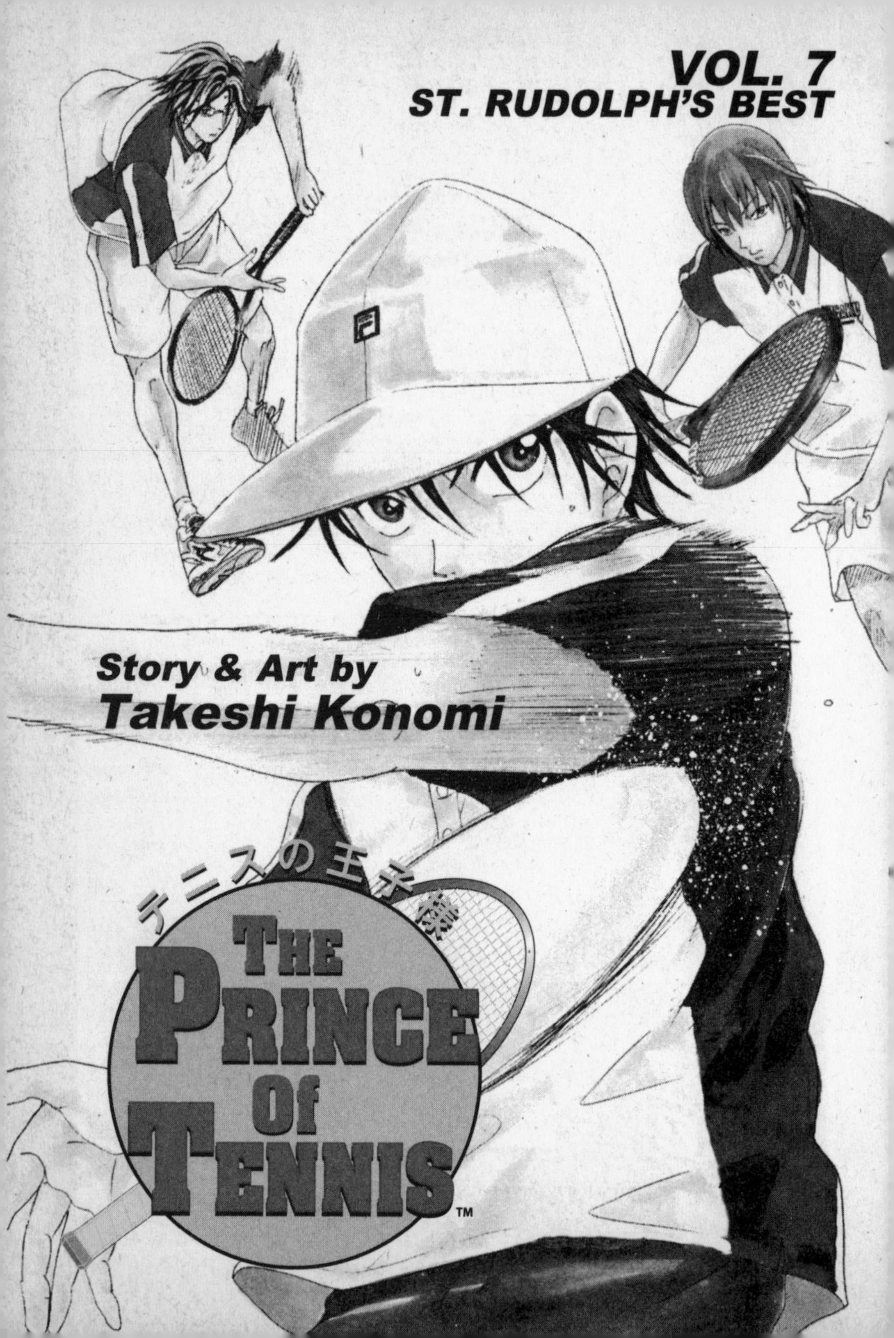
VOL. 7
ST. RUDOLPH'S BEST
Story & Art by
Takeshi Konomi
THE PRINCE of TENNIS™

THE PRINCE OF TENNIS

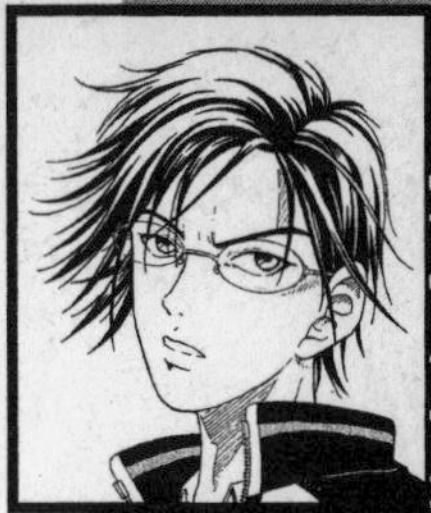

Kunimitsu Tezuka

Seishun Academy Tennis Team Captain (9th Grade)

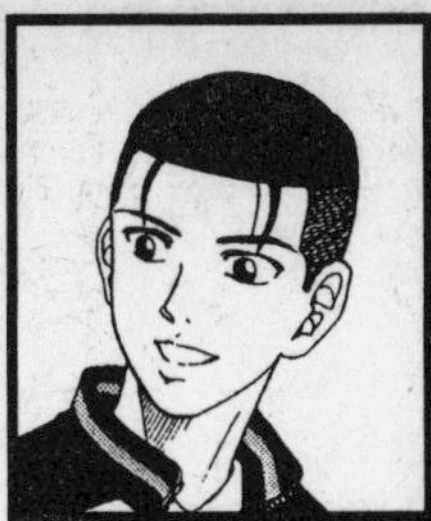

Shuichiro Oishi

Seishun Academy Tennis Team Alternate Captain (9th Grade)

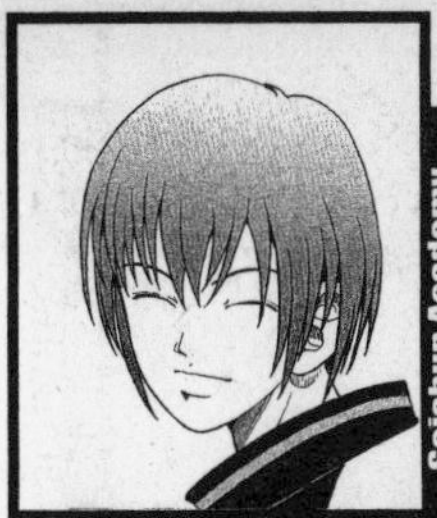

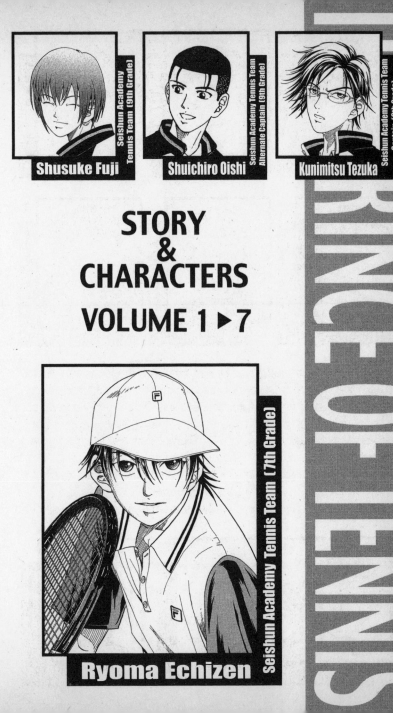

Shusuke Fuji

Seishun Academy Tennis Team (9th Grade)

STORY & CHARACTERS

VOLUME 1 ▶ 7

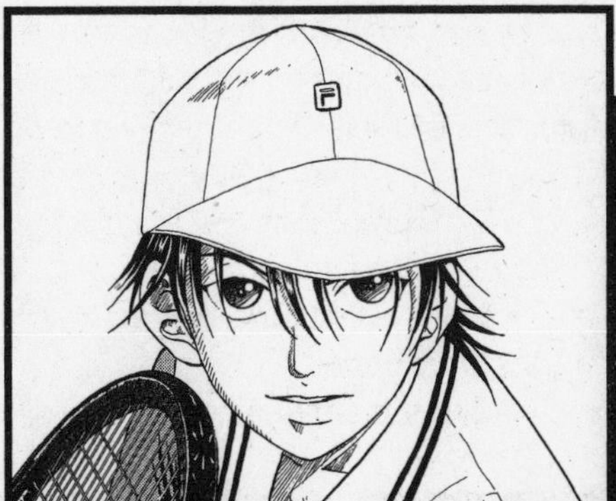

Ryoma Echizen

Seishun Academy Tennis Team (7th Grade)

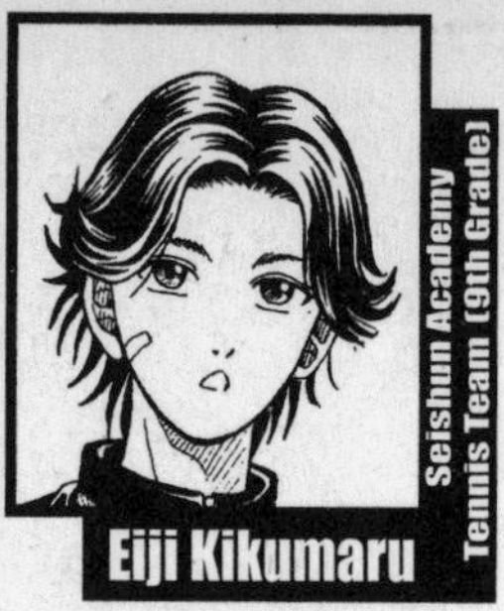
Eiji Kikumaru
Seishun Academy Tennis Team (9th Grade)

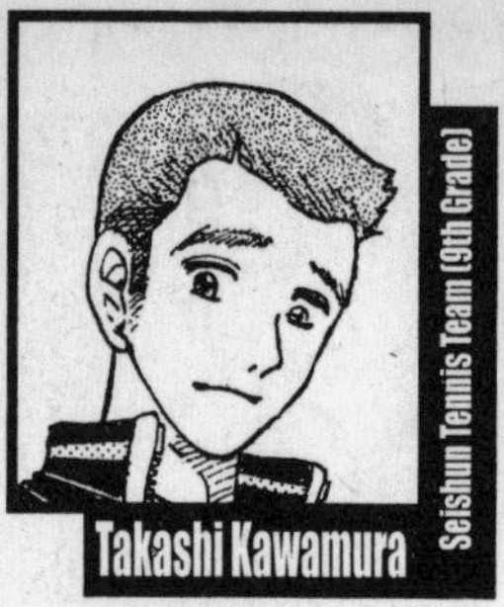
Takashi Kawamura
Seishun Tennis Team (9th Grade)

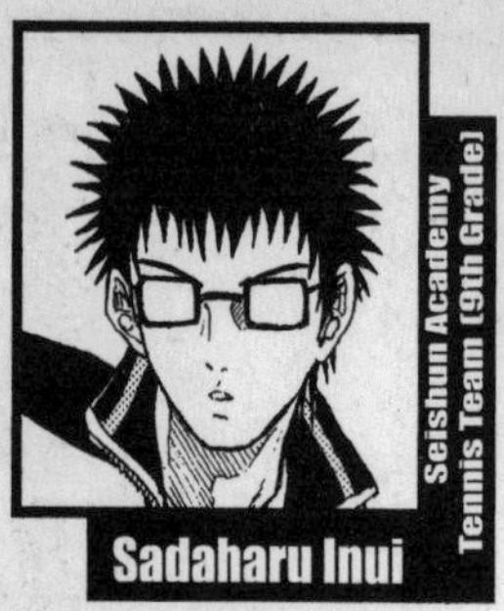
Sadaharu Inui
Seishun Academy Tennis Team (9th Grade)

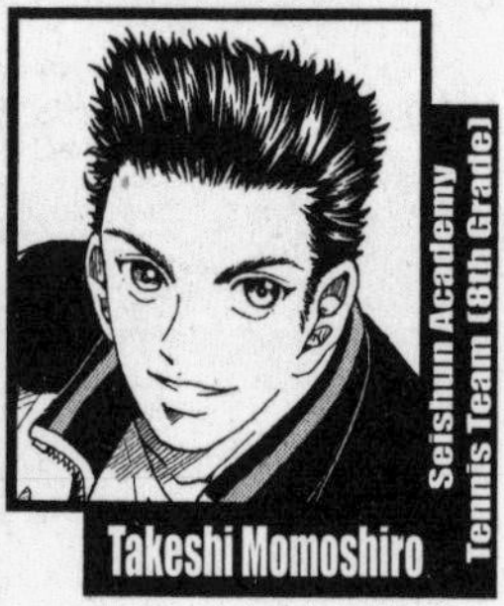
Takeshi Momoshiro
Seishun Academy Tennis Team (8th Grade)

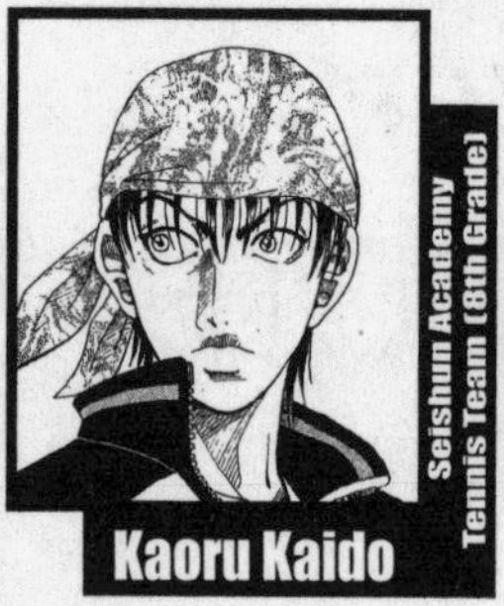
Kaoru Kaido
Seishun Academy Tennis Team (8th Grade)

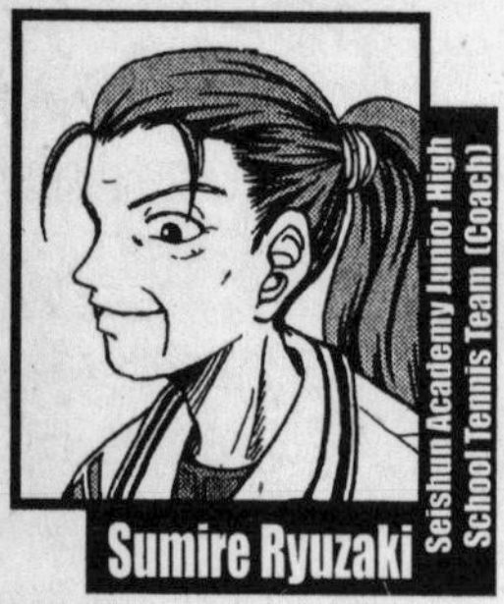
Sumire Ryuzaki
Seishun Academy Junior High School Tennis Team (Coach)

Ryoma Echizen, a tennis prodigy and winner of four consecutive US Junior tournaments, has returned to Japan and enrolled at Seishun Academy Junior High. He became the first 7th grader ever to be a starter in the District Preliminaries, where he overcame a series of accidents to earn a berth in the City Tournament. But in a challenge match against his Team Captain, Kunimitsu, Ryoma realized the difference in their skills and for the first time found himself wishing he were better.

And now, the City Tournament begins!!

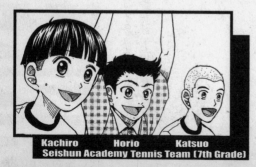

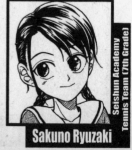

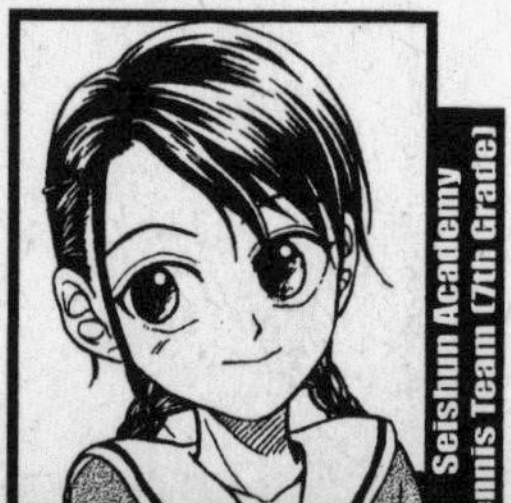
Sakuno Ryuzaki
Seishun Academy Tennis Team (7th Grade)

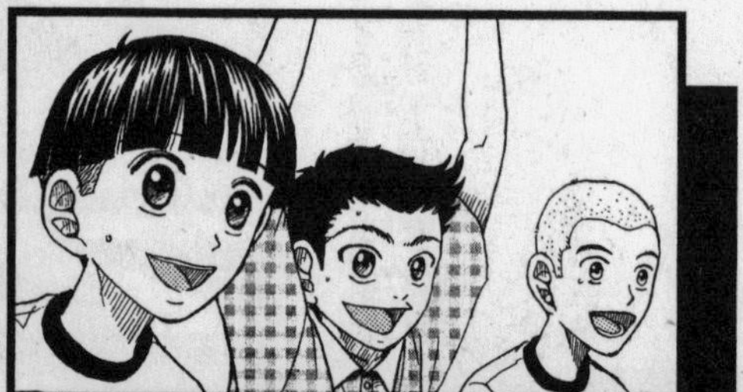
Kachiro
Horio
Katsuo
Seishun Academy Tennis Team (7th Grade)

CONTENTS

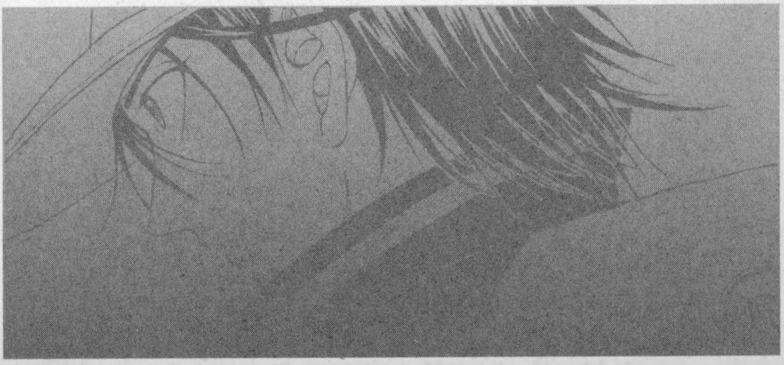

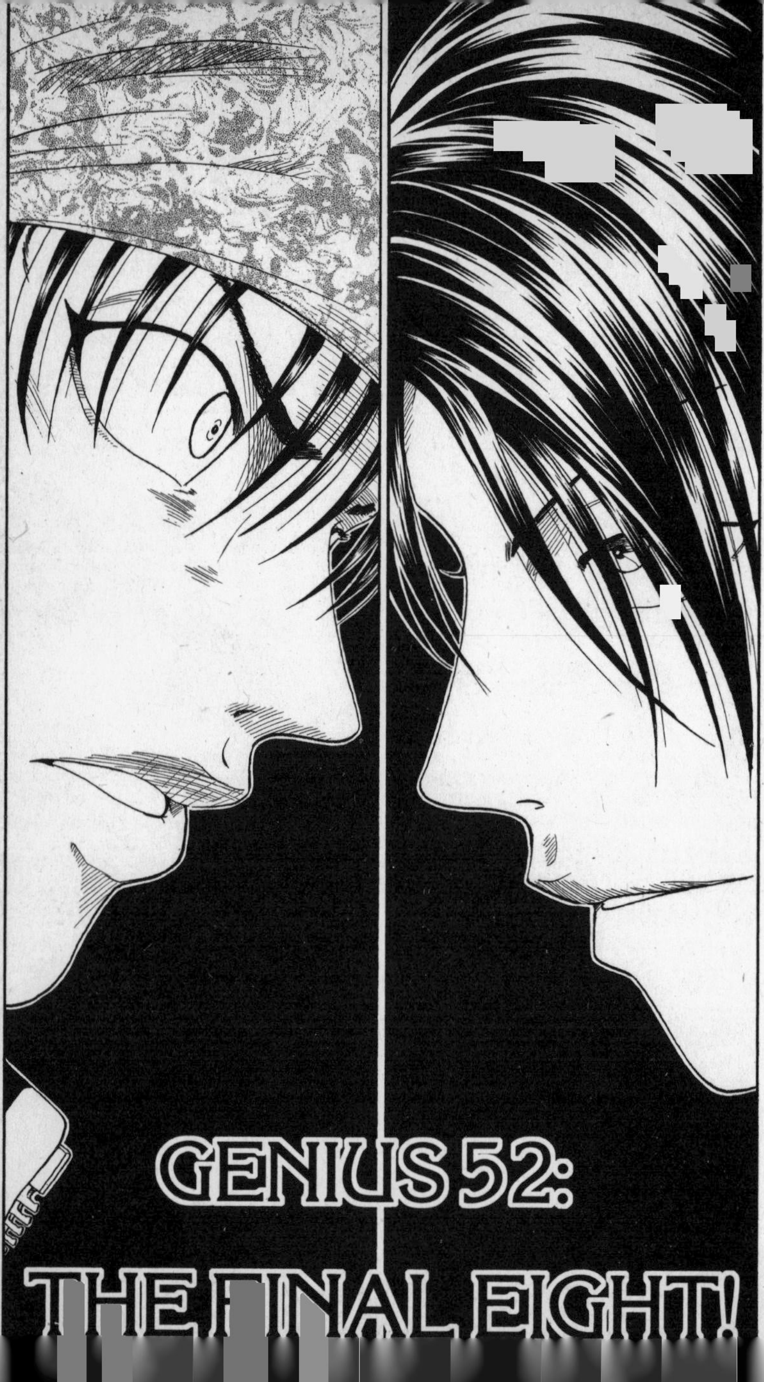
GENIUS 52:
THE FINAL EIGHT!

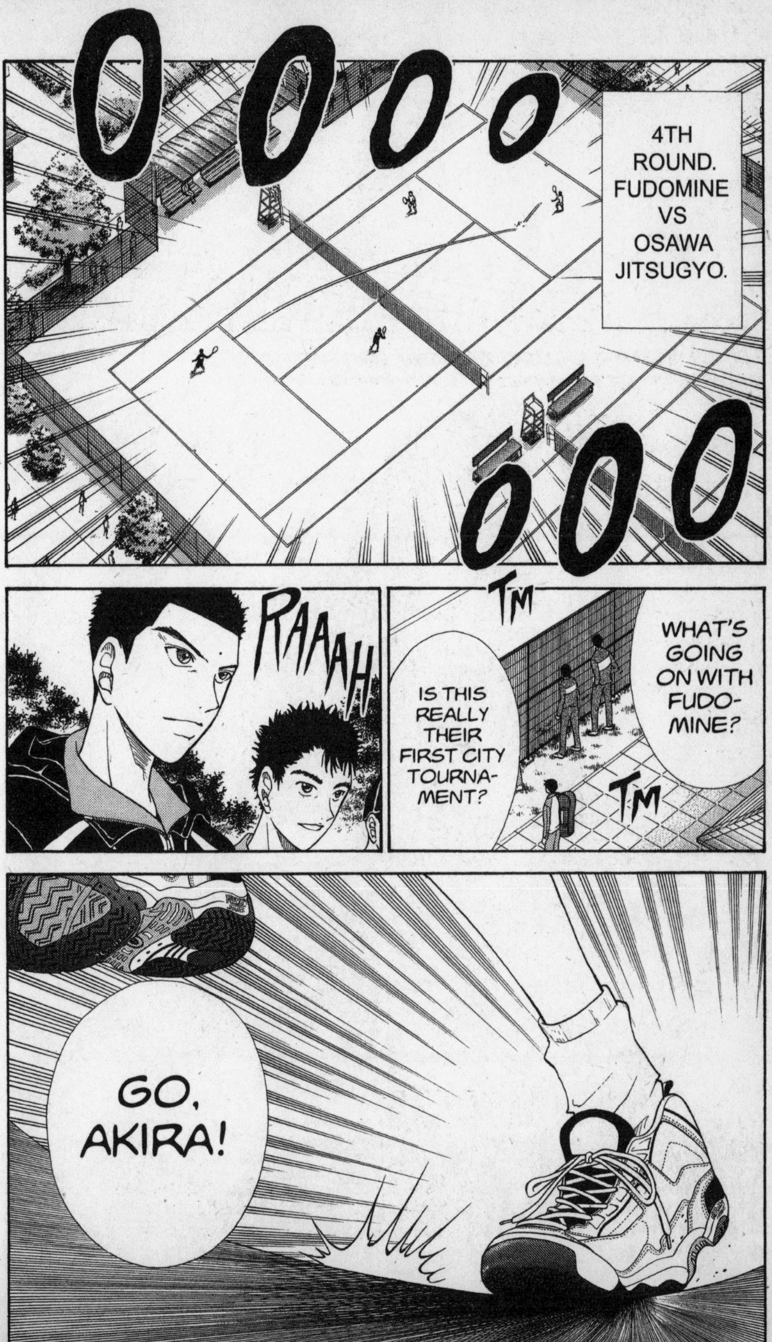
OOOO
4TH ROUND. FUDOMINE VS OSAWA JITSUGYO.
OOO
TM
WHAT'S GOING ON WITH FUDO-MINE?
IS THIS REALLY THEIR FIRST CITY TOURNA-MENT?
TM
RAAAH
GO, AKIRA!

READ THIS WAY

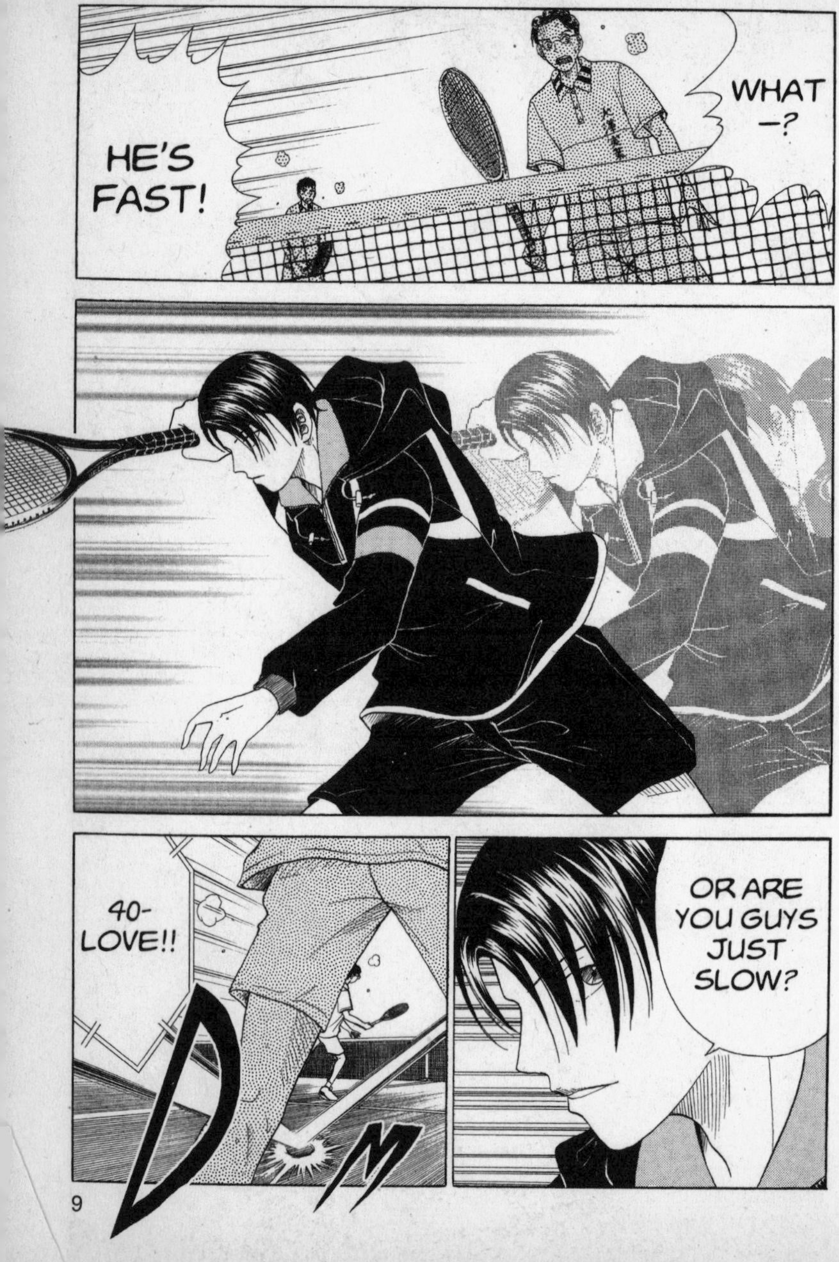
WHAT —?
HE'S FAST!
OR ARE YOU GUYS JUST SLOW?
40-LOVE!!
DM

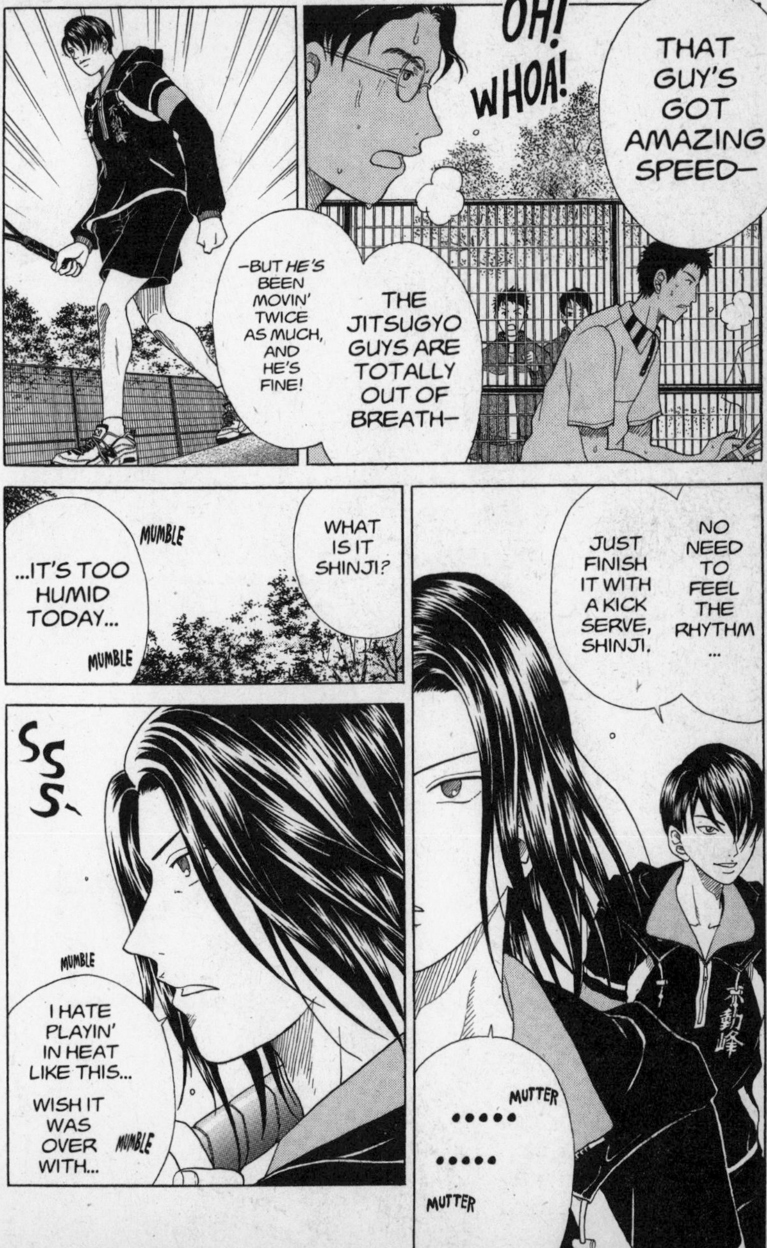
OH!
WHOA!
THAT GUY'S GOT AMAZING SPEED—
THE JITSUGYO GUYS ARE TOTALLY OUT OF BREATH—
—BUT HE'S BEEN MOVIN' TWICE AS MUCH, AND HE'S FINE!
NO NEED TO FEEL THE RHYTHM...
JUST FINISH IT WITH A KICK SERVE, SHINJI.
MUTTER
.....
.....
MUTTER
WHAT IS IT SHINJI?
MUMBLE
...IT'S TOO HUMID TODAY...
MUMBLE
SSS
MUMBLE
I HATE PLAYIN' IN HEAT LIKE THIS...
WISH IT WAS OVER WITH...
MUMBLE

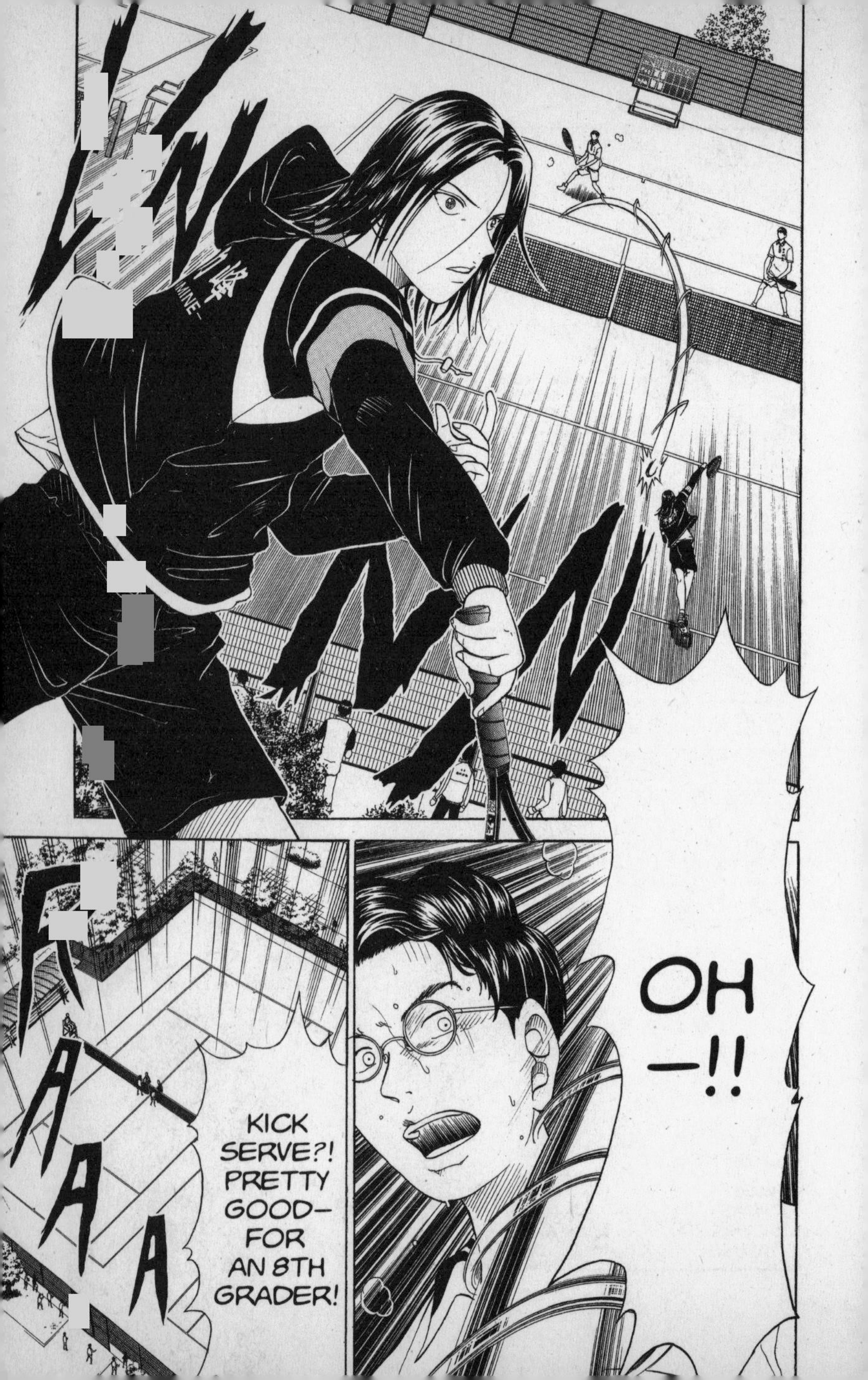
OH —!!
KICK SERVE?! PRETTY GOOD— FOR AN 8TH GRADER!
FAAAA

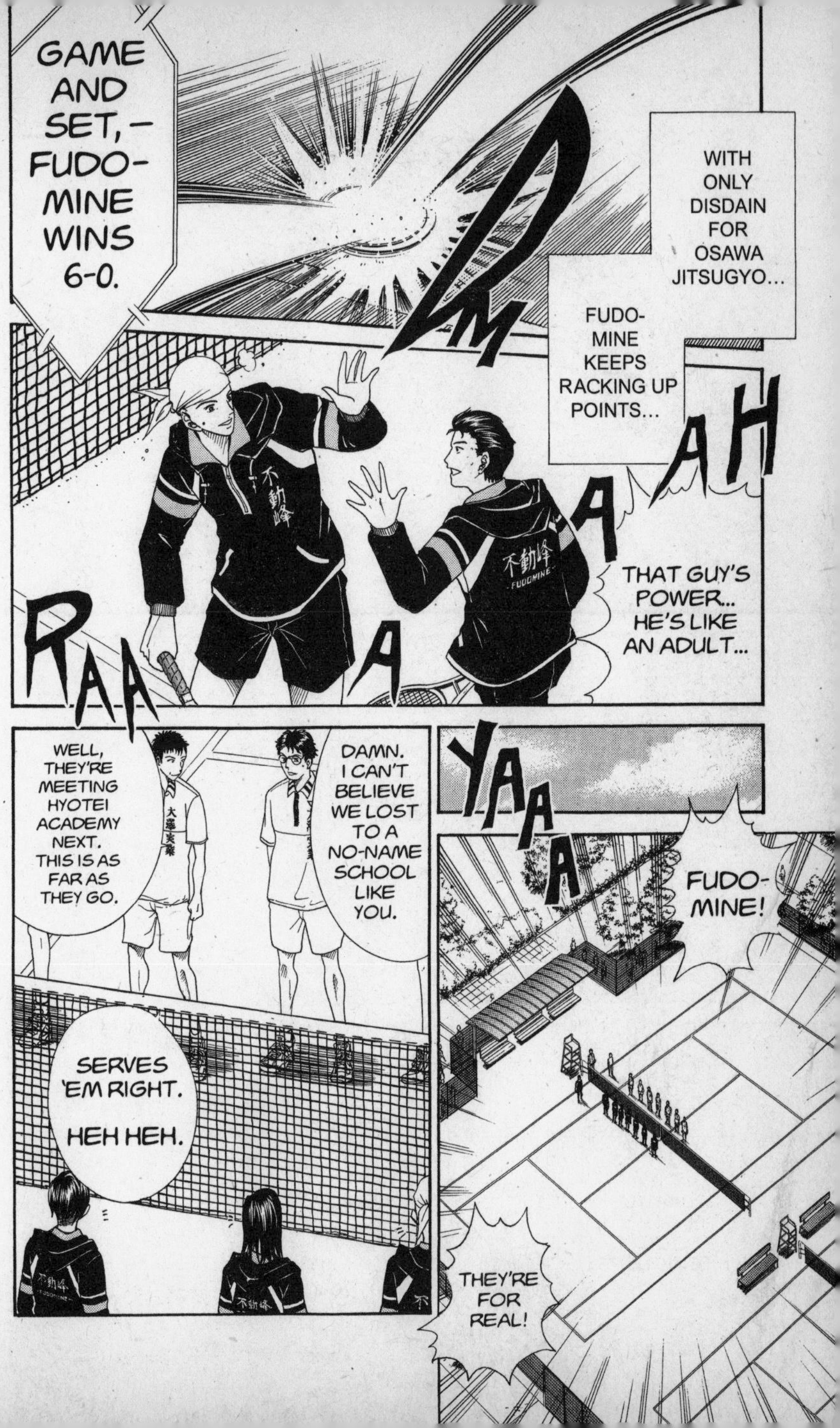
GAME AND SET, – FUDO-MINE WINS 6-0.
DM
WITH ONLY DISDAIN FOR OSAWA JITSUGYO...
FUDO-MINE KEEPS RACKING UP POINTS...
RAAAAAH
THAT GUY'S POWER... HE'S LIKE AN ADULT...
YAAAA
FUDO-MINE!
THEY'RE FOR REAL!
DAMN. I CAN'T BELIEVE WE LOST TO A NO-NAME SCHOOL LIKE YOU.
WELL, THEY'RE MEETING HYOTEI ACADEMY NEXT. THIS IS AS FAR AS THEY GO.
SERVES 'EM RIGHT.
HEH HEH.

READ THIS WAY

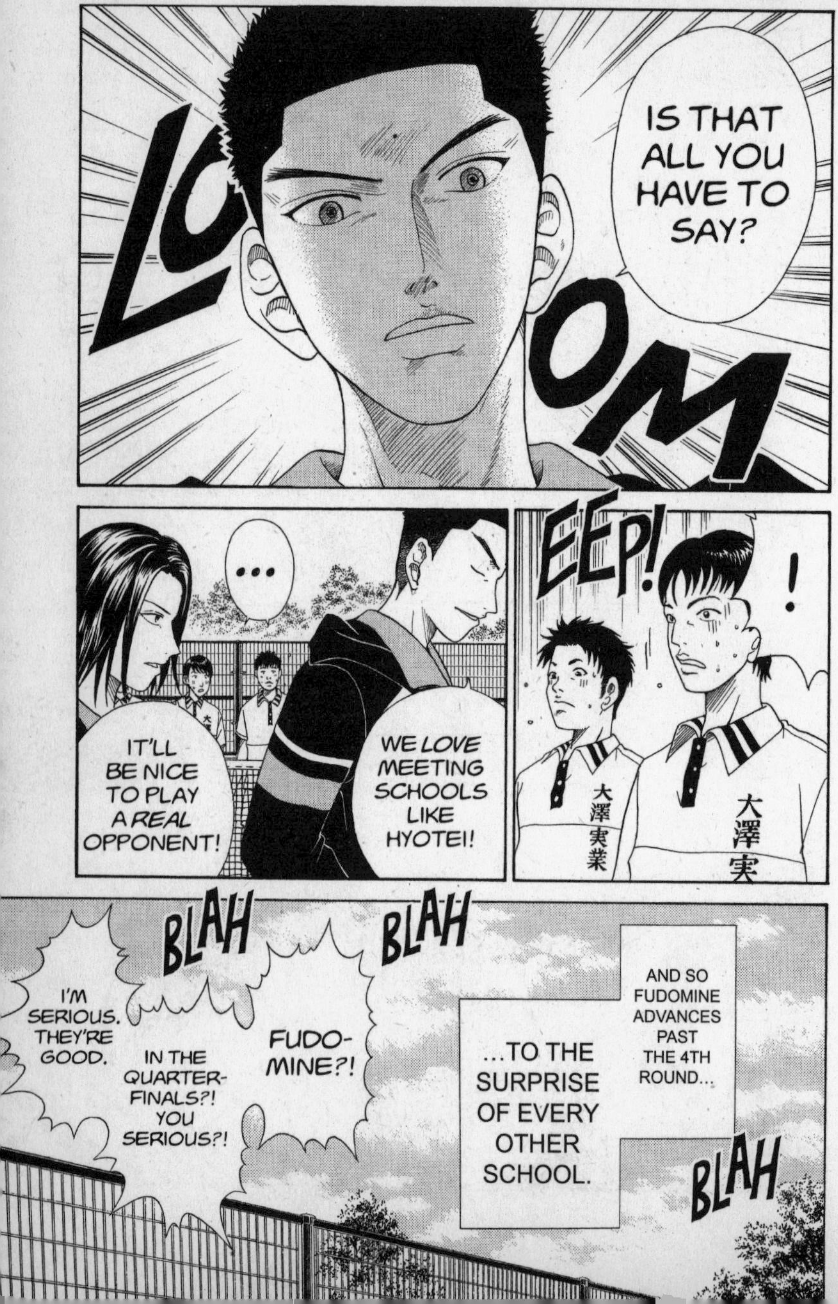
LOOM
IS THAT ALL YOU HAVE TO SAY?
EEP!
!
大澤実業
大澤実
...
WE LOVE MEETING SCHOOLS LIKE HYOTEI!
IT'LL BE NICE TO PLAY A REAL OPPONENT!
AND SO FUDOMINE ADVANCES PAST THE 4TH ROUND...
...TO THE SURPRISE OF EVERY OTHER SCHOOL.
BLAH
BLAH
FUDO-MINE?!
BLAH
IN THE QUARTER-FINALS?! YOU SERIOUS?!
I'M SERIOUS. THEY'RE GOOD.

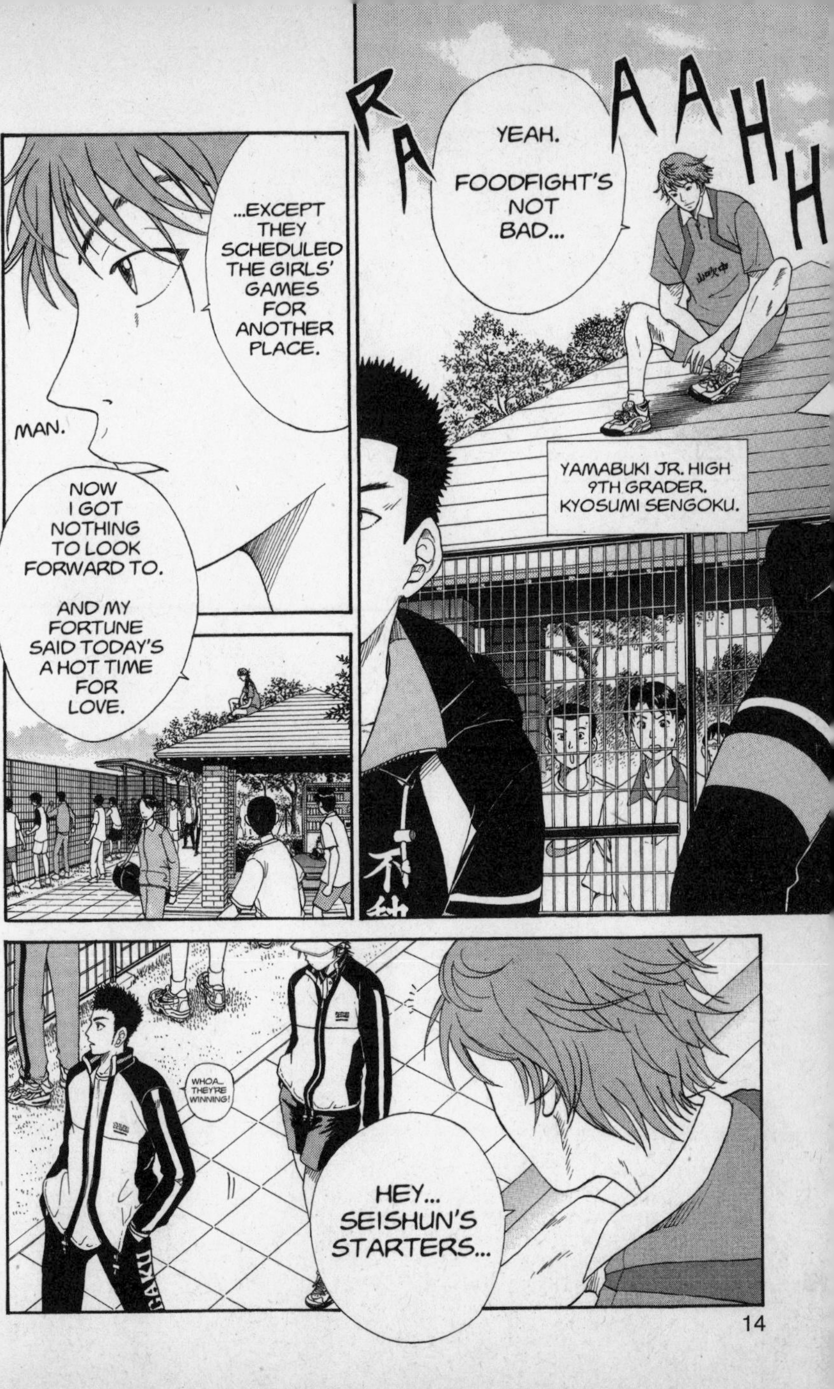
RAAAHHH
YEAH.
FOODFIGHT'S NOT BAD...
YAMABUKI JR. HIGH 9TH GRADER. KYOSUMI SENGOKU.
...EXCEPT THEY SCHEDULED THE GIRLS' GAMES FOR ANOTHER PLACE.
MAN.
NOW I GOT NOTHING TO LOOK FORWARD TO.
AND MY FORTUNE SAID TODAY'S A HOT TIME FOR LOVE.
HEY... SEISHUN'S STARTERS...
WHOA... THEY'RE WINNING!

READ THIS WAY

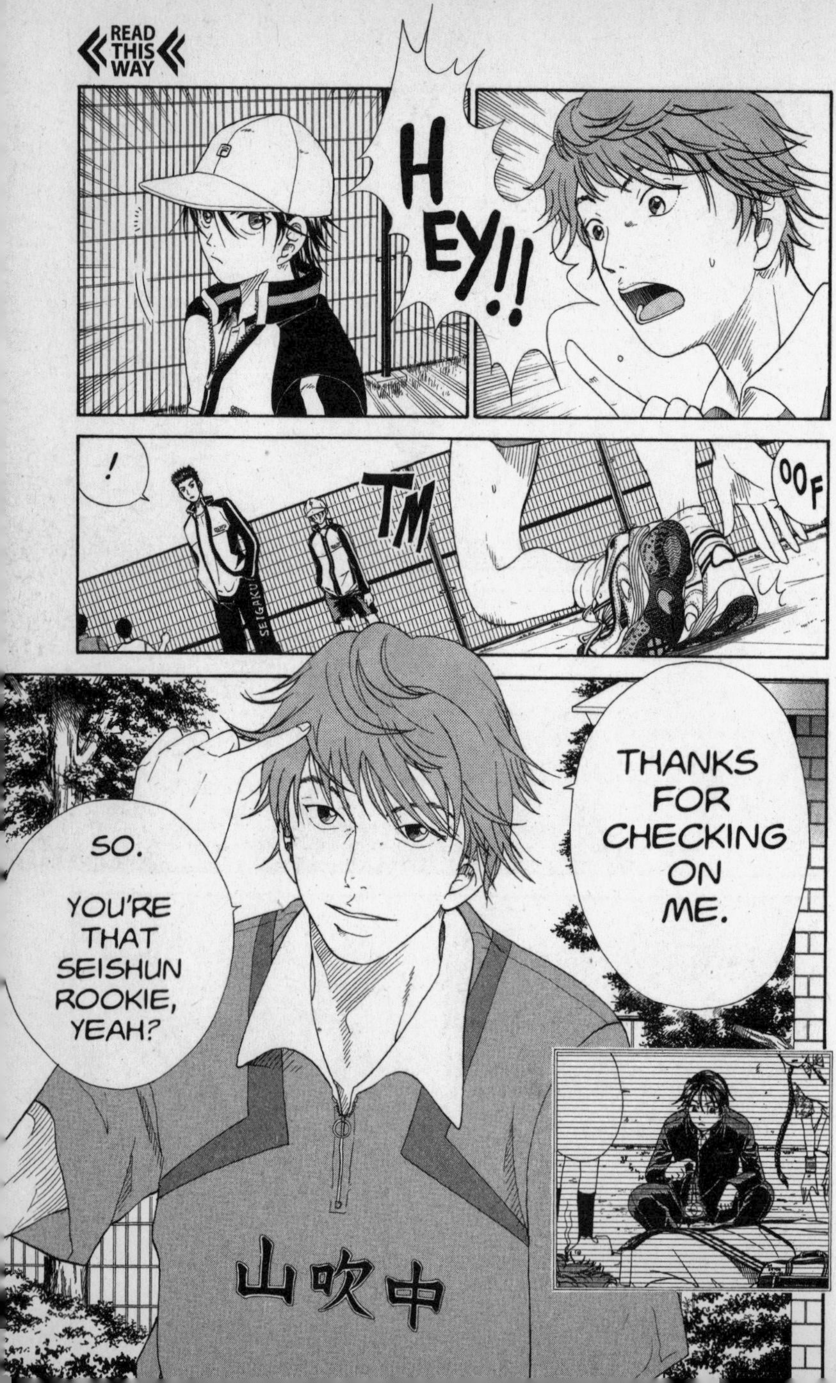
HEY!!
OOF
TM
!
SEIGAKU
THANKS FOR CHECKING ON ME.
SO. YOU'RE THAT SEISHUN ROOKIE, YEAH?
山吹中

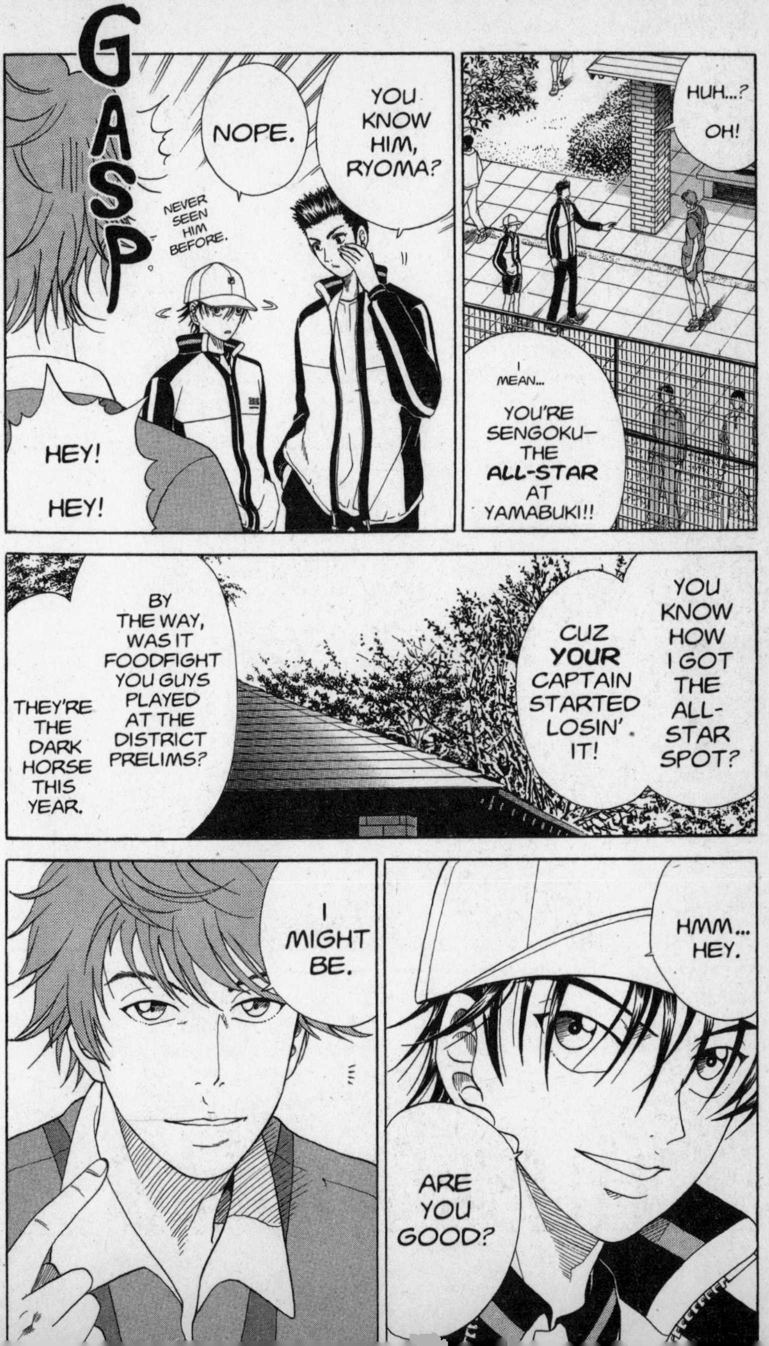
HUH...?
OH!
I MEAN...
YOU'RE SENGOKU—THE ALL-STAR AT YAMABUKI!!
YOU KNOW HIM, RYOMA?
NOPE.
NEVER SEEN HIM BEFORE.
GASP
HEY!
HEY!
YOU KNOW HOW I GOT THE ALL-STAR SPOT?
CUZ YOUR CAPTAIN STARTED LOSIN' IT!
BY THE WAY, WAS IT FOODFIGHT YOU GUYS PLAYED AT THE DISTRICT PRELIMS?
THEY'RE THE DARK HORSE THIS YEAR.
HMM... HEY.
ARE YOU GOOD?
I MIGHT BE.

READ THIS WAY

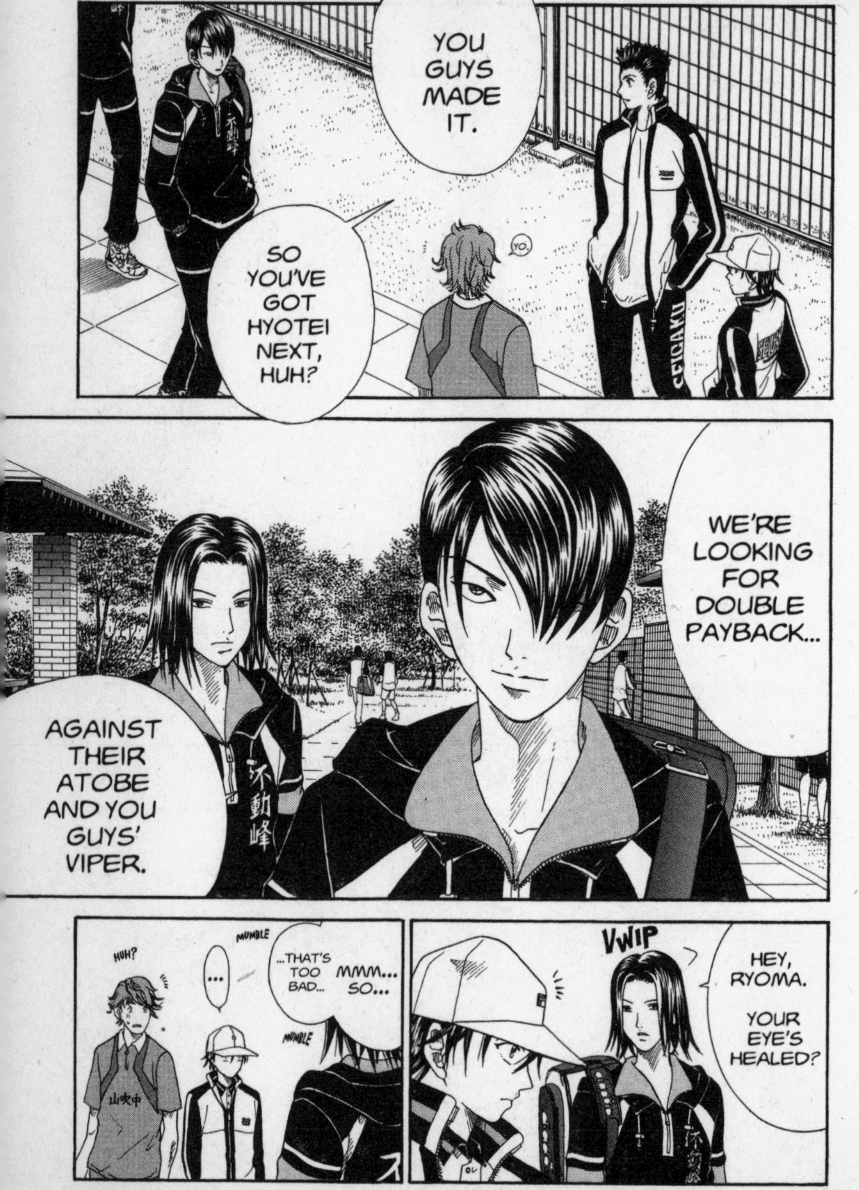
HEY. YOU GUYS MADE IT.
YO.
SO YOU'VE GOT HYOTEI NEXT, HUH?
WE'RE LOOKING FOR DOUBLE PAYBACK...
AGAINST THEIR ATOBE AND YOU GUYS' VIPER.
VWIP
HEY, RYOMA. YOUR EYE'S HEALED?
MMM... SO...
...THAT'S TOO BAD...
MUMBLE
MUMBLE
...
HUH?

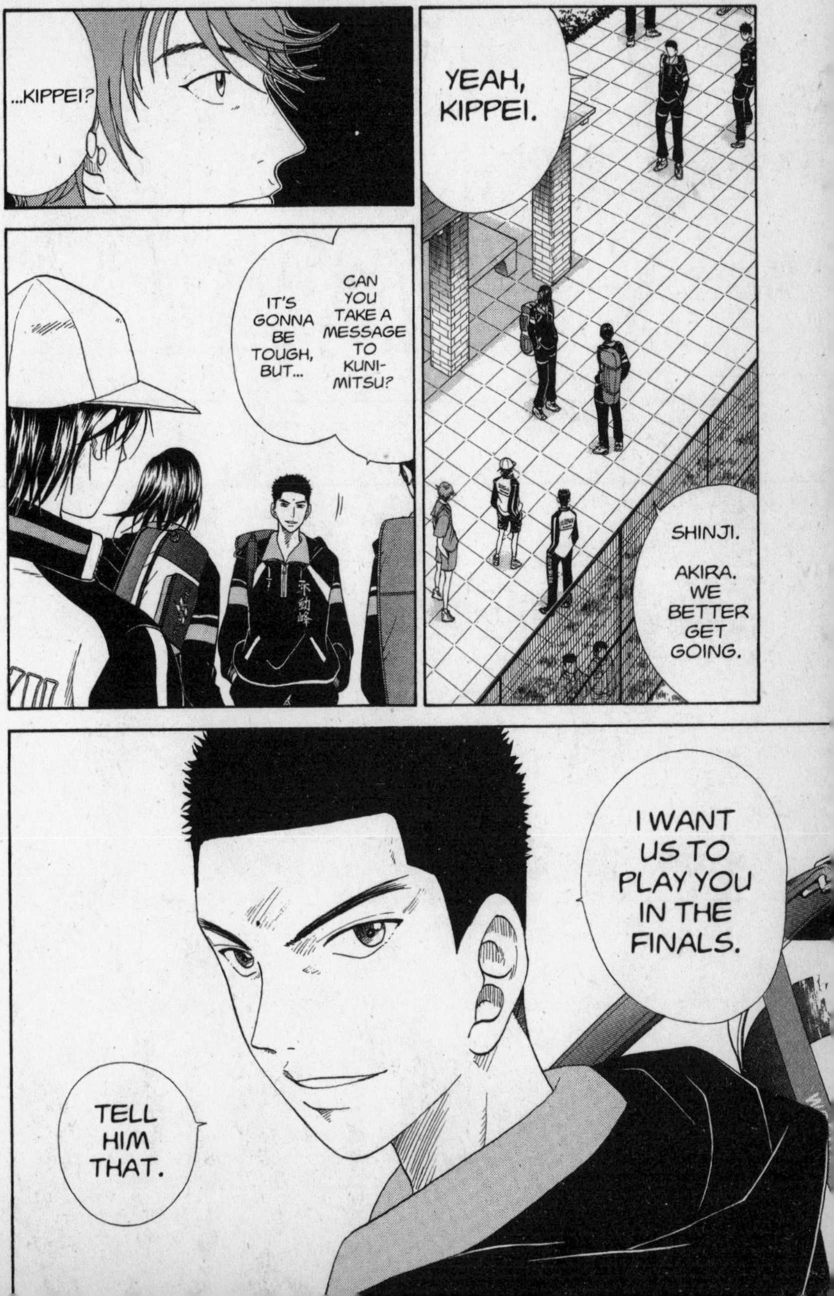
YEAH, KIPPEI.
SHINJI.
AKIRA. WE BETTER GET GOING.
...KIPPEI?
IT'S GONNA BE TOUGH, BUT... CAN YOU TAKE A MESSAGE TO KUNI-MITSU?
I WANT US TO PLAY YOU IN THE FINALS.
TELL HIM THAT.

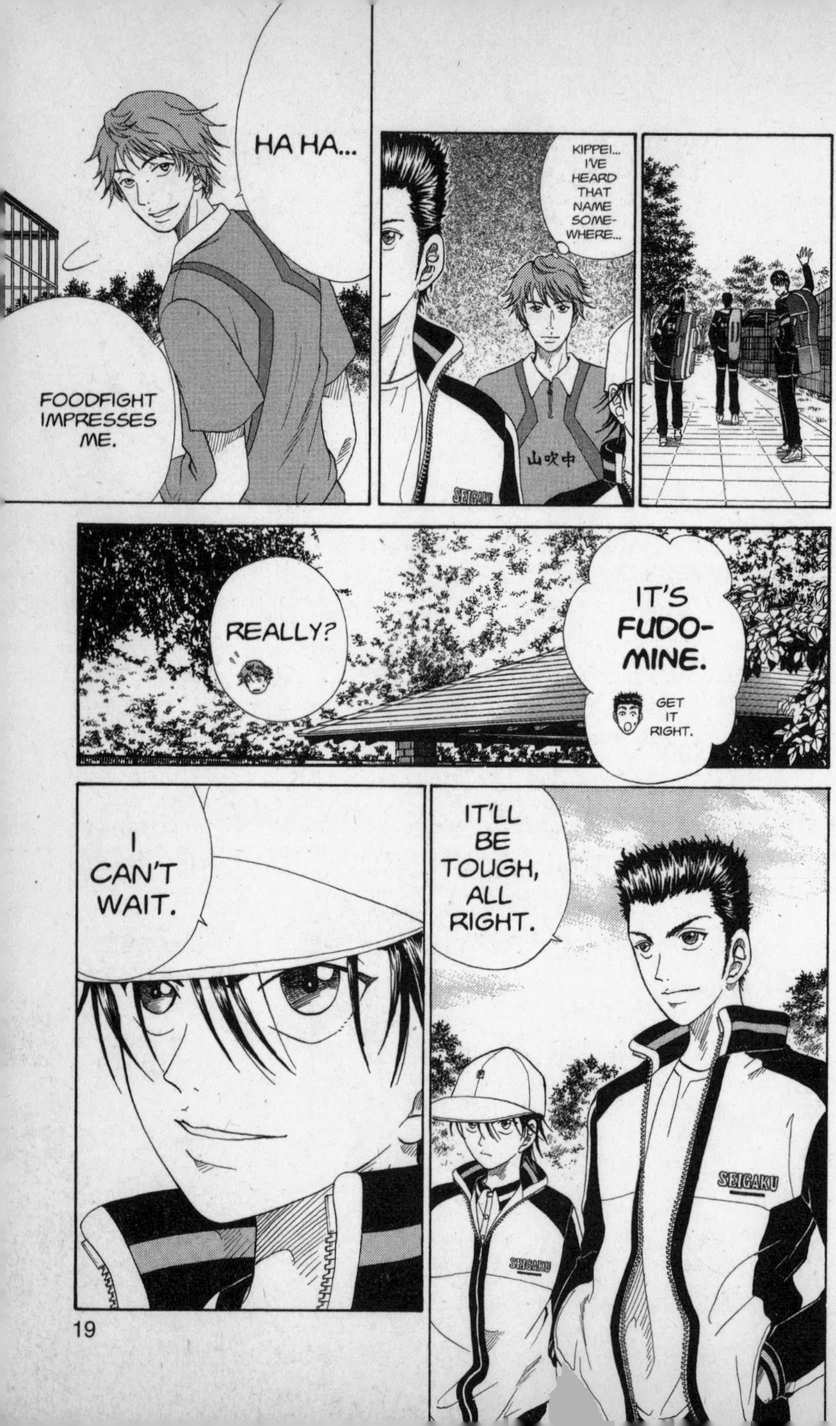
KIPPEI... I'VE HEARD THAT NAME SOME-WHERE...
HA HA...
FOODFIGHT IMPRESSES ME.
IT'S FUDO-MINE.
GET IT RIGHT.
REALLY?
IT'LL BE TOUGH, ALL RIGHT.
I CAN'T WAIT.

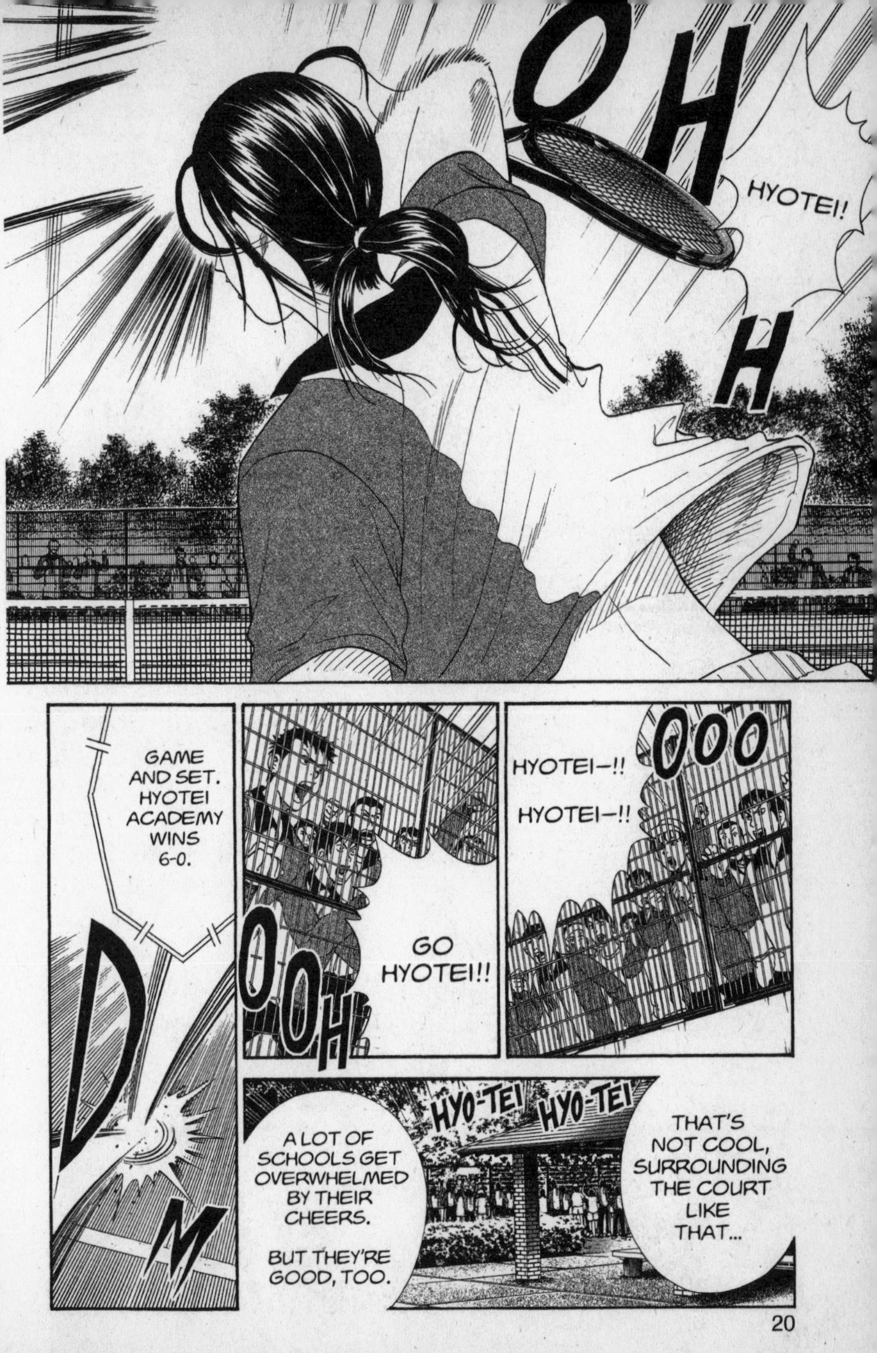
OOH
H
HYOTEI!
OOO
HYOTEI–!!
HYOTEI–!!
GO HYOTEI!!
OOH
THAT'S NOT COOL, SURROUNDING THE COURT LIKE THAT...
HYO-TEI
HYO-TEI
A LOT OF SCHOOLS GET OVERWHELMED BY THEIR CHEERS.
BUT THEY'RE GOOD, TOO.
GAME AND SET. HYOTEI ACADEMY WINS 6-0.
D
M

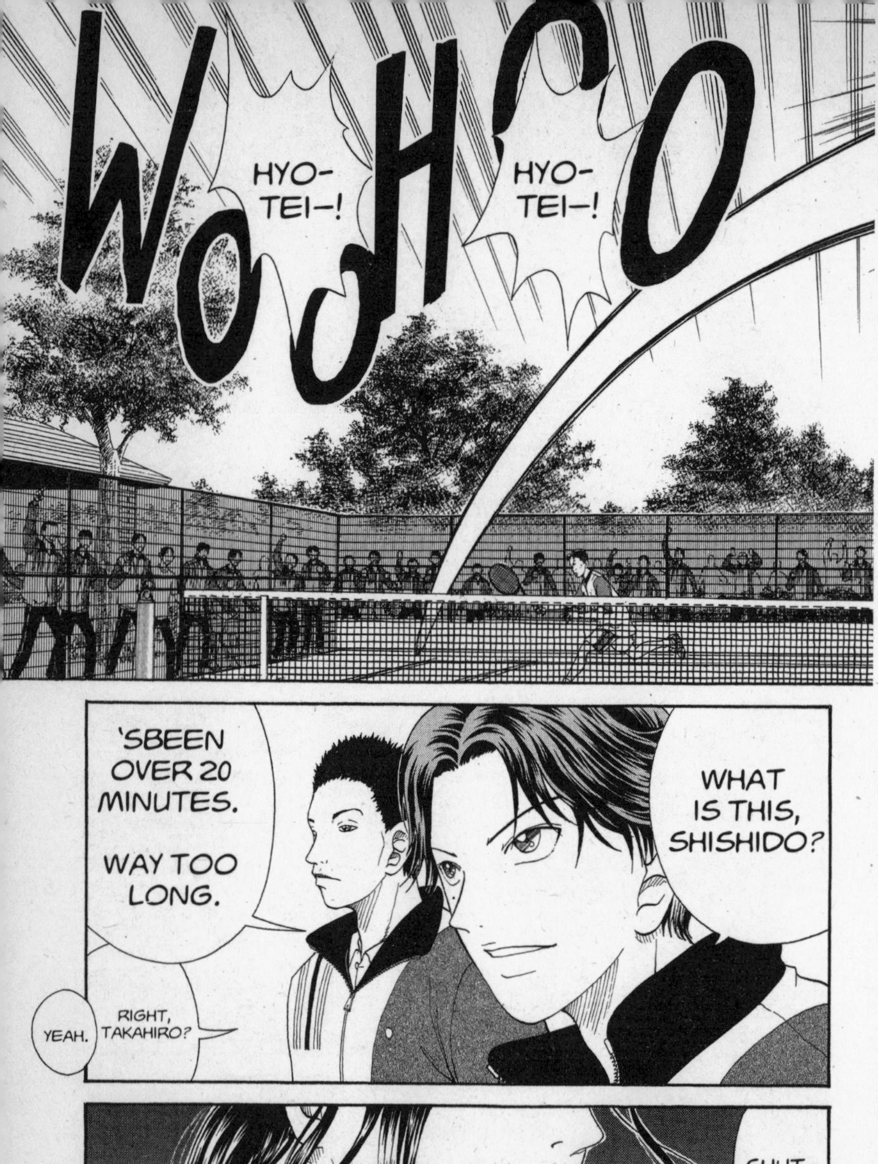
HYO-TEI—!
HYO-TEI—!
WHAT IS THIS, SHISHIDO?
'SBEEN OVER 20 MINUTES.
WAY TOO LONG.
RIGHT, TAKAHIRO?
YEAH.
SHUT—

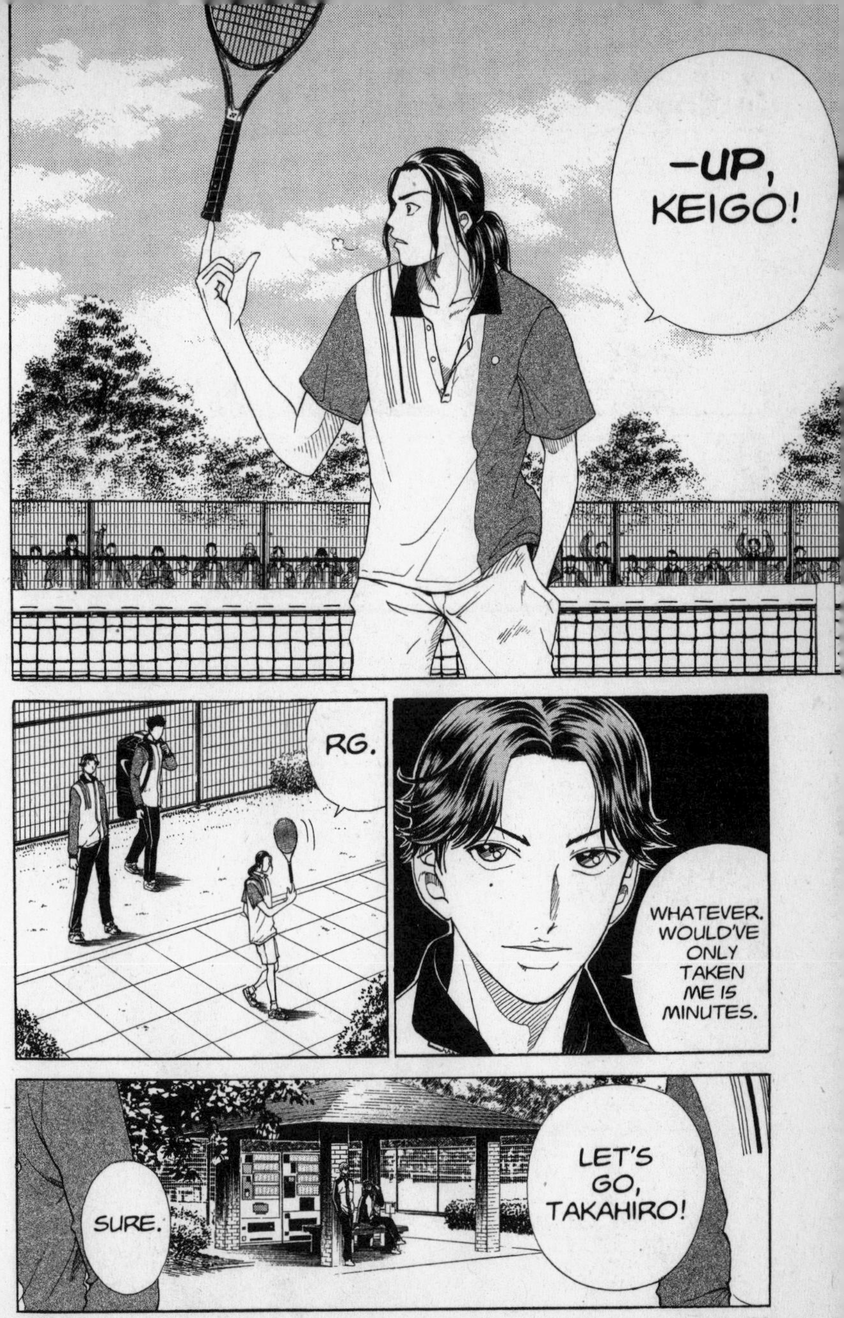
–UP, KEIGO!
WHATEVER. WOULD'VE ONLY TAKEN ME 15 MINUTES.
RG.
LET'S GO, TAKAHIRO!
SURE.

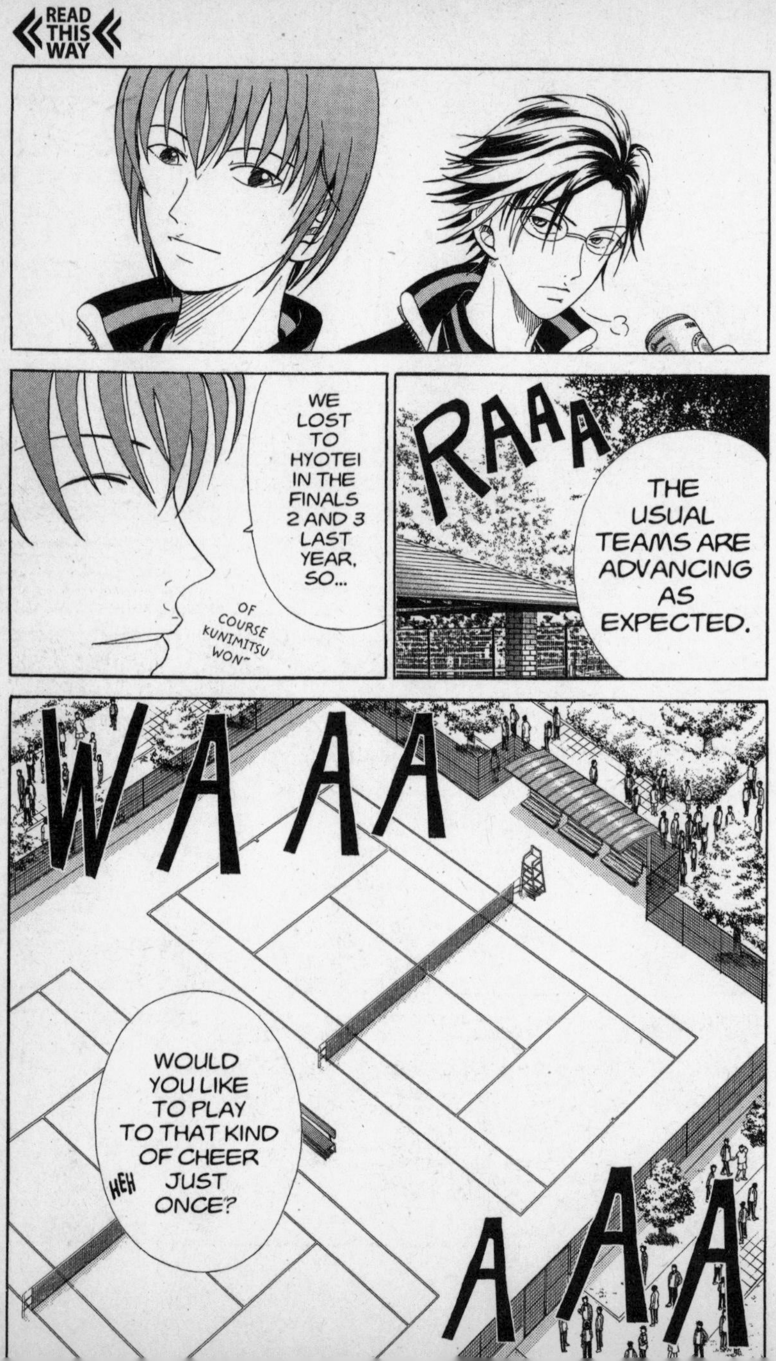
READ THIS WAY
RAAA
THE USUAL TEAMS ARE ADVANCING AS EXPECTED.
WE LOST TO HYOTEI IN THE FINALS 2 AND 3 LAST YEAR, SO...
OF COURSE KUNIMITSU WON~
WAAA
AAA
WOULD YOU LIKE TO PLAY TO THAT KIND OF CHEER JUST ONCE?
HEH

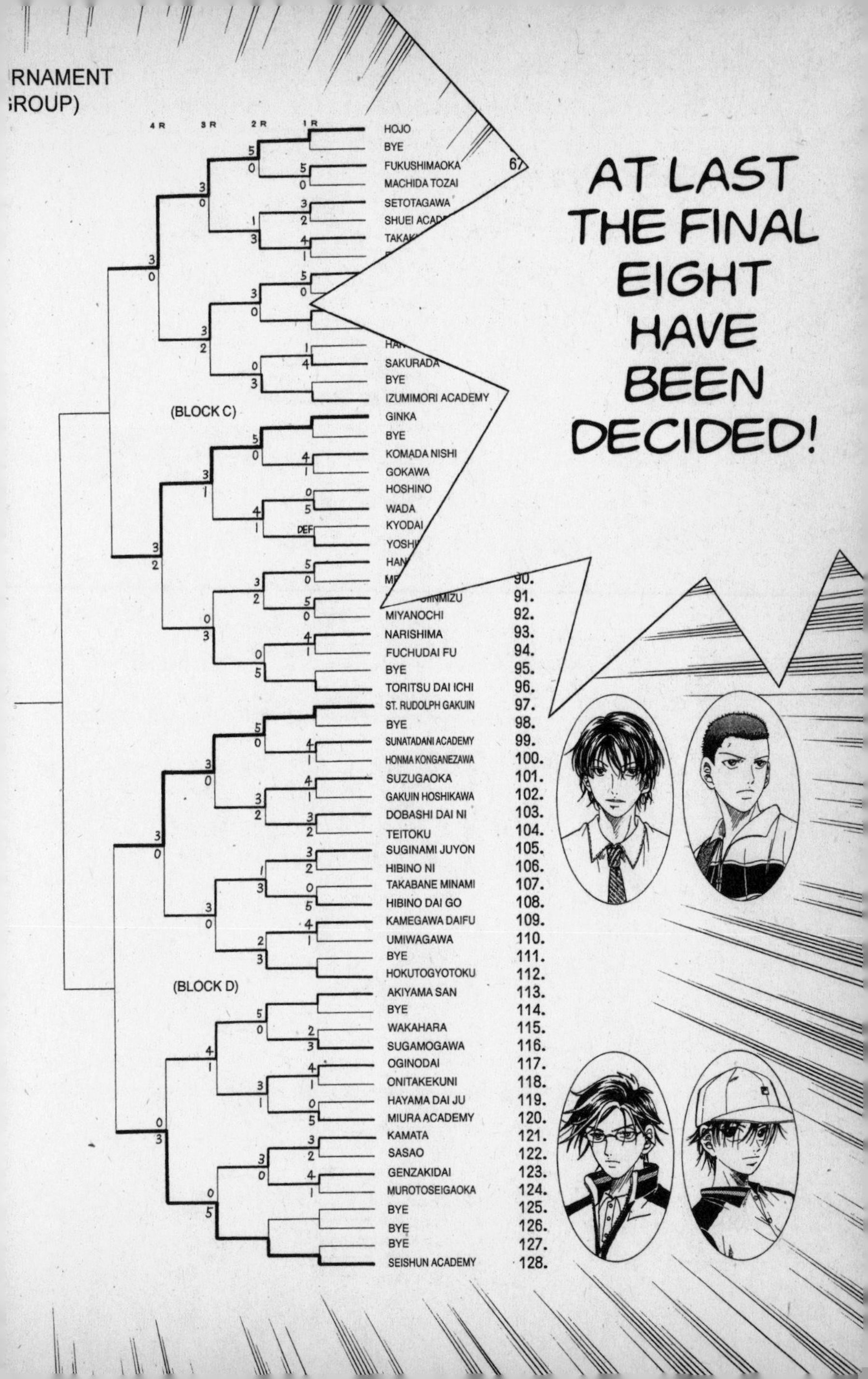
AT LAST THE FINAL EIGHT HAVE BEEN DECIDED!
RNAMENT
ROUP)
4 R
3 R
2 R
1 R
HOJO
BYE
FUKUSHIMAOKA 67
MACHIDA TOZAI
SETOTAGAWA
SAKURADA
BYE
IZUMIMORI ACADEMY
(BLOCK C)
GINKA
BYE
KOMADA NISHI
GOKAWA
HOSHINO
WADA
KYODAI
DEF
90.
91.
MIYANOCHI 92.
NARISHIMA 93.
FUCHUDAI FU 94.
BYE 95.
TORITSU DAI ICHI 96.
ST. RUDOLPH GAKUIN 97.
BYE 98.
SUNATADANI ACADEMY 99.
HONMA KONGANEZAWA 100.
SUZUGAOKA 101.
GAKUIN HOSHIKAWA 102.
DOBASHI DAI NI 103.
TEITOKU 104.
SUGINAMI JUYON 105.
HIBINO NI 106.
TAKABANE MINAMI 107.
HIBINO DAI GO 108.
KAMEGAWA DAIFU 109.
UMIWAGAWA 110.
BYE 111.
HOKUTOGYOTOKU 112.
(BLOCK D)
AKIYAMA SAN 113.
BYE 114.
WAKAHARA 115.
SUGAMOGAWA 116.
OGINODAI 117.
ONITAKEKUNI 118.
HAYAMA DAI JU 119.
MIURA ACADEMY 120.
KAMATA 121.
SASAO 122.
GENZAKIDAI 123.
MUROTOSEIGAOKA 124.
BYE 125.
BYE 126.
BYE 127.
SEISHUN ACADEMY 128.

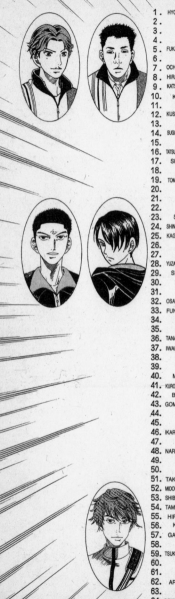

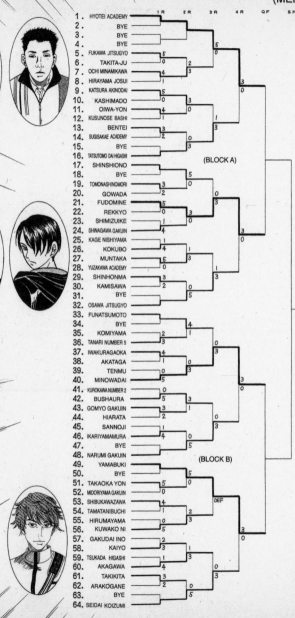

1. HYOTEI ACADEMY
2. BYE
3. BYE
4. BYE
5. FUKAWA JITSUGYO
6. TAKITA-JU
7. OCHI MINAMIKAWA
8. HIRAYAMA JOSUI
9. KATSURA AKINODAI
10. KASHIMADO
11. OIWA-YON
12. KUSUNOSE BASHI
13. BENTEI
14. SUGISAKAE ACADEMY
15. BYE
16. TATSUTOMO DAI HIGASHI
17. SHINSHIONO
18. BYE
19. TOMONASHINOMORI
20. GOWADA
21. FUDOMINE
22. REKKYO
23. SHIMIZUIKE
24. SHINAGAWA GAKUIN
25. KAGE NISHIYAMA
26. KOKUBO
27. MUNTAKA
28. YUZAKAWA ACADEMY
29. SHINHONMA
30. KAMISAWA
31. BYE
32. OSAWA JITSUGYO
33. FUNATSUMOTO
34. BYE
35. KOMIYAMA
36. TANARI NUMBER 5
37. IWAKURAGAOKA
38. AKATAGA
39. TENMU
40. MINOWADAI
41. KUROKAWA NUMBER 2
42. BUSHAURA
43. GOMYO GAKUIN
44. HIARATA
45. SANNOJI
46. IKARIYAMAMURA
47. BYE
48. NARUMI GAKUIN
49. YAMABUKI
50. BYE
51. TAKAOKA YON
52. MIDORIYAMA GAKUIN
53. SHIBUKAWAZAWA
54. TAMATANIBUCHI
55. HIRUMAYAMA
56. KUWAKO NI
57. GAKUDAI INO
58. KAIYO
59. TSUKADA HIGASHI
60. AKAGAWA
61. TAKIKITA
62. ARAKOGANE
63. BYE
64. SEIDAI KOIZUMI

(BLOCK A)

(BLOCK B)

1R   2R   3R   4R   QF   SF   F

SHUSUKE FUJI - RIGHT-HANDED

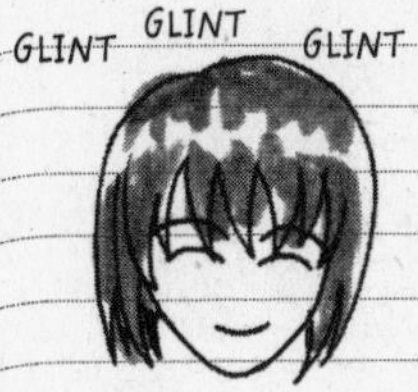
GLINT
GLINT
GLINT

SEISHUN ACADEMY 9TH GRADE CLASS 6
HEIGHT: 167CM - BLOOD TYPE: B - BORN: 2/29
FAVORITE BRAND SHOES: NIKE
(AIR BISCAYNE MID III)
RACKET: PRINCE (TRIPLE THREAT RIP)
PRINCE (MICHAEL CHANG TITANIUM)
BEST SHOT: TRIPLE COUNTER
FAVORITE FOOD: APPLES, CAJUN FOOD,
SPICY RAMEN
HOBBIES: COLLECTING CACTUS, PHOTOGRAPHY

TAKASHI KAWAMURA - RIGHT - HANDED

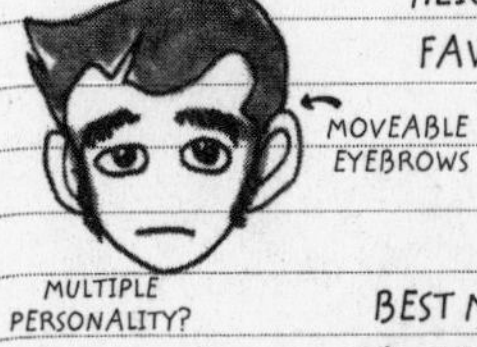
MOVEABLE
EYEBROWS
MULTIPLE
PERSONALITY?

SEISHUN ACADEMY 9TH GRADE CLASS 4
HEIGHT: 180CM - BLOOD TYPE : A - BORN : 11/18
FAVORITE BRAND SHOES: ASICS
(GELSTROKE)
RACKET: DUNLOP OP
(RIMBREED XL)
BEST MOVE: BURNING SERVE
FAVORITE FOOD : MATSUTAKE DOBINMUSHI, RAW IKURA
HOBBIES: MONOPOLY, SHARPENING KNIVES

GENIUS 53: DARK CLOUDS

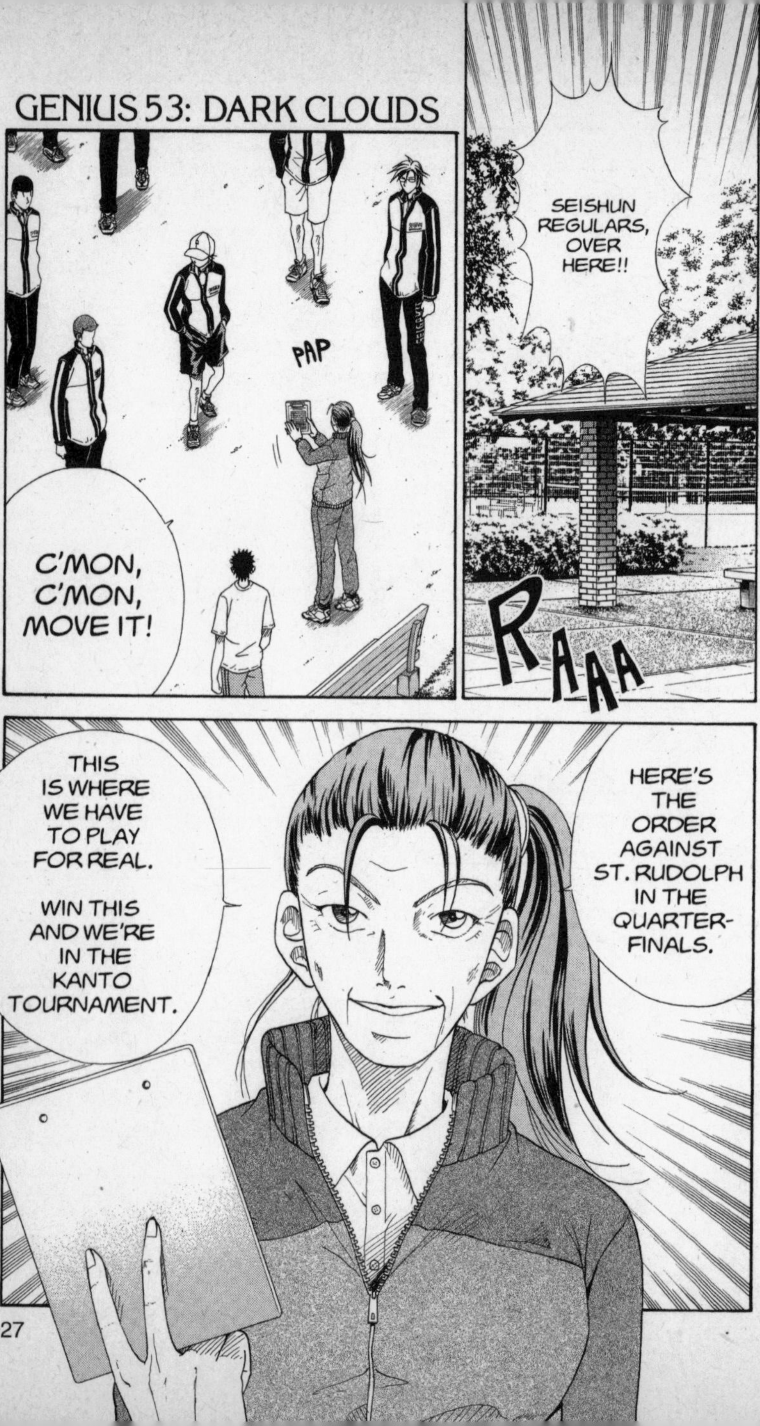
SEISHUN REGULARS, OVER HERE!!
RAAA
PAP
C'MON, C'MON, MOVE IT!
HERE'S THE ORDER AGAINST ST. RUDOLPH IN THE QUARTER-FINALS.
THIS IS WHERE WE HAVE TO PLAY FOR REAL.
WIN THIS AND WE'RE IN THE KANTO TOURNAMENT.

GENIUS 53: DARK CLOUDS

NO. 2 DOUBLES

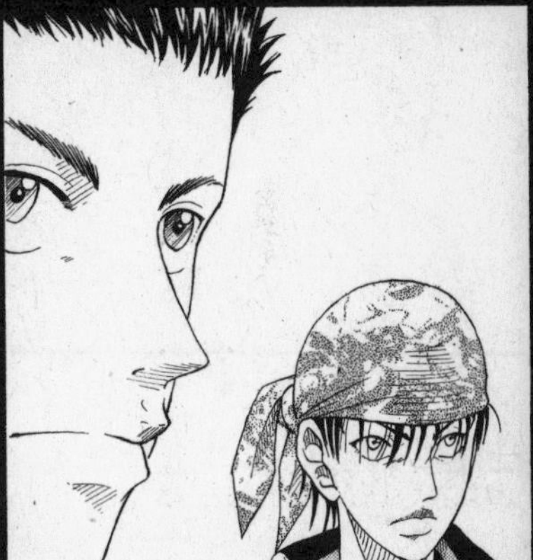

SEIGAKU

TAKESHI MOMOSHIRO (8TH GRADE)

KAORU KAIDO (8TH GRADE)

NO. 1 DOUBLES

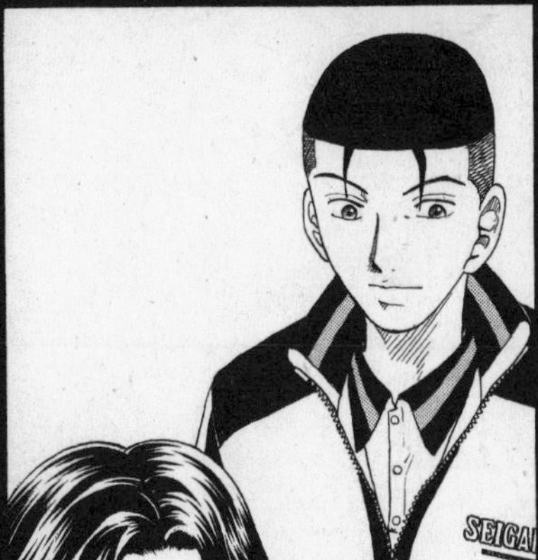

SEIGAKU

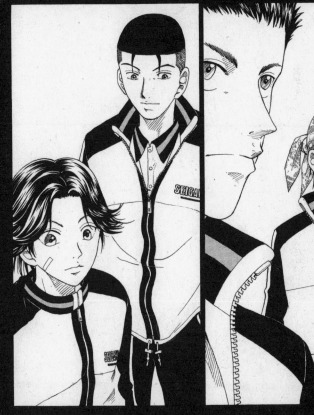

EIJI KIKUMARU (9TH GRADE)

SHUICHIRO OISHI (9TH GRADE)

NO. 1 SINGLES

NO. 2 SINGLES

NO. 3 SINGLES

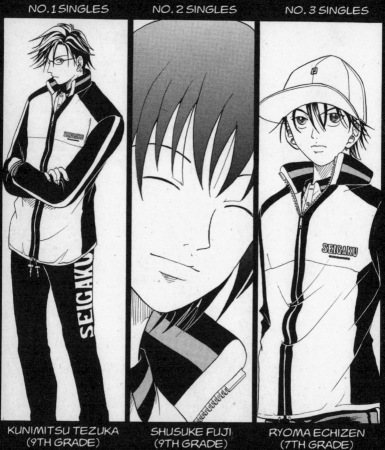

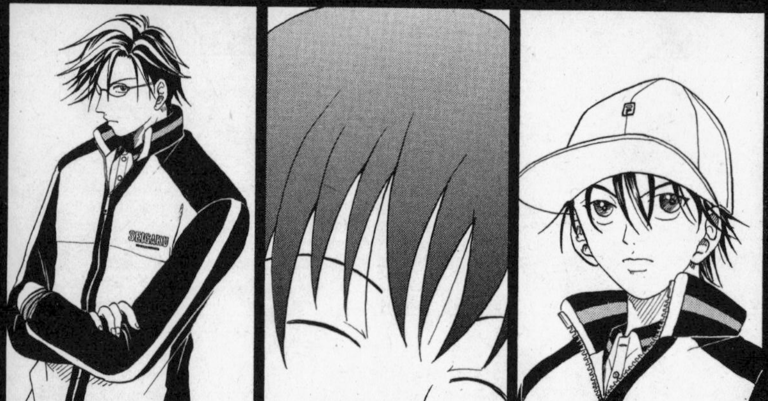
SEIGAKU
SEIGAKU
SEIGAKU

KUNIMITSU TEZUKA
(9TH GRADE)

SHUSUKE FUJI
(9TH GRADE)

RYOMA ECHIZEN
(7TH GRADE)

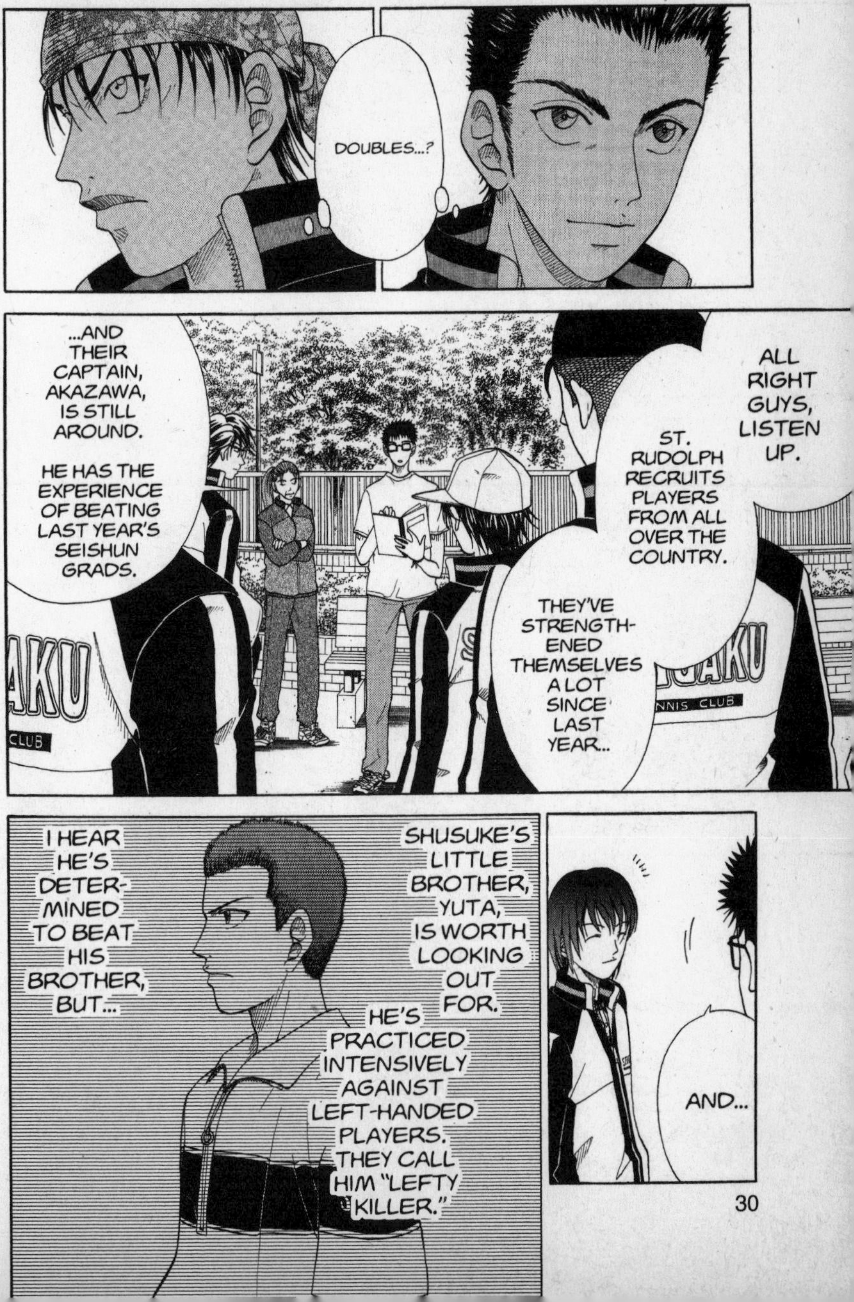
DOUBLES...?
ALL RIGHT GUYS, LISTEN UP.
ST. RUDOLPH RECRUITS PLAYERS FROM ALL OVER THE COUNTRY.
THEY'VE STRENGTH-ENED THEMSELVES A LOT SINCE LAST YEAR...
...AND THEIR CAPTAIN, AKAZAWA, IS STILL AROUND.
HE HAS THE EXPERIENCE OF BEATING LAST YEAR'S SEISHUN GRADS.
AND...
SHUSUKE'S LITTLE BROTHER, YUTA, IS WORTH LOOKING OUT FOR.
HE'S PRACTICED INTENSIVELY AGAINST LEFT-HANDED PLAYERS. THEY CALL HIM "LEFTY KILLER."
I HEAR HE'S DETER-MINED TO BEAT HIS BROTHER, BUT...

READ THIS WAY

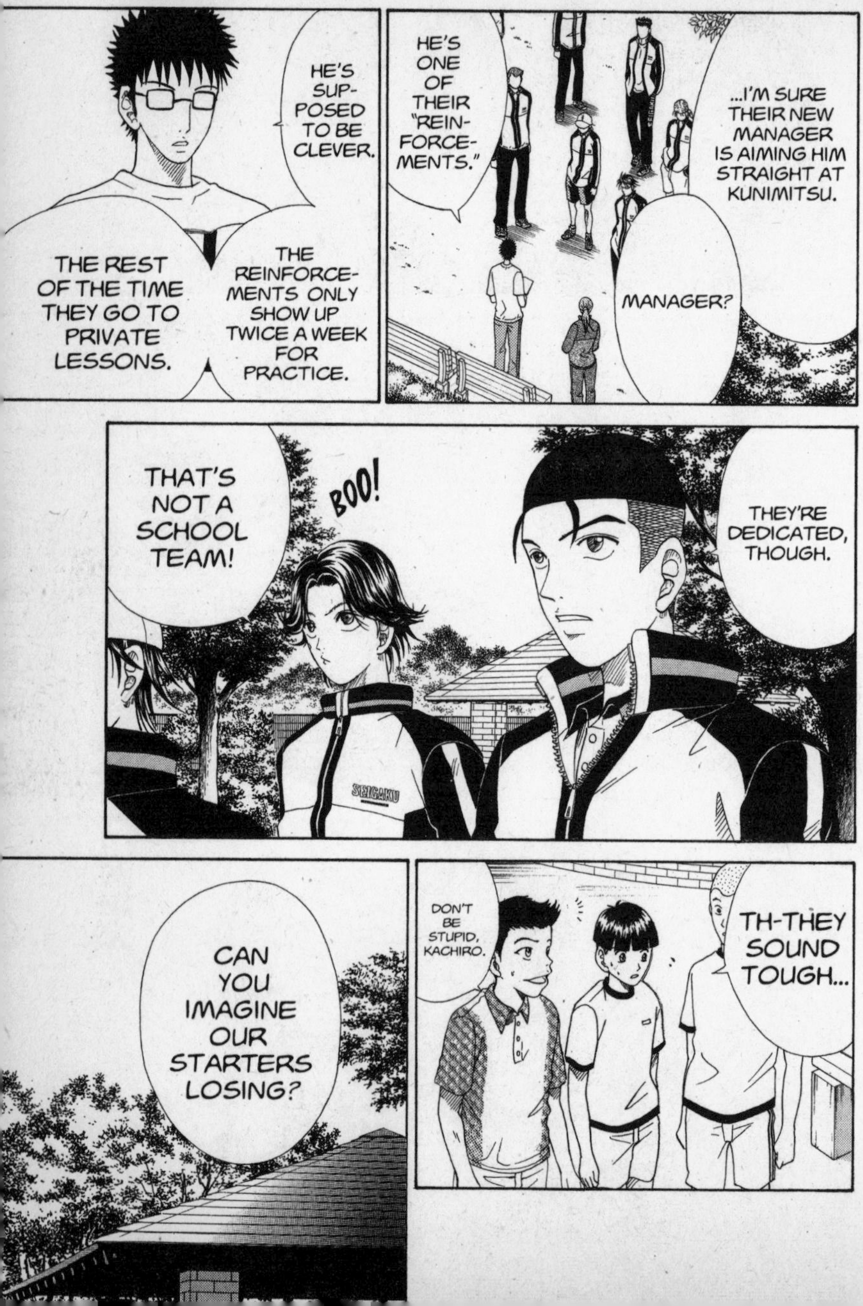
HE'S ONE OF THEIR "REINFORCEMENTS."
...I'M SURE THEIR NEW MANAGER IS AIMING HIM STRAIGHT AT KUNIMITSU.
MANAGER?
HE'S SUPPOSED TO BE CLEVER.
THE REINFORCEMENTS ONLY SHOW UP TWICE A WEEK FOR PRACTICE.
THE REST OF THE TIME THEY GO TO PRIVATE LESSONS.
THEY'RE DEDICATED, THOUGH.
BOO!
THAT'S NOT A SCHOOL TEAM!
SEIGAKU
TH-THEY SOUND TOUGH...
DON'T BE STUPID, KACHIRO.
CAN YOU IMAGINE OUR STARTERS LOSING?

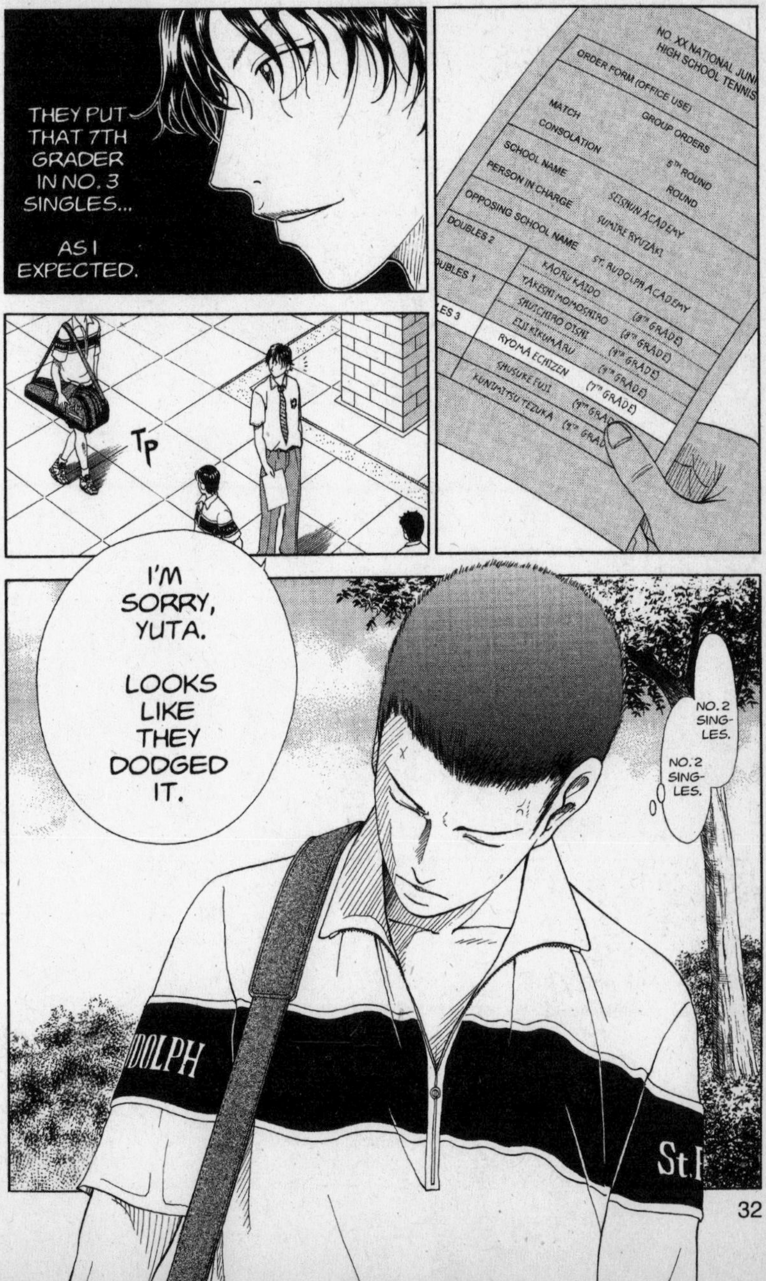
NO. XX NATIONAL JUNI
HIGH SCHOOL TENNIS
ORDER FORM (OFFICE USE)
MATCH
GROUP ORDERS
CONSOLATION
5TH ROUND
ROUND
SCHOOL NAME
SEISHUN ACADEMY
PERSON IN CHARGE
SUMIRE RYUZAKI
OPPOSING SCHOOL NAME
ST. RUDOLPH ACADEMY
DOUBLES 2
KAORU KAIDO (8TH GRADE)
TAKESHI MOMOSHIRO (8TH GRADE)
UBLES 1
SHUICHIRO OISHI (9TH GRADE)
EIJI KIKUMARU (9TH GRADE)
LES 3
RYOMA ECHIZEN (7TH GRADE)
SHUSUKE FUJI (9TH GRADE)
KUNIMITSU TEZUKA (9TH GRAD
THEY PUT THAT 7TH GRADER IN NO. 3 SINGLES...
AS I EXPECTED.
TP
NO. 2 SINGLES.
NO. 2 SINGLES.
I'M SORRY, YUTA.
LOOKS LIKE THEY DODGED IT.
DOLPH
St.R

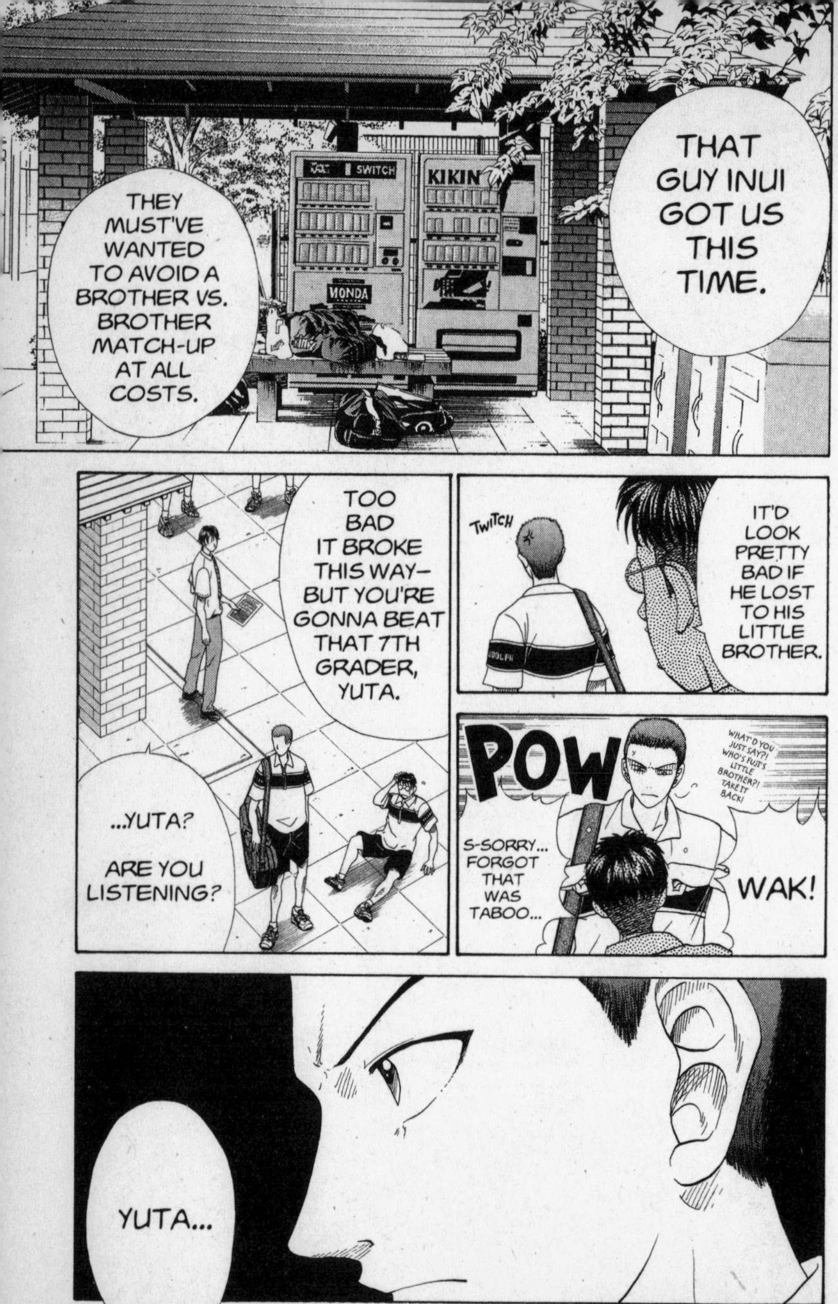
THAT GUY INUI GOT US THIS TIME.
THEY MUST'VE WANTED TO AVOID A BROTHER VS. BROTHER MATCH-UP AT ALL COSTS.
SWITCH
KIKIN
TWITCH
IT'D LOOK PRETTY BAD IF HE LOST TO HIS LITTLE BROTHER.
WHAT'D YOU JUST SAY?! WHO'S FUJI'S LITTLE BROTHER?! TAKE IT BACK!
POW
WAK!
S-SORRY... FORGOT THAT WAS TABOO...
TOO BAD IT BROKE THIS WAY— BUT YOU'RE GONNA BEAT THAT 7TH GRADER, YUTA.
...YUTA?
ARE YOU LISTENING?
YUTA...

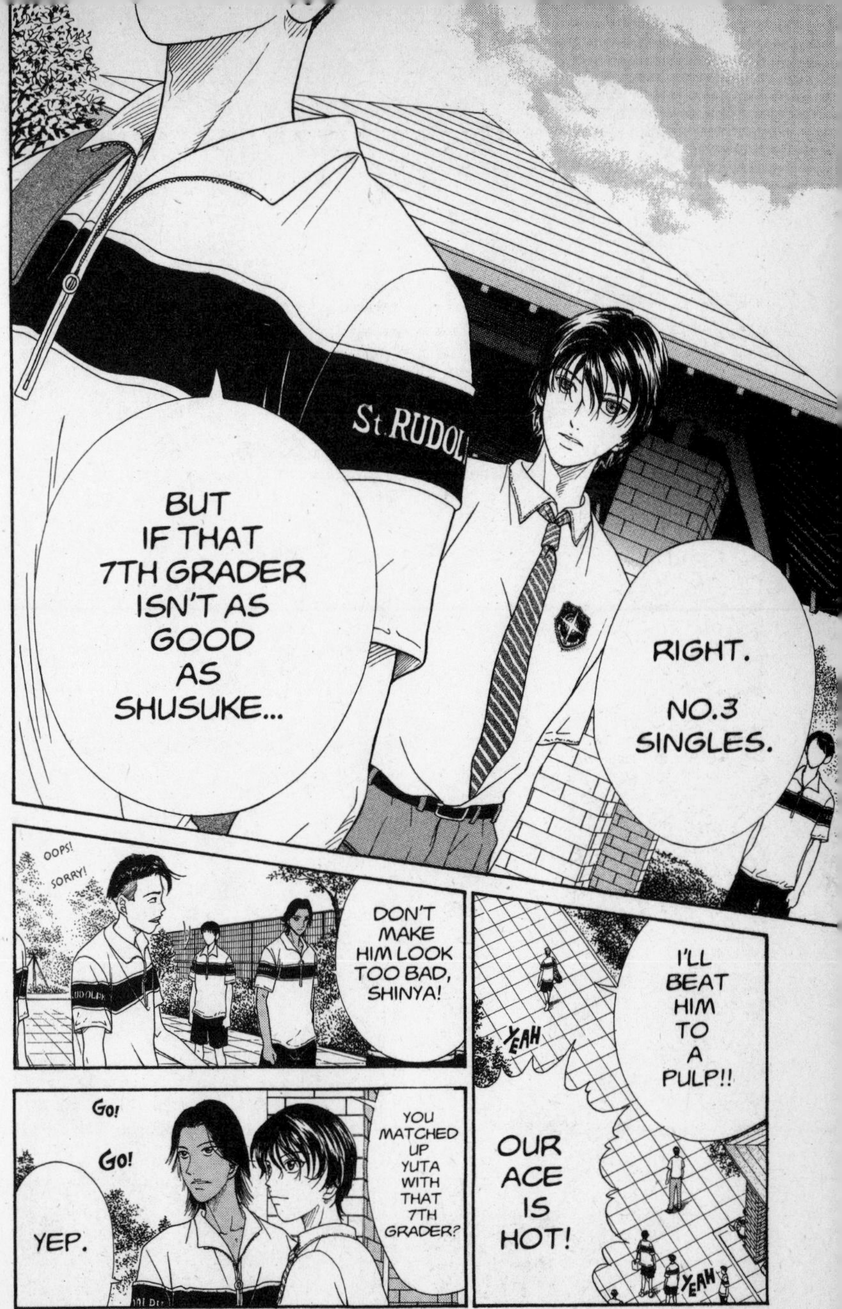
St. RUDOL
RIGHT. NO.3 SINGLES.
BUT IF THAT 7TH GRADER ISN'T AS GOOD AS SHUSUKE...
I'LL BEAT HIM TO A PULP!!
YEAH
OUR ACE IS HOT!
YEAH
DON'T MAKE HIM LOOK TOO BAD, SHINYA!
OOPS!
SORRY!
YOU MATCHED UP YUTA WITH THAT 7TH GRADER?
GO!
GO!
YEP.

READ THIS WAY

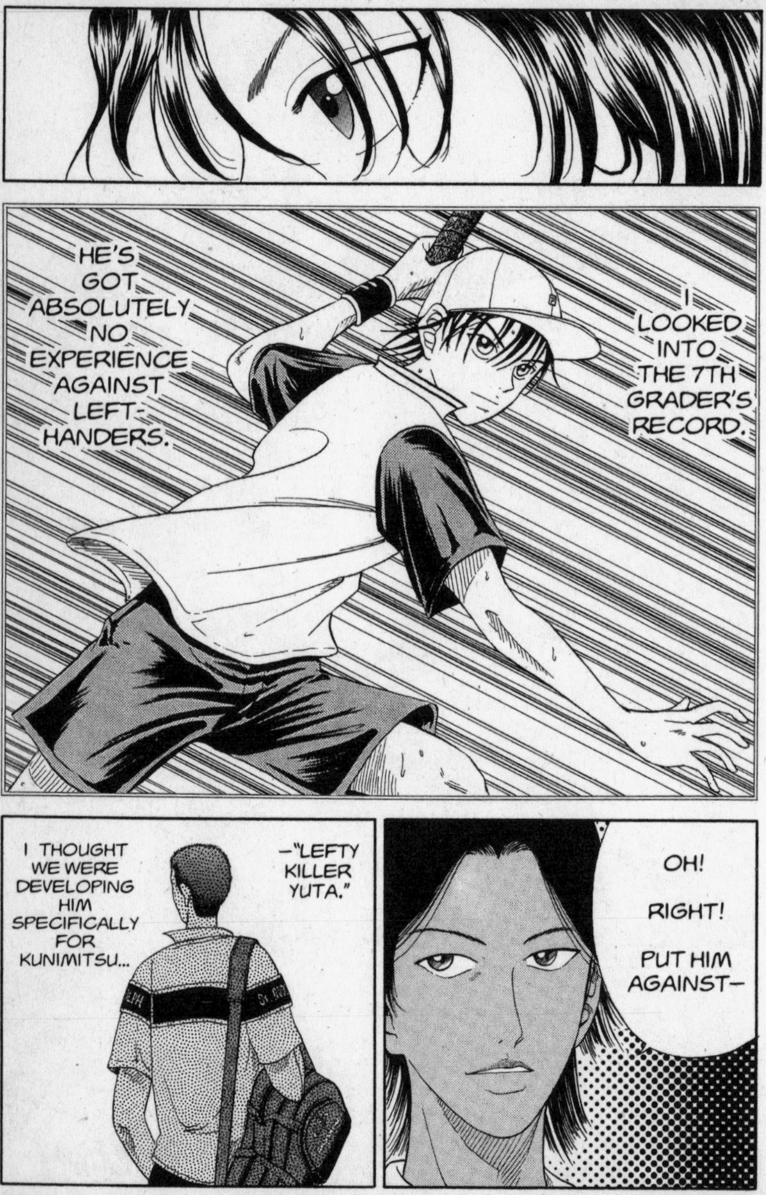
I LOOKED INTO THE 7TH GRADER'S RECORD.
HE'S GOT ABSOLUTELY NO EXPERIENCE AGAINST LEFT-HANDERS.
OH!
RIGHT!
PUT HIM AGAINST—
—"LEFTY KILLER YUTA."
I THOUGHT WE WERE DEVELOPING HIM SPECIFICALLY FOR KUNIMITSU...

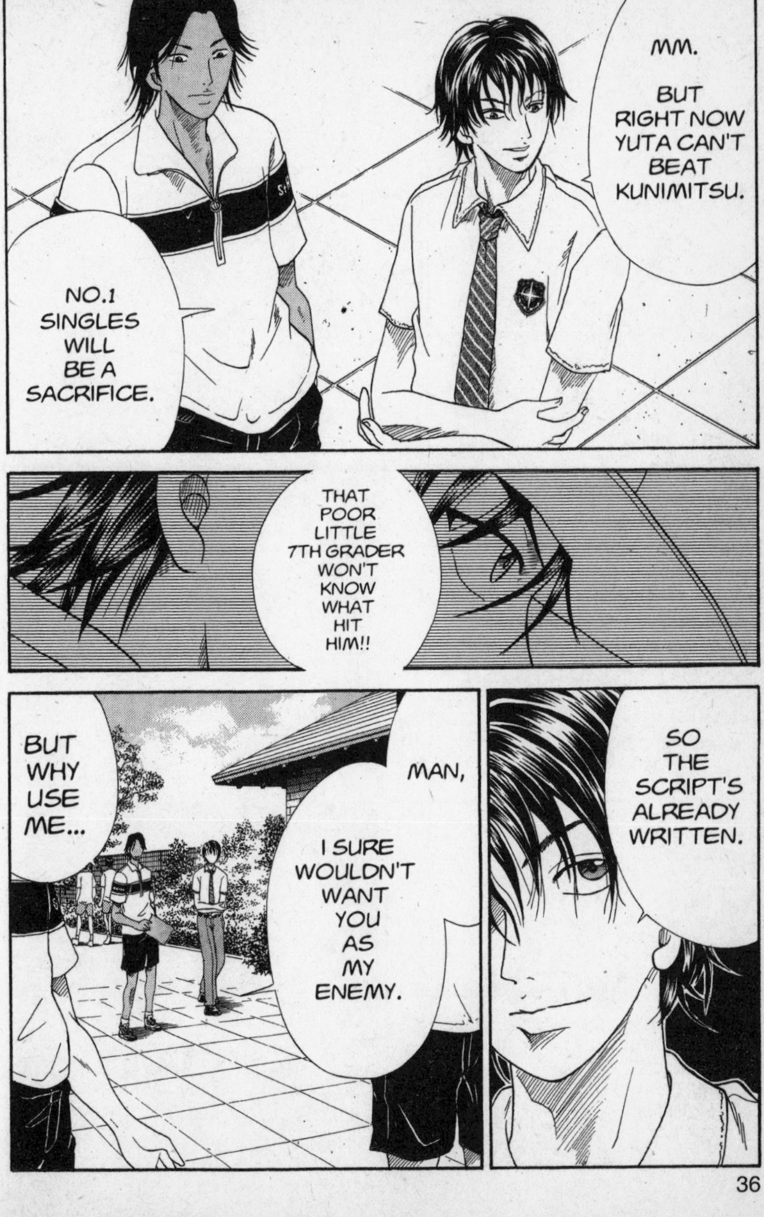
MM.
BUT RIGHT NOW YUTA CAN'T BEAT KUNIMITSU.
NO.1 SINGLES WILL BE A SACRIFICE.
THAT POOR LITTLE 7TH GRADER WON'T KNOW WHAT HIT HIM!!
SO THE SCRIPT'S ALREADY WRITTEN.
MAN,
I SURE WOULDN'T WANT YOU AS MY ENEMY.
BUT WHY USE ME...

READ THIS WAY

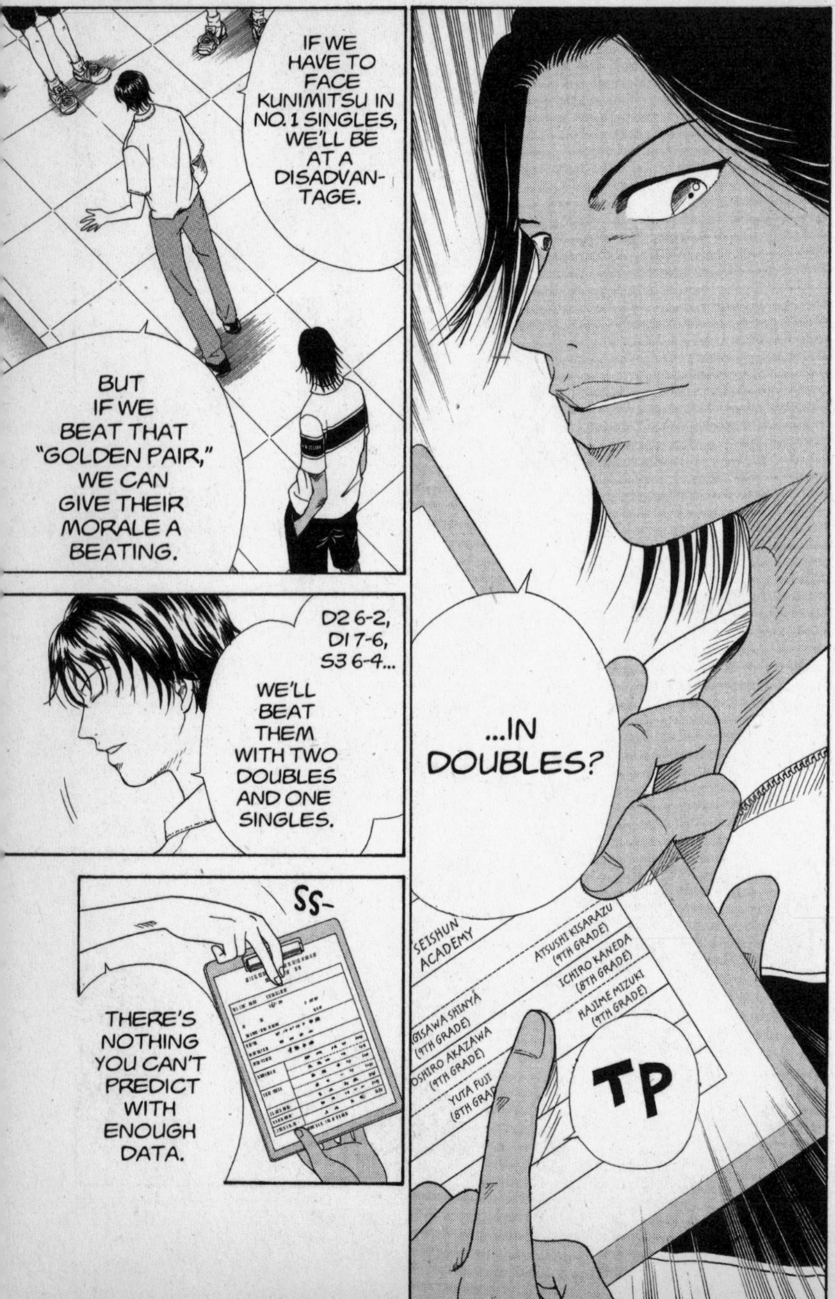
...IN DOUBLES?
SEISHUN ACADEMY
ATSUSHI KISARAZU (9TH GRADE)
ICHIRO KANEDA (8TH GRADE)
HAJIME MIZUKI (9TH GRADE)
OSHIRO AKAZAWA (9TH GRADE)
YUTA FUJI (8TH GRAD
TP
IF WE HAVE TO FACE KUNIMITSU IN NO.1 SINGLES, WE'LL BE AT A DISADVANTAGE.
BUT IF WE BEAT THAT "GOLDEN PAIR," WE CAN GIVE THEIR MORALE A BEATING.
D2 6-2, D1 7-6, S3 6-4...
WE'LL BEAT THEM WITH TWO DOUBLES AND ONE SINGLES.
SS-
THERE'S NOTHING YOU CAN'T PREDICT WITH ENOUGH DATA.

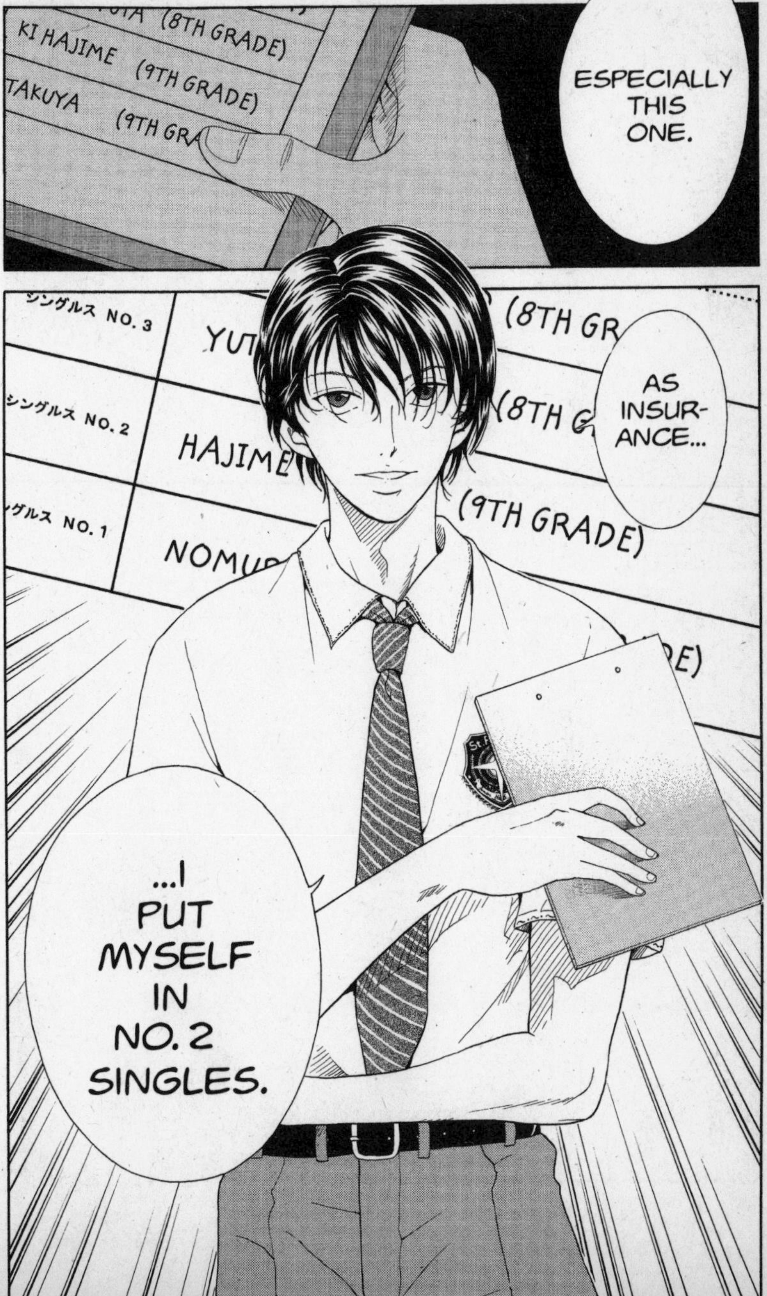
ESPECIALLY THIS ONE.
KI HAJIME (9TH GRADE)
シングルス NO. 3
シングルス NO. 2
HAJIME
(9TH GRADE)
AS INSURANCE...
...I PUT MYSELF IN NO. 2 SINGLES.

READ THIS WAY

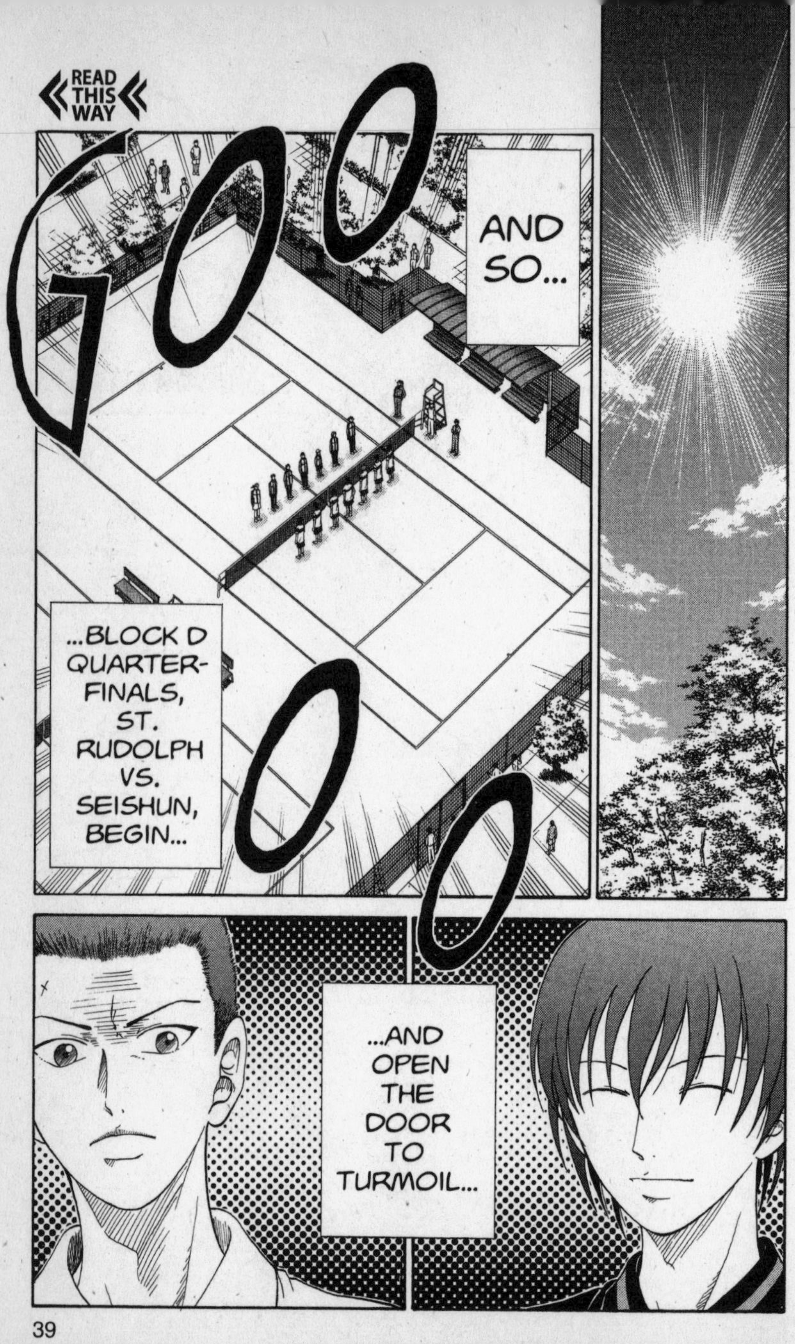
AND SO...
...BLOCK D QUARTER-FINALS, ST. RUDOLPH VS. SEISHUN, BEGIN...
GOOOO
...AND OPEN THE DOOR TO TURMOIL...

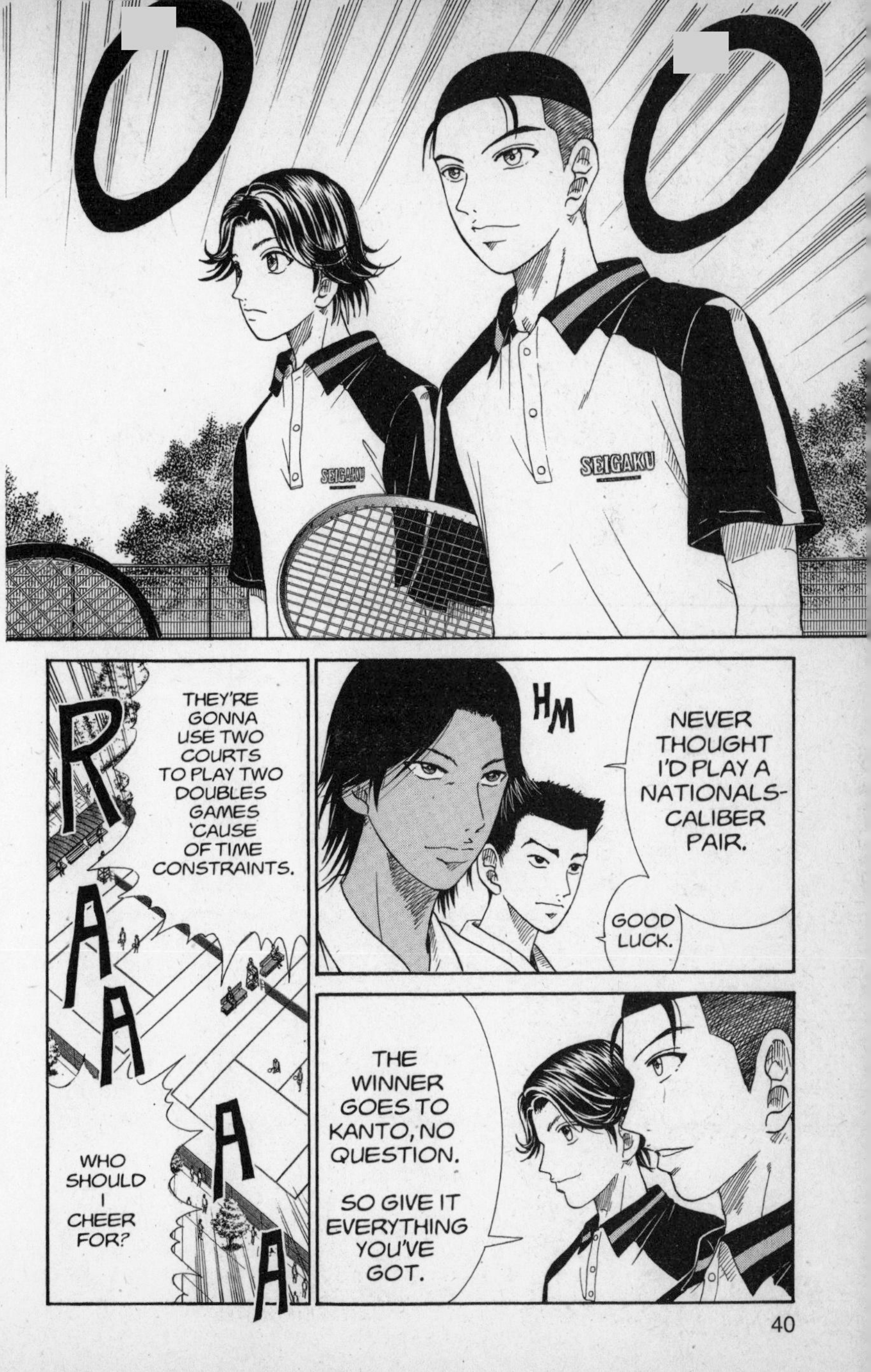
HM
NEVER THOUGHT I'D PLAY A NATIONALS-CALIBER PAIR.
GOOD LUCK.
THE WINNER GOES TO KANTO, NO QUESTION.
SO GIVE IT EVERYTHING YOU'VE GOT.
RAAAAA
THEY'RE GONNA USE TWO COURTS TO PLAY TWO DOUBLES GAMES 'CAUSE OF TIME CONSTRAINTS.
WHO SHOULD I CHEER FOR?

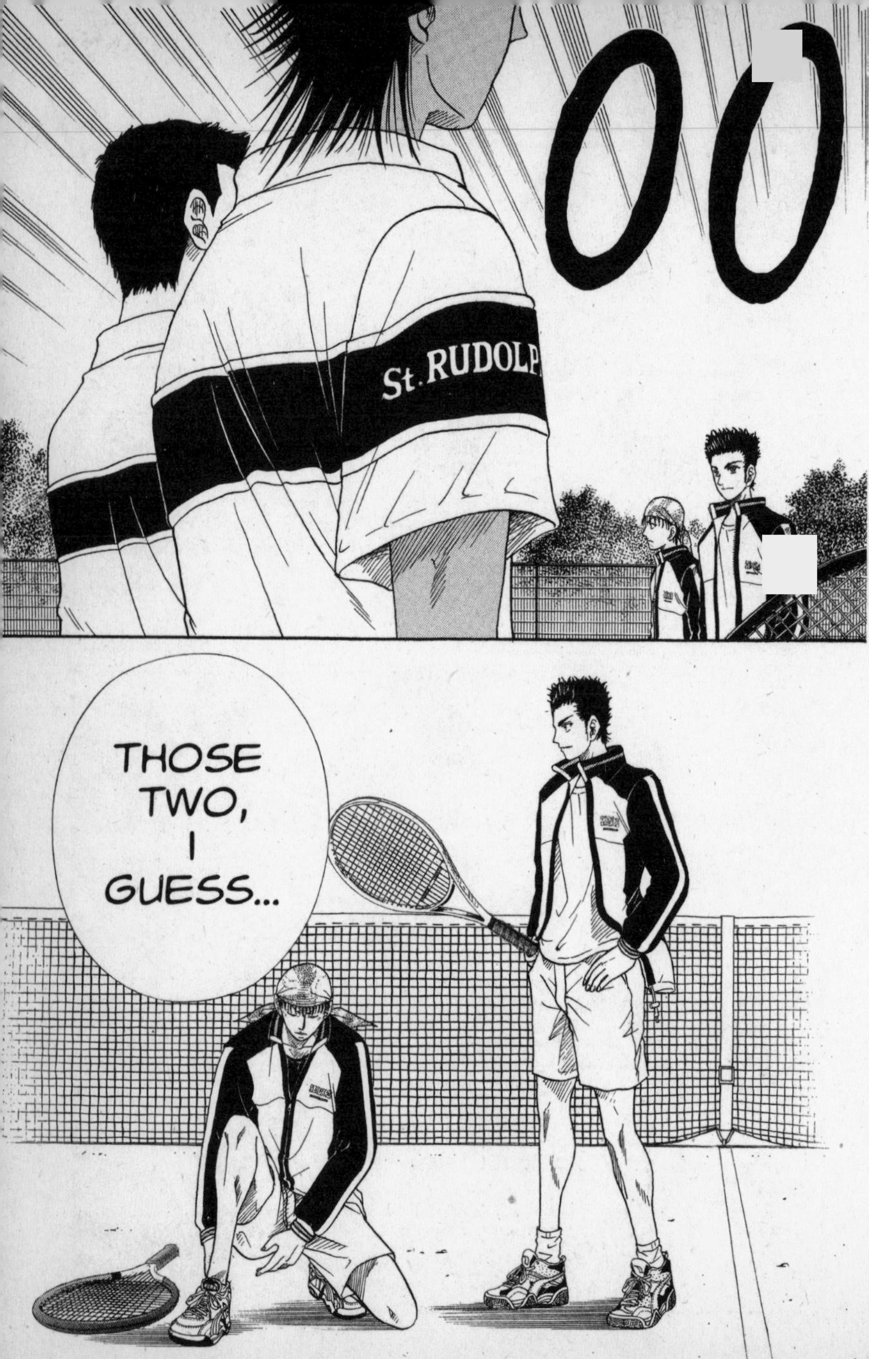
St.RUDOLP
THOSE TWO, I GUESS...

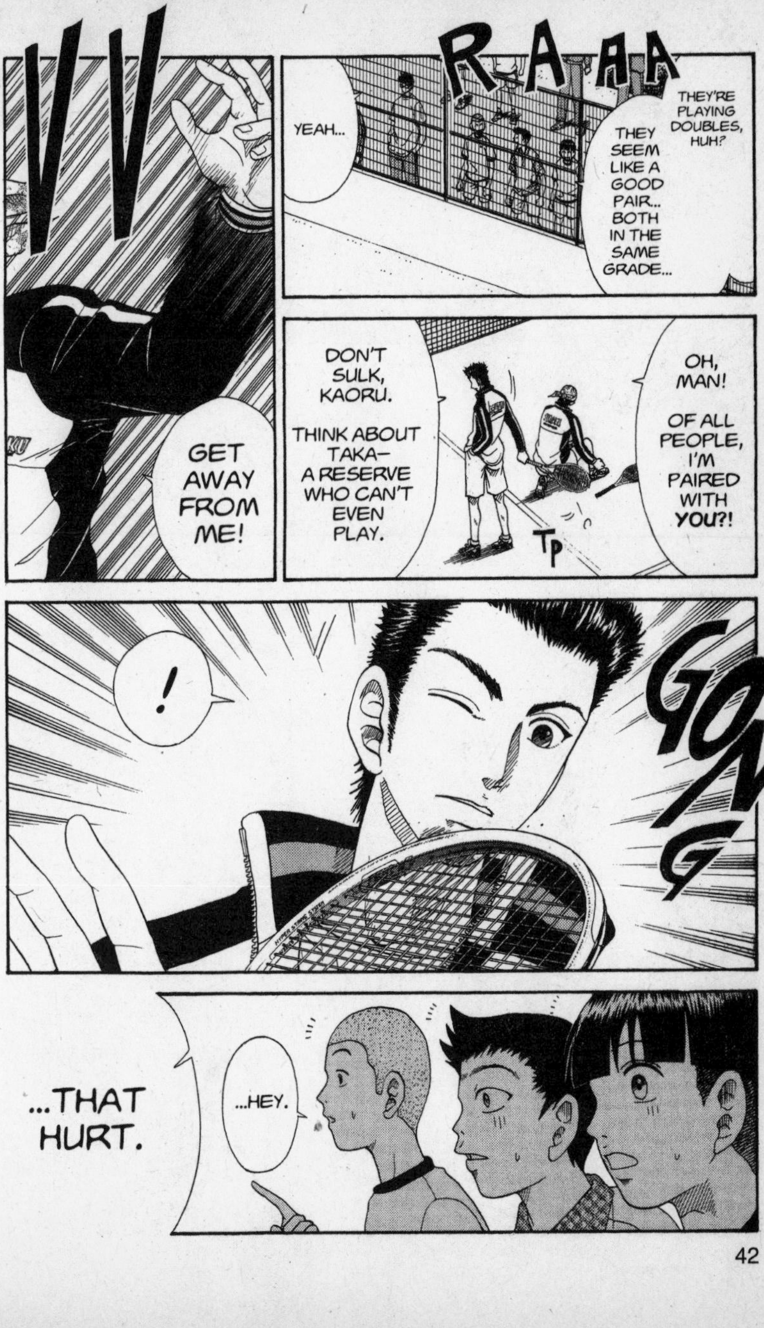
RAAA
THEY'RE PLAYING DOUBLES, HUH?
THEY SEEM LIKE A GOOD PAIR... BOTH IN THE SAME GRADE...
YEAH...
OH, MAN! OF ALL PEOPLE, I'M PAIRED WITH **YOU**?!
TP
DON'T SULK, KAORU. THINK ABOUT TAKA— A RESERVE WHO CAN'T EVEN PLAY.
VV
GET AWAY FROM ME!
GONG
!
...HEY.
...THAT HURT.

READ THIS WAY

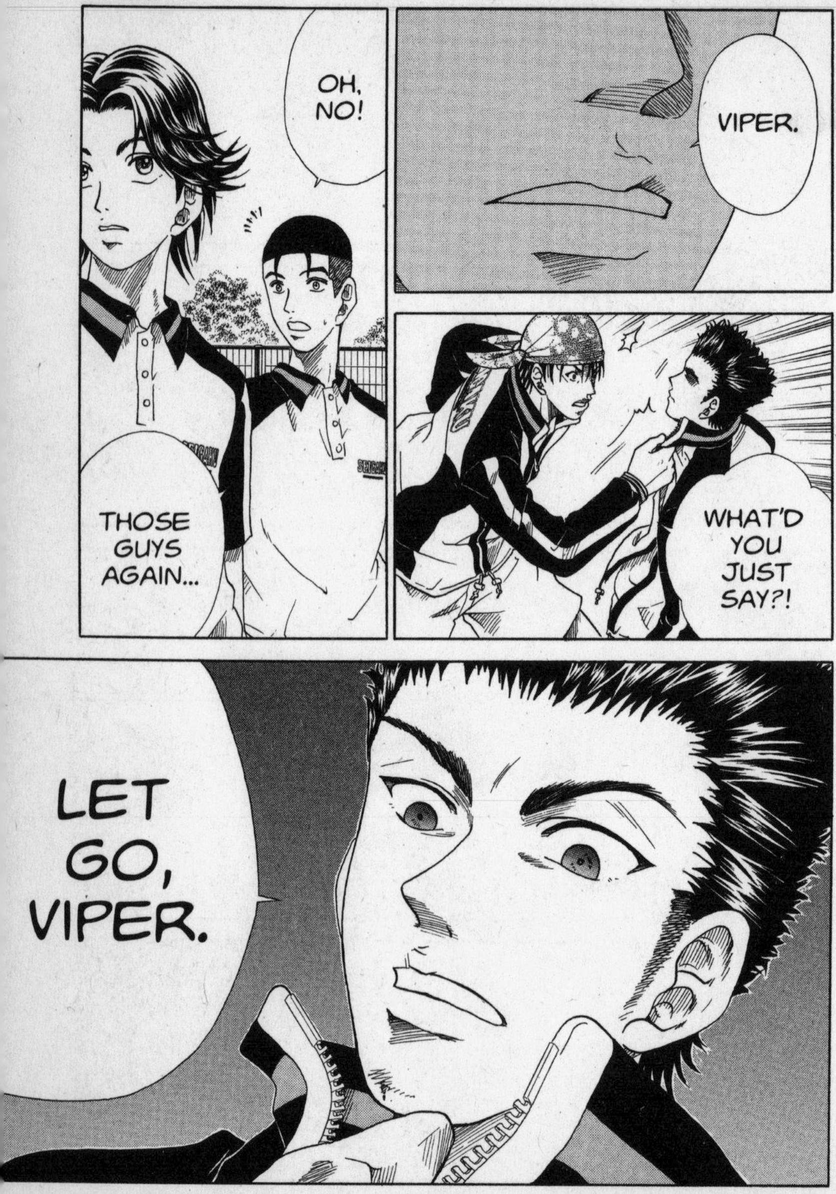
VIPER.
WHAT'D YOU JUST SAY?!
OH, NO!
THOSE GUYS AGAIN...
LET GO, VIPER.

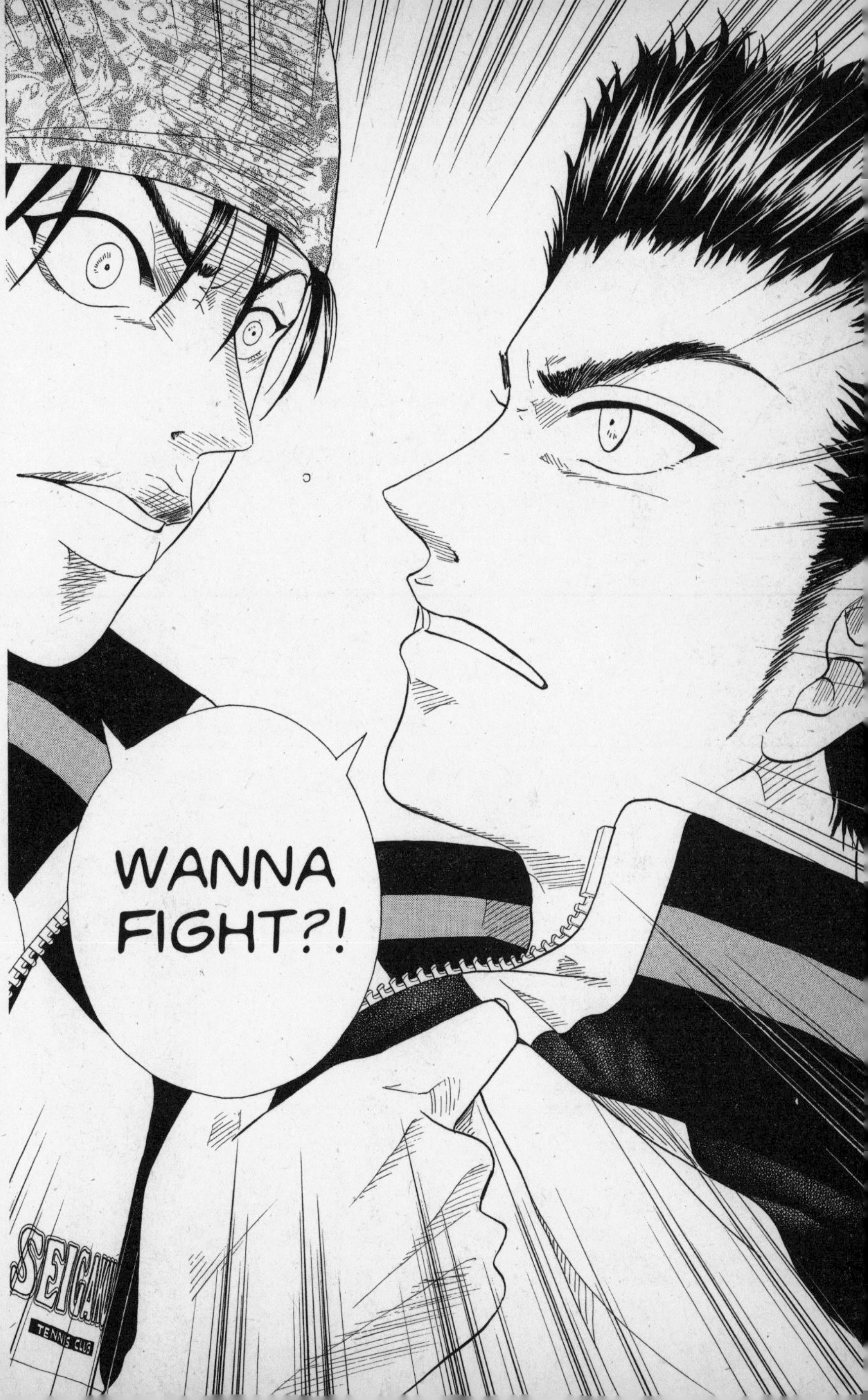
WANNA FIGHT?!
SEIGAKU
TENNIS CLUB

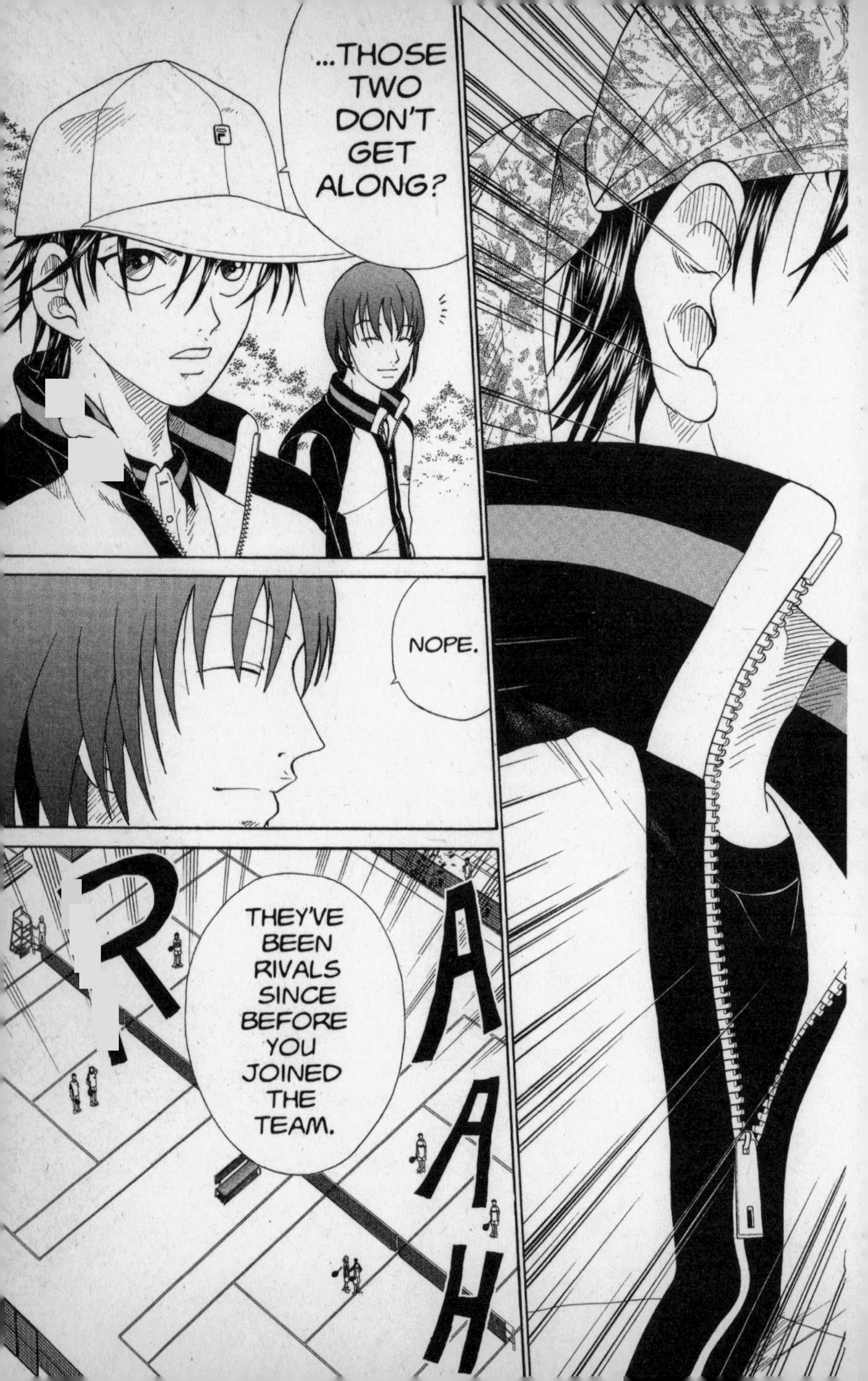
...THOSE TWO DON'T GET ALONG?
NOPE.
THEY'VE BEEN RIVALS SINCE BEFORE YOU JOINED THE TEAM.
RAAH

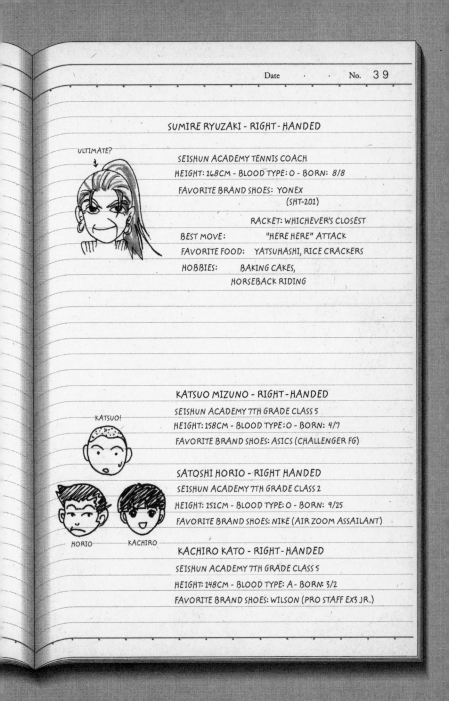

SUMIRE RYUZAKI - RIGHT-HANDED

ULTIMATE?

SEISHUN ACADEMY TENNIS COACH
HEIGHT: 168CM - BLOOD TYPE: O - BORN: 8/8
FAVORITE BRAND SHOES: YONEX
                                    (SHT-201)
                        RACKET: WHICHEVER'S CLOSEST
BEST MOVE: "HERE HERE" ATTACK
FAVORITE FOOD: YATSUHASHI, RICE CRACKERS
HOBBIES: BAKING CAKES,
                    HORSEBACK RIDING

KATSUO MIZUNO - RIGHT-HANDED

KATSUO!

SEISHUN ACADEMY 7TH GRADE CLASS 5
HEIGHT: 158CM - BLOOD TYPE: O - BORN: 4/7
FAVORITE BRAND SHOES: ASICS (CHALLENGER FG)

SATOSHI HORIO - RIGHT HANDED

SEISHUN ACADEMY 7TH GRADE CLASS 2
HEIGHT: 151CM - BLOOD TYPE: O - BORN: 9/25
FAVORITE BRAND SHOES: NIKE (AIR ZOOM ASSAILANT)

HORIO   KACHIRO

KACHIRO KATO - RIGHT-HANDED

SEISHUN ACADEMY 7TH GRADE CLASS 5
HEIGHT: 148CM - BLOOD TYPE: A - BORN: 3/2
FAVORITE BRAND SHOES: WILSON (PRO STAFF EX3 JR.)

GENIUS 54: MOMO & KAIDO

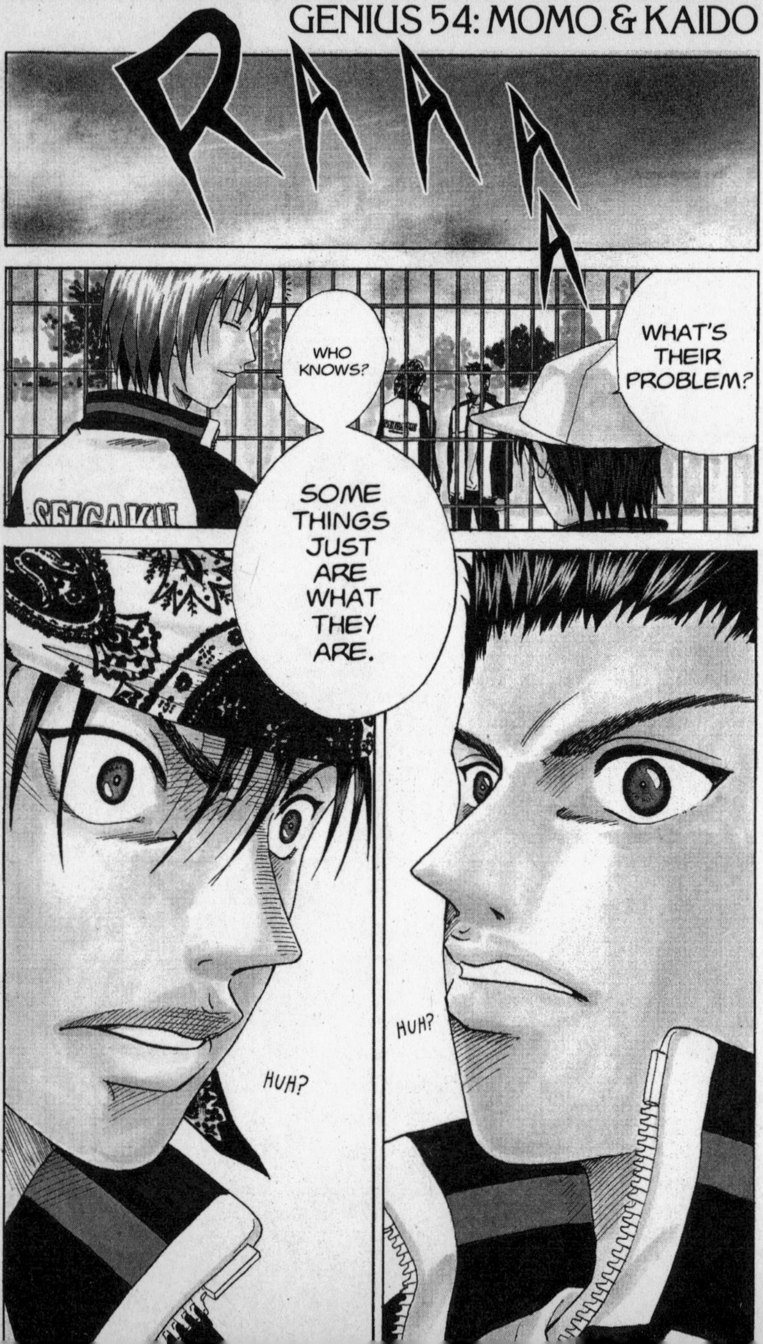
RAAAA
WHAT'S THEIR PROBLEM?
WHO KNOWS?
SOME THINGS JUST ARE WHAT THEY ARE.
SEIGAKU
HUH?
HUH?

GENIUS 54: MOMO & KAIDO

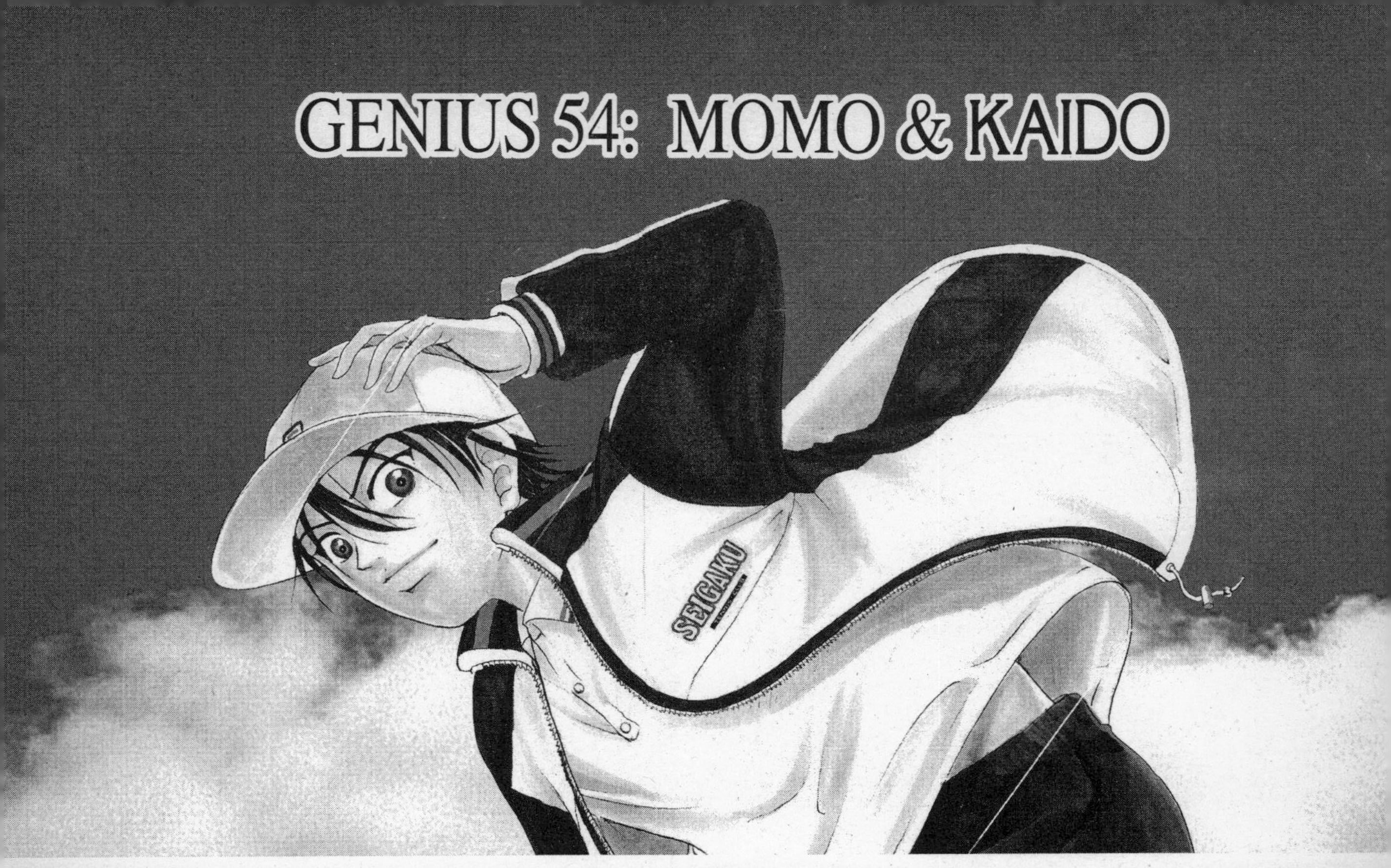
SEIGAKU

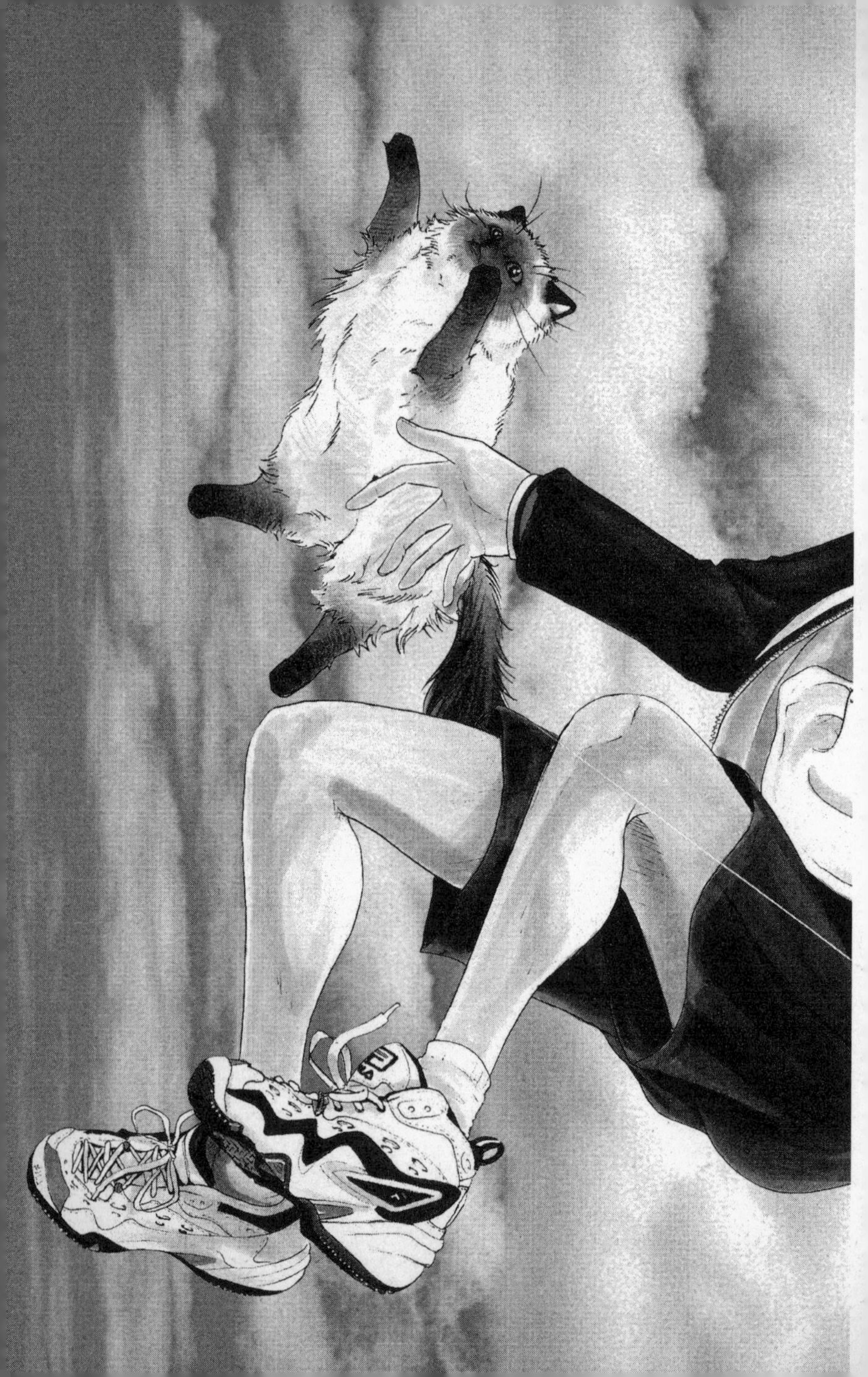

テニスの王子様

THE PRINCE OF TENNIS™

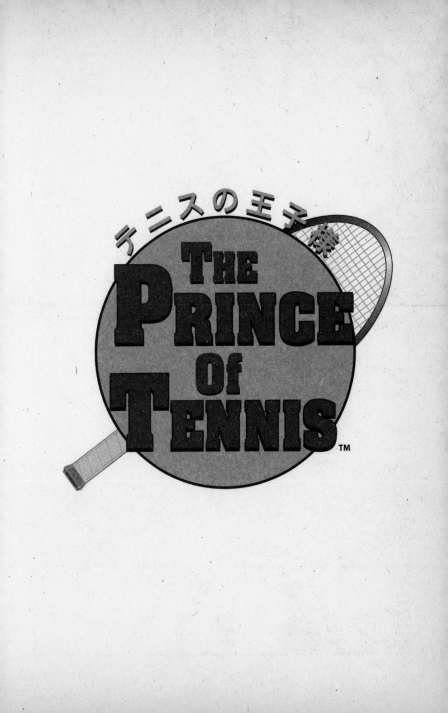

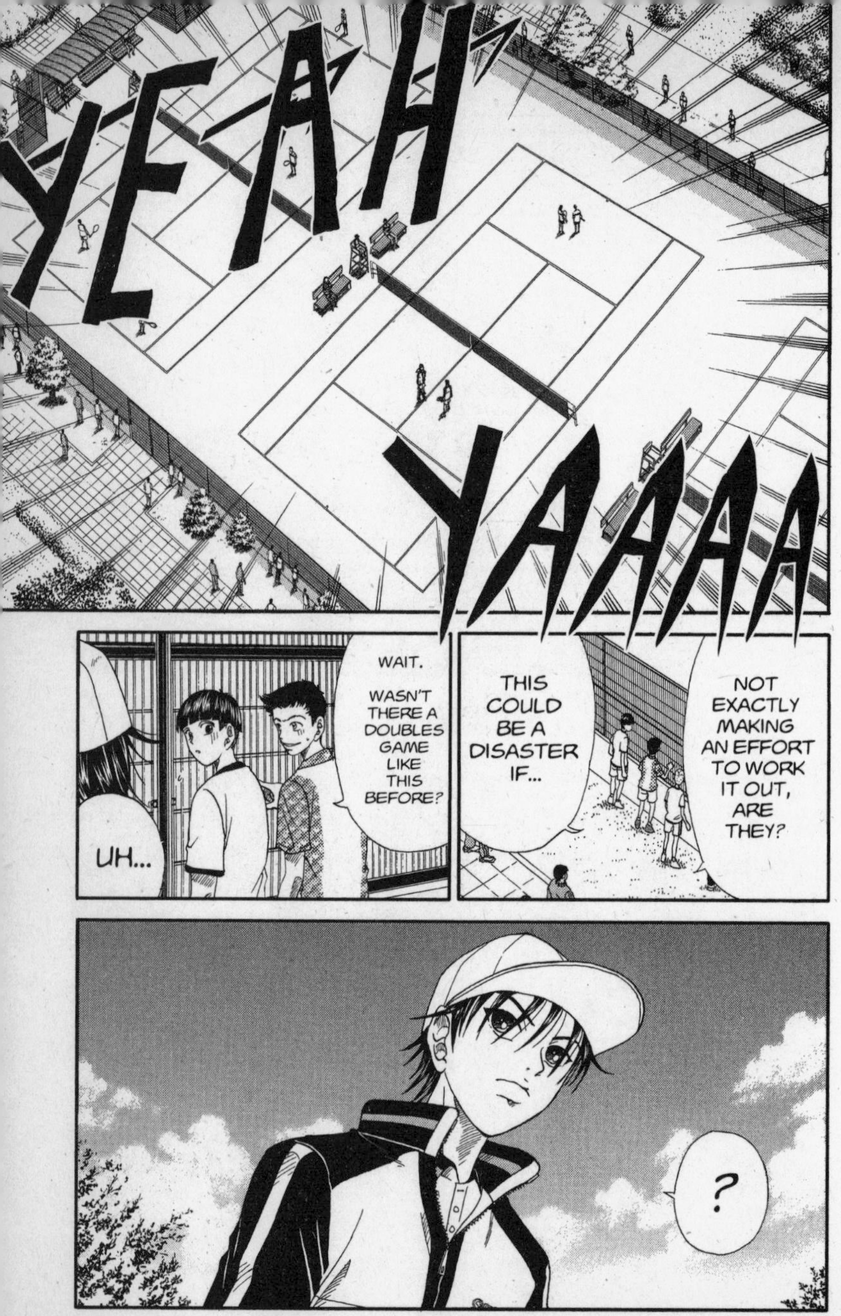
YE-A-H
YAAAA
NOT EXACTLY MAKING AN EFFORT TO WORK IT OUT, ARE THEY?
THIS COULD BE A DISASTER IF...
WAIT.
WASN'T THERE A DOUBLES GAME LIKE THIS BEFORE?
UH...
?

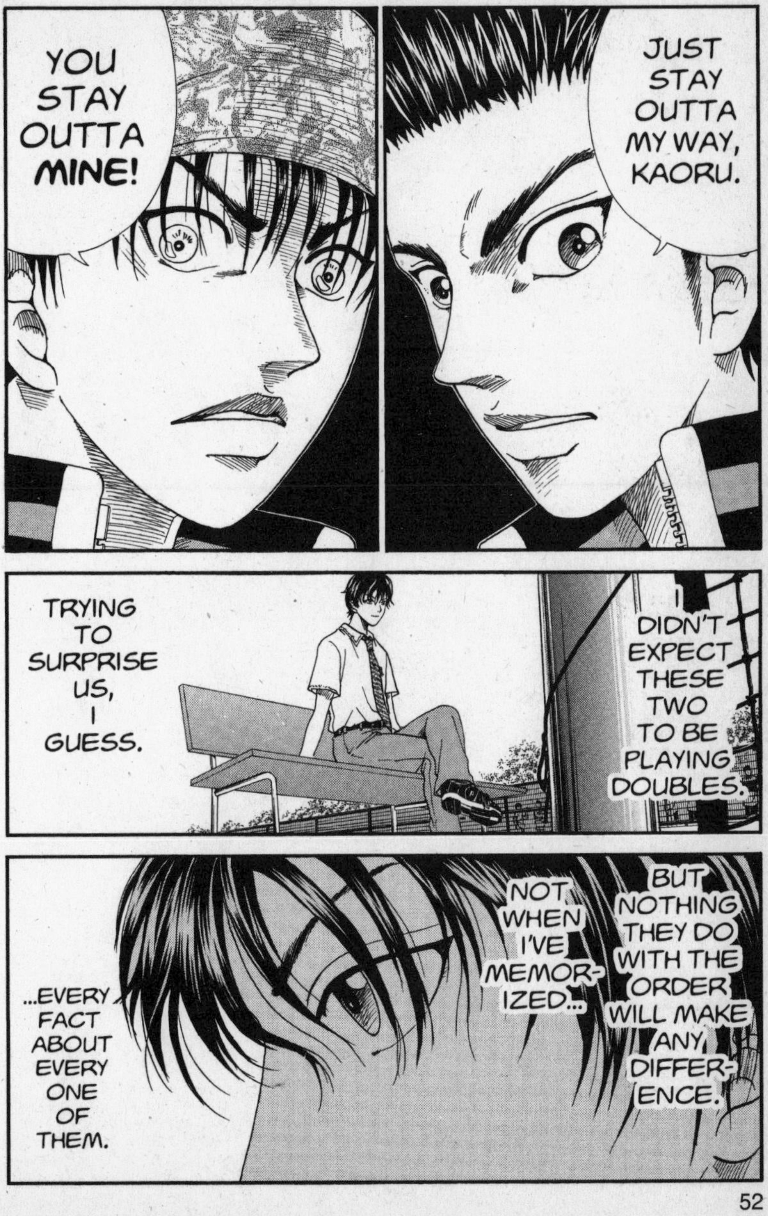
JUST STAY OUTTA MY WAY, KAORU.
YOU STAY OUTTA MINE!
I DIDN'T EXPECT THESE TWO TO BE PLAYING DOUBLES.
TRYING TO SURPRISE US, I GUESS.
BUT NOTHING THEY DO WITH THE ORDER WILL MAKE ANY DIFFERENCE.
NOT WHEN I'VE MEMORIZED...
...EVERY FACT ABOUT EVERY ONE OF THEM.

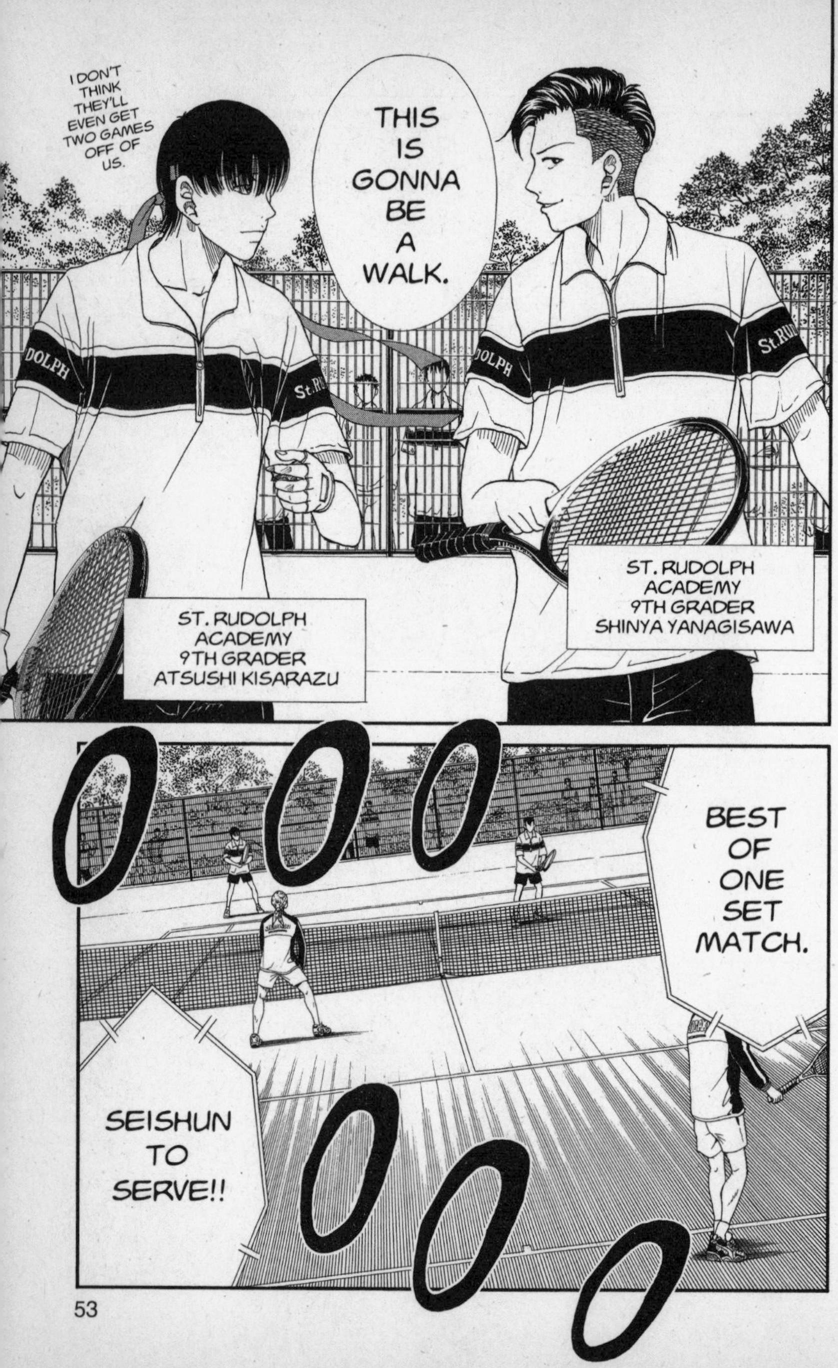
ST. RUDOLPH ACADEMY 9TH GRADER SHINYA YANAGISAWA
THIS IS GONNA BE A WALK.
I DON'T THINK THEY'LL EVEN GET TWO GAMES OFF OF US.
ST. RUDOLPH ACADEMY 9TH GRADER ATSUSHI KISARAZU
BEST OF ONE SET MATCH.
SEISHUN TO SERVE!!

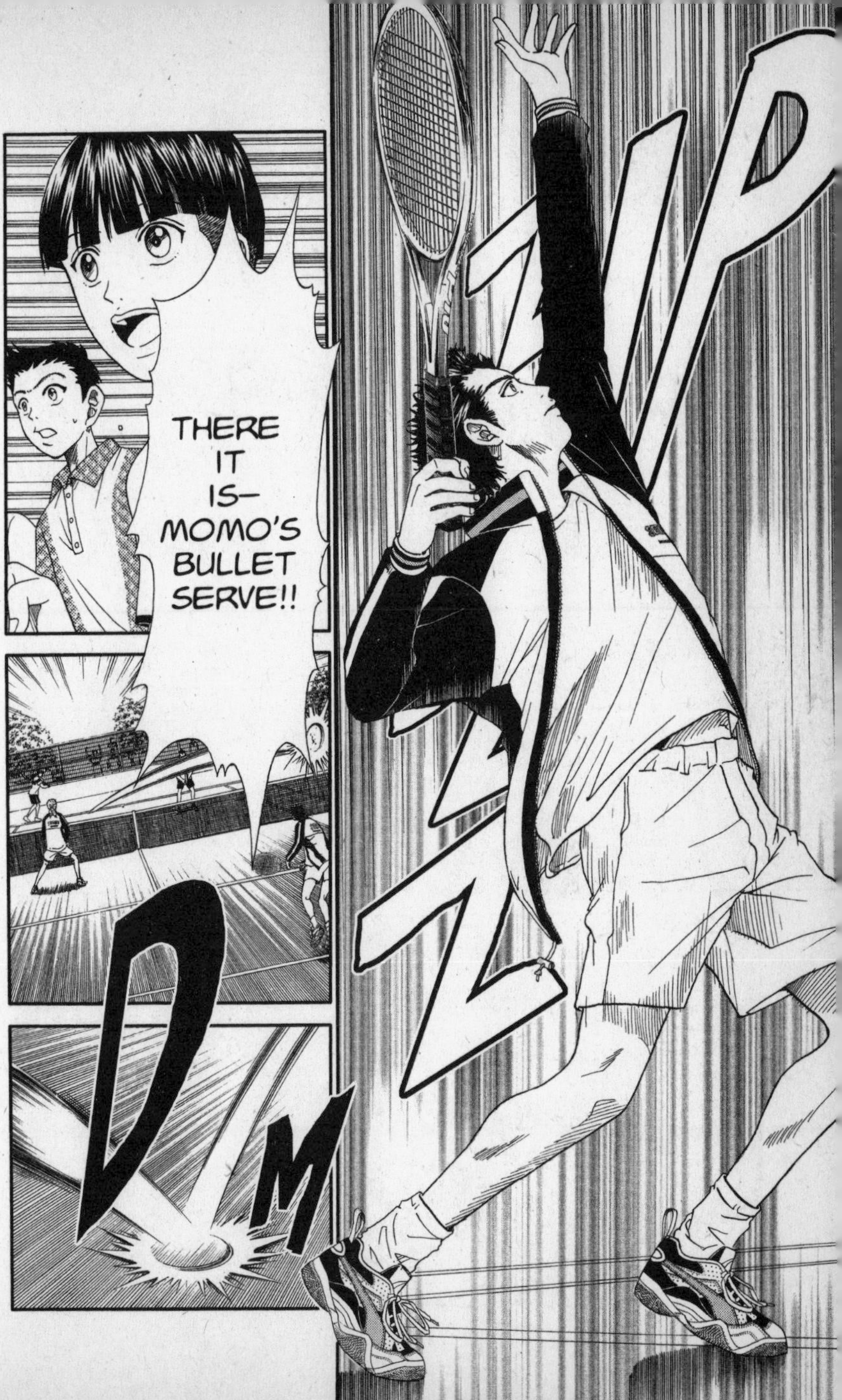
THERE IT IS— MOMO'S BULLET SERVE!!

READ THIS WAY

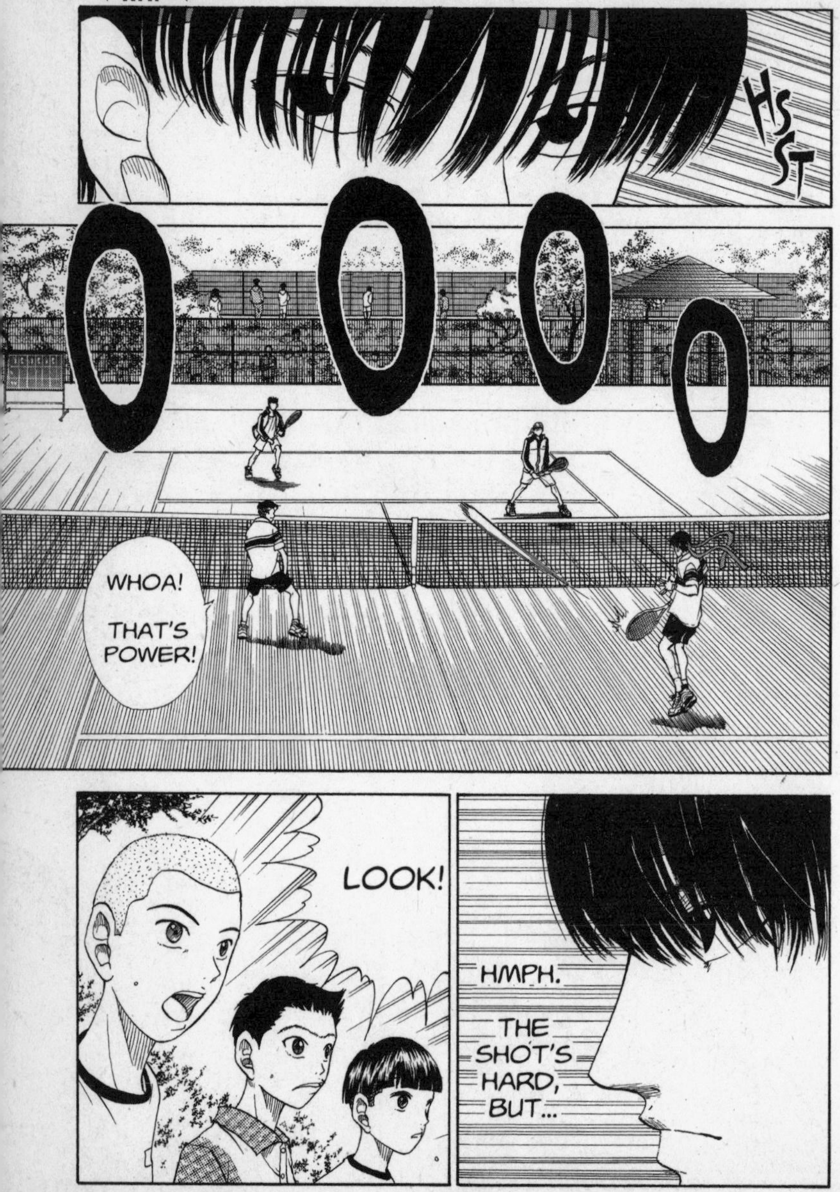
HSST
WHOA! THAT'S POWER!
HMPH. THE SHOT'S HARD, BUT...
LOOK!

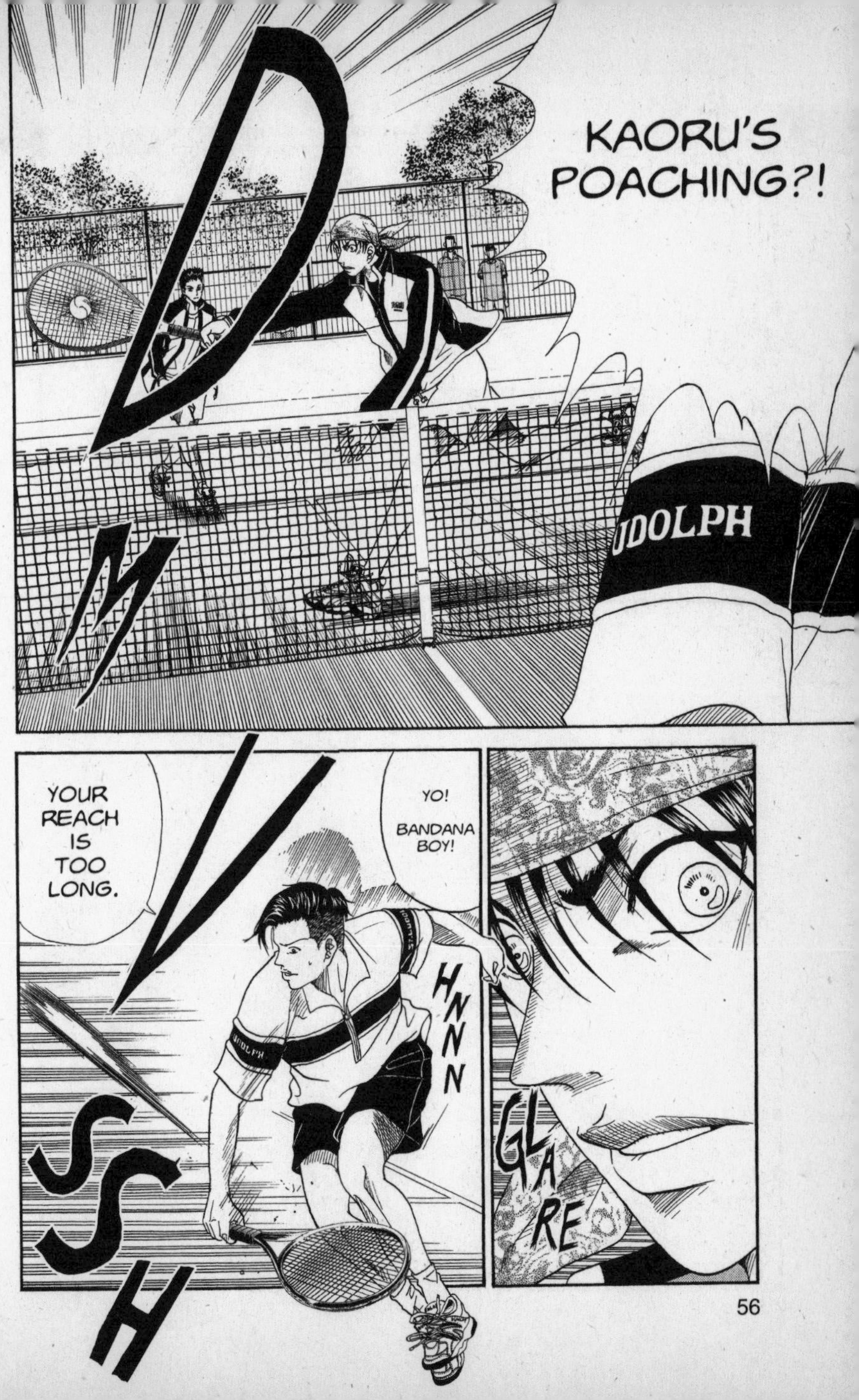
KAORU'S POACHING?!
DM
UDOLPH
GLARE
YO! BANDANA BOY!
YOUR REACH IS TOO LONG.
HNNN
SSH

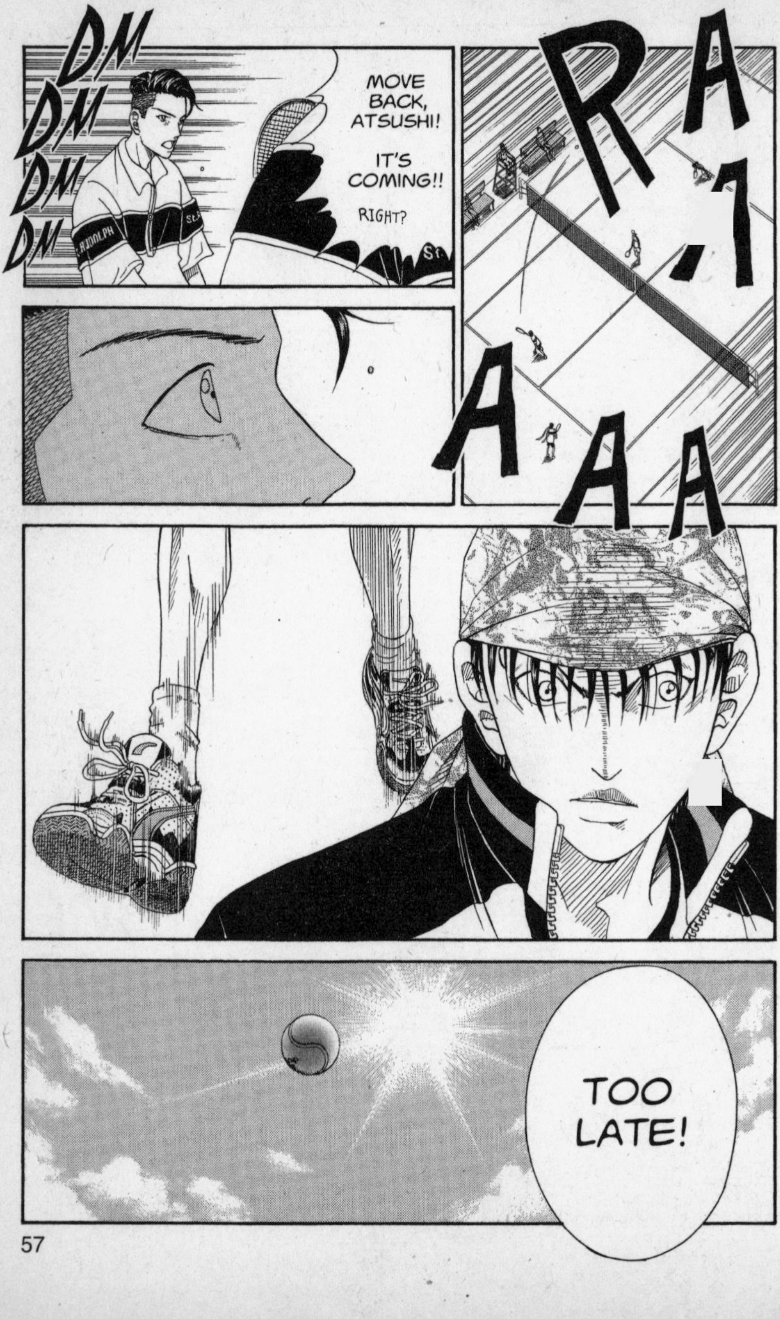
RA
AAA
DM DM DM DM DM
MOVE BACK, ATSUSHI!
IT'S COMING!!
RIGHT?
TOO LATE!

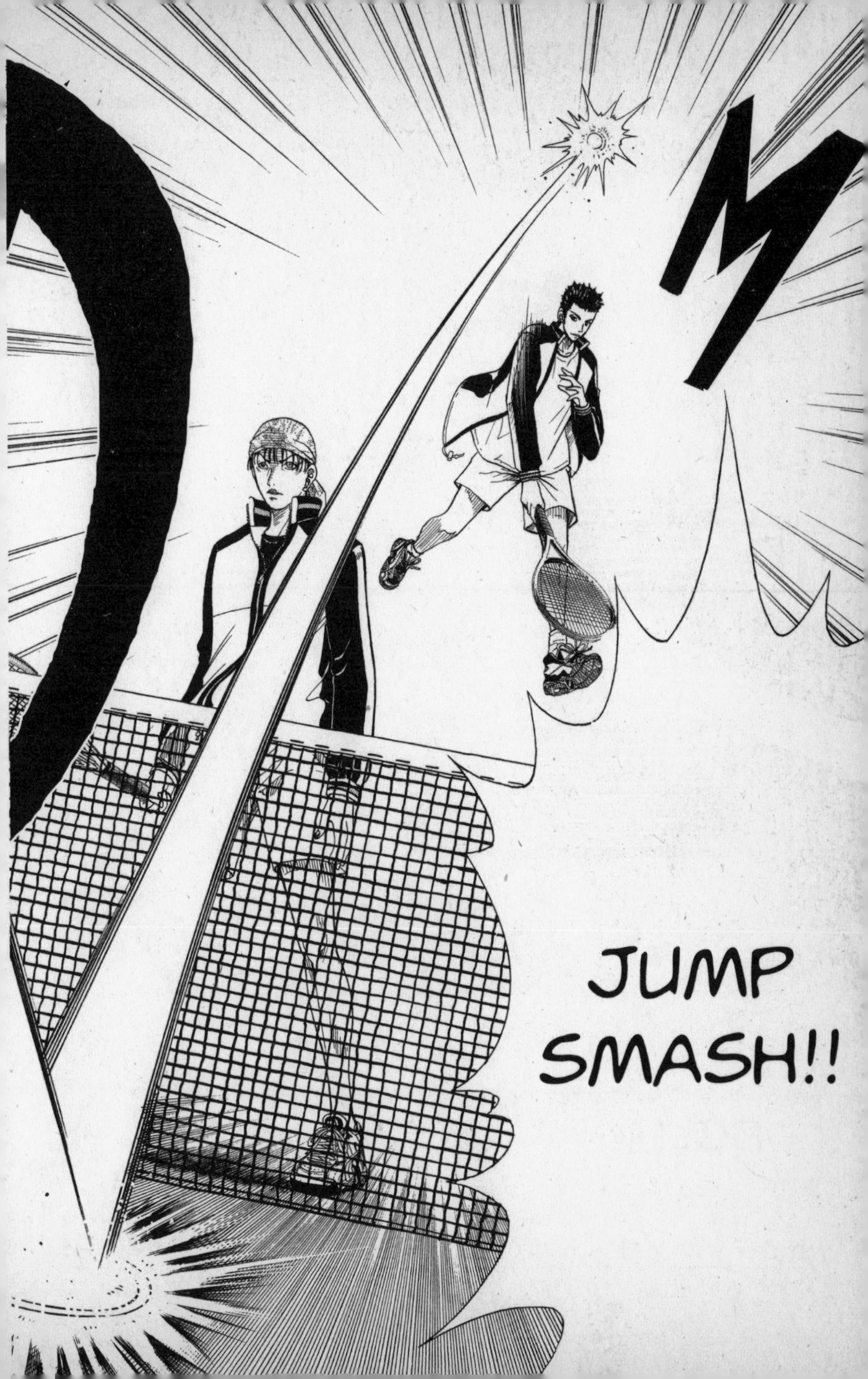
M
JUMP SMASH!!

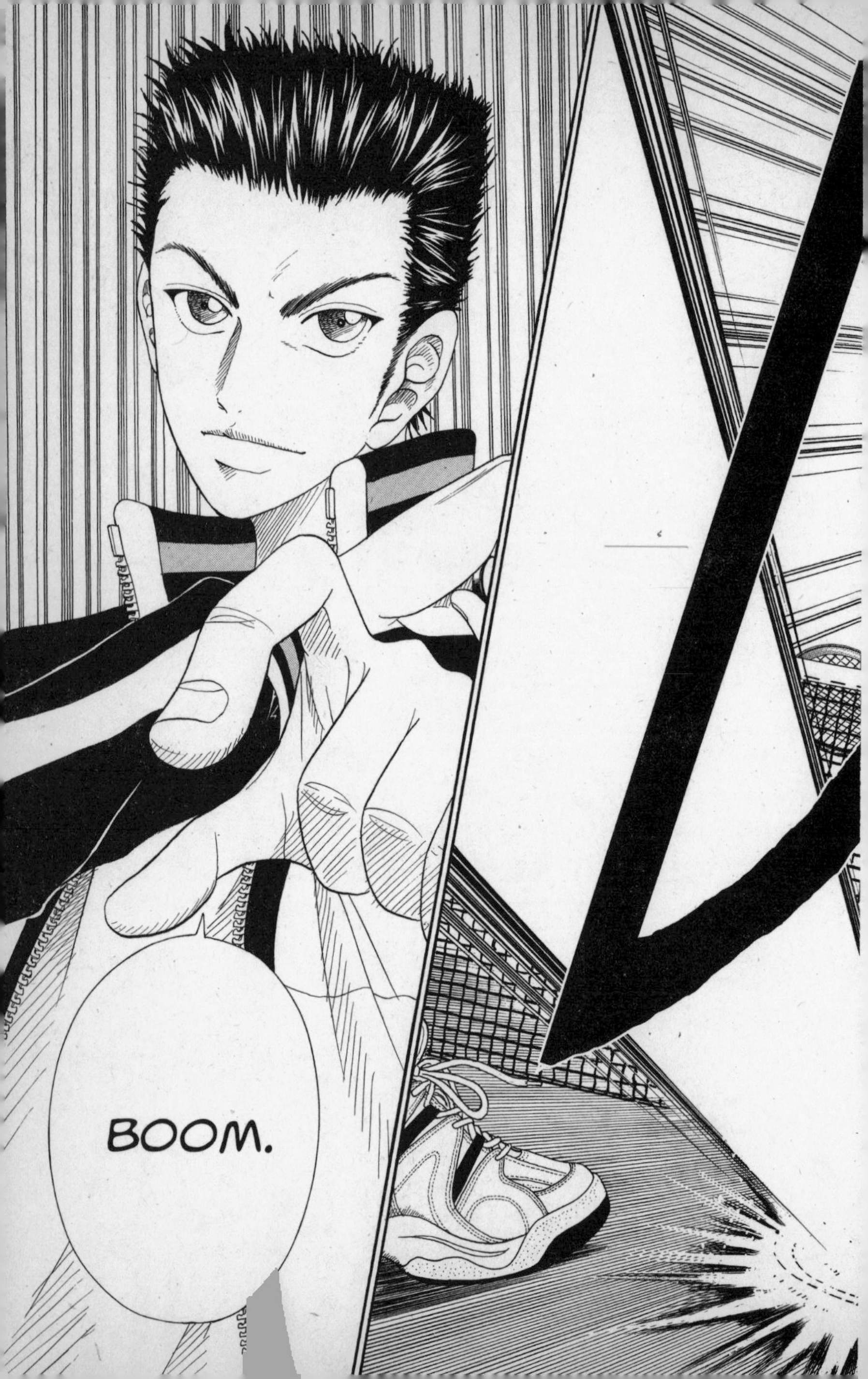
BOOM.

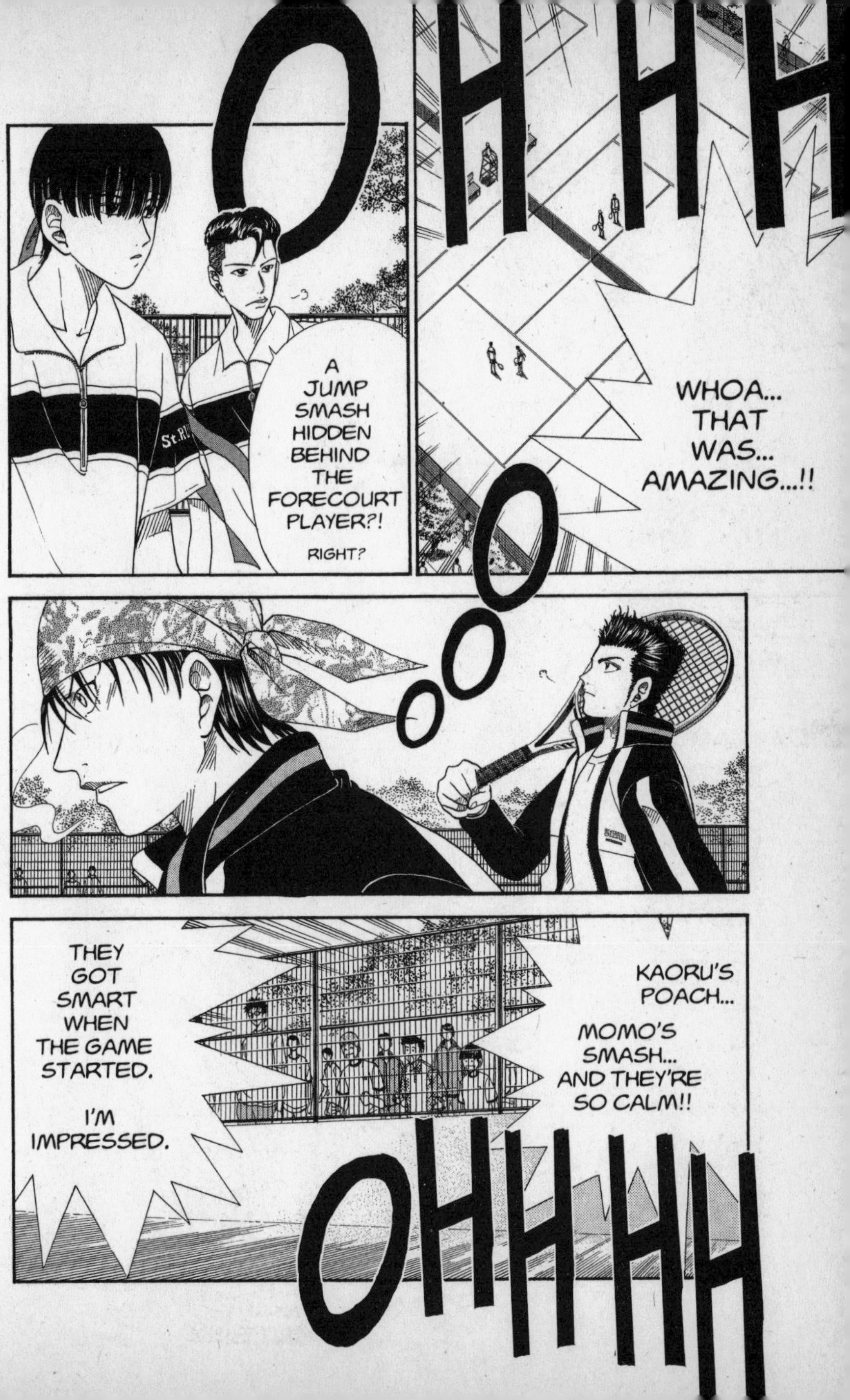

OHHH
WHOA... THAT WAS... AMAZING...!!
A JUMP SMASH HIDDEN BEHIND THE FORECOURT PLAYER?!
RIGHT?
KAORU'S POACH...
MOMO'S SMASH... AND THEY'RE SO CALM!!
THEY GOT SMART WHEN THE GAME STARTED.
I'M IMPRESSED.
OHHHH

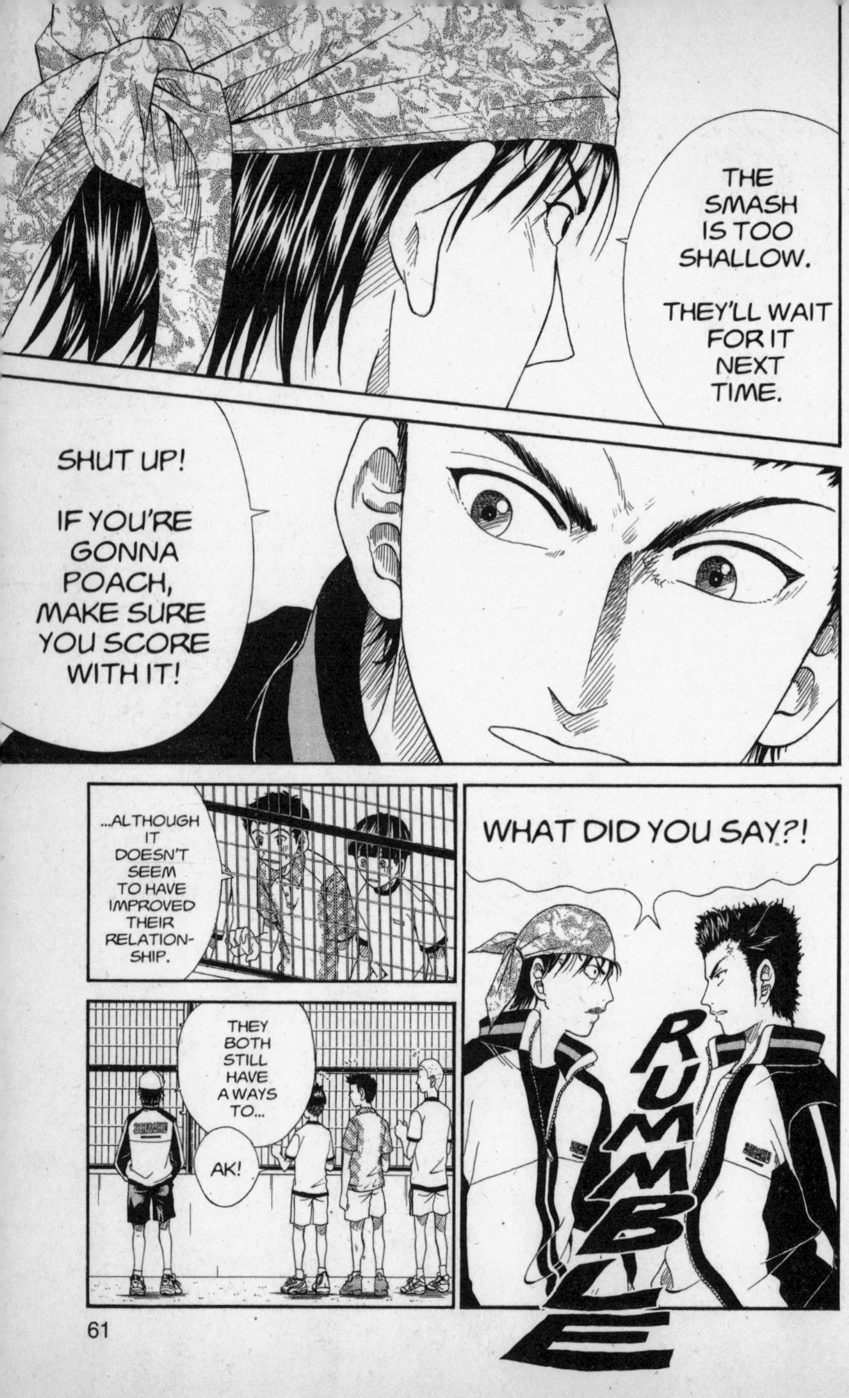
THE SMASH IS TOO SHALLOW.
THEY'LL WAIT FOR IT NEXT TIME.
SHUT UP!
IF YOU'RE GONNA POACH, MAKE SURE YOU SCORE WITH IT!
WHAT DID YOU SAY?!
RUMBLE
...ALTHOUGH IT DOESN'T SEEM TO HAVE IMPROVED THEIR RELATIONSHIP.
THEY BOTH STILL HAVE A WAYS TO...
AK!

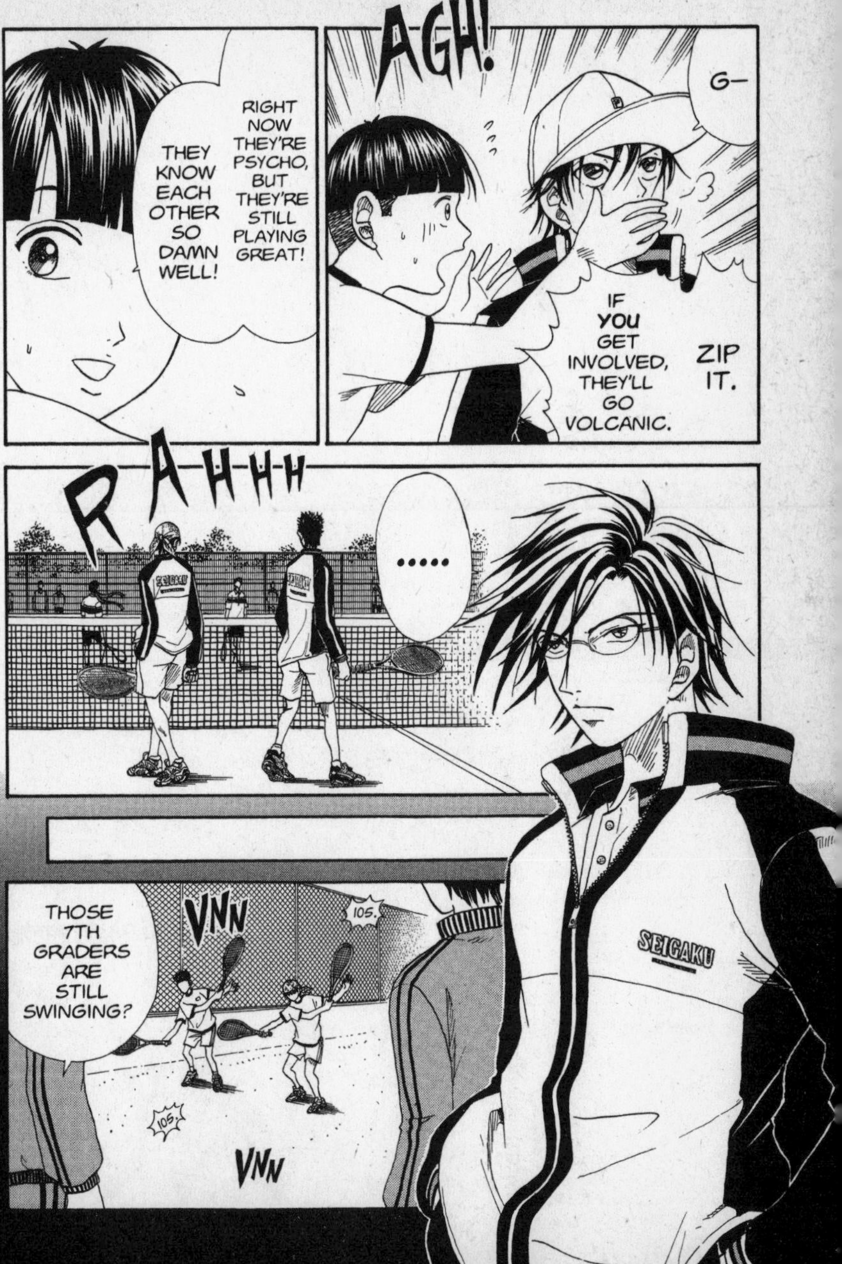
G—
AGH!
ZIP IT.
IF YOU GET INVOLVED, THEY'LL GO VOLCANIC.
RIGHT NOW THEY'RE PSYCHO, BUT THEY'RE STILL PLAYING GREAT!
THEY KNOW EACH OTHER SO DAMN WELL!
.....
RAHHH
105.
VNN
THOSE 7TH GRADERS ARE STILL SWINGING?
105.
VNN

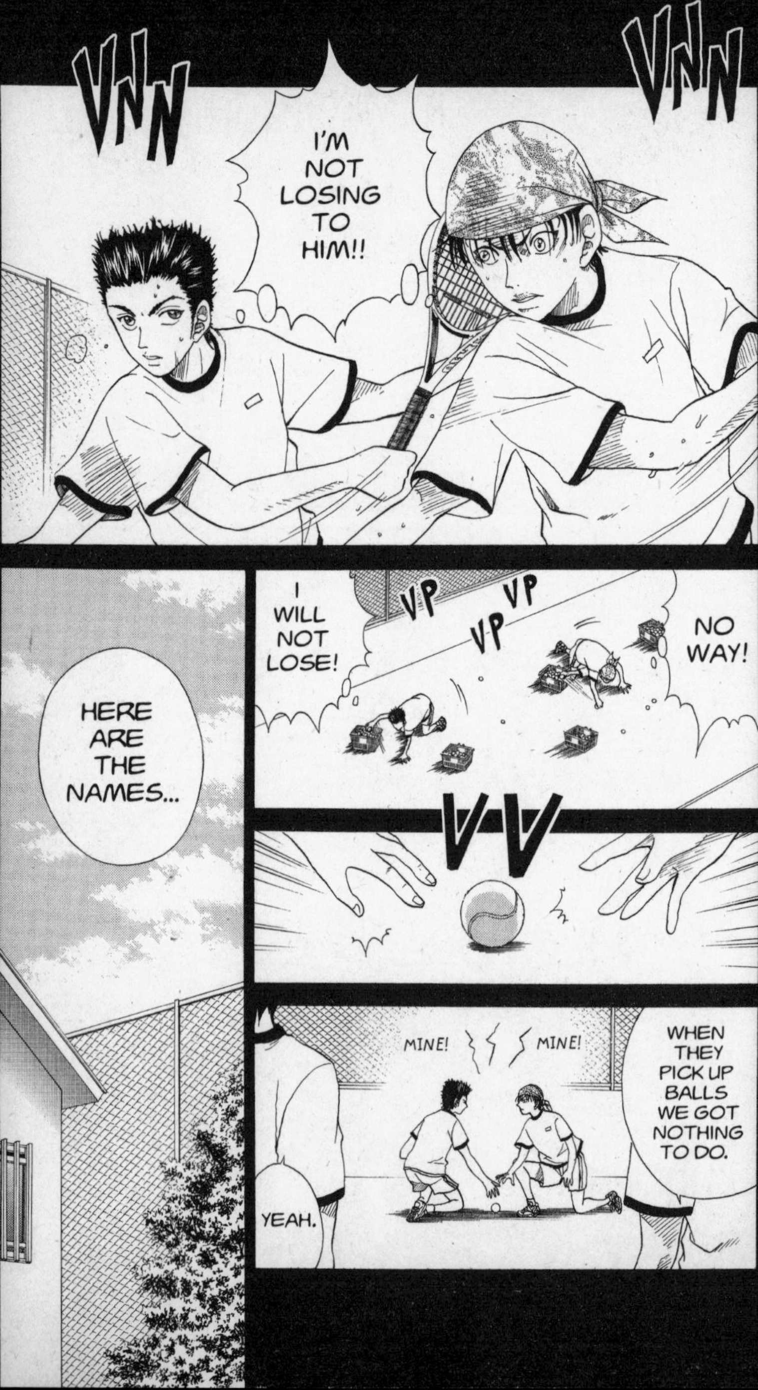
VNN
I'M NOT LOSING TO HIM!!
VNN
NO WAY!
VP VP VP
I WILL NOT LOSE!
VV
WHEN THEY PICK UP BALLS WE GOT NOTHING TO DO.
MINE!
MINE!
YEAH.
HERE ARE THE NAMES...

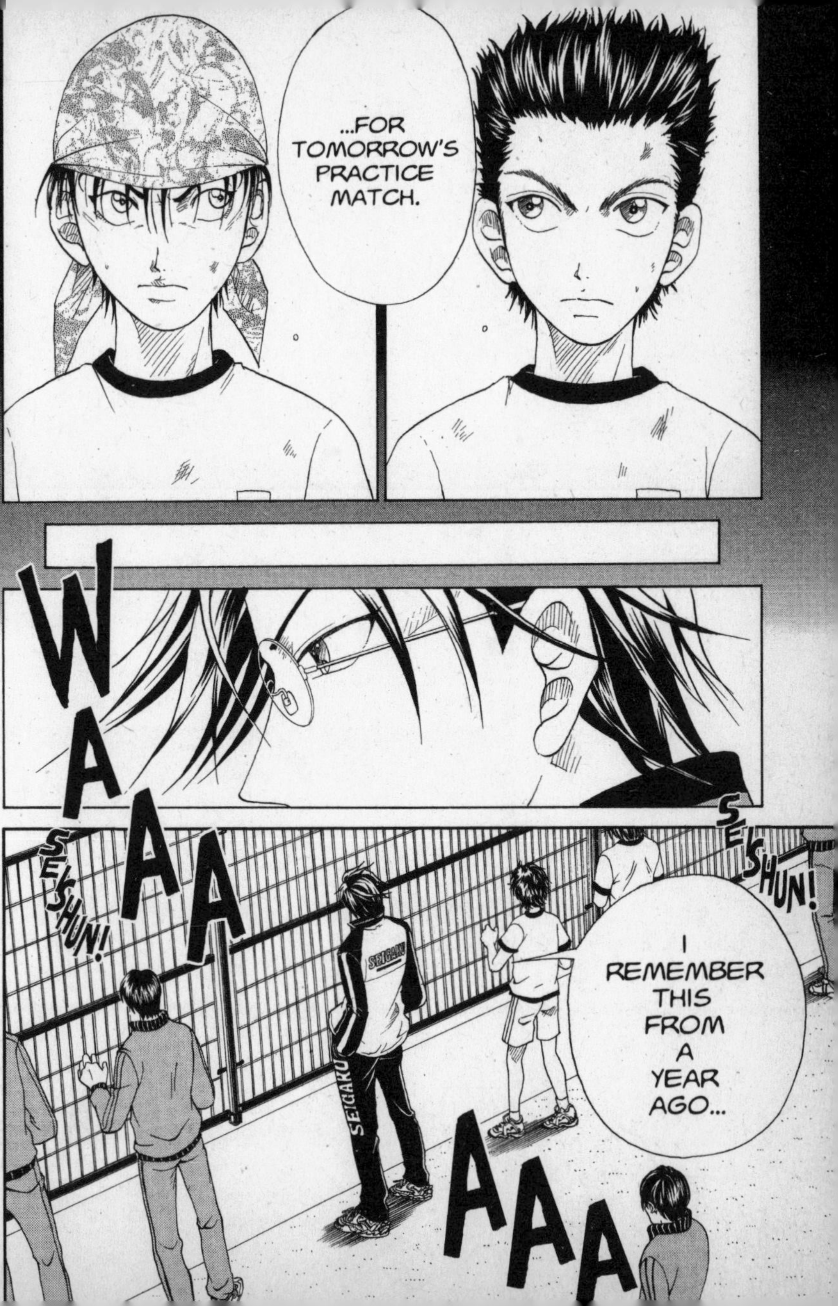
...FOR TOMORROW'S PRACTICE MATCH.
WAAAA
SEISHUN!
SEISHUN!
I REMEMBER THIS FROM A YEAR AGO...
SEIGAKU
SEIGAKU
AAA

READ THIS WAY

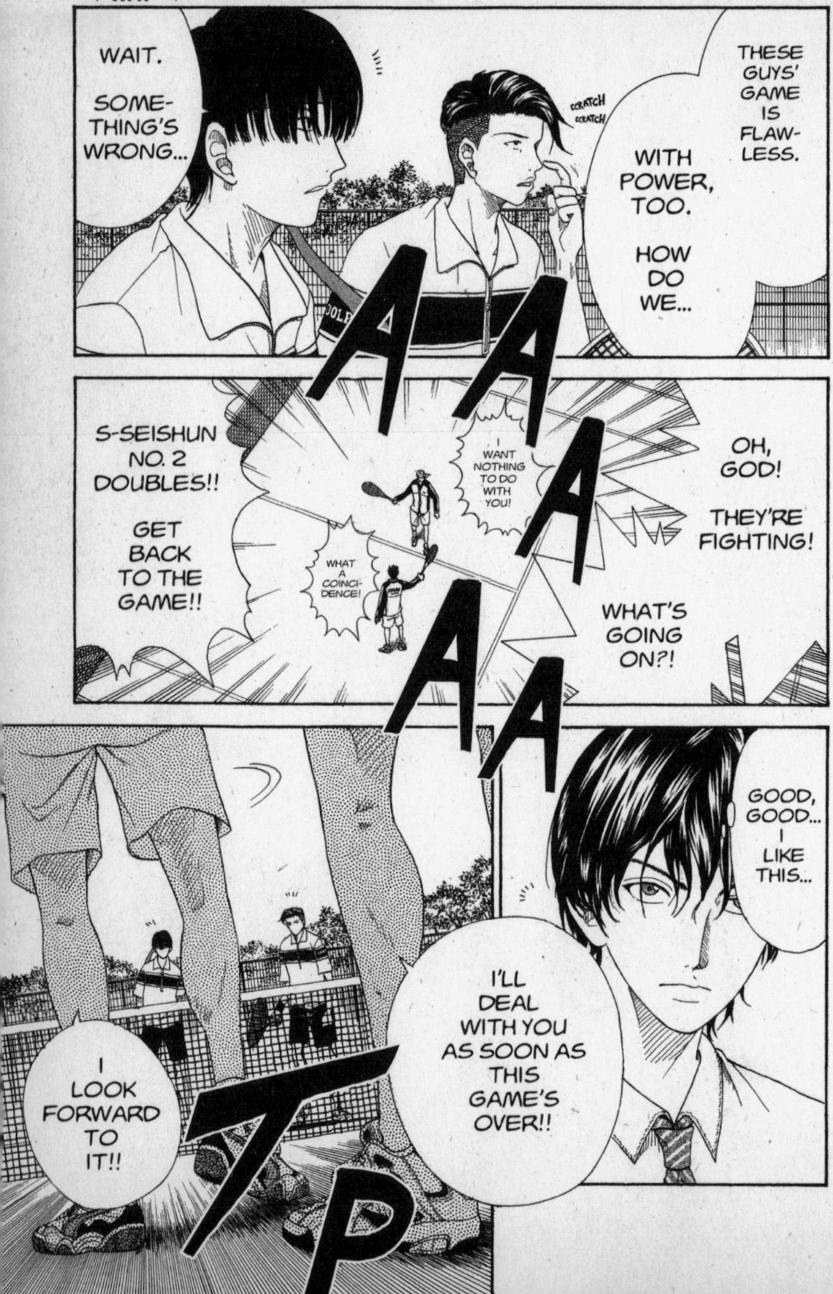

THESE GUYS' GAME IS FLAWLESS.
WITH POWER, TOO.
HOW DO WE...
SCRATCH SCRATCH
WAIT.
SOMETHING'S WRONG...
AAAAAA
OH, GOD!
THEY'RE FIGHTING!
WHAT'S GOING ON?!
I WANT NOTHING TO DO WITH YOU!
WHAT A COINCIDENCE!
S-SEISHUN NO. 2 DOUBLES!!
GET BACK TO THE GAME!!
GOOD, GOOD... I LIKE THIS...
I'LL DEAL WITH YOU AS SOON AS THIS GAME'S OVER!!
I LOOK FORWARD TO IT!!
TP

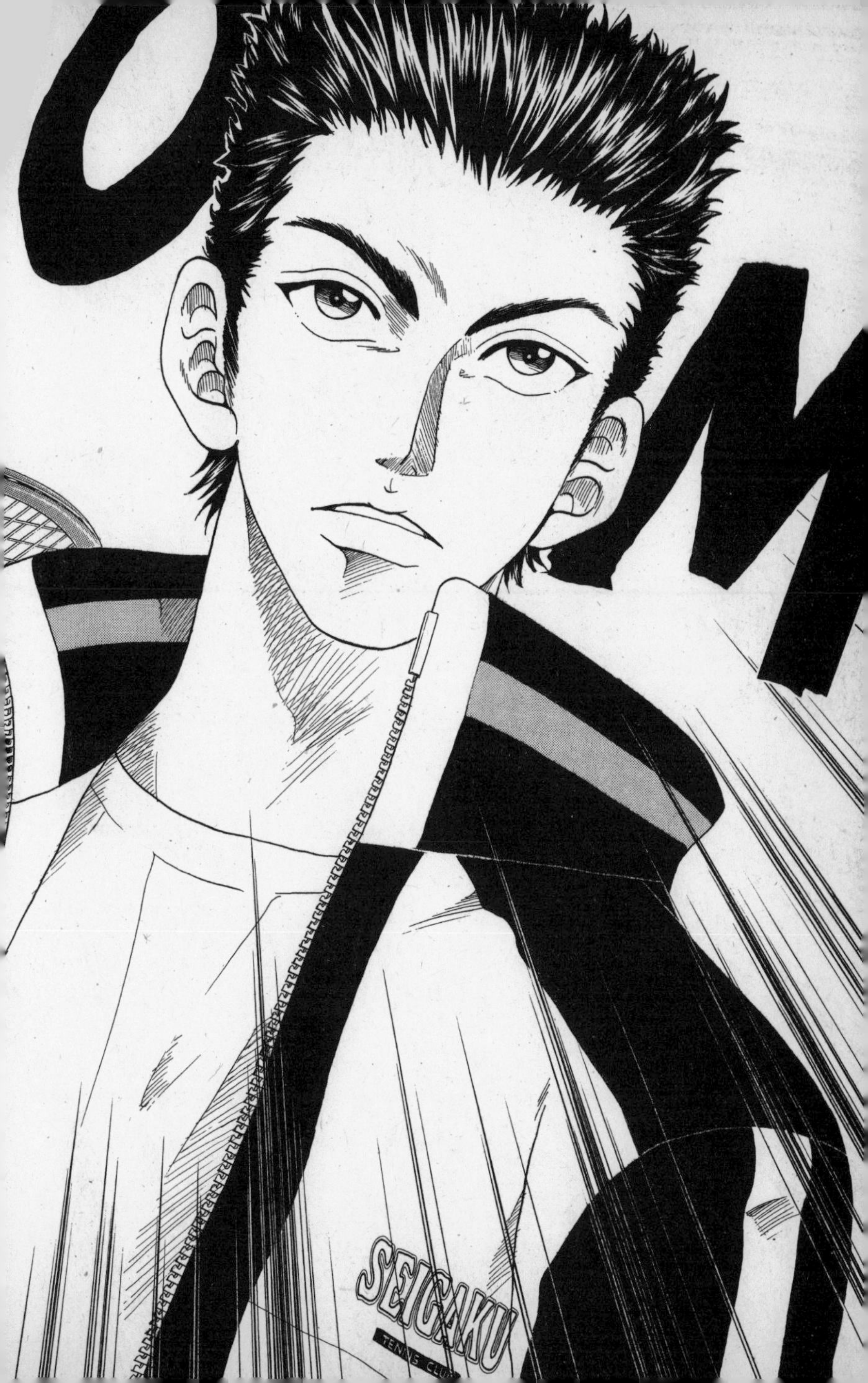
SEIGAKU

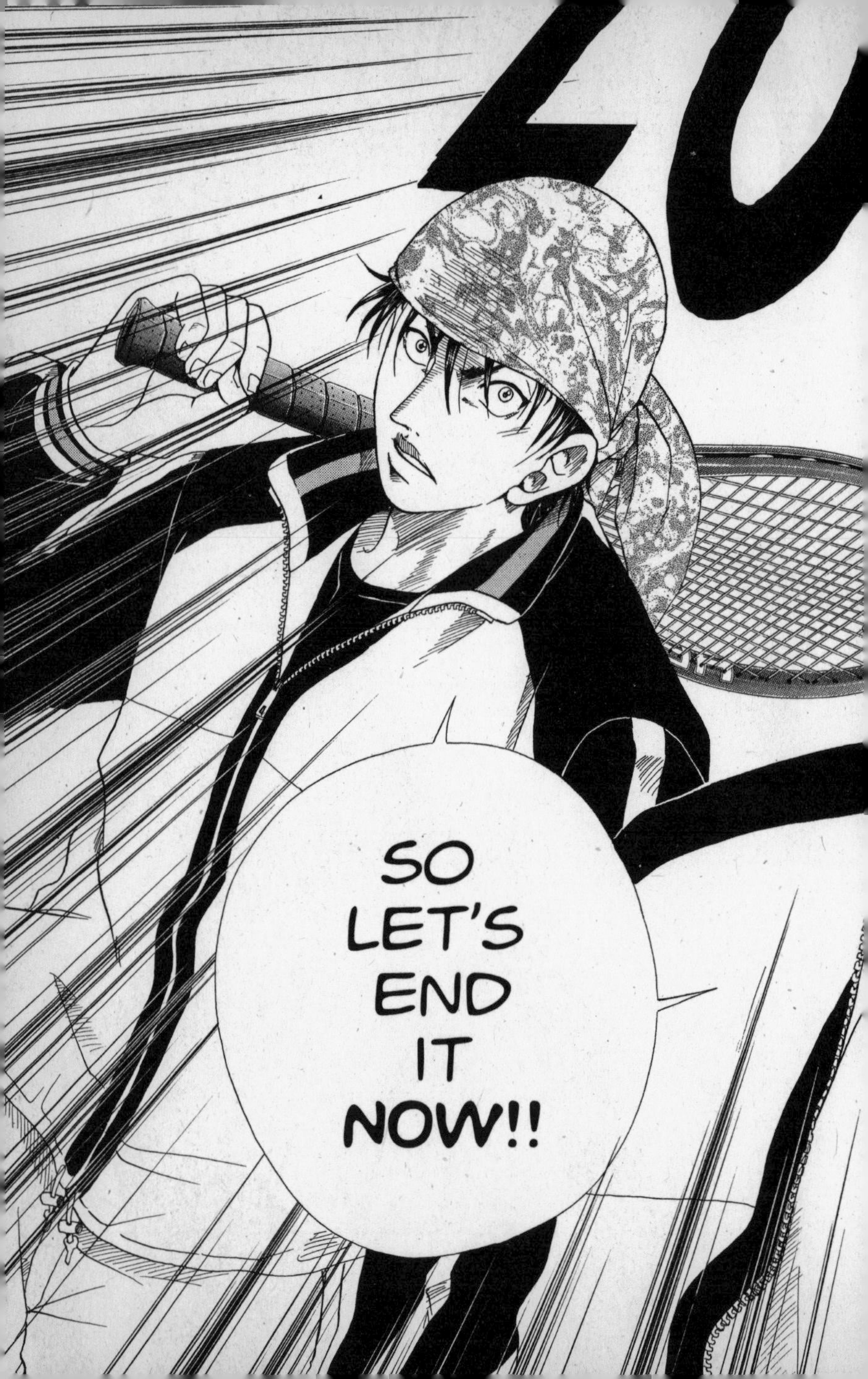
SO LET'S END IT NOW!!

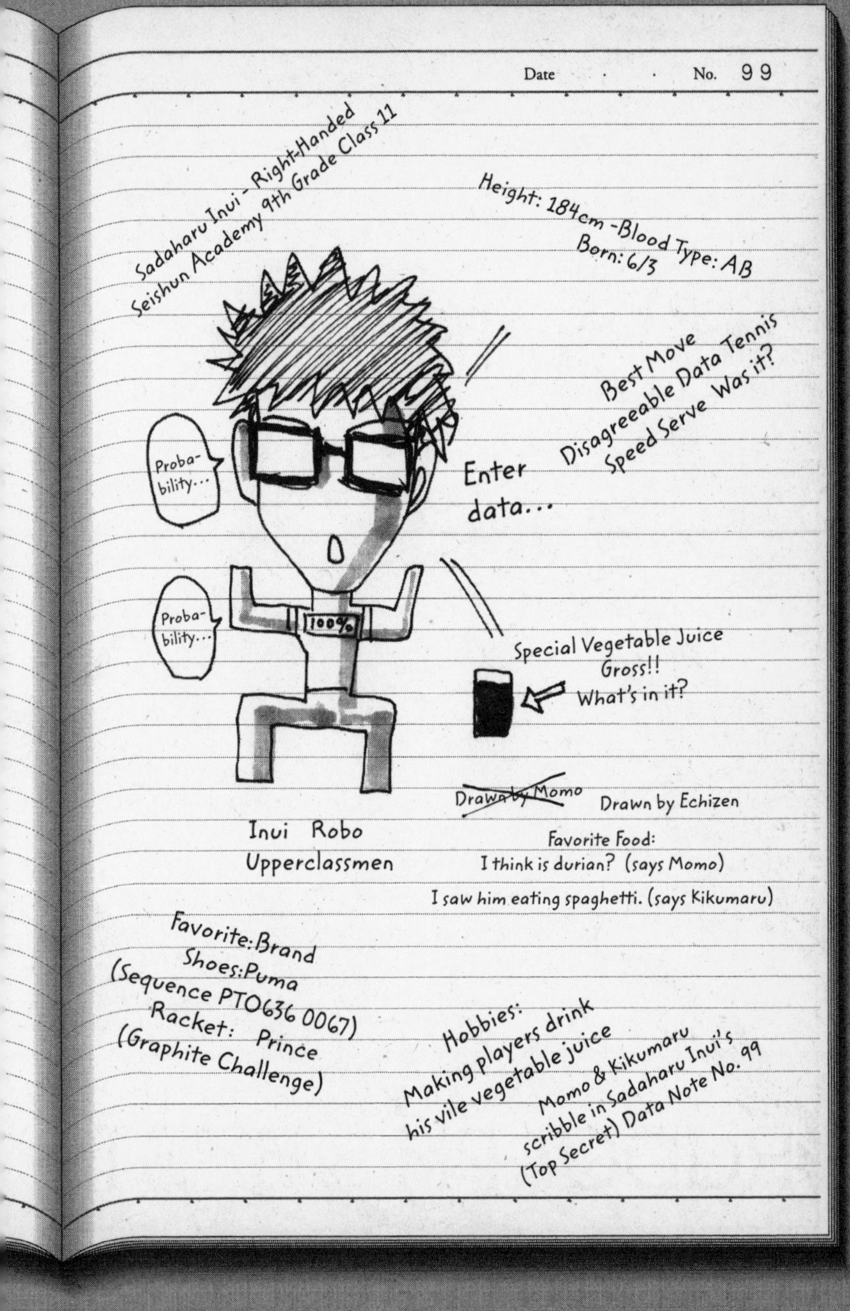
Date . . No. 99
Sadaharu Inui - Right-Handed
Seishun Academy 9th Grade Class 11
Height: 184cm -Blood Type: AB
Born: 6/3
Proba-bility...
Proba-bility...
100%
Enter data...
Best Move
Disagreeable Data Tennis
Speed Serve Was it?
Special Vegetable Juice
Gross!!
What's in it?
~~Drawn by Momo~~
Drawn by Echizen
Inui Robo
Upperclassmen
Favorite Food:
I think is durian? (says Momo)
I saw him eating spaghetti. (says Kikumaru)
Favorite: Brand
Shoes: Puma
(Sequence PTO636 0067)
Racket: Prince
(Graphite Challenge)
Hobbies:
Making players drink
his vile vegetable juice
Momo & Kikumaru
scribble in Sadaharu Inui's
(Top Secret) Data Note No. 99

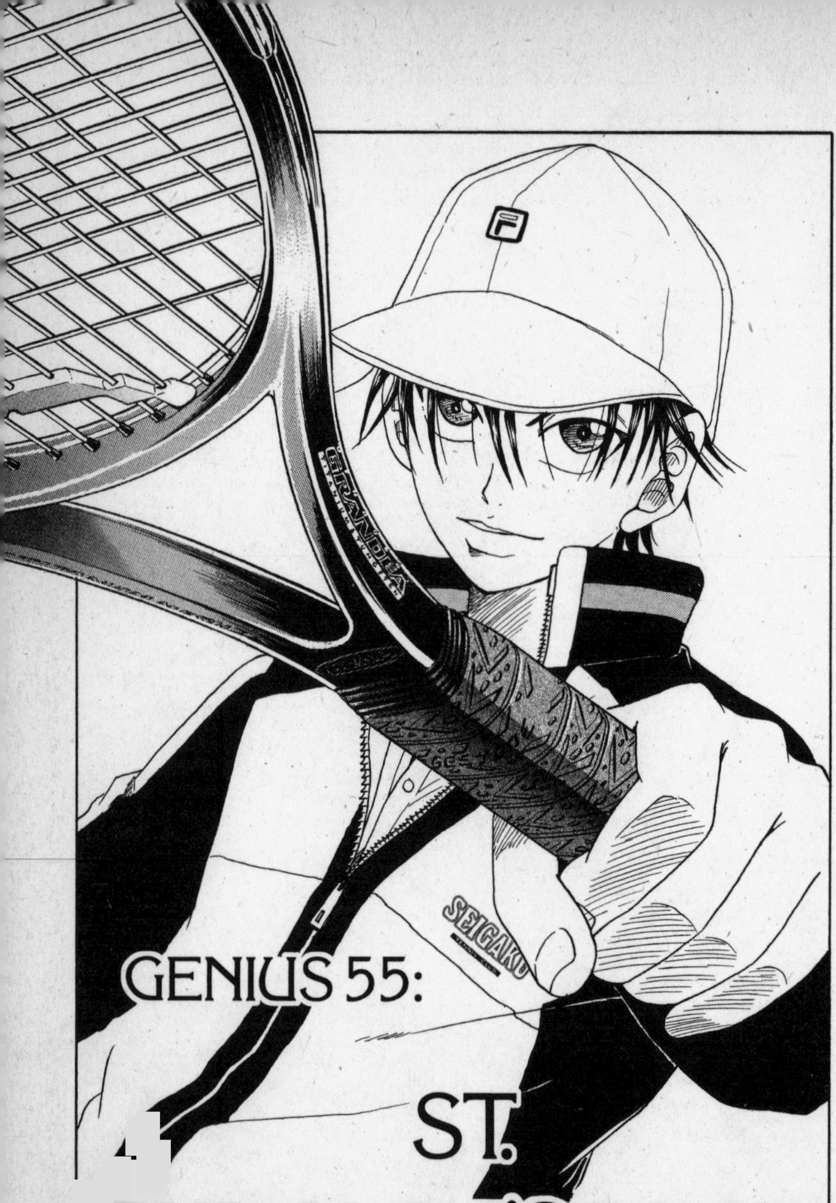

GENIUS 55: ST. RUDOLPH'S BEST

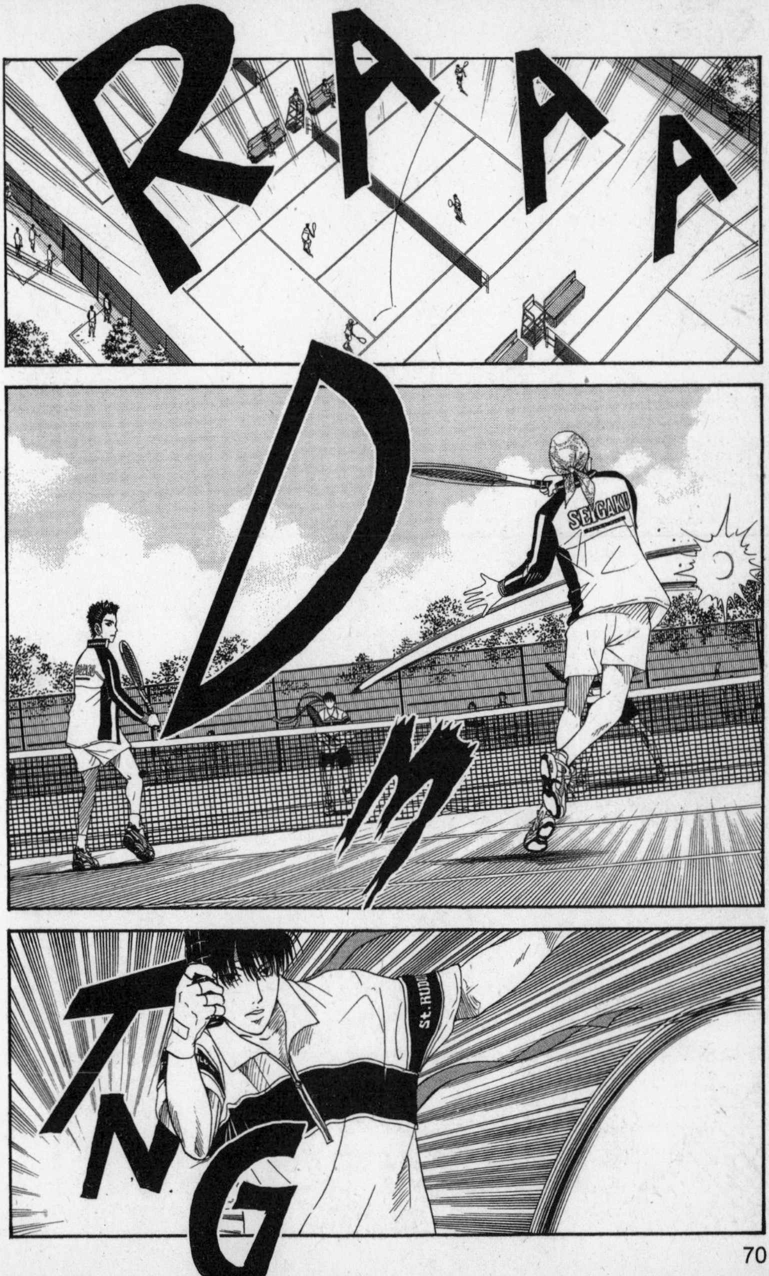
RAAAA
DM
SEIGAKU
TNG

READ THIS WAY

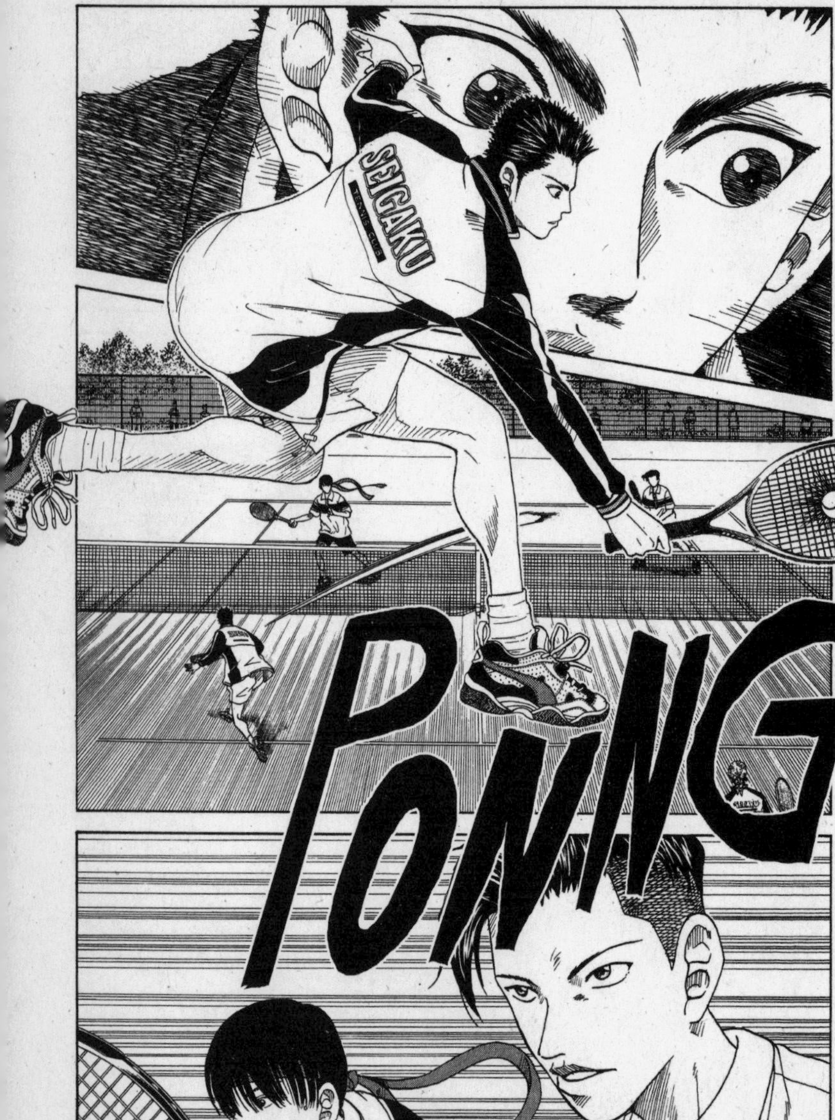
SEIGAKU
TENNIS CLUB
PONNG

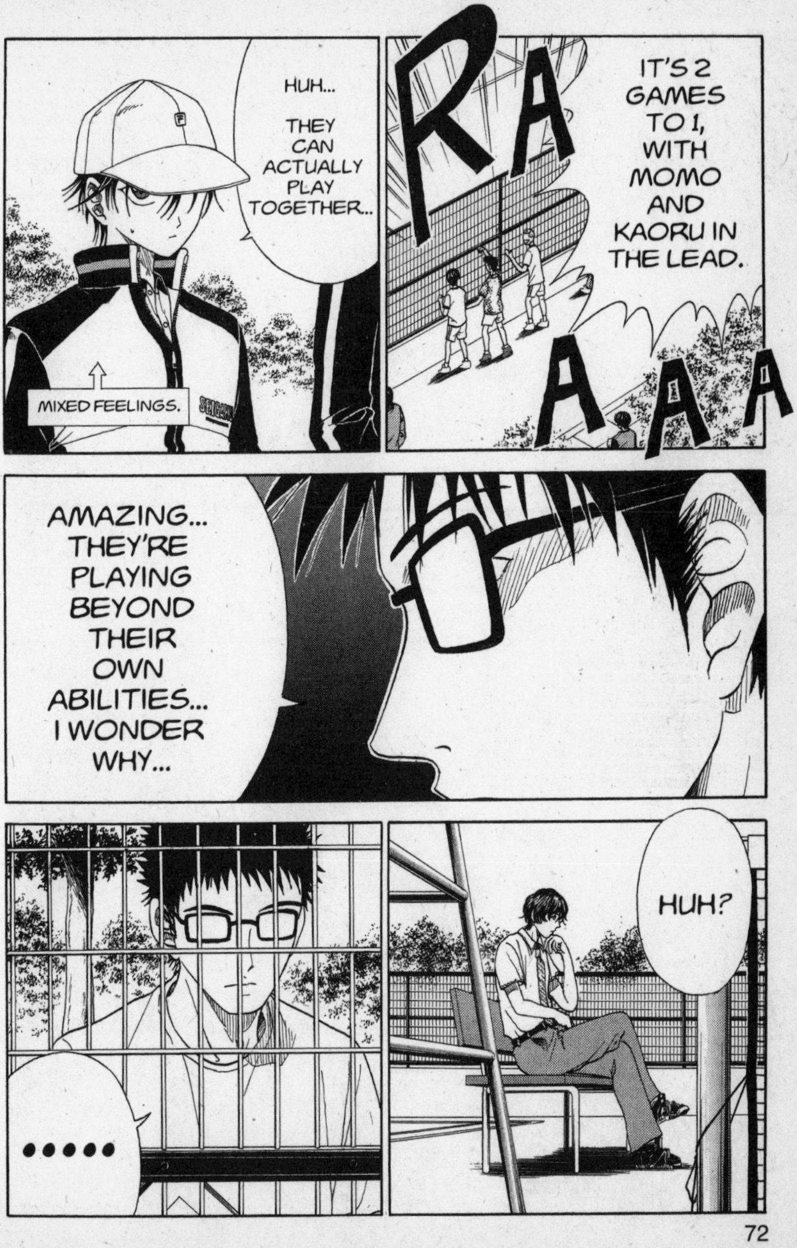
RA
AAA
IT'S 2 GAMES TO 1, WITH MOMO AND KAORU IN THE LEAD.
HUH... THEY CAN ACTUALLY PLAY TOGETHER...
MIXED FEELINGS.
AMAZING... THEY'RE PLAYING BEYOND THEIR OWN ABILITIES... I WONDER WHY...
HUH?
.....

READ THIS WAY

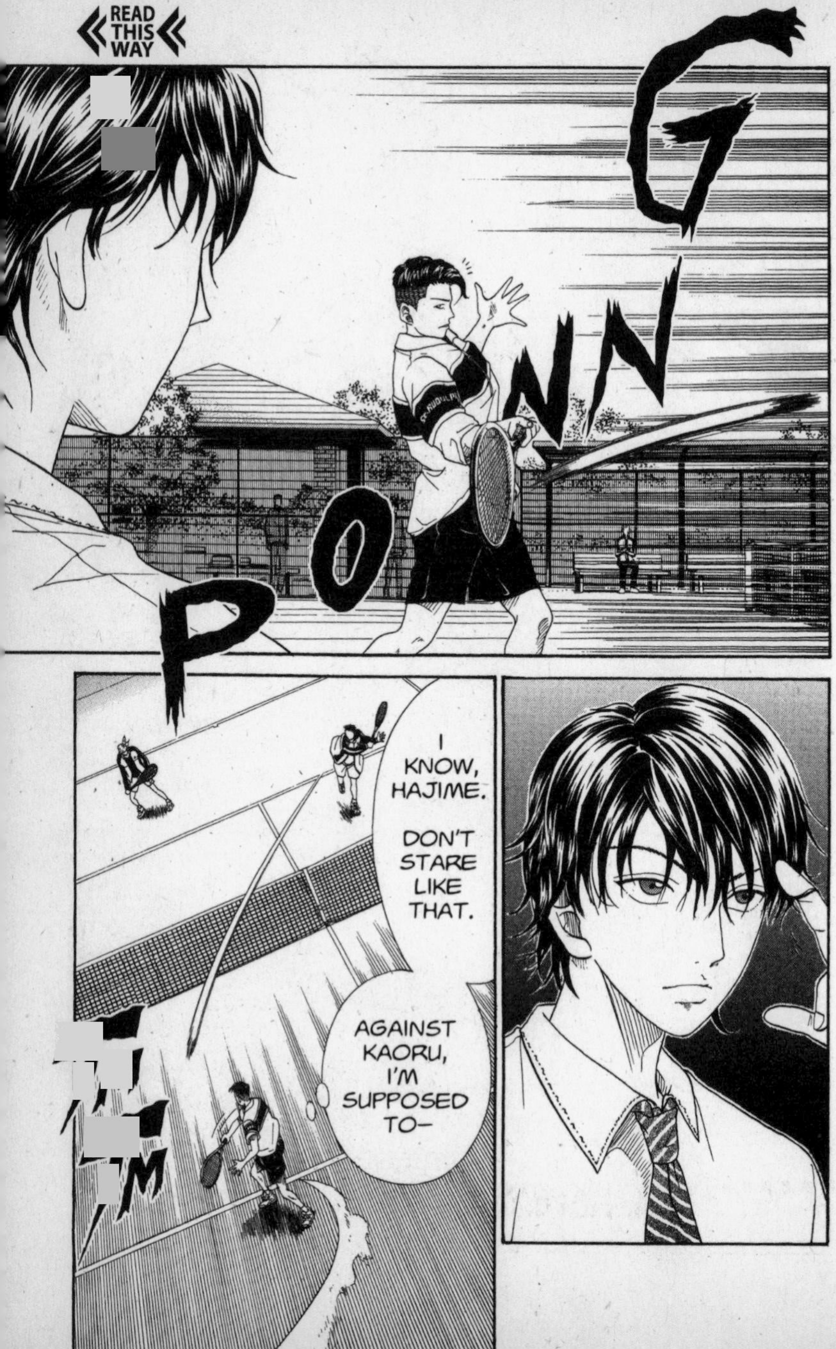
I KNOW, HAJIME.
DON'T STARE LIKE THAT.
AGAINST KAORU, I'M SUPPOSED TO–

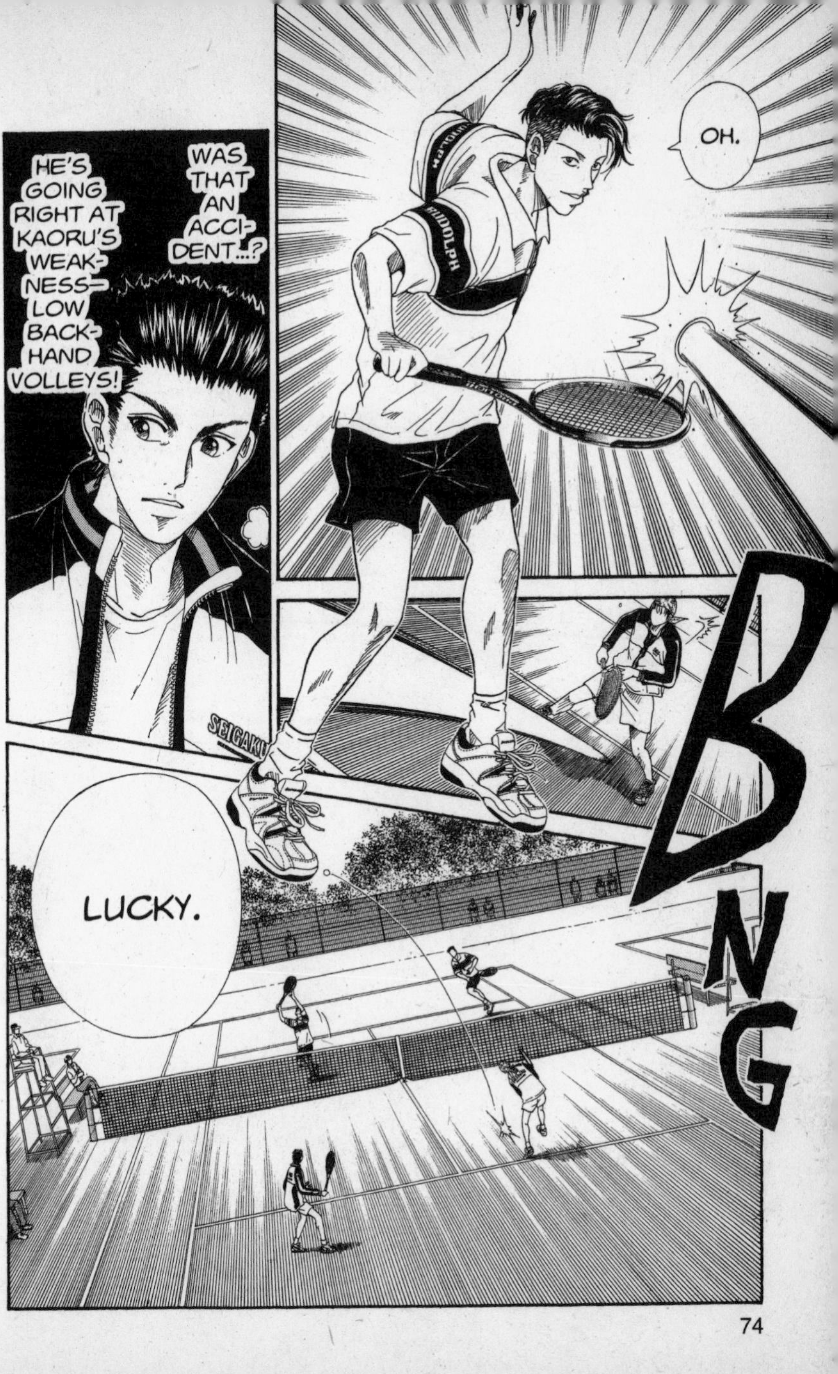
OH.
WAS THAT AN ACCI-DENT...?
HE'S GOING RIGHT AT KAORU'S WEAK-NESS—LOW BACK-HAND VOLLEYS!
RUDOLPH
SEIGAKU
BNG
LUCKY.

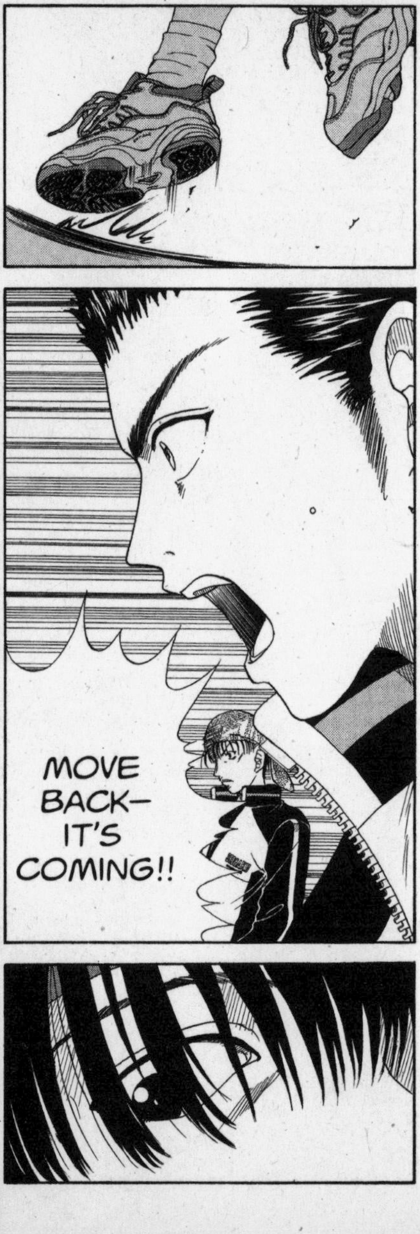
MOVE BACK— IT'S COMING!!

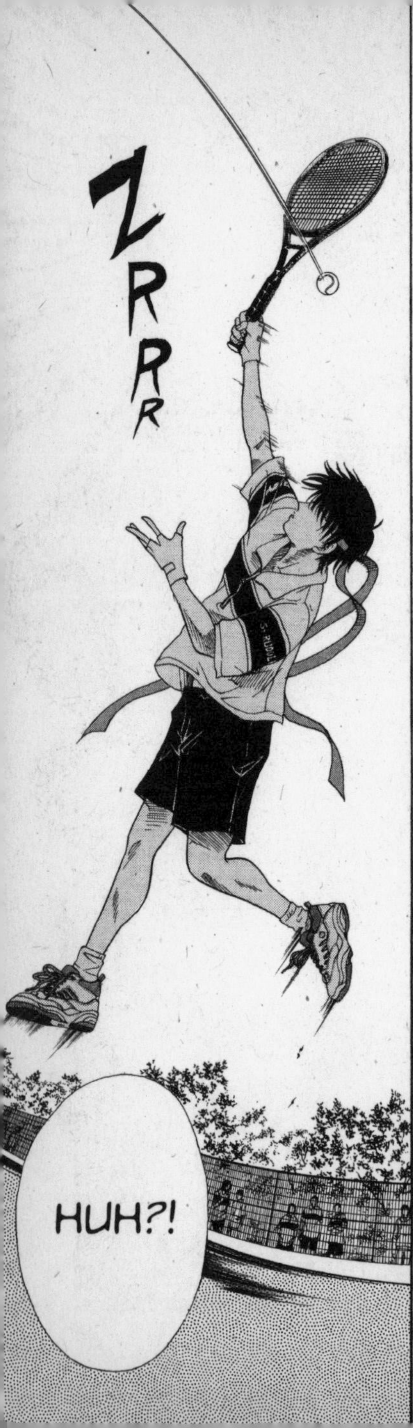
ZRRR
HUH?!

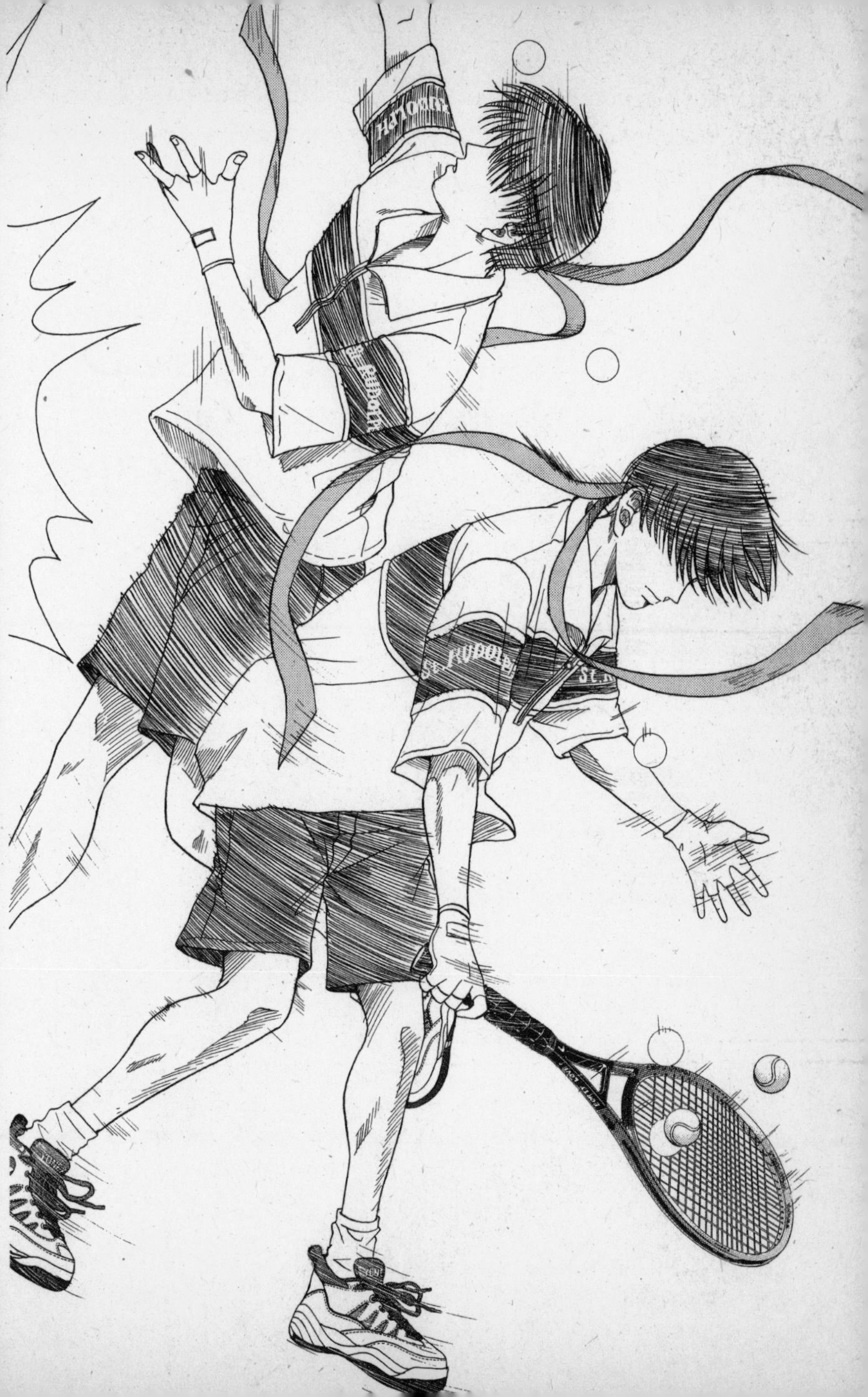

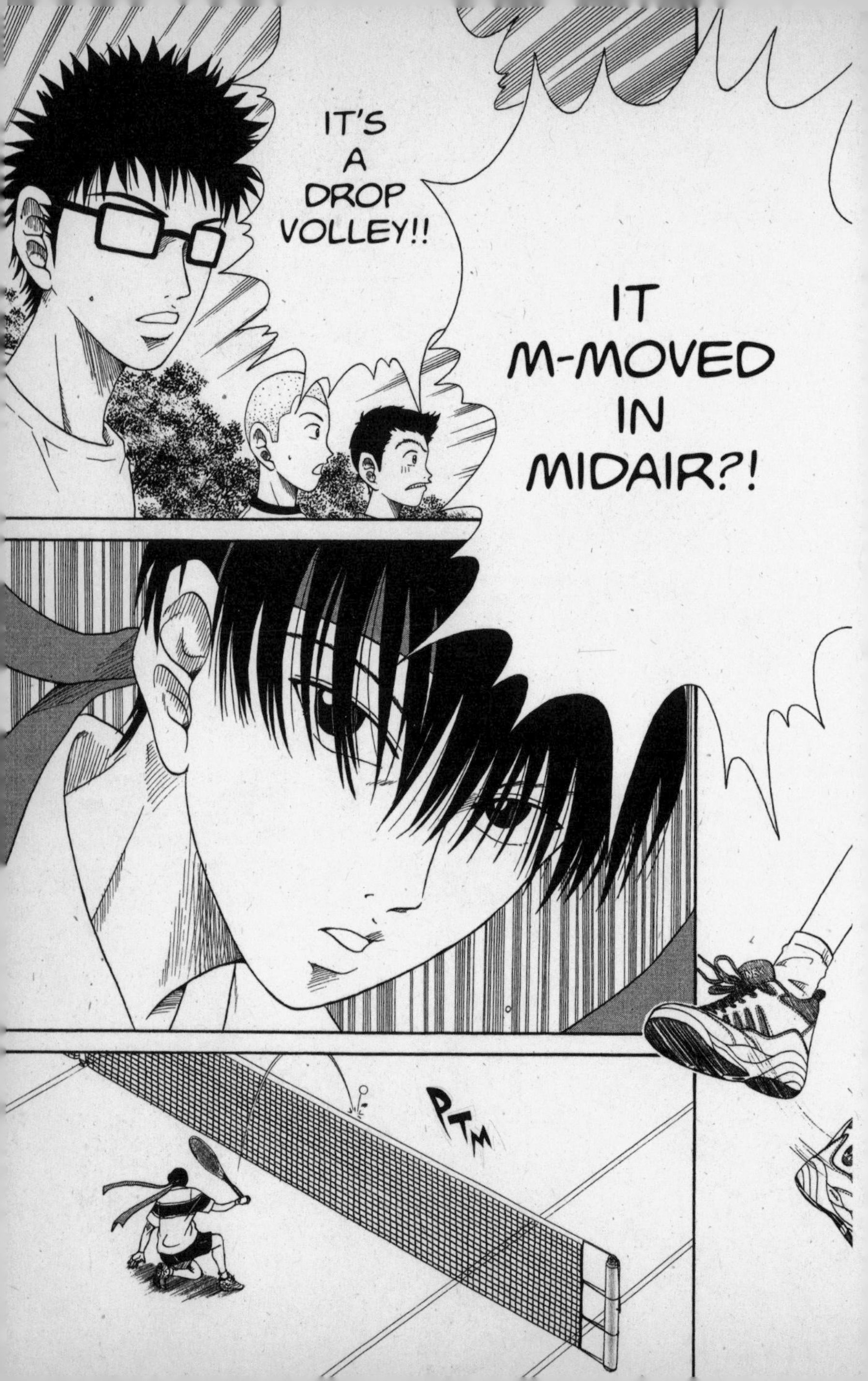
IT M-MOVED IN MIDAIR?!
IT'S A DROP VOLLEY!!
PTM

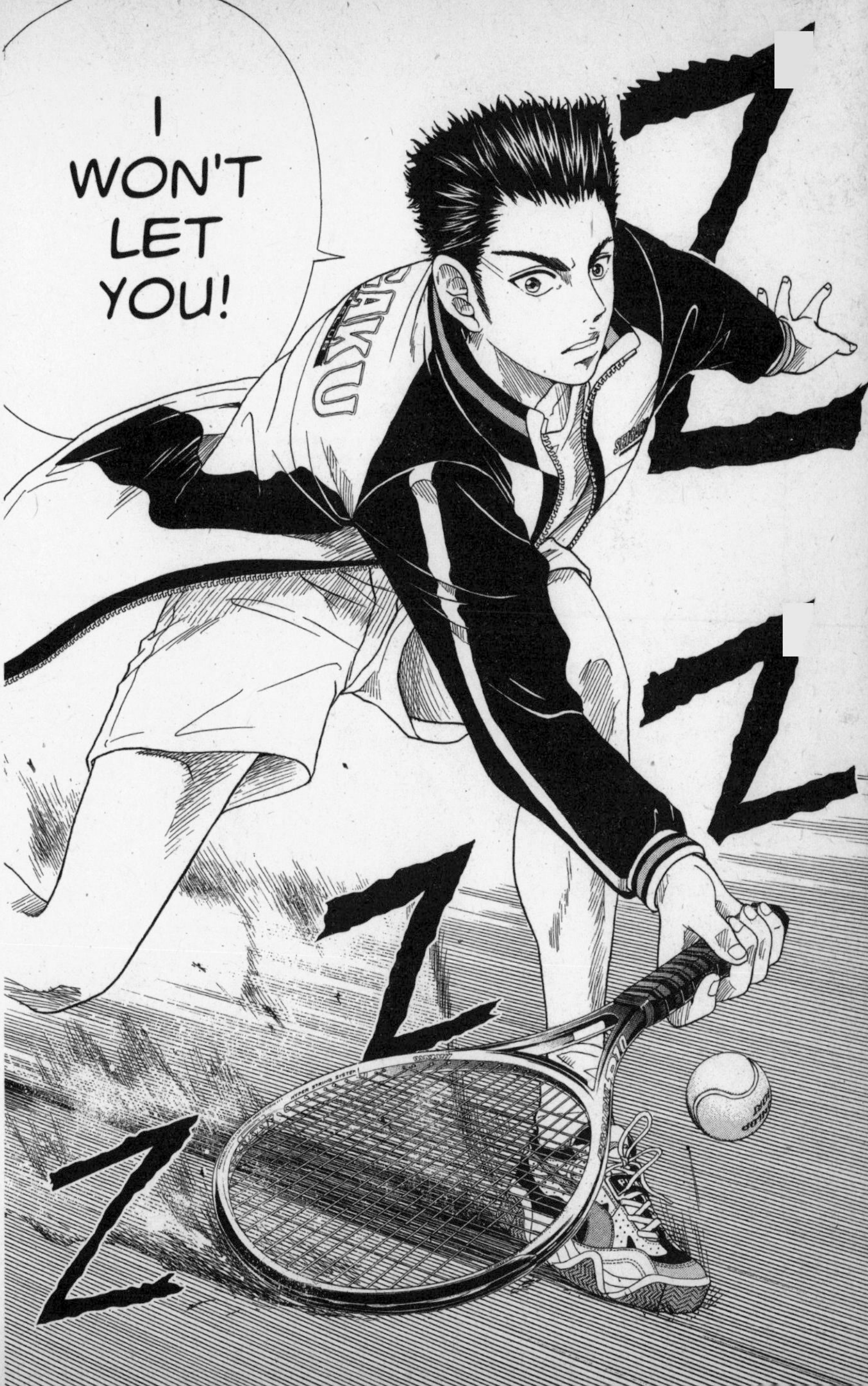
I WON'T LET YOU!
ZZZZ

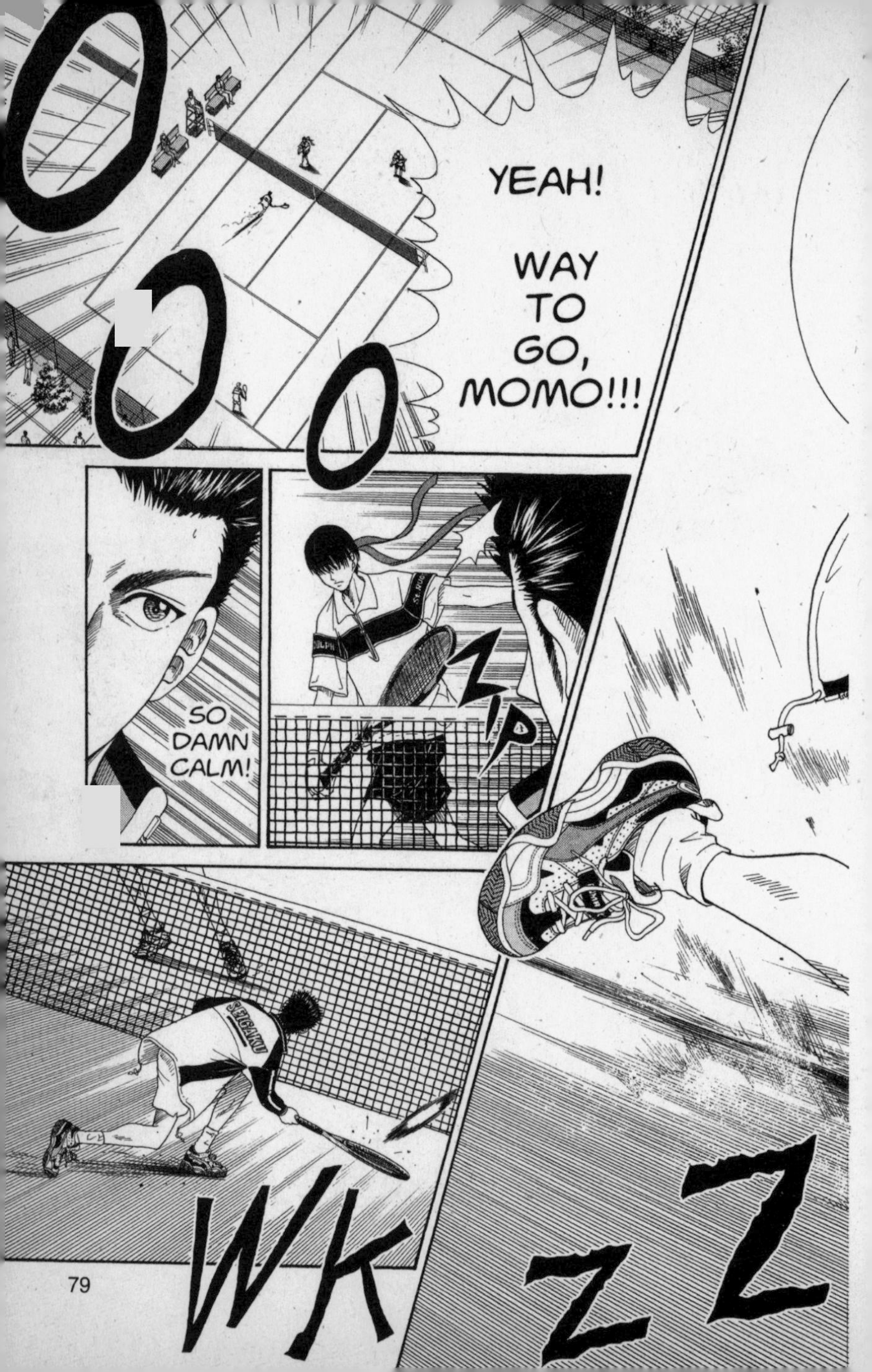
YEAH!
WAY TO GO, MOMO!!!
OOO
ZZ
ZIP
SO DAMN CALM!
WK

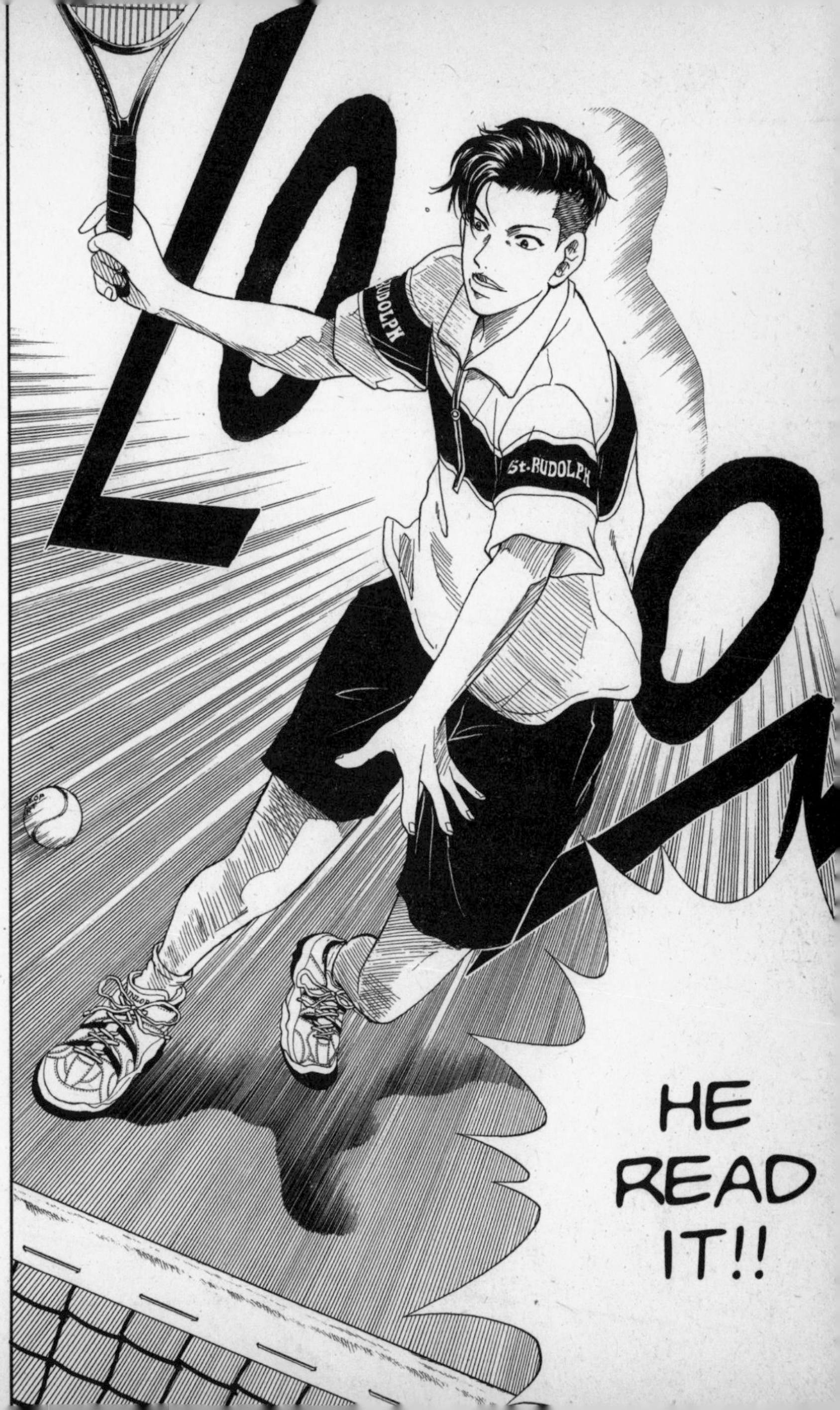
St.RUDOLPH
HE READ IT!!

READ THIS WAY

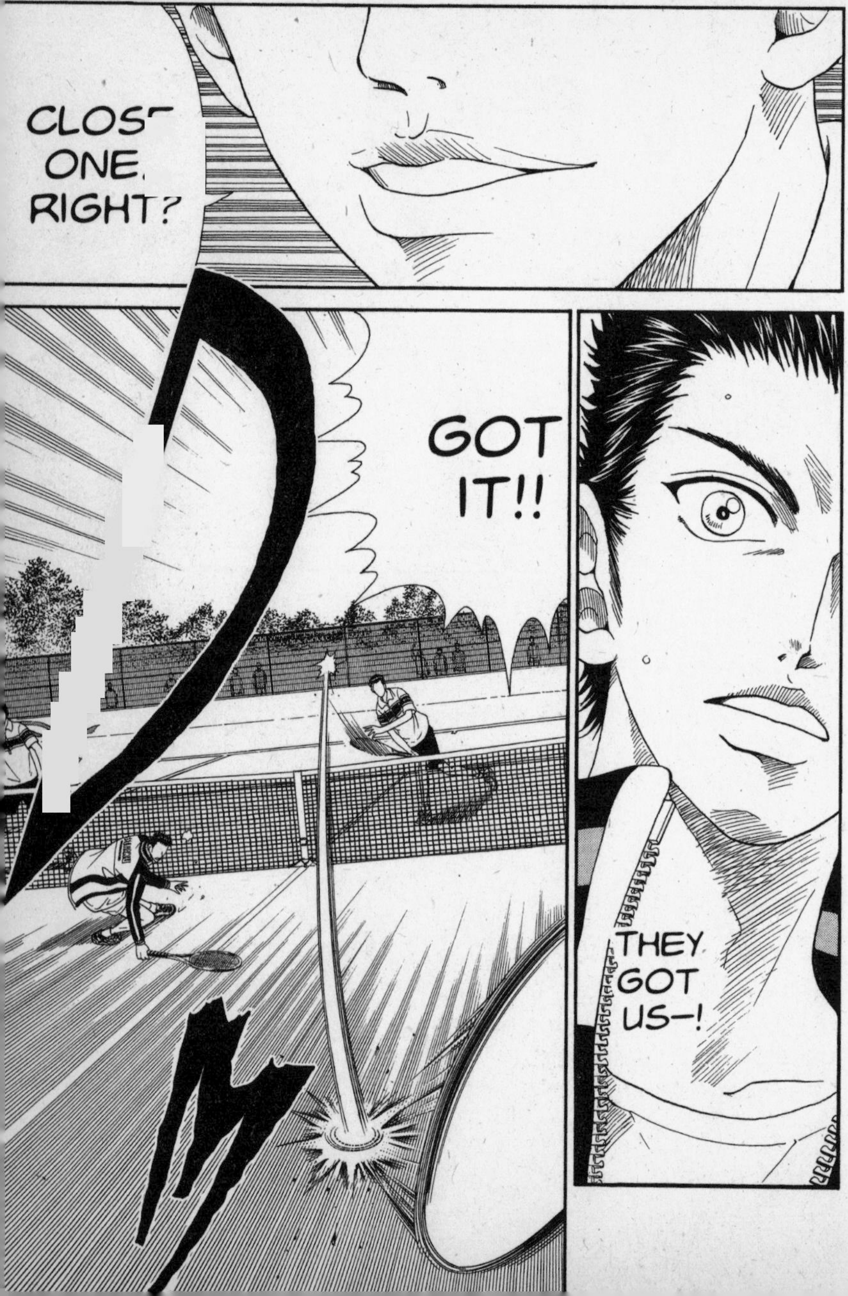
CLOS
ONE
RIGHT?
THEY GOT US—!
GOT IT!!

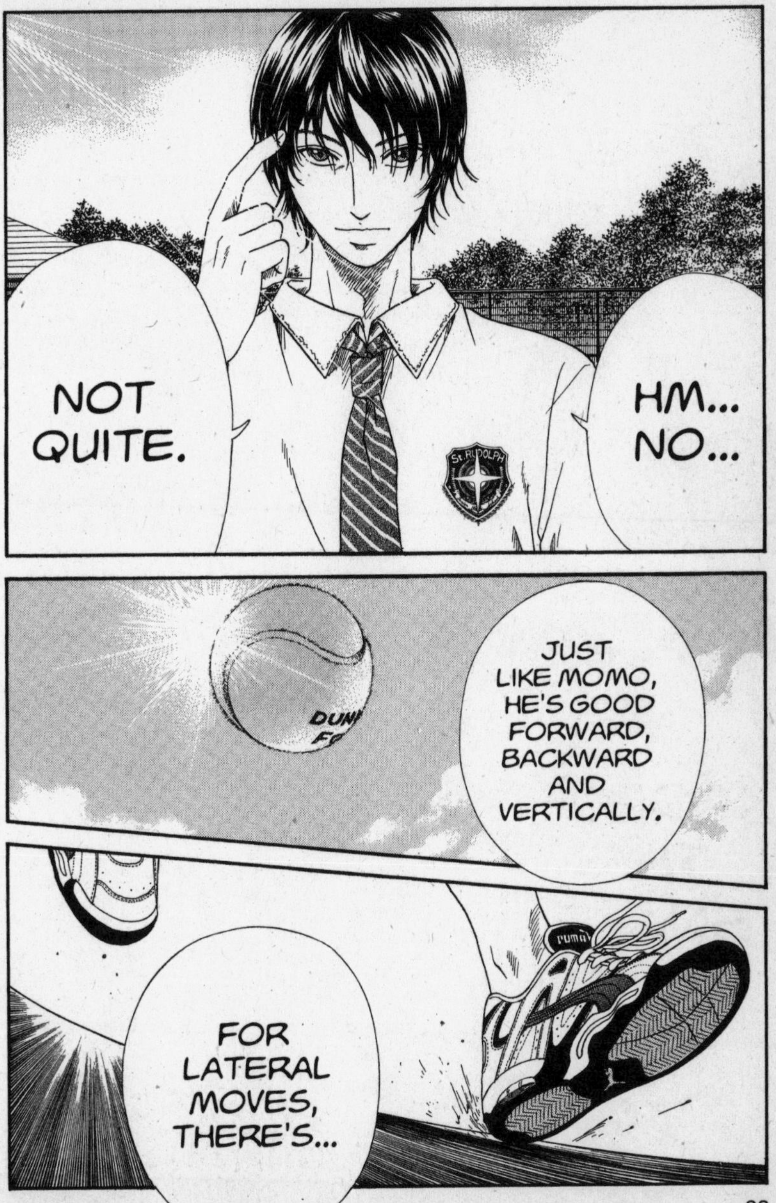
HM... NO...
NOT QUITE.
JUST LIKE MOMO, HE'S GOOD FORWARD, BACKWARD AND VERTICALLY.
FOR LATERAL MOVES, THERE'S...

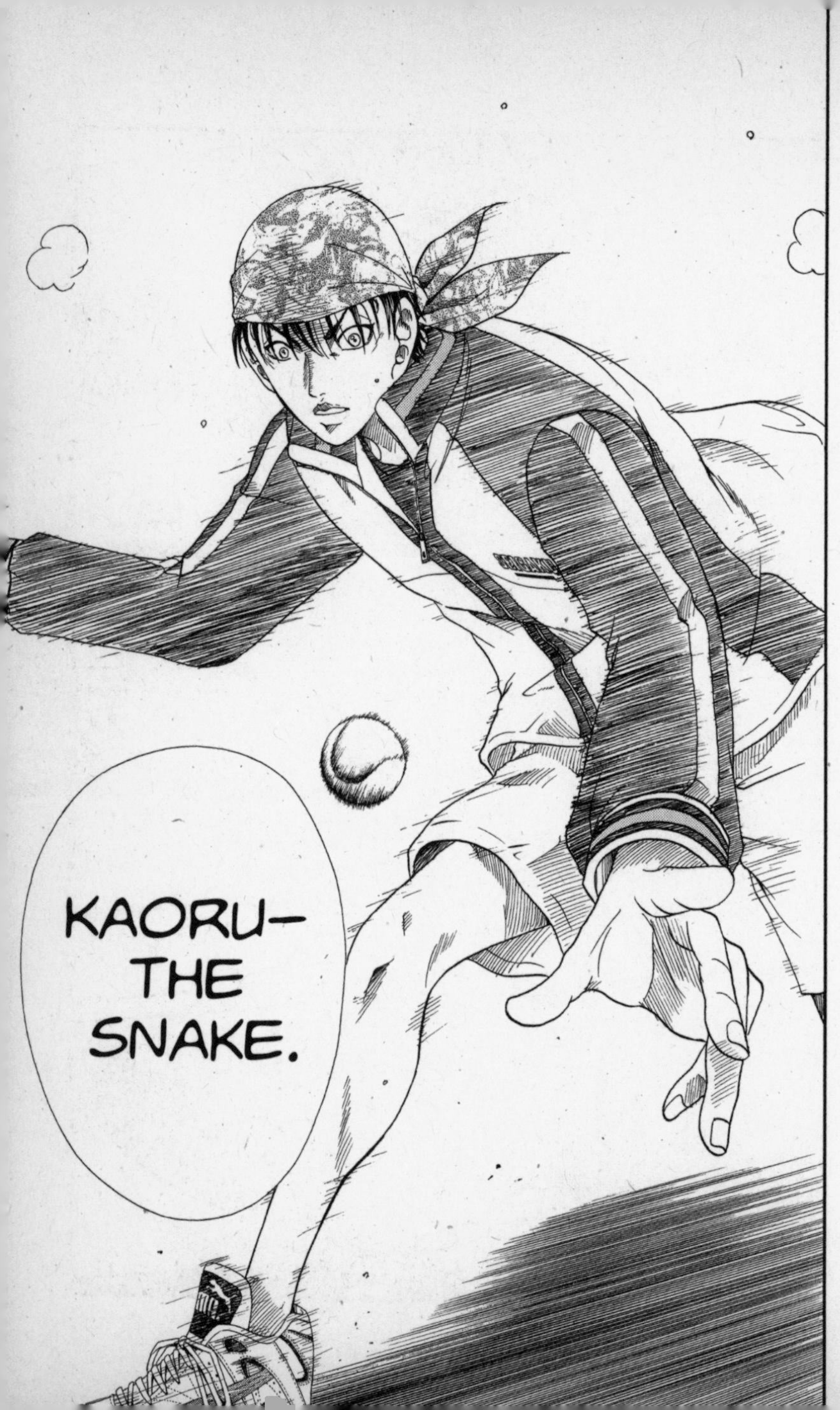
KAORU-
THE
SNAKE.

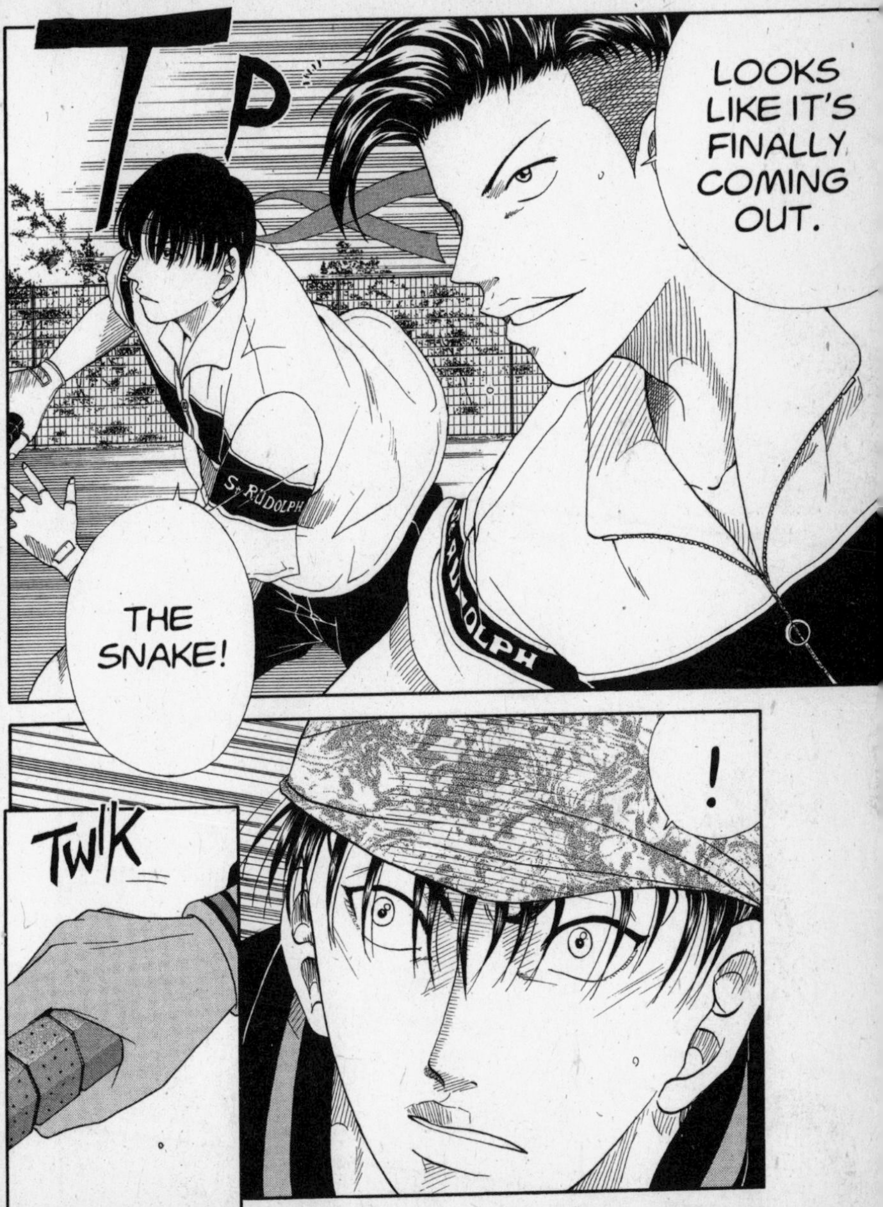
TP
LOOKS LIKE IT'S FINALLY COMING OUT.
THE SNAKE!
!
TWIK

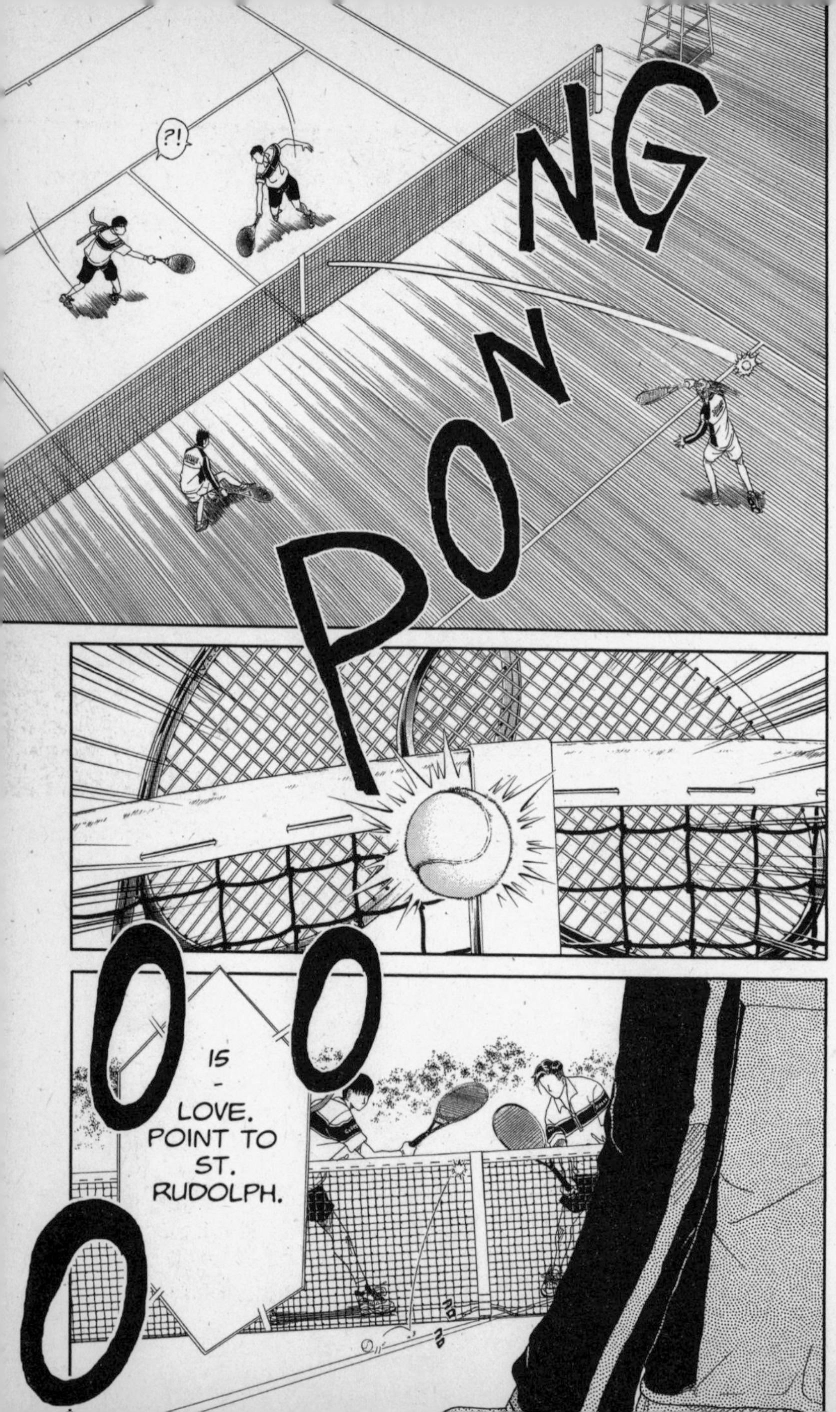
?!
PONG
POOO
15 - LOVE. POINT TO ST. RUDOLPH.

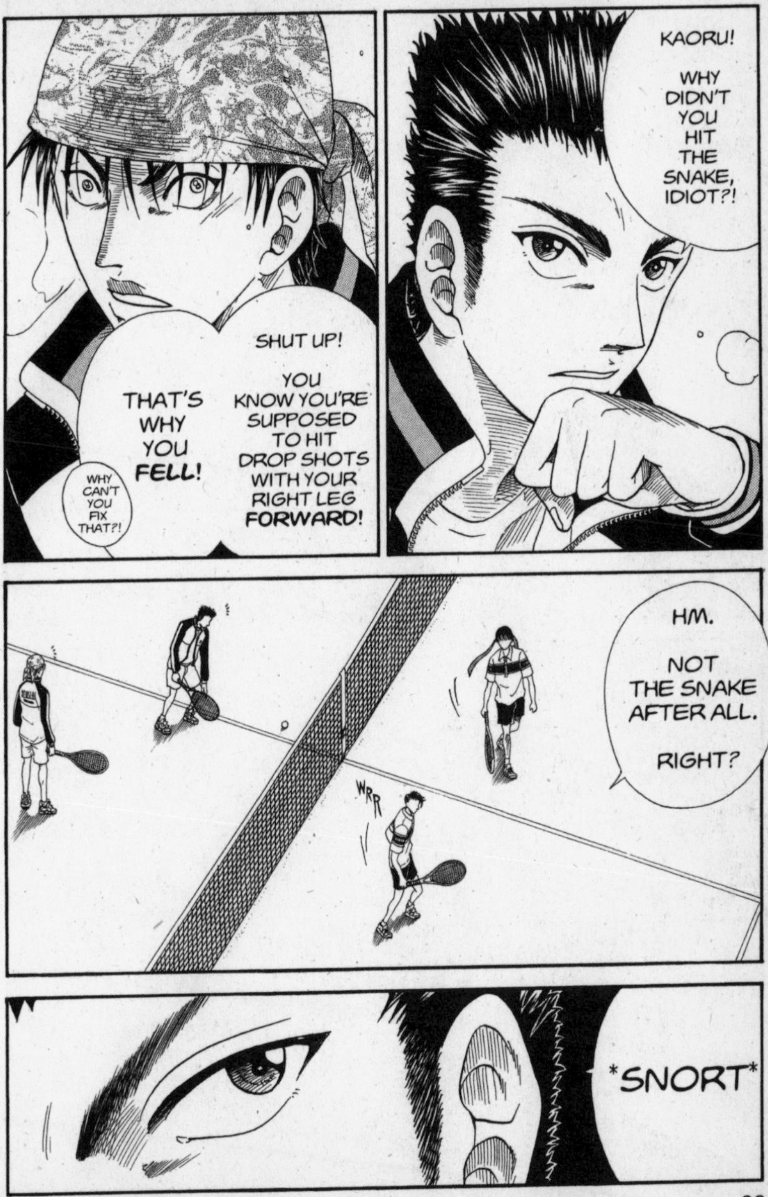
KAORU! WHY DIDN'T YOU HIT THE SNAKE, IDIOT?!
SHUT UP! YOU KNOW YOU'RE SUPPOSED TO HIT DROP SHOTS WITH YOUR RIGHT LEG FORWARD!
THAT'S WHY YOU FELL!
WHY CAN'T YOU FIX THAT?!
HM. NOT THE SNAKE AFTER ALL. RIGHT?
WRR
SNORT

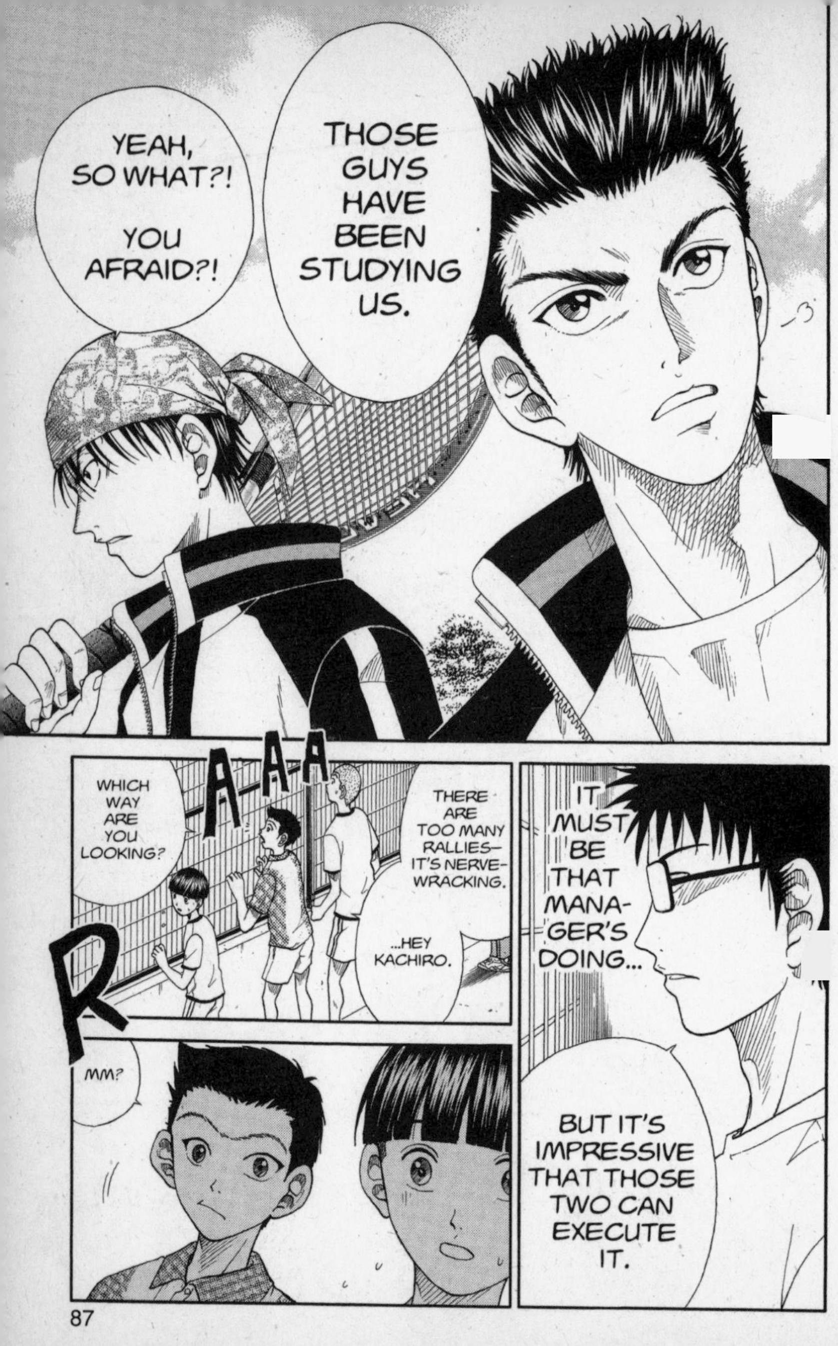
THOSE GUYS HAVE BEEN STUDYING US.
YEAH, SO WHAT?! YOU AFRAID?!
IT MUST BE THAT MANAGER'S DOING...
BUT IT'S IMPRESSIVE THAT THOSE TWO CAN EXECUTE IT.
THERE ARE TOO MANY RALLIES— IT'S NERVE-WRACKING.
...HEY KACHIRO.
WHICH WAY ARE YOU LOOKING?
AAA
R
MM?

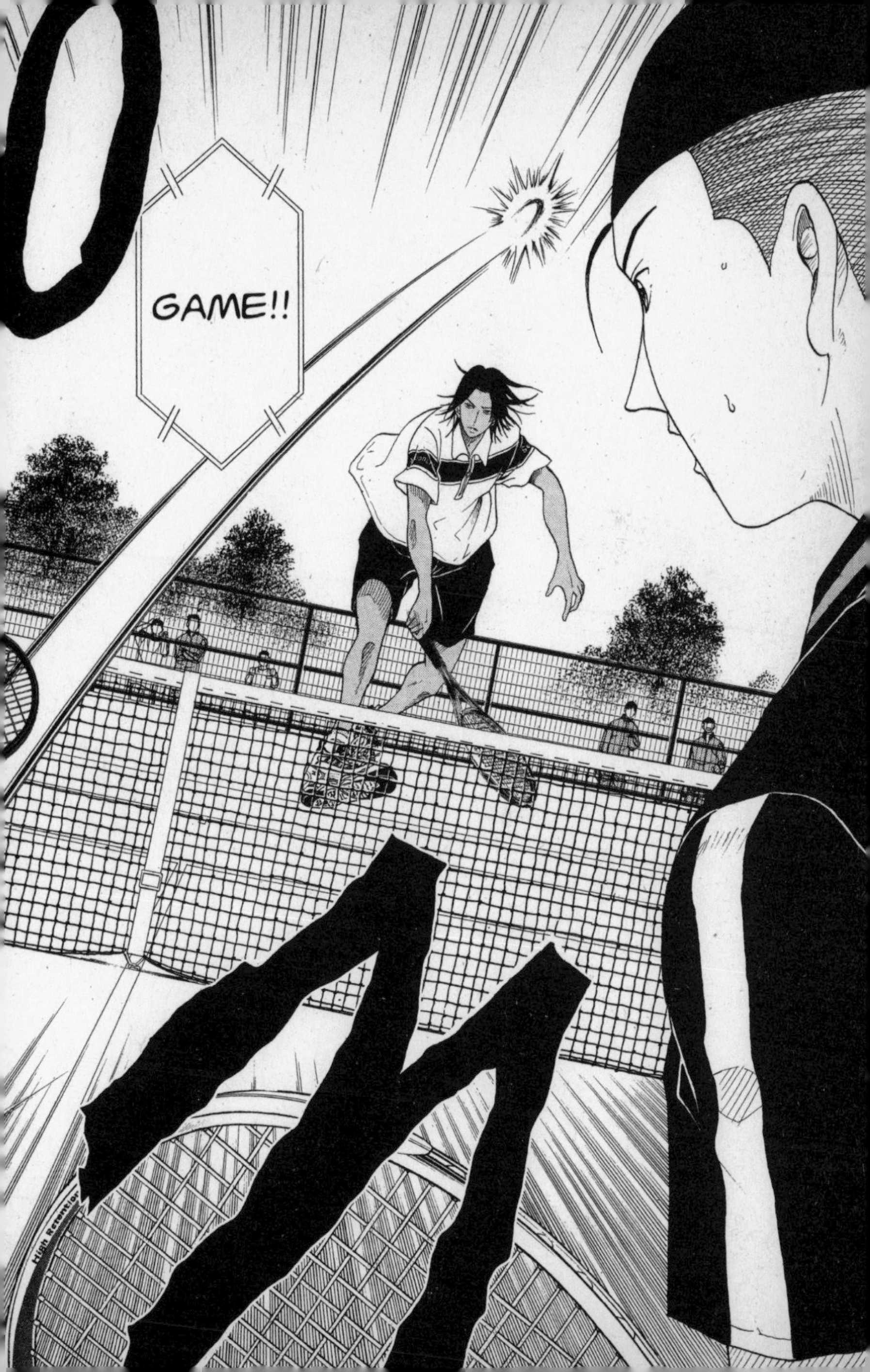
GAME!!

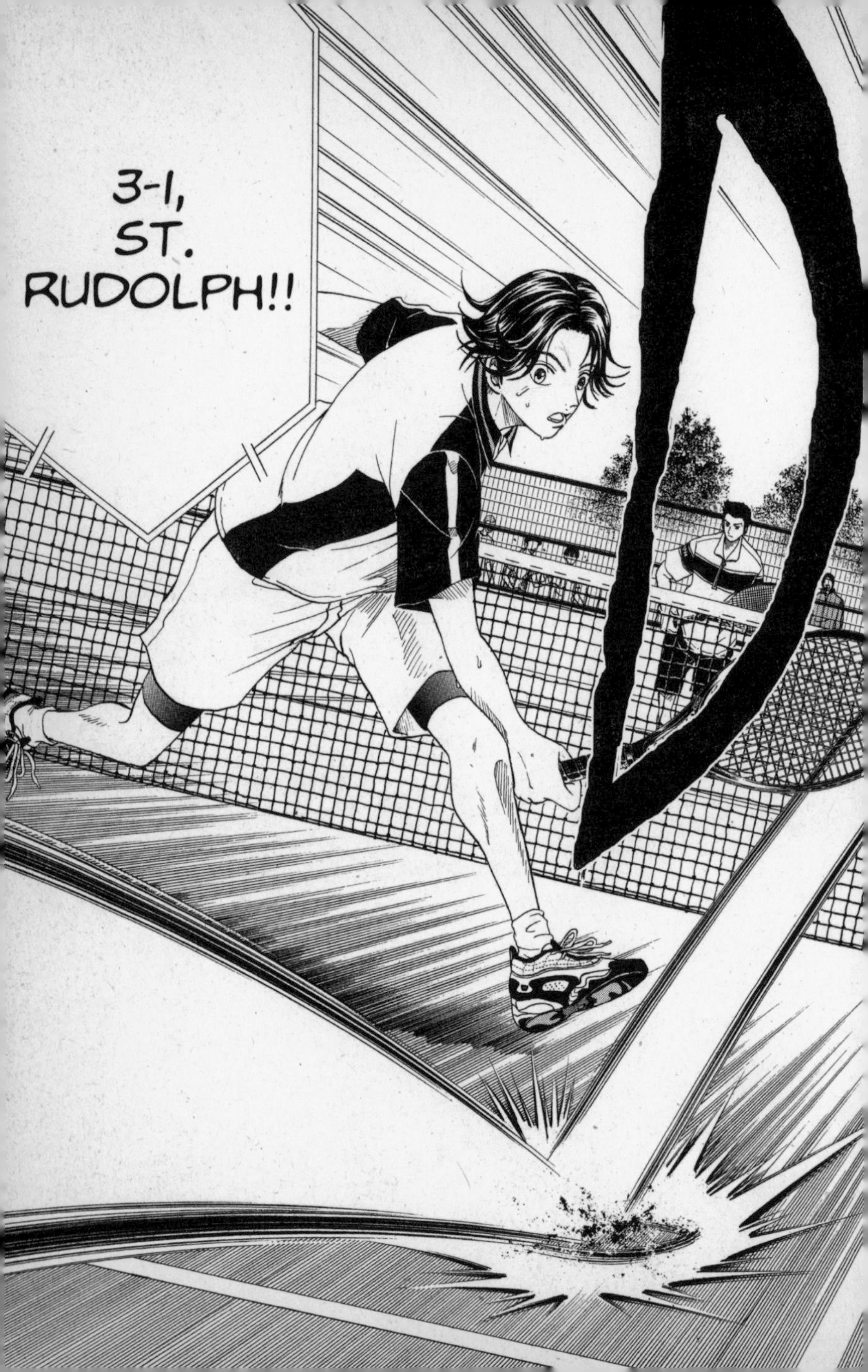
3-1, ST. RUDOLPH!!

テニスの王子様

THE PRINCE OF TENNIS™

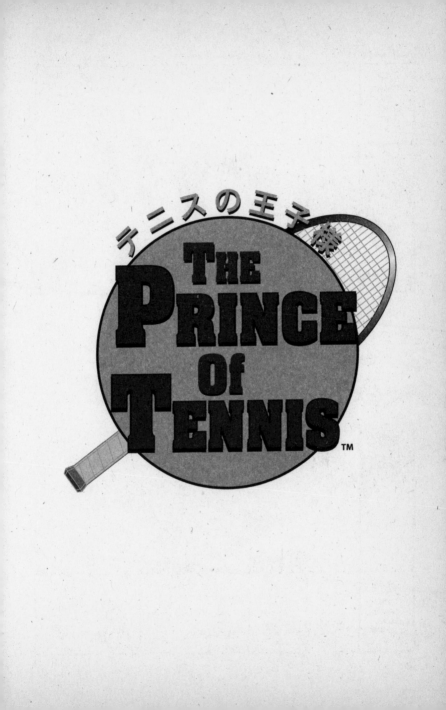

NO: 1 SINGLES	NO: 2 SINGLES	NO: 3 SINGLES	2ND GAME NO:1 DOUBLES		1ST GAME NO:2 DOUBLES	
KUNIMITSU TEZUKA (9TH GRADE) BLOOD TYPE: O	SHUSUKE FUJI (9TH GRADE) BLOOD TYPE: B	RYOMA ECHIZEN (7TH GRADE) BLOOD TYPE: O	SHUICHIRO OISHI (9TH GRADE) BLOOD TYPE: O	EIJI KIKUMARU (9TH GRADE) BLOOD TYPE: A	KAORU KAIDO (8TH GRADE) BLOOD TYPE: B	TAKESHI MOMO-SHIRO (8TH GRADE) BLOOD TYPE: O

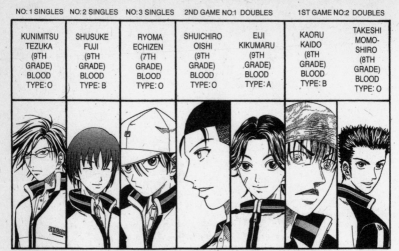

GENIUS 56:

AKAZAWA MAGIC

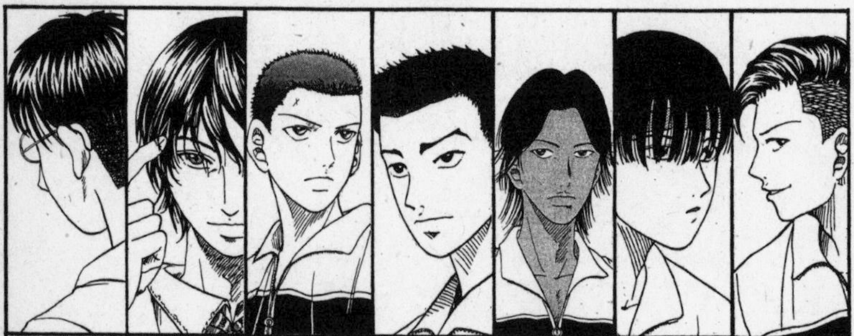

TAKUYA NOMURA (9TH GRADE) BLOOD TYPE: B	HAJIME MIZUKI (9TH GRADE) BLOOD TYPE: B	YUTA FUJI (8TH GRADE) BLOOD TYPE: O	ICHIRO KANDEA (8TH GRADE) BLOOD TYPE: AB	YOSHIRO AKAZAWA (9TH GRADE) BLOOD TYPE: O	ATSUSHI KISARAZU (9TH GRADE) BLOOD TYPE: O	SHINYA YANAGISAWA (9TH GRADE) BLOOD TYPE: O

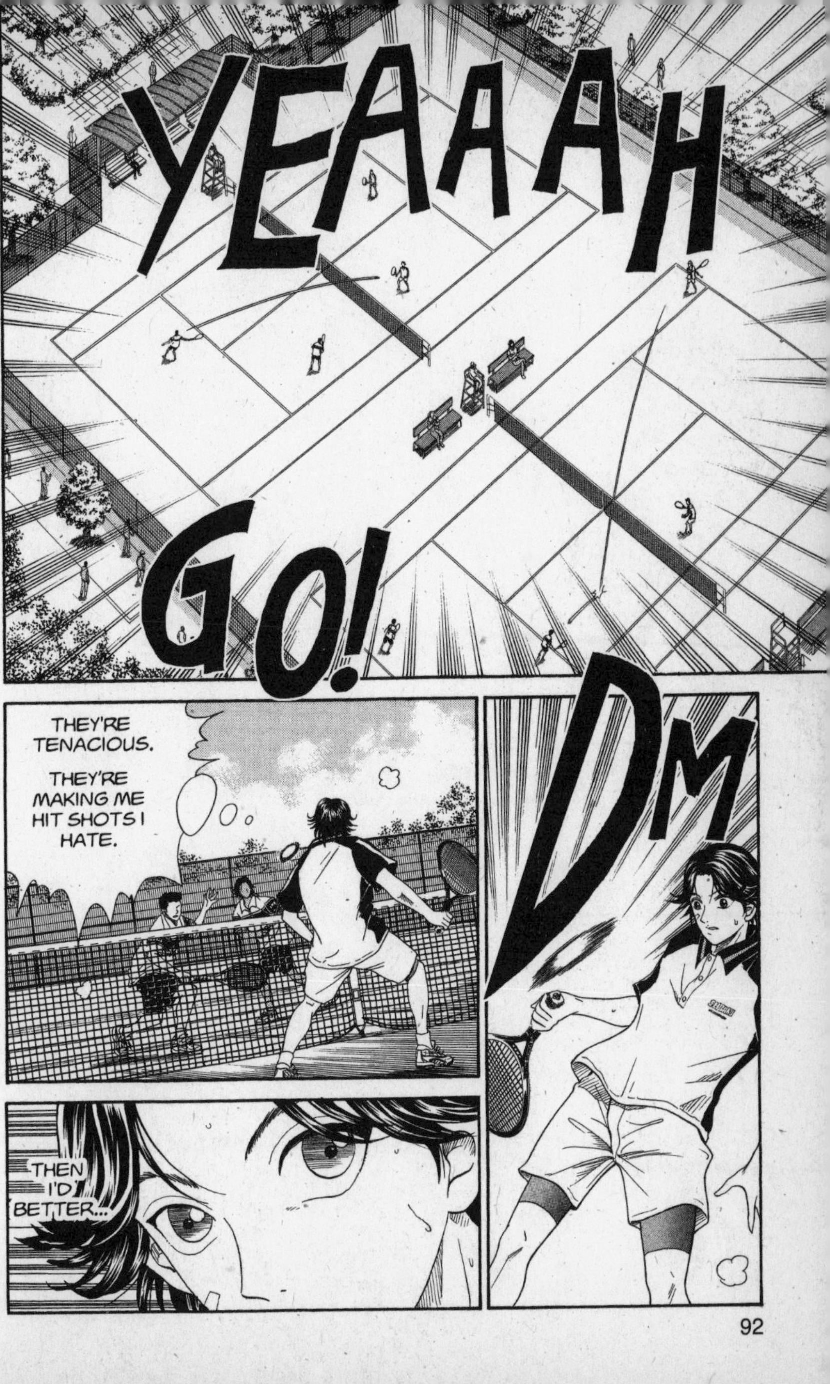
YEAAAH
GO!
DM
THEY'RE TENACIOUS.
THEY'RE MAKING ME HIT SHOTS I HATE.
THEN I'D BETTER...

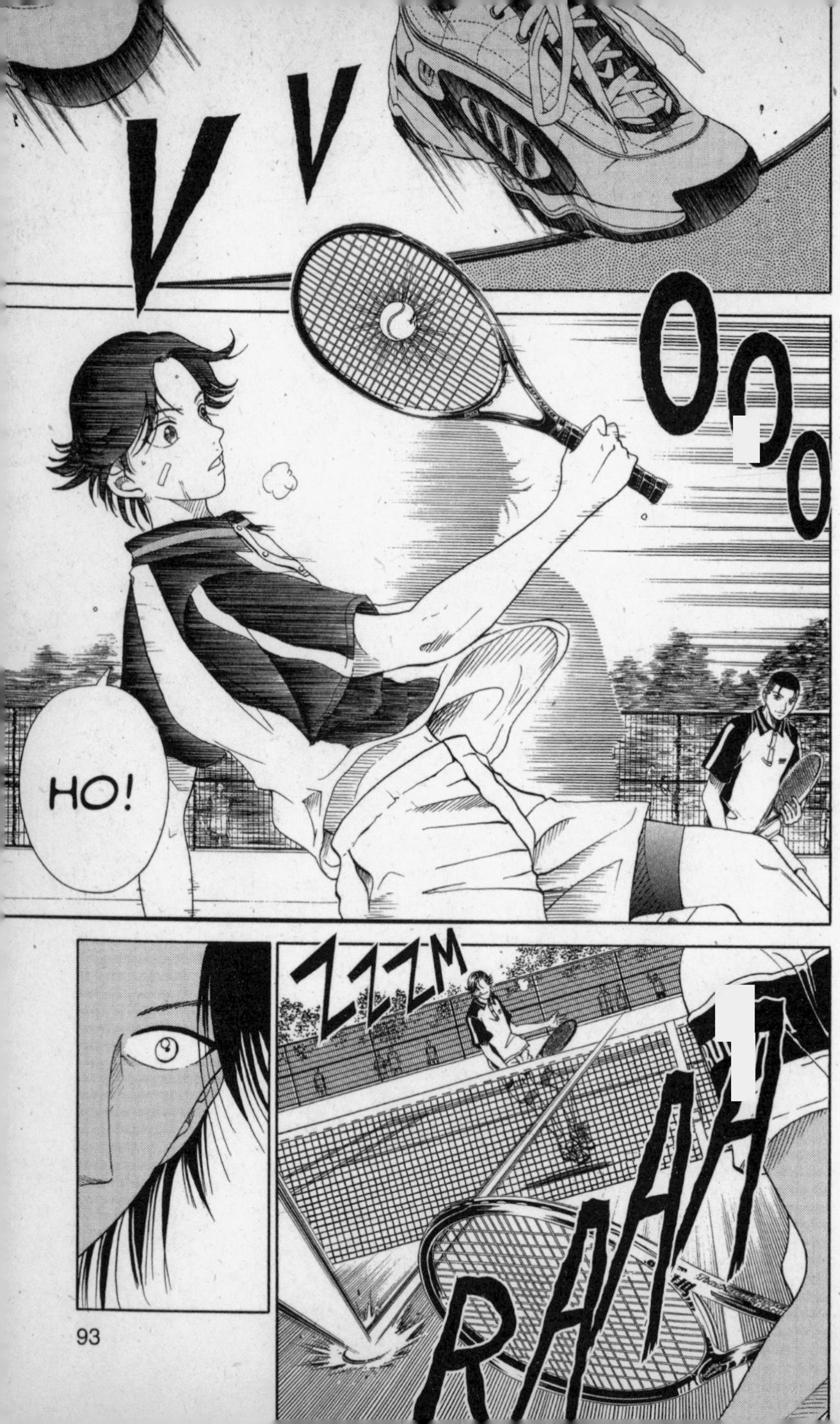
VV
OOO
HO!
ZZZM
RAAH

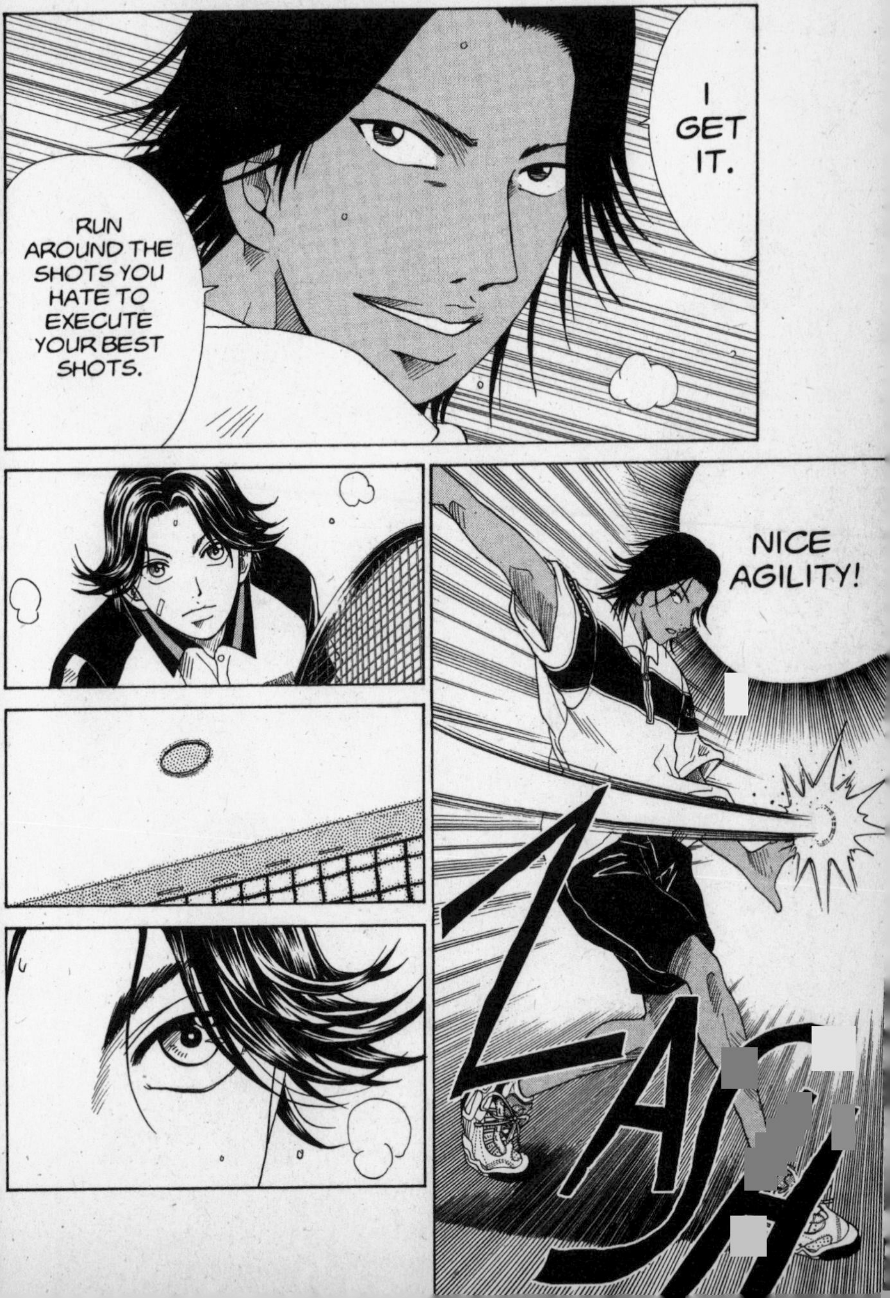
I GET IT.
RUN AROUND THE SHOTS YOU HATE TO EXECUTE YOUR BEST SHOTS.
NICE AGILITY!

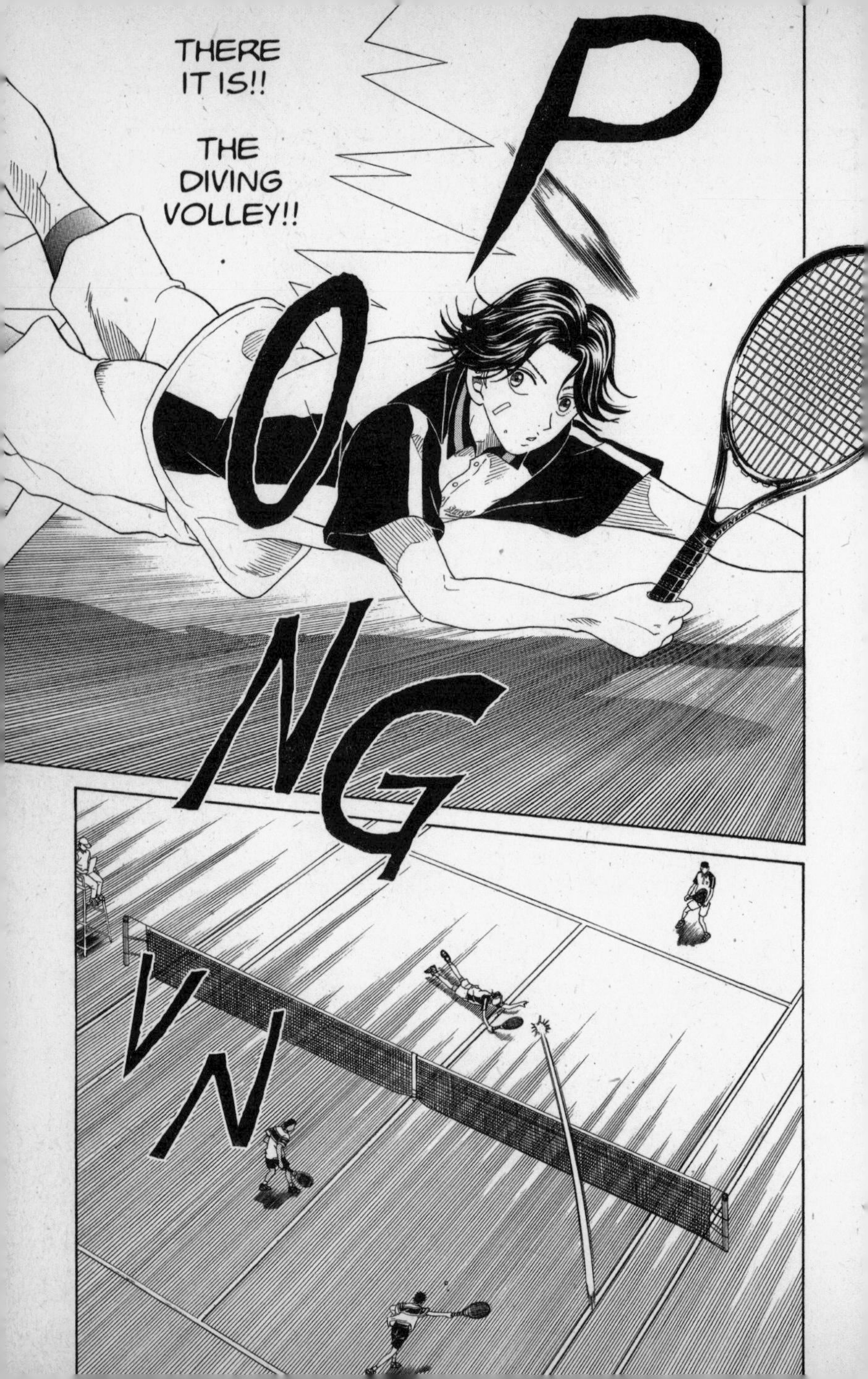
PONG
THERE IT IS!!
THE DIVING VOLLEY!!
VN

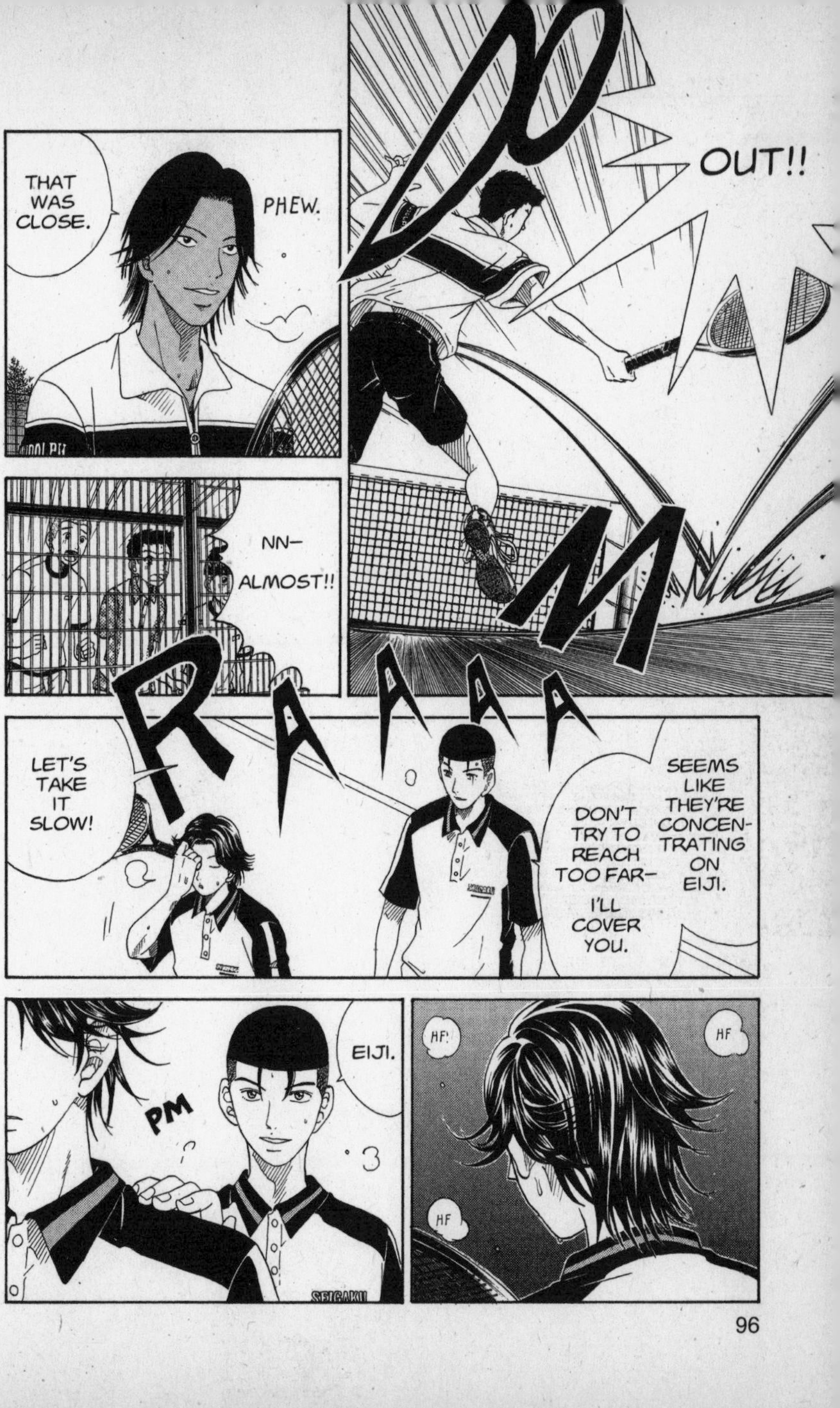
OUT!!
THAT WAS CLOSE.
PHEW.
NN—
ALMOST!!
SEEMS LIKE THEY'RE CONCEN-TRATING ON EIJI.
DON'T TRY TO REACH TOO FAR—
I'LL COVER YOU.
LET'S TAKE IT SLOW!
HF!
HF
HF
EIJI.
PM

READ THIS WAY

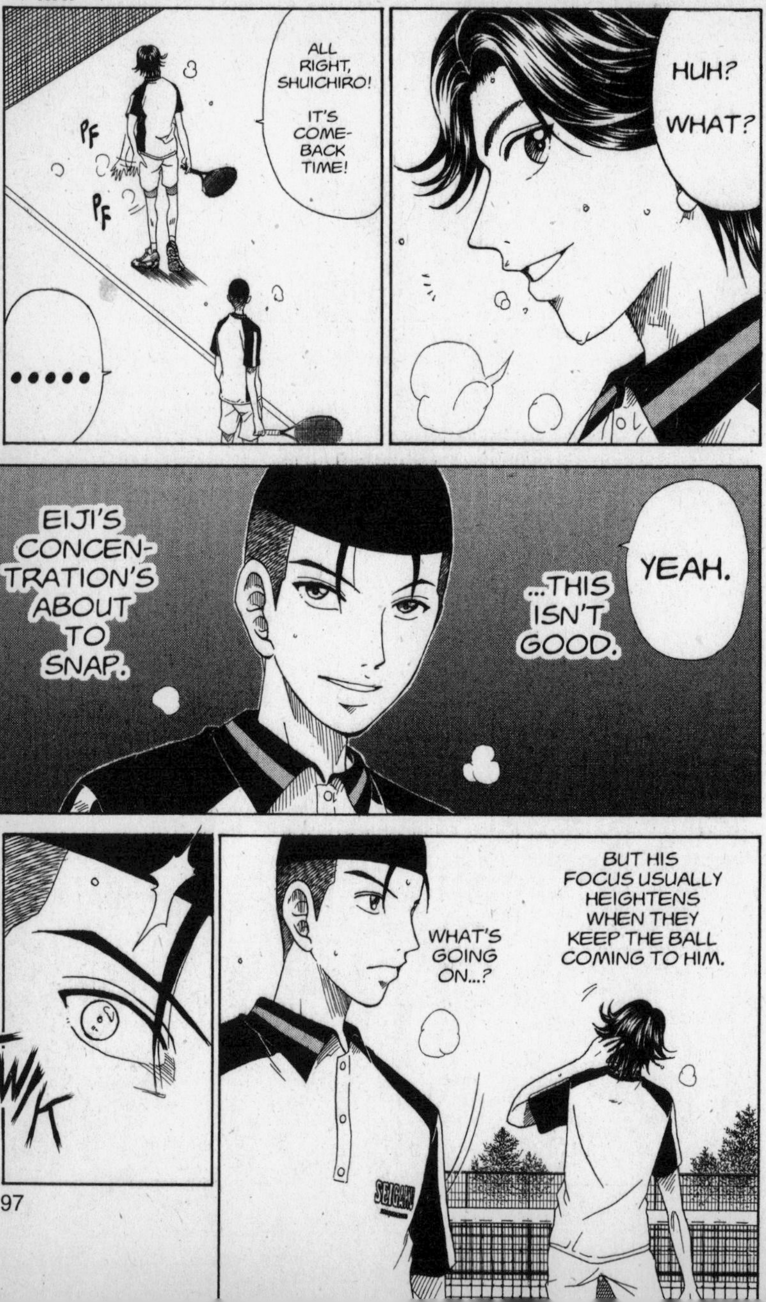

HUH?
WHAT?
ALL RIGHT, SHUICHIRO!
IT'S COME-BACK TIME!
PF
PF
.....
YEAH.
...THIS ISN'T GOOD.
EIJI'S CONCEN-TRATION'S ABOUT TO SNAP.
BUT HIS FOCUS USUALLY HEIGHTENS WHEN THEY KEEP THE BALL COMING TO HIM.
WHAT'S GOING ON...?
SEIGAKU
TWIK

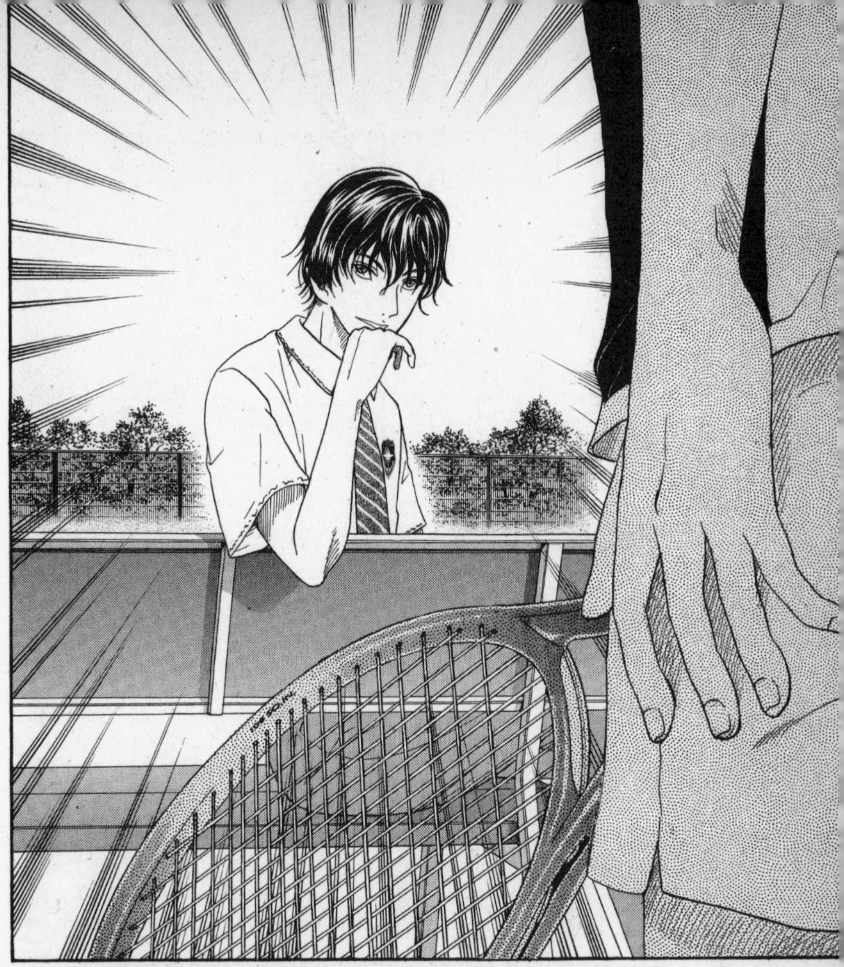

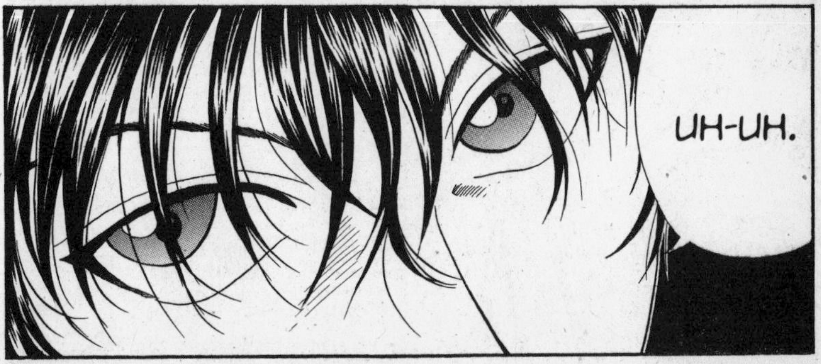
UH-UH.

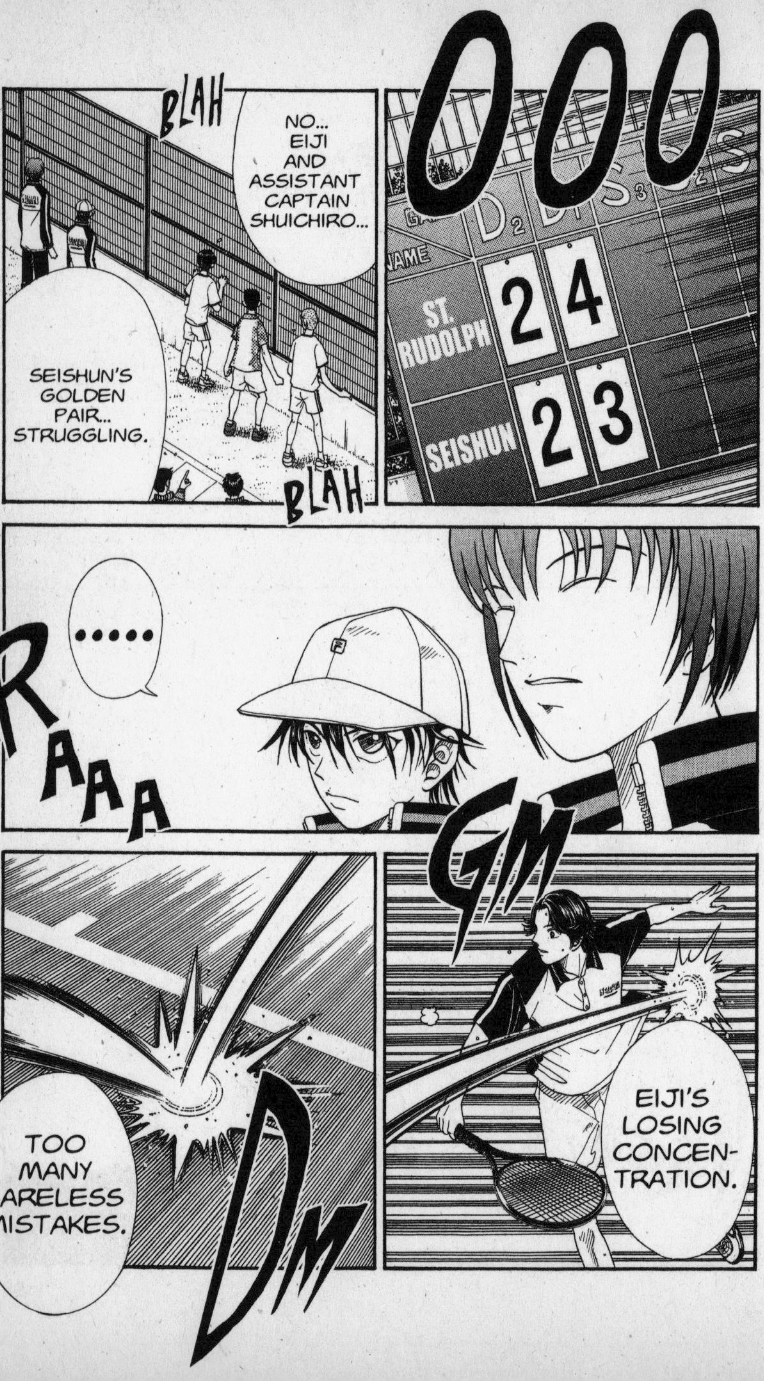
OOO
D2 D1 S3 S2 S
NAME
ST. RUDOLPH 2 4
SEISHUN 2 3
BLAH
NO... EIJI AND ASSISTANT CAPTAIN SHUICHIRO...
SEISHUN'S GOLDEN PAIR... STRUGGLING.
BLAH
......
RAAA
GM
EIJI'S LOSING CONCEN-TRATION.
TOO MANY CARELESS MISTAKES.
DM

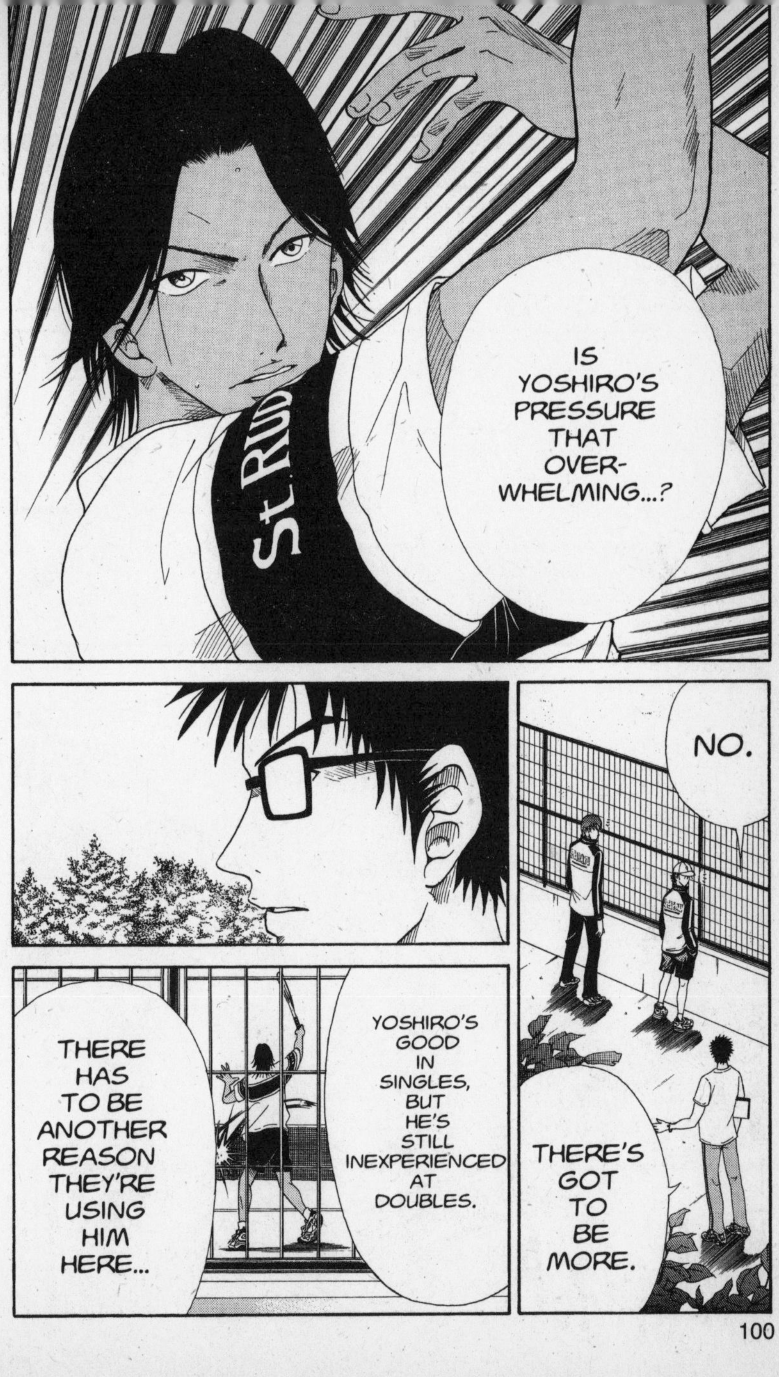
IS YOSHIRO'S PRESSURE THAT OVER-WHELMING...?
NO.
THERE'S GOT TO BE MORE.
YOSHIRO'S GOOD IN SINGLES, BUT HE'S STILL INEXPERIENCED AT DOUBLES.
THERE HAS TO BE ANOTHER REASON THEY'RE USING HIM HERE...

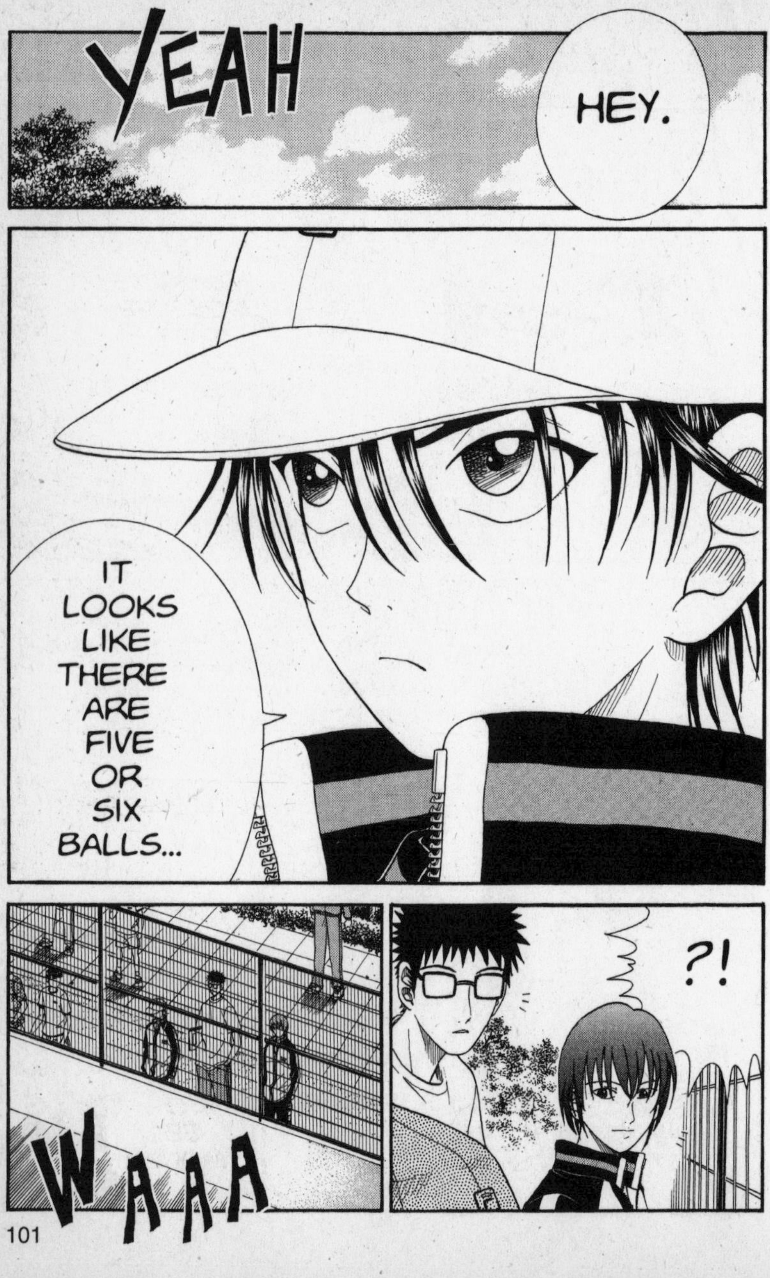
HEY.
YEAH
IT LOOKS LIKE THERE ARE FIVE OR SIX BALLS...
?!
WAAA

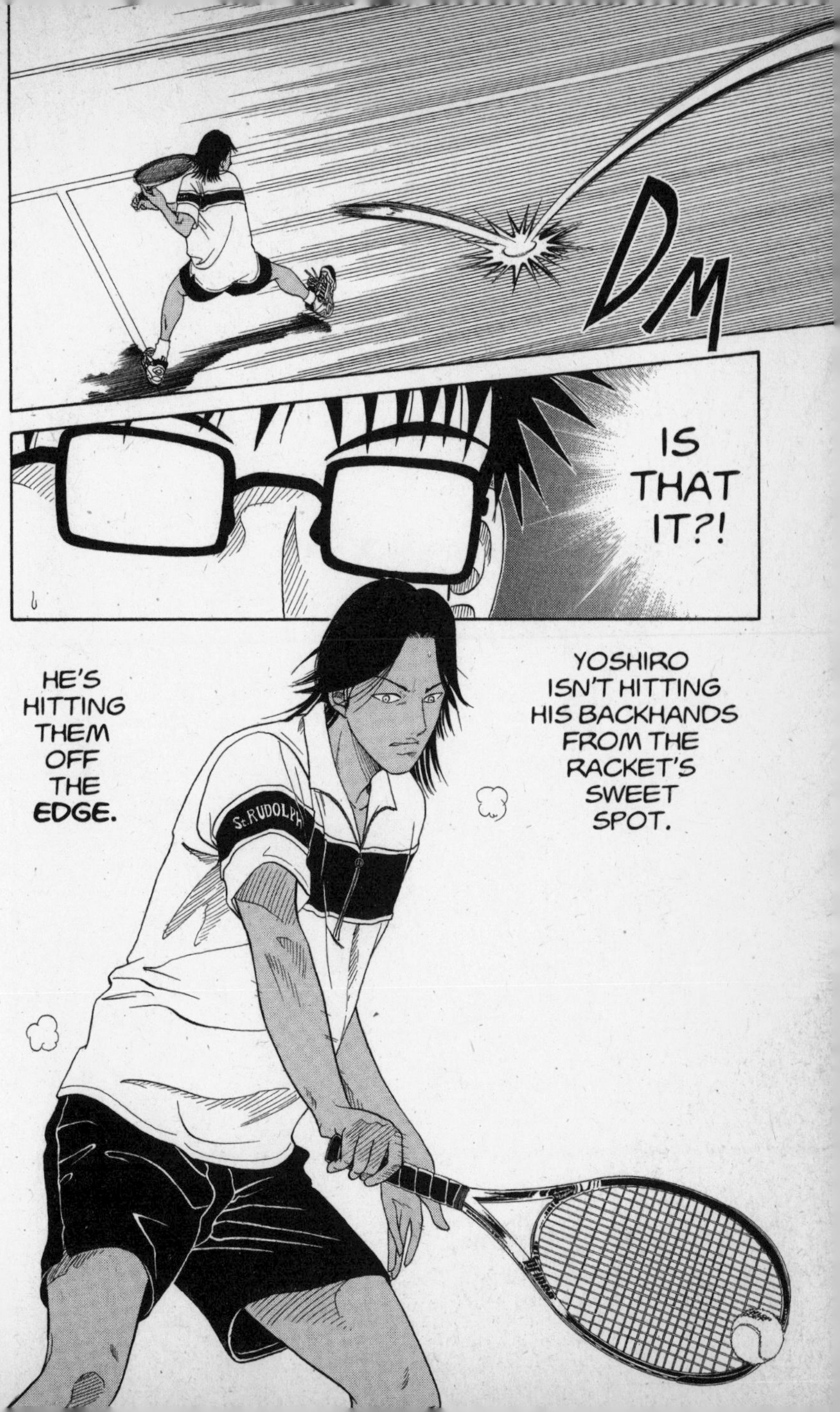
DM
IS THAT IT?!
YOSHIRO ISN'T HITTING HIS BACKHANDS FROM THE RACKET'S SWEET SPOT.
HE'S HITTING THEM OFF THE EDGE.
St. RUDOLPH

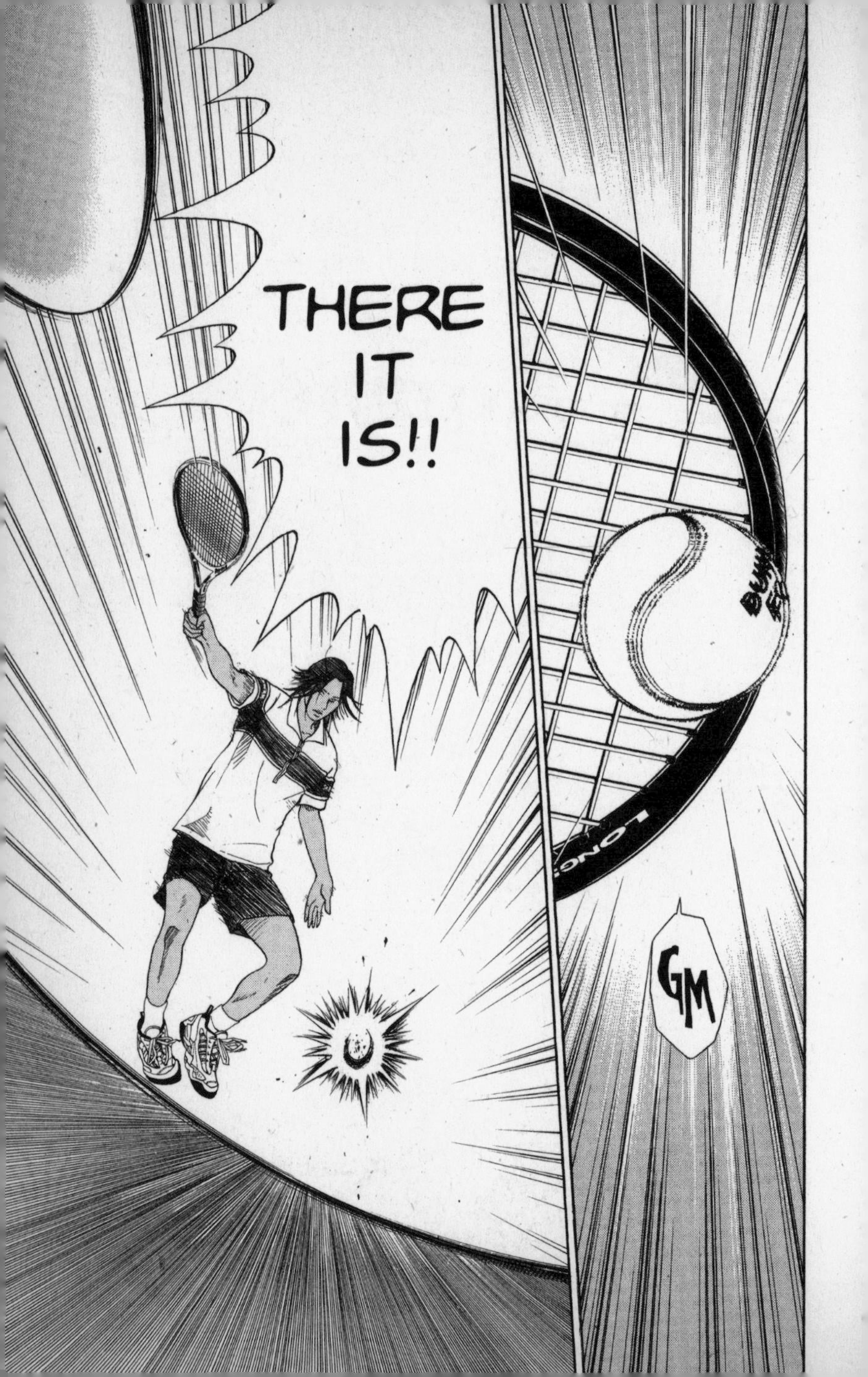
GM
THERE IT IS!!

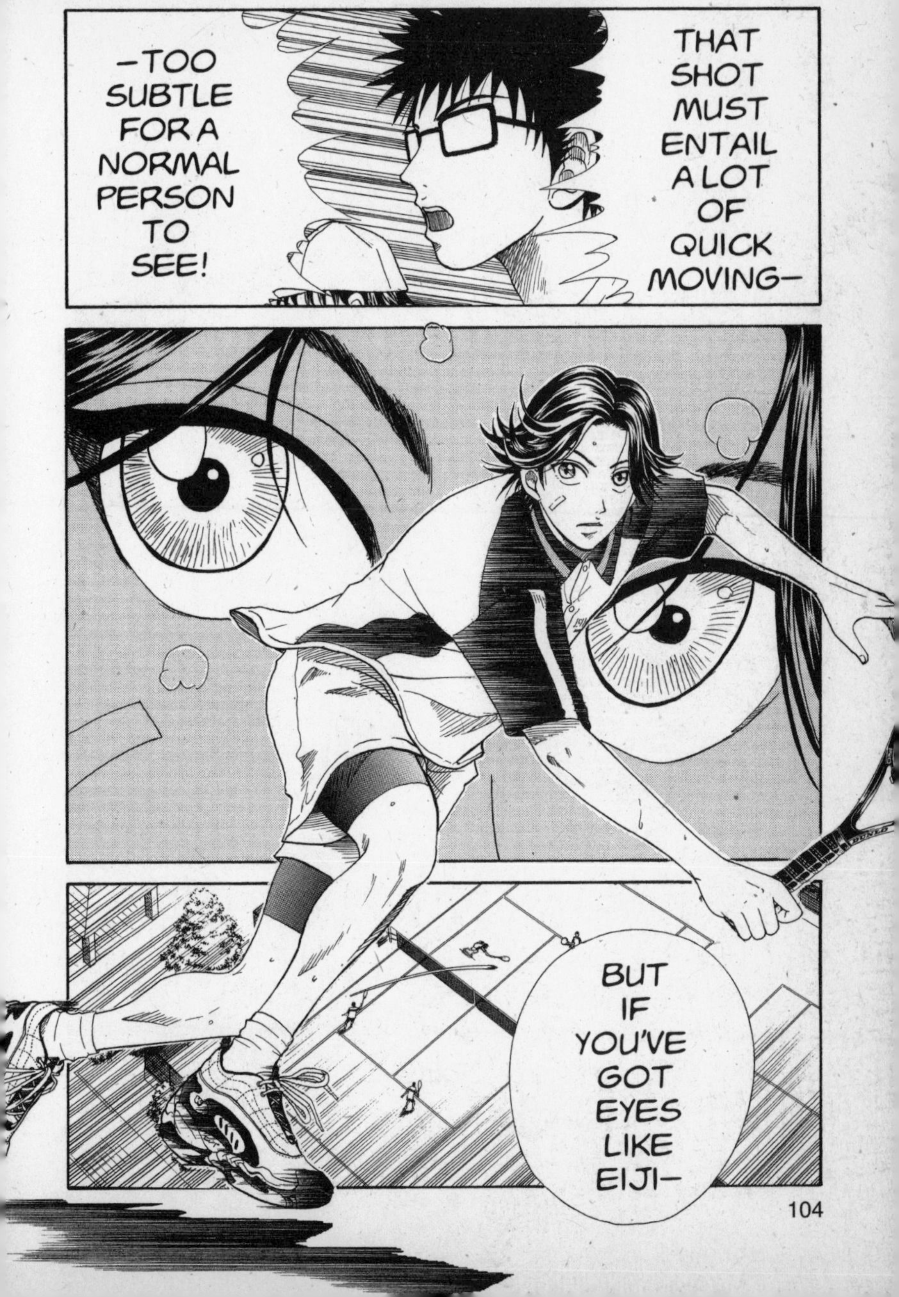
THAT SHOT MUST ENTAIL A LOT OF QUICK MOVING—
—TOO SUBTLE FOR A NORMAL PERSON TO SEE!
BUT IF YOU'VE GOT EYES LIKE EIJI—

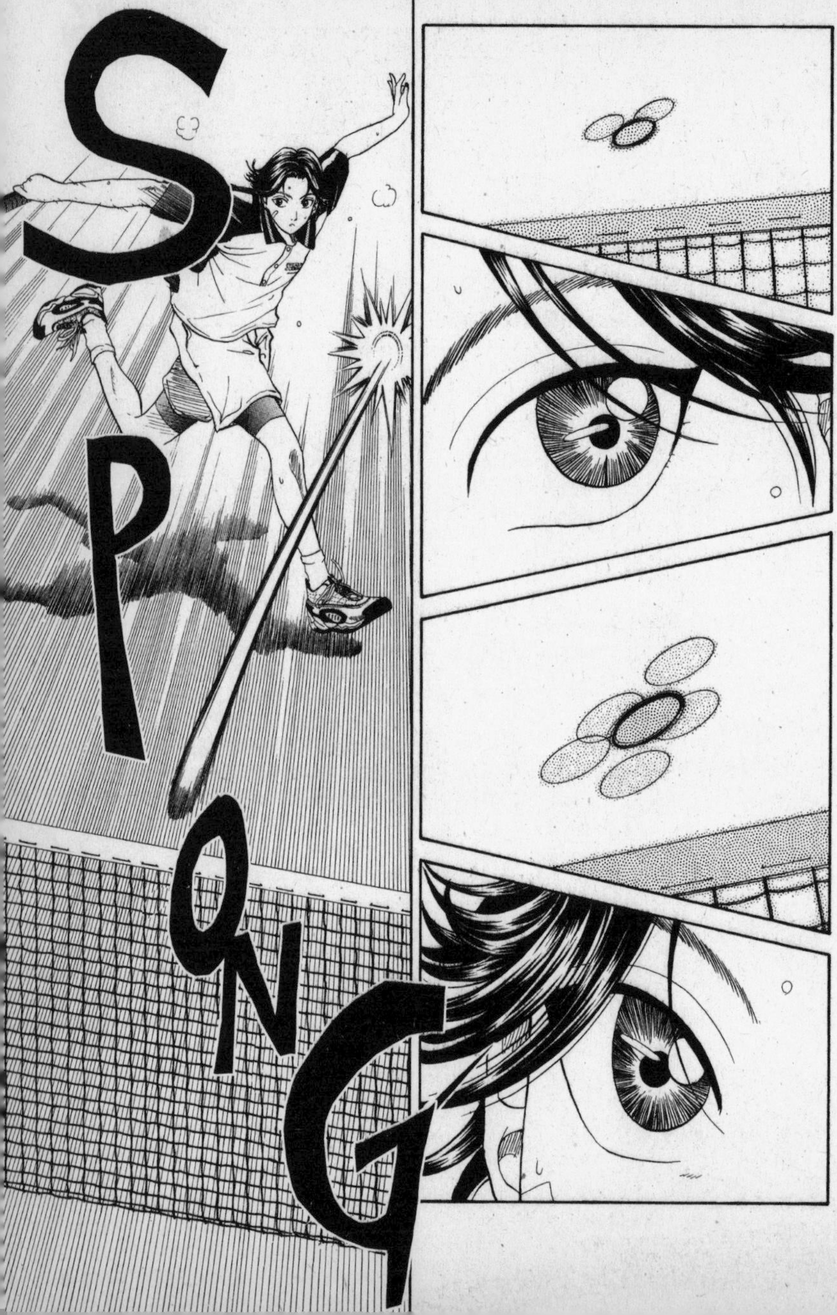
SPONG

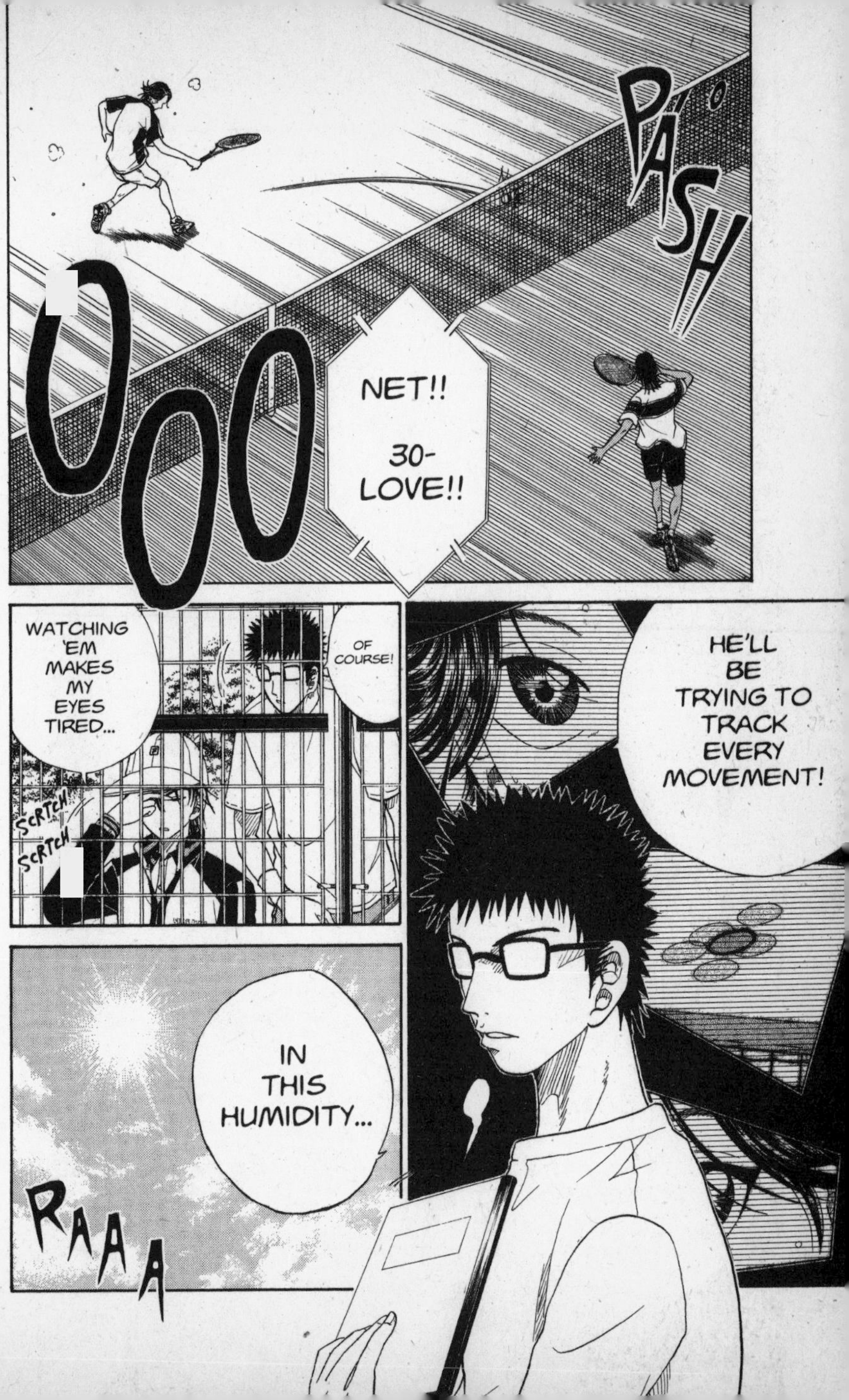
PASH
OOO
NET!!
30-LOVE!!
HE'LL BE TRYING TO TRACK EVERY MOVEMENT!
OF COURSE!
WATCHING 'EM MAKES MY EYES TIRED...
SCRTCH SCRTCH
IN THIS HUMIDITY...
RAAA

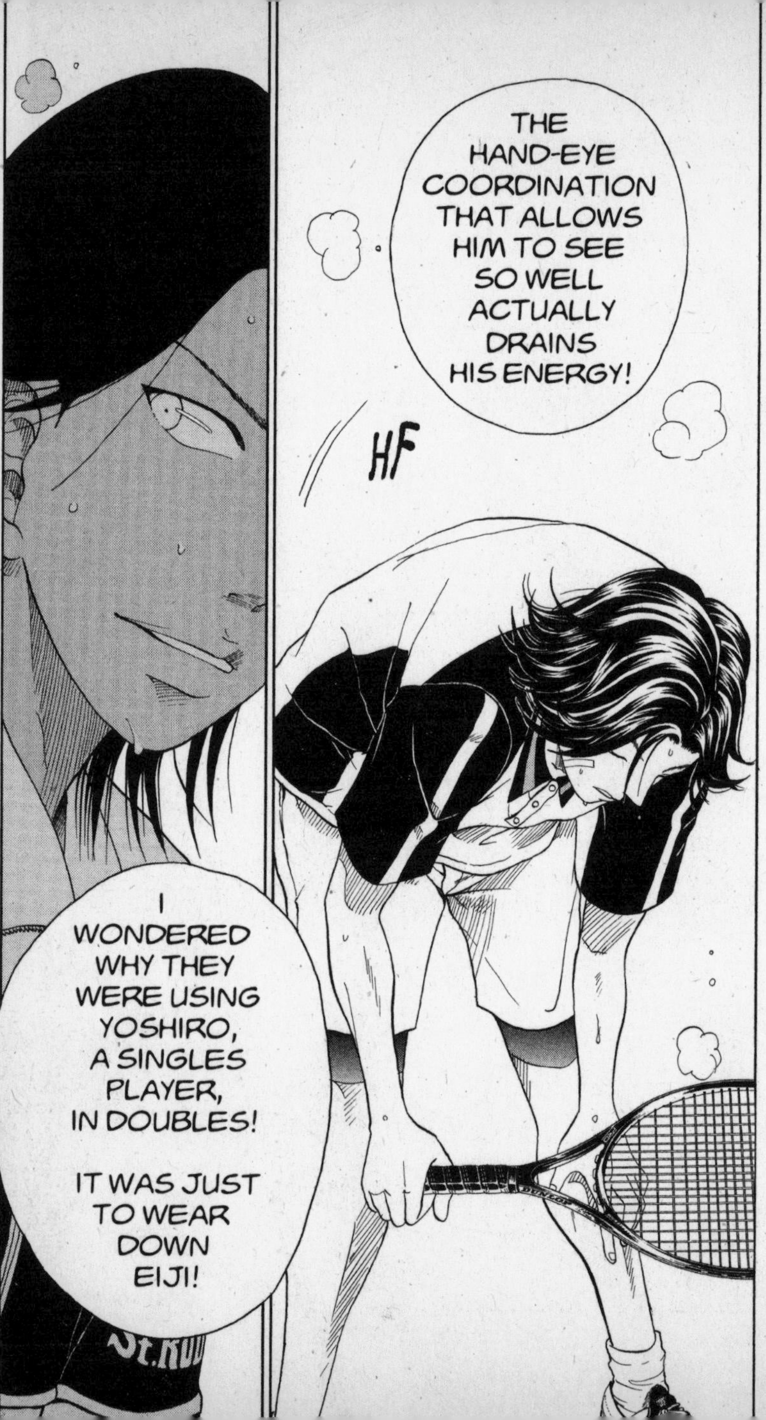
THE HAND-EYE COORDINATION THAT ALLOWS HIM TO SEE SO WELL ACTUALLY DRAINS HIS ENERGY!
HF
I WONDERED WHY THEY WERE USING YOSHIRO, A SINGLES PLAYER, IN DOUBLES!
IT WAS JUST TO WEAR DOWN EIJI!

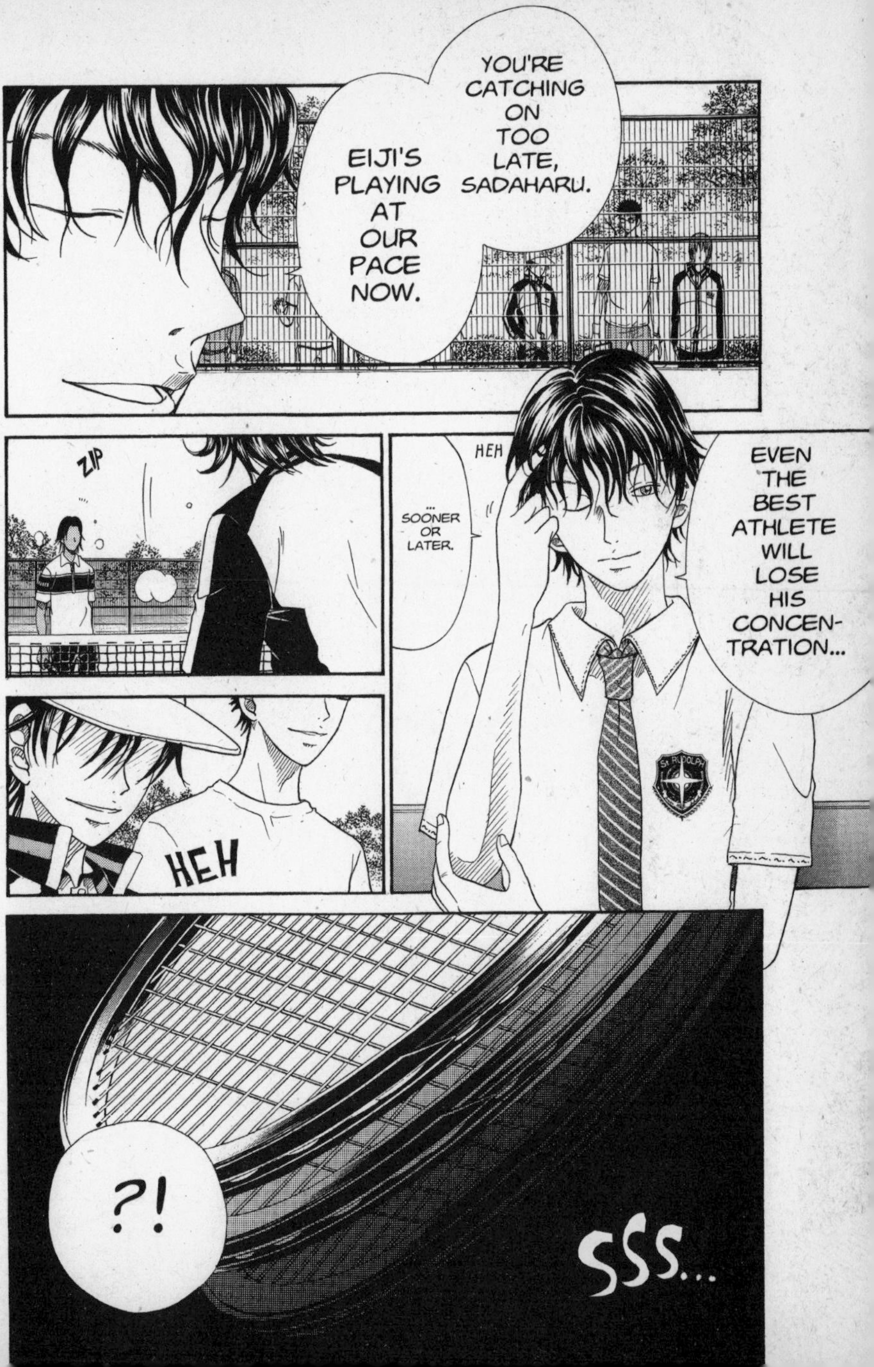
YOU'RE CATCHING ON TOO LATE, SADAHARU.
EIJI'S PLAYING AT OUR PACE NOW.
EVEN THE BEST ATHLETE WILL LOSE HIS CONCENTRATION...
HEH
...SOONER OR LATER.
ZIP
HEH
?!
SSS...

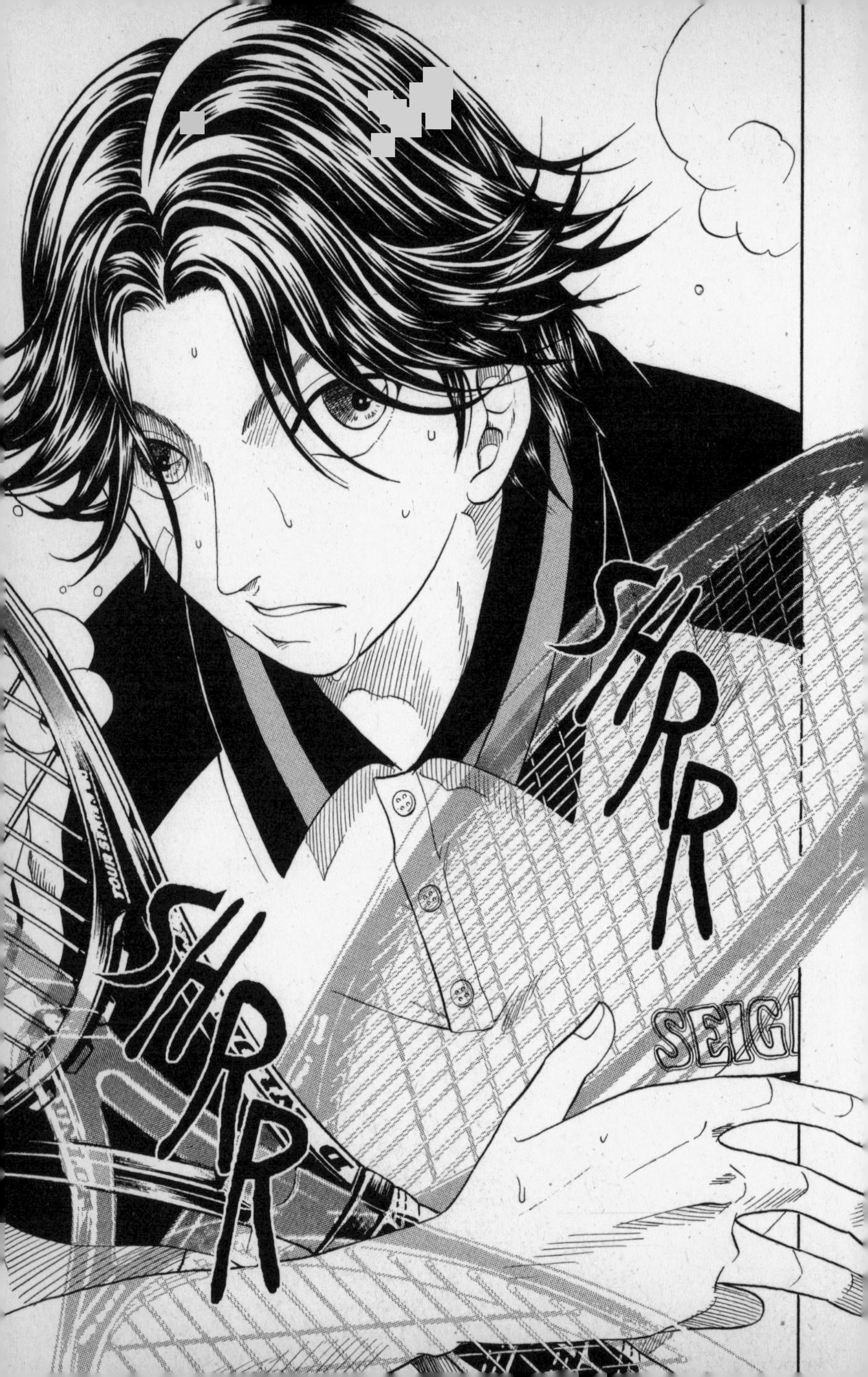
SHRR
SHRR

テニスの王子様

THE PRINCE OF TENNIS™

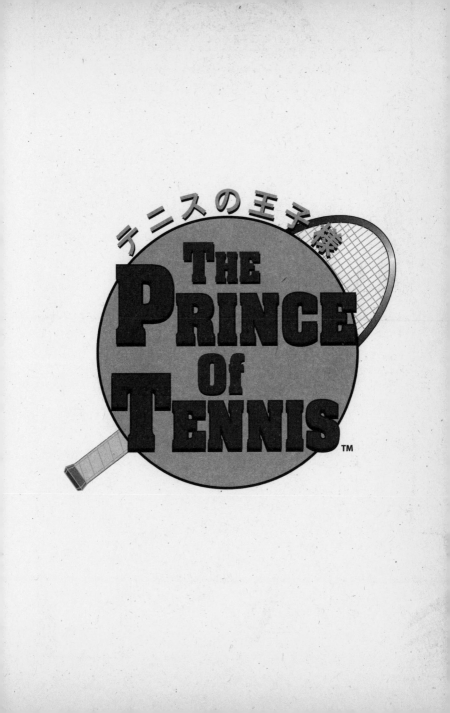

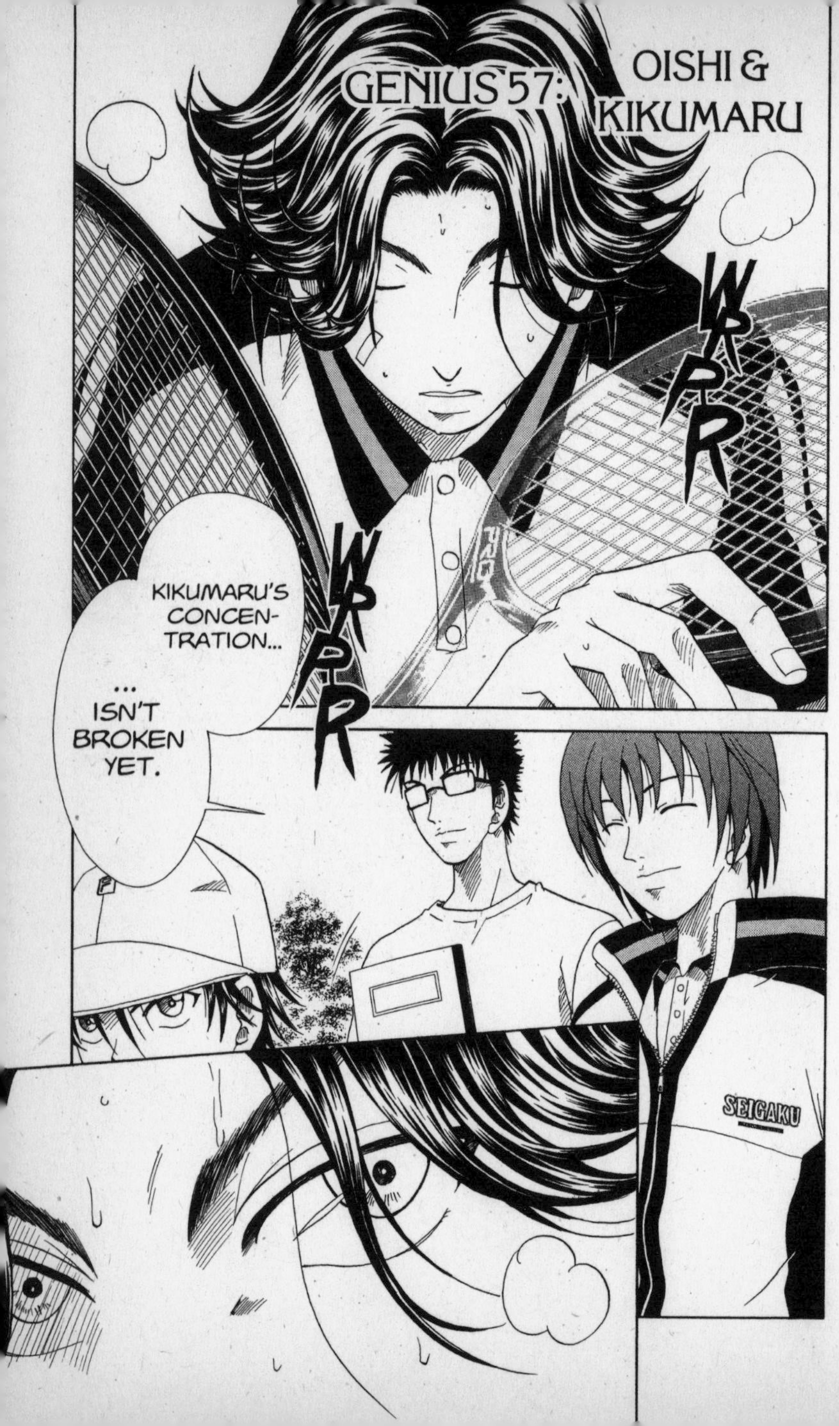
GENIUS 57: OISHI & KIKUMARU
WRPR
WRPR
KIKUMARU'S CONCEN-TRATION...
... ISN'T BROKEN YET.
SEIGAKU

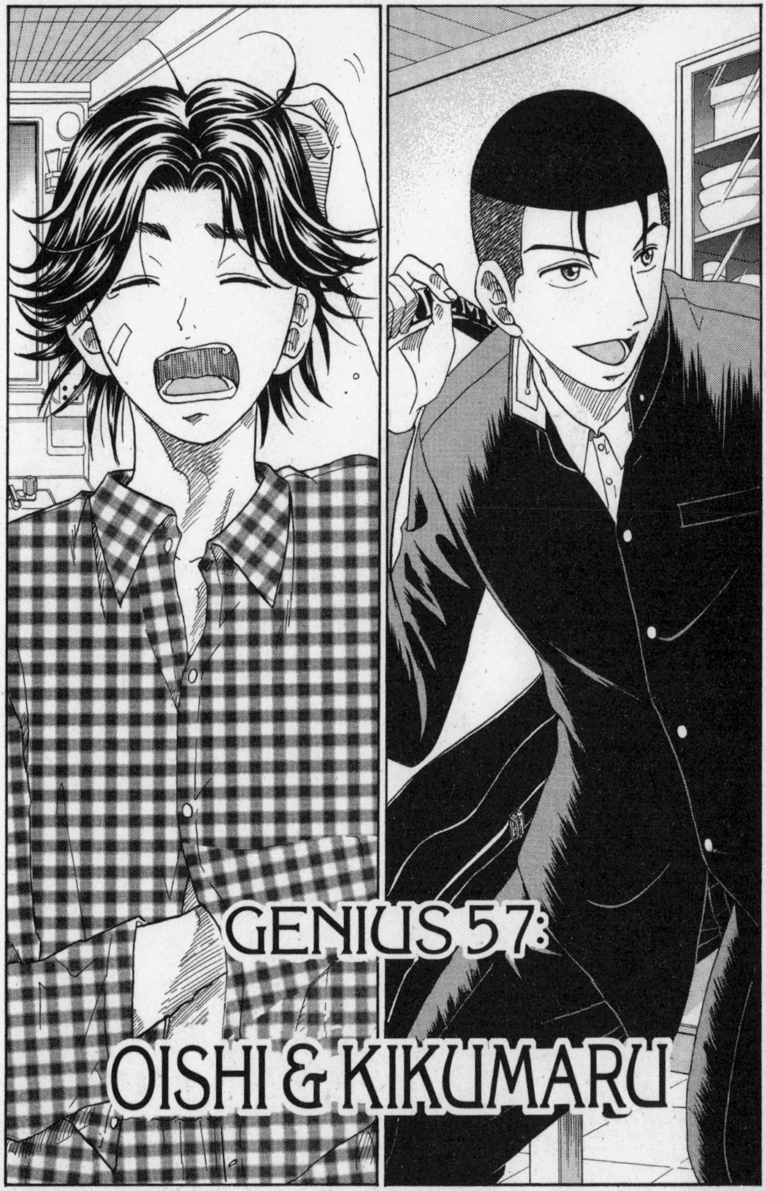
GENIUS 57:
OISHI & KIKUMARU

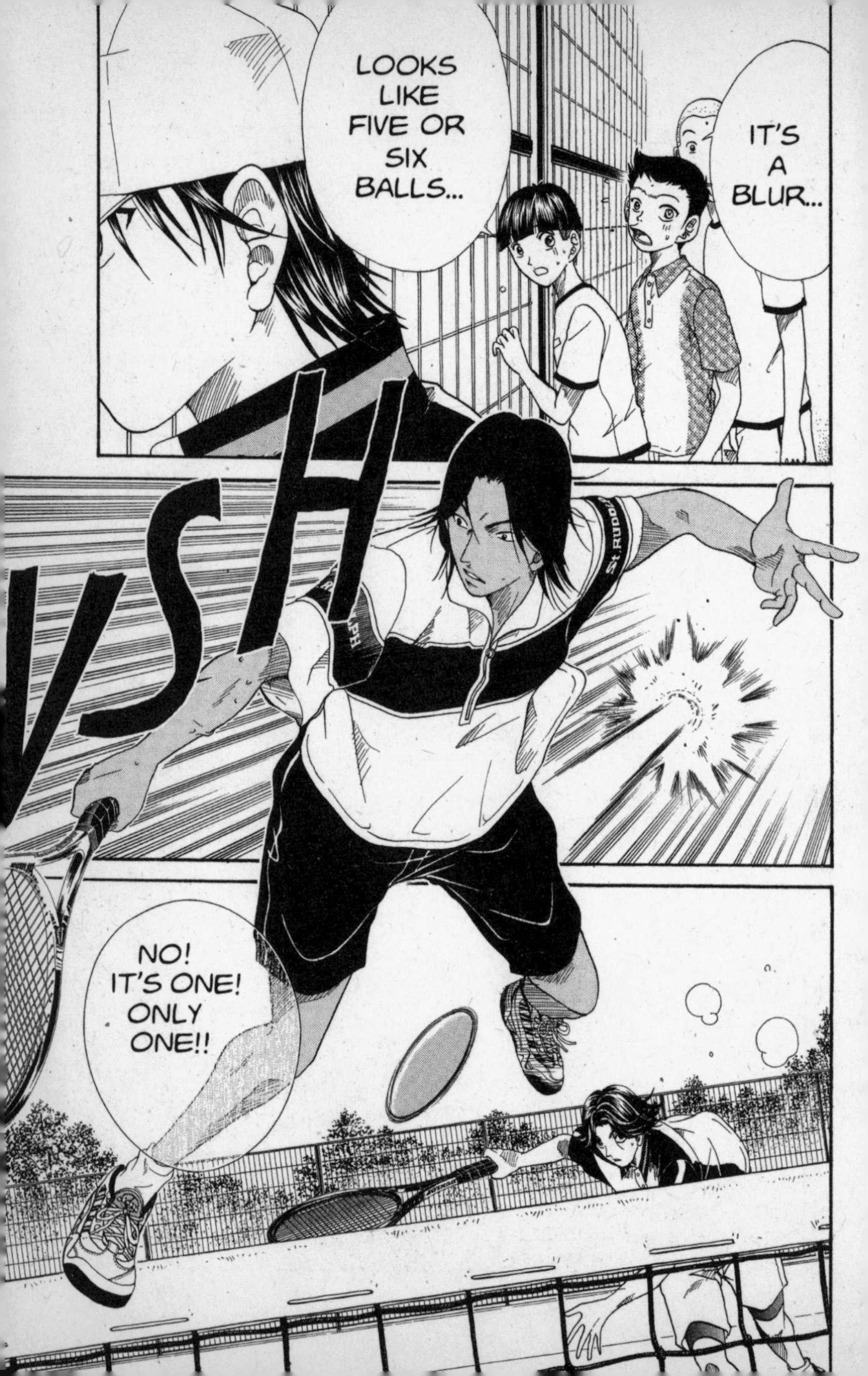
IT'S A BLUR...
LOOKS LIKE FIVE OR SIX BALLS...
VSH
NO! IT'S ONE! ONLY ONE!!

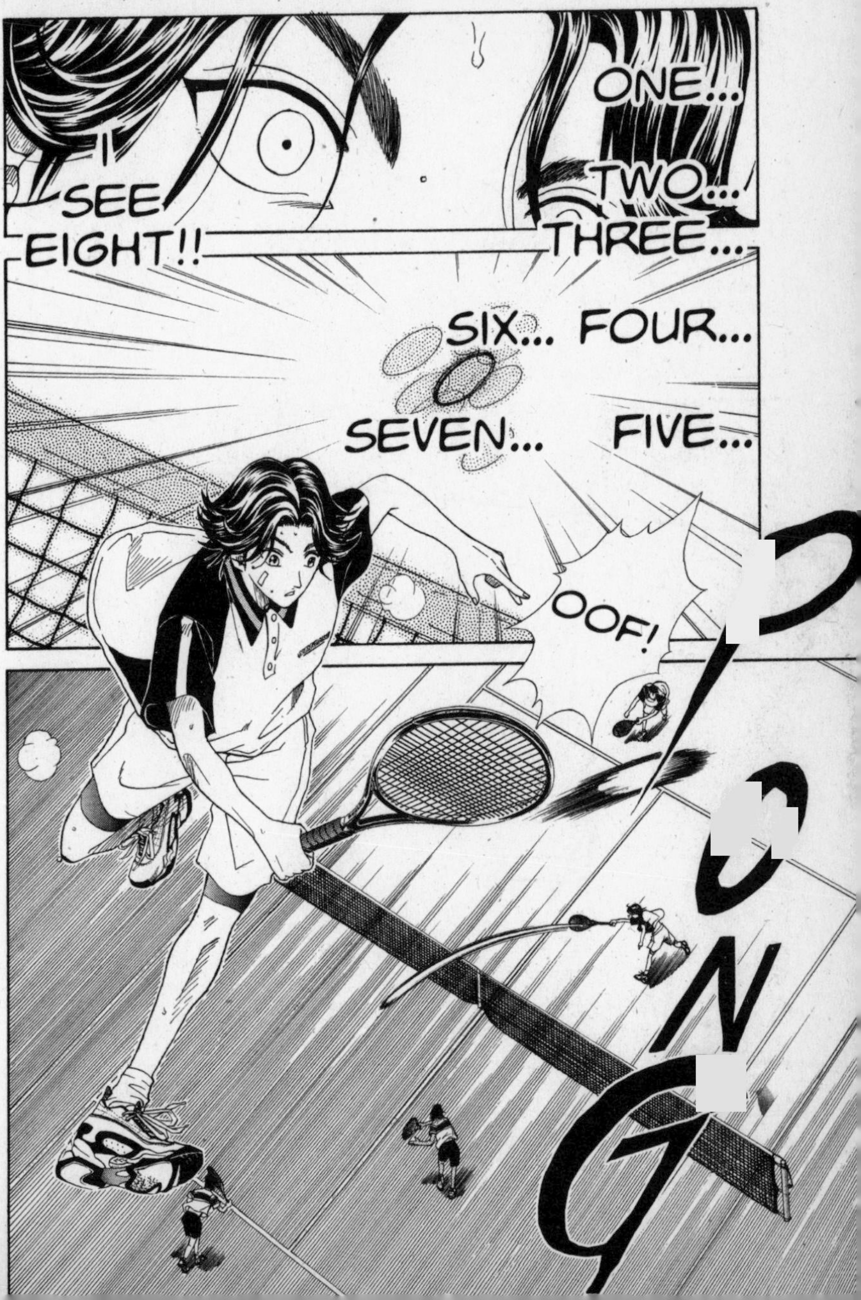
ONE...
TWO...
THREE...
I SEE EIGHT!!
FOUR...
FIVE...
SIX...
SEVEN...
OOF!
PONG

READ THIS WAY

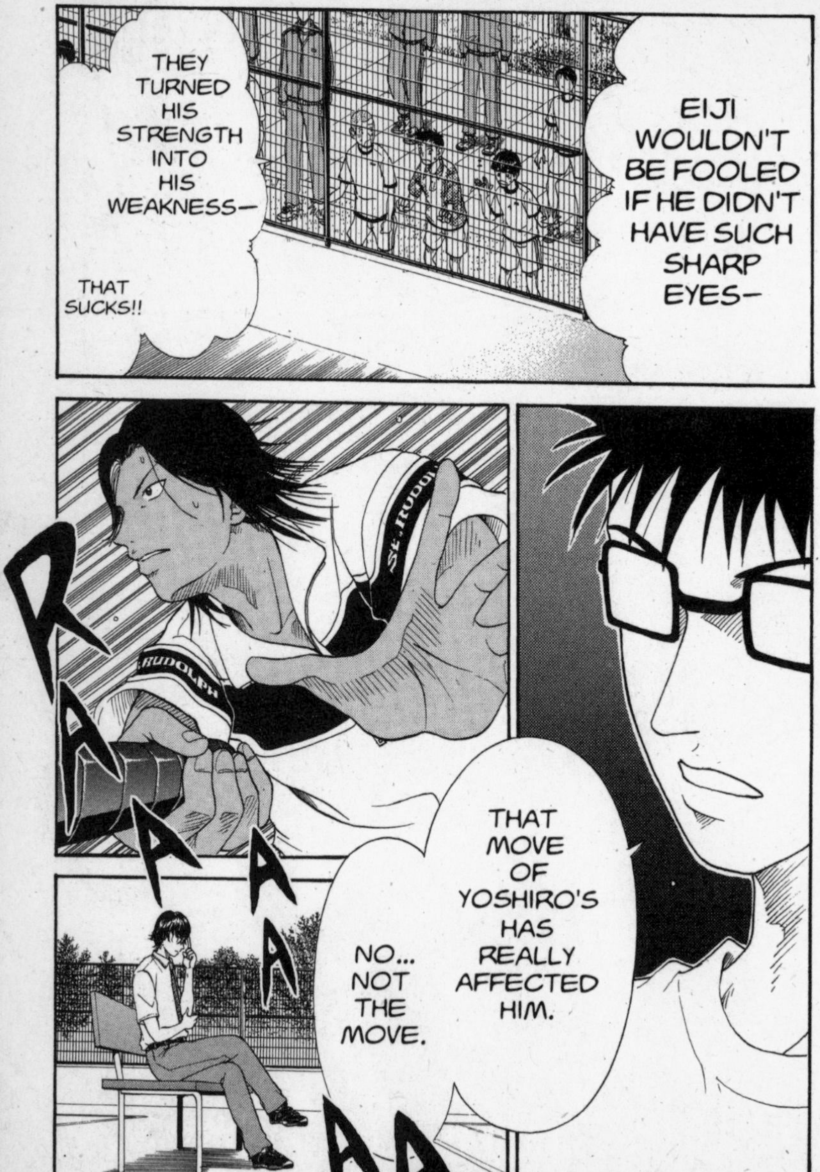
EIJI WOULDN'T BE FOOLED IF HE DIDN'T HAVE SUCH SHARP EYES—
THEY TURNED HIS STRENGTH INTO HIS WEAKNESS—
THAT SUCKS!!
THAT MOVE OF YOSHIRO'S HAS REALLY AFFECTED HIM.
NO... NOT THE MOVE.
RAAAAAAA

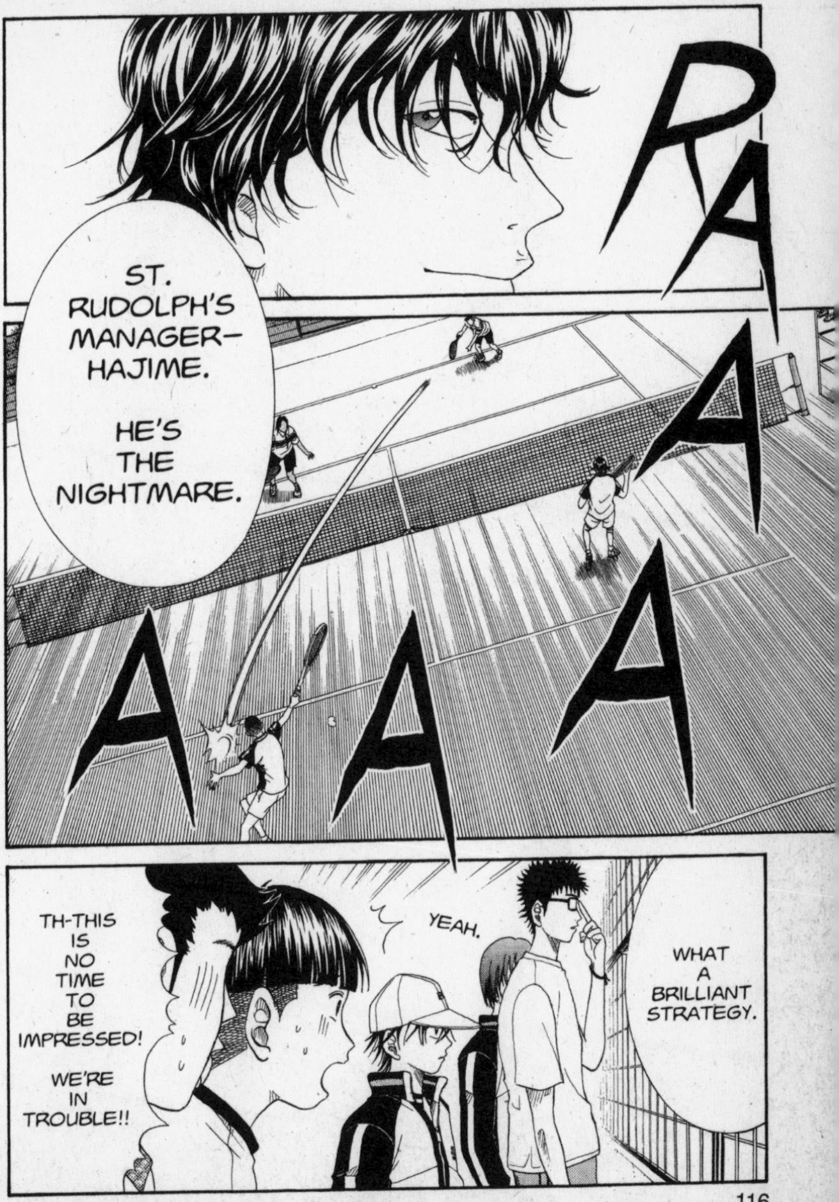
ST. RUDOLPH'S MANAGER— HAJIME.
HE'S THE NIGHTMARE.
RAAAAAA
WHAT A BRILLIANT STRATEGY.
YEAH.
TH-THIS IS NO TIME TO BE IMPRESSED!
WE'RE IN TROUBLE!!

READ THIS WAY

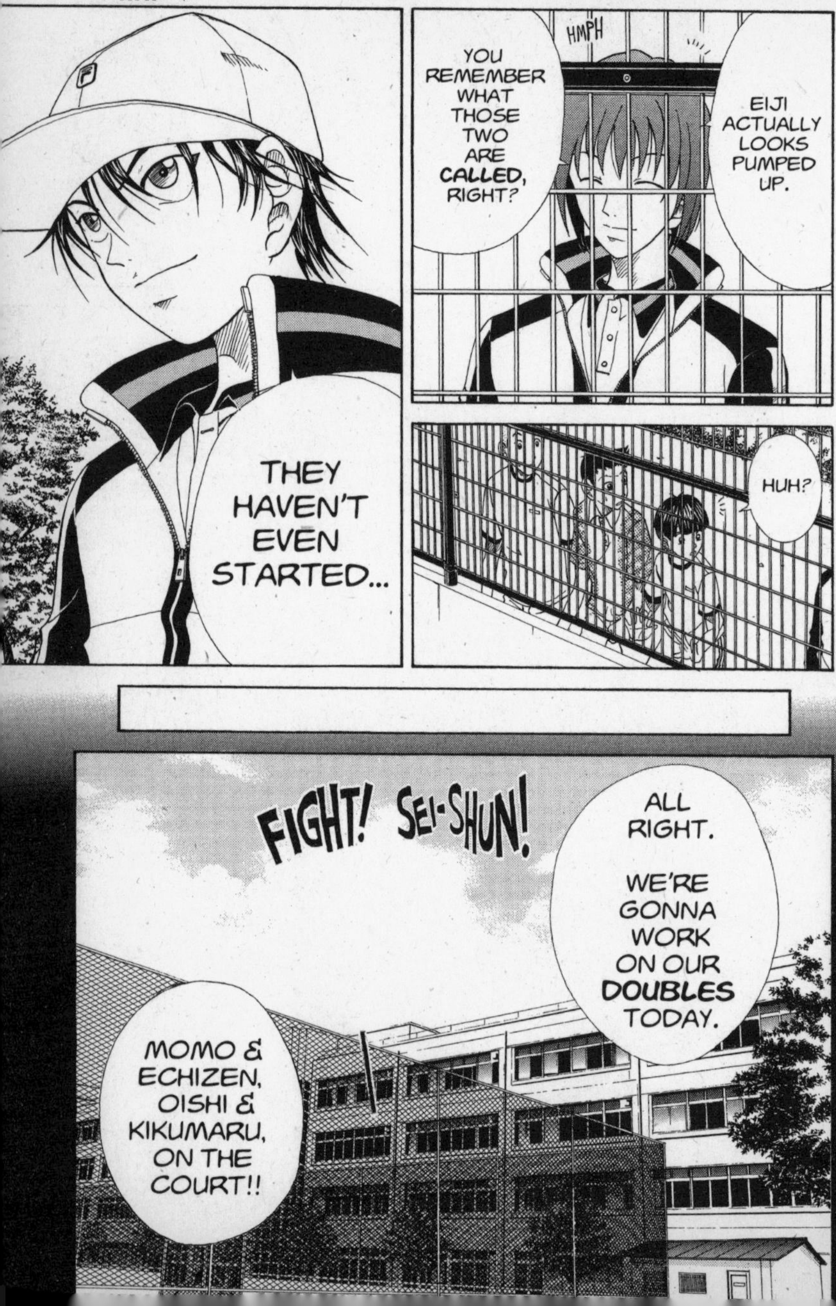

EIJI ACTUALLY LOOKS PUMPED UP.
HMPH
YOU REMEMBER WHAT THOSE TWO ARE CALLED, RIGHT?
HUH?
THEY HAVEN'T EVEN STARTED...
FIGHT! SEI-SHUN!
ALL RIGHT.
WE'RE GONNA WORK ON OUR DOUBLES TODAY.
MOMO & ECHIZEN, OISHI & KIKUMARU, ON THE COURT!!

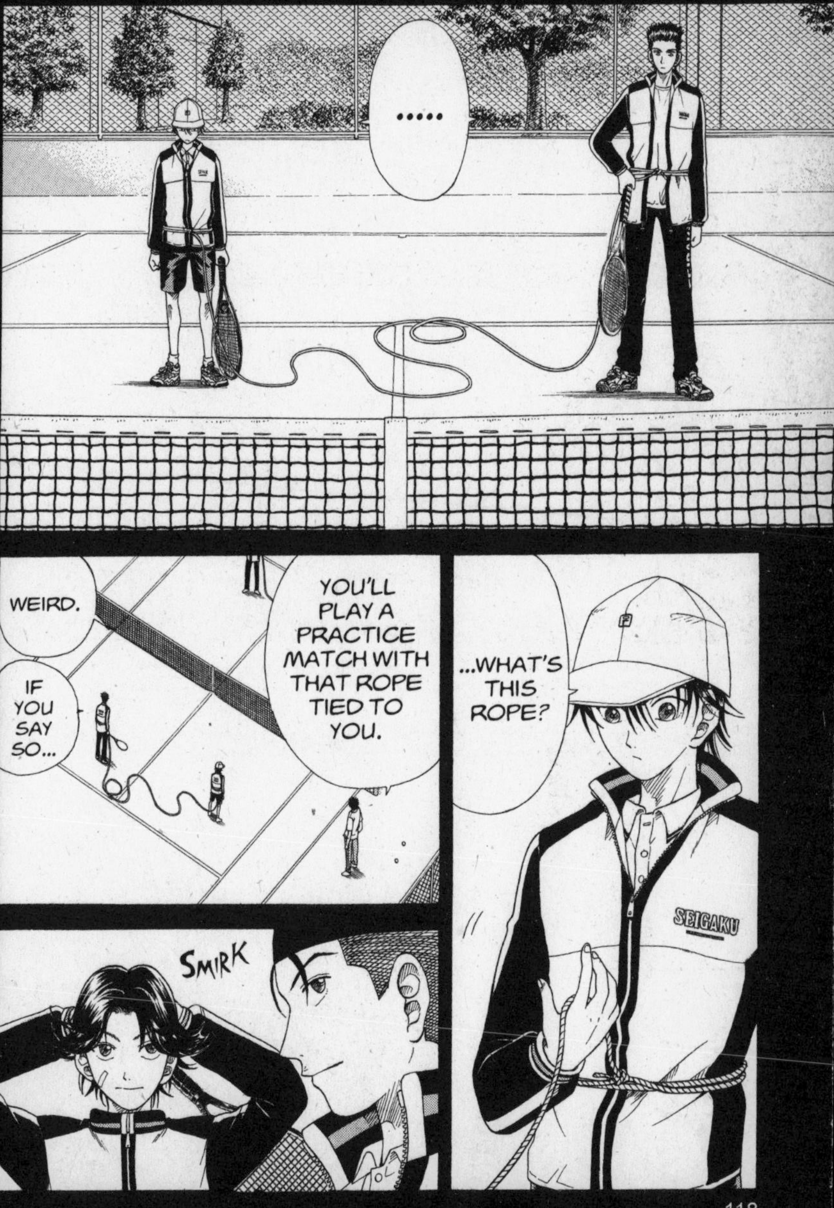
.....
...WHAT'S THIS ROPE?
YOU'LL PLAY A PRACTICE MATCH WITH THAT ROPE TIED TO YOU.
WEIRD.
IF YOU SAY SO...
SMIRK

READ THIS WAY

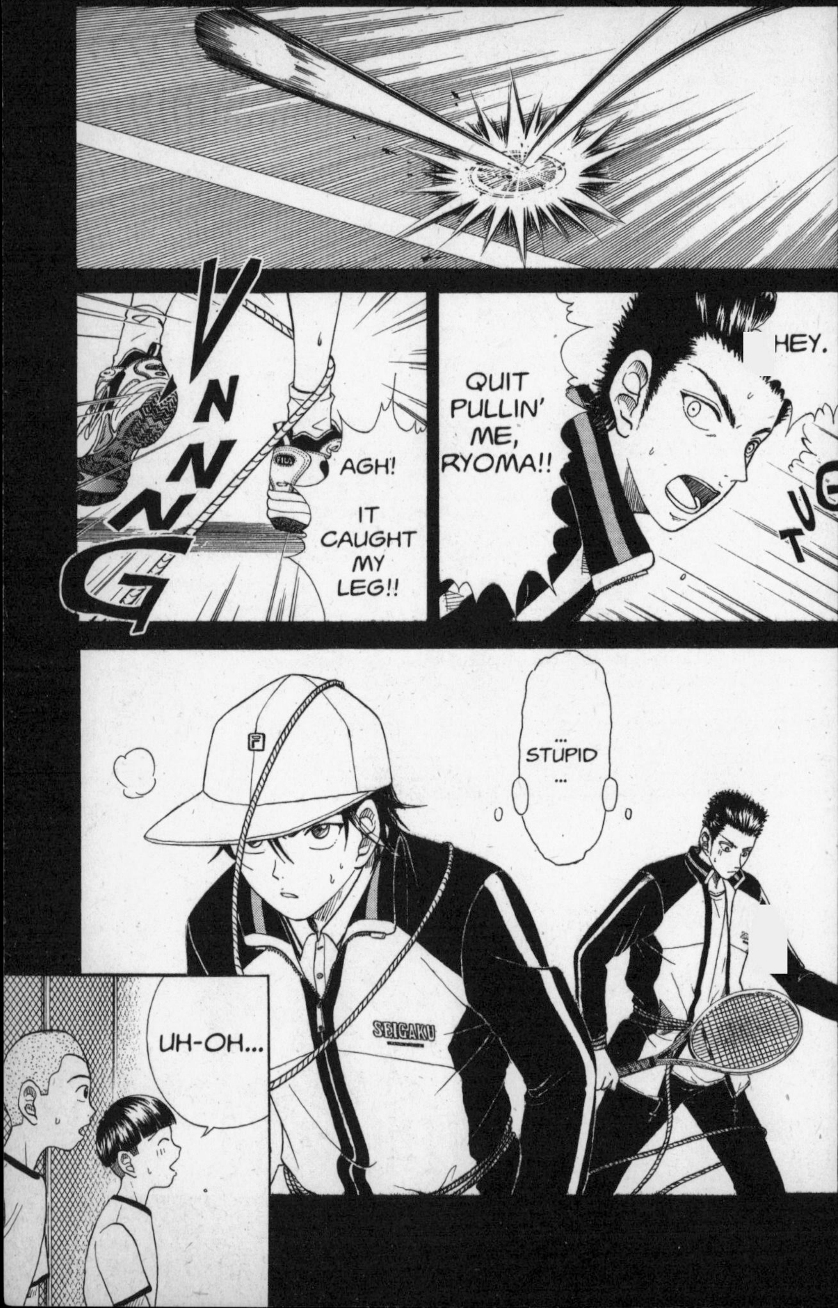
HEY.
TUG
QUIT PULLIN' ME, RYOMA!!
AGH!
IT CAUGHT MY LEG!!
VNNNG
... STUPID ...
UH-OH...

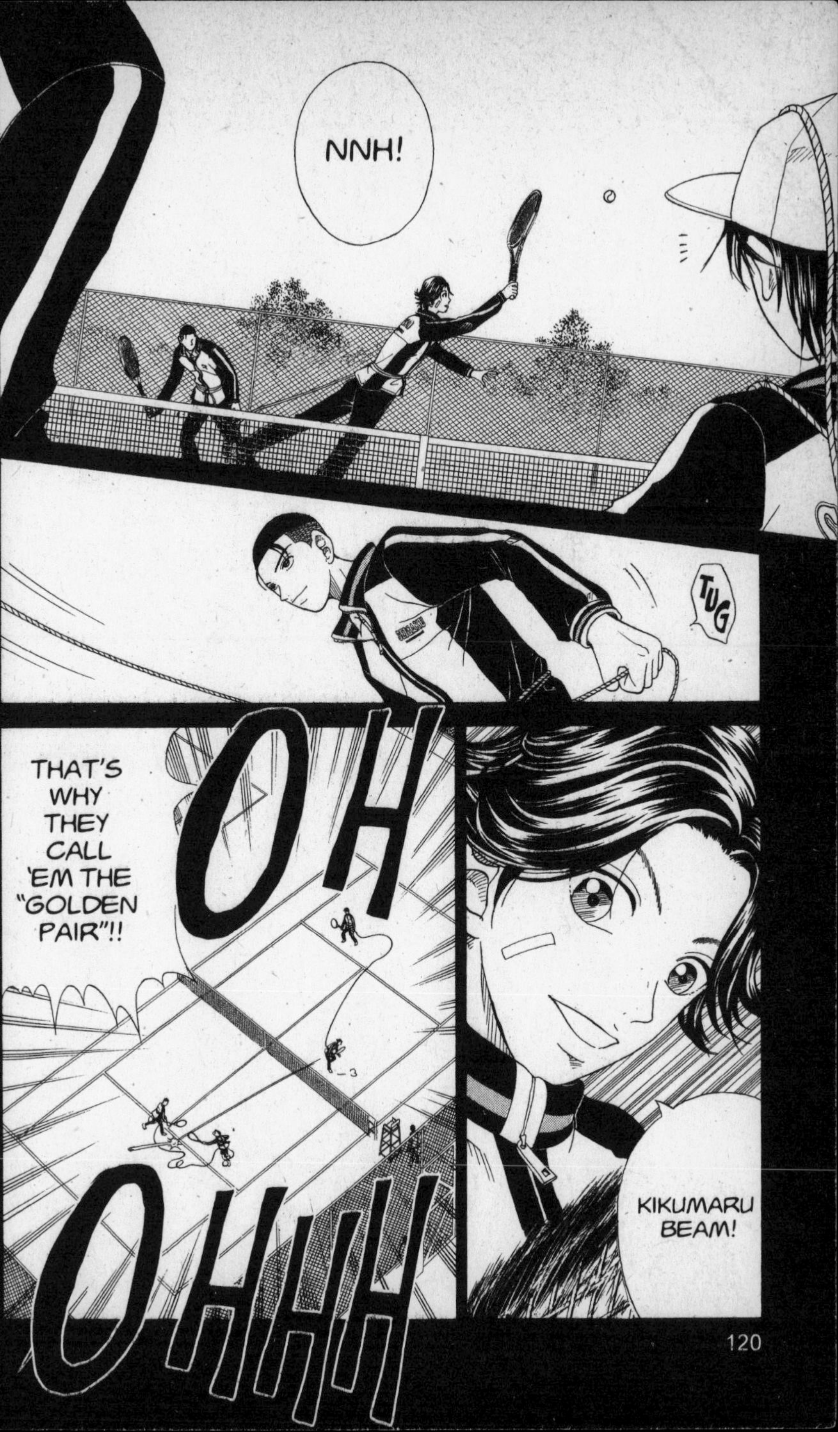
NNH!
TUG
KIKUMARU BEAM!
OH
OHHHH
THAT'S WHY THEY CALL 'EM THE "GOLDEN PAIR"!!

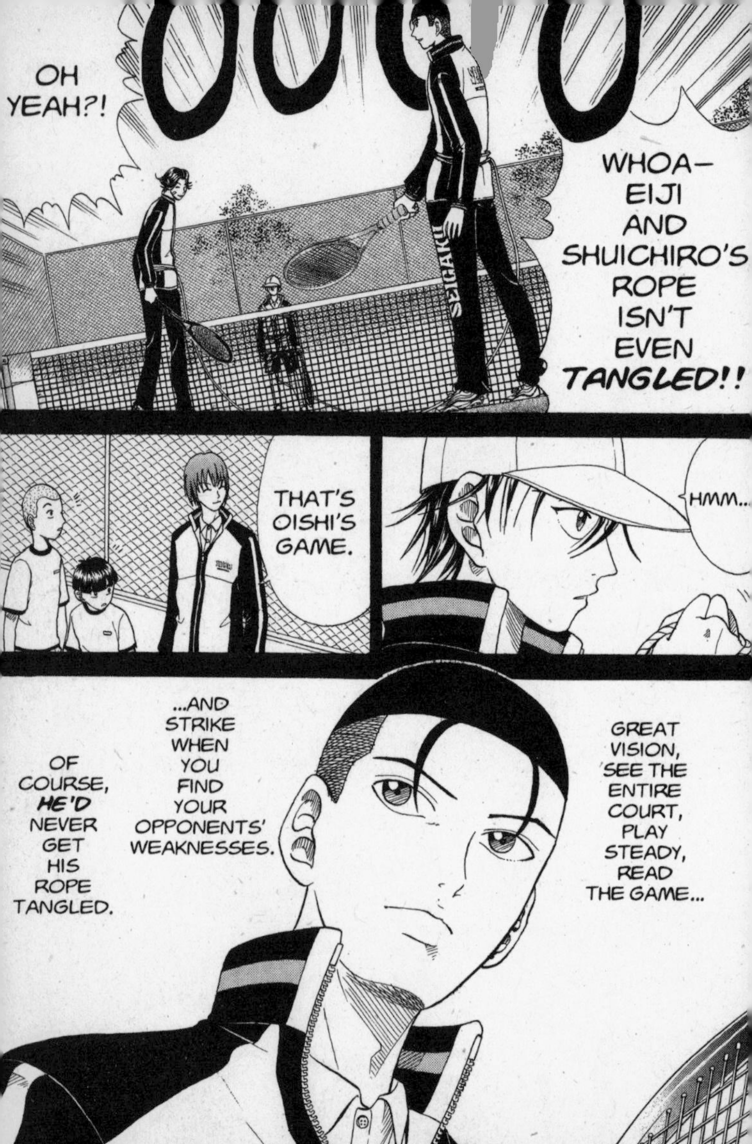
WHOA- EIJI AND SHUICHIRO'S ROPE ISN'T EVEN **TANGLED!!**
OH YEAH?!
HMM...
THAT'S OISHI'S GAME.
GREAT VISION, SEE THE ENTIRE COURT, PLAY STEADY, READ THE GAME...
...AND STRIKE WHEN YOU FIND YOUR OPPONENTS' WEAKNESSES.
OF COURSE, **HE'D** NEVER GET HIS ROPE TANGLED.

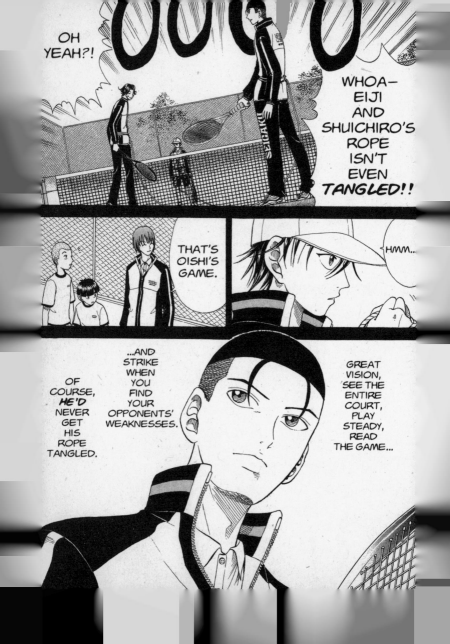

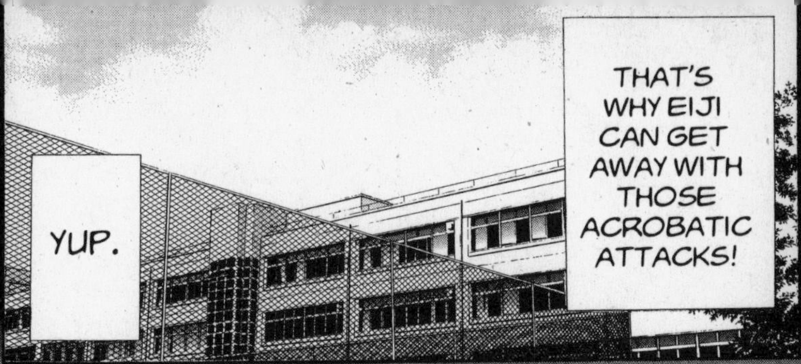
THAT'S WHY EIJI CAN GET AWAY WITH THOSE ACROBATIC ATTACKS!
YUP.

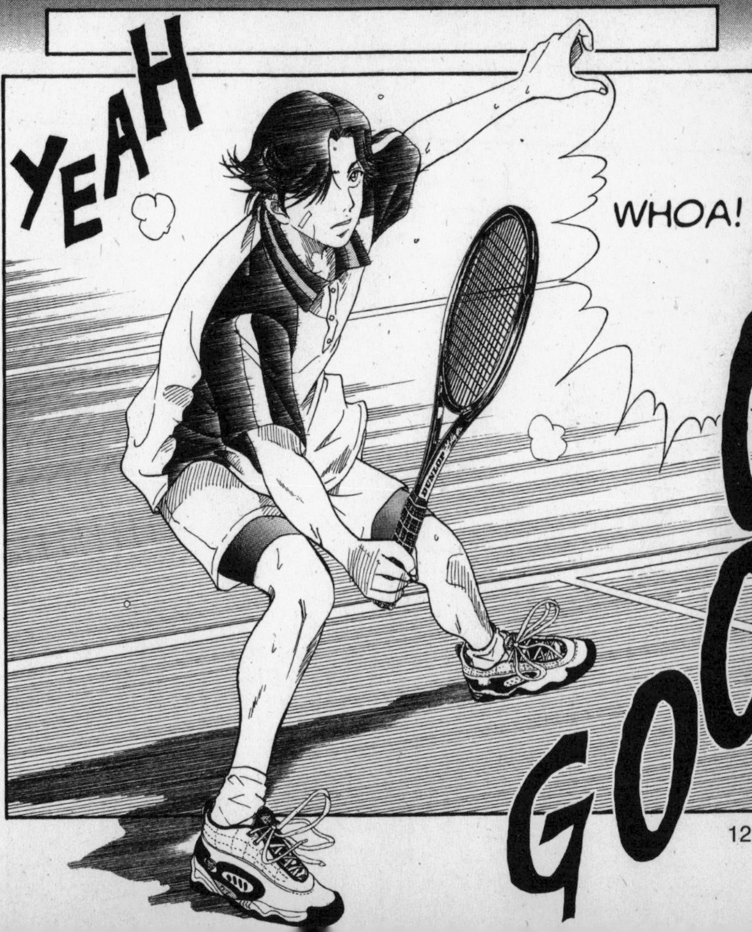
YEAH
WHOA!
GOOOO

READ THIS WAY

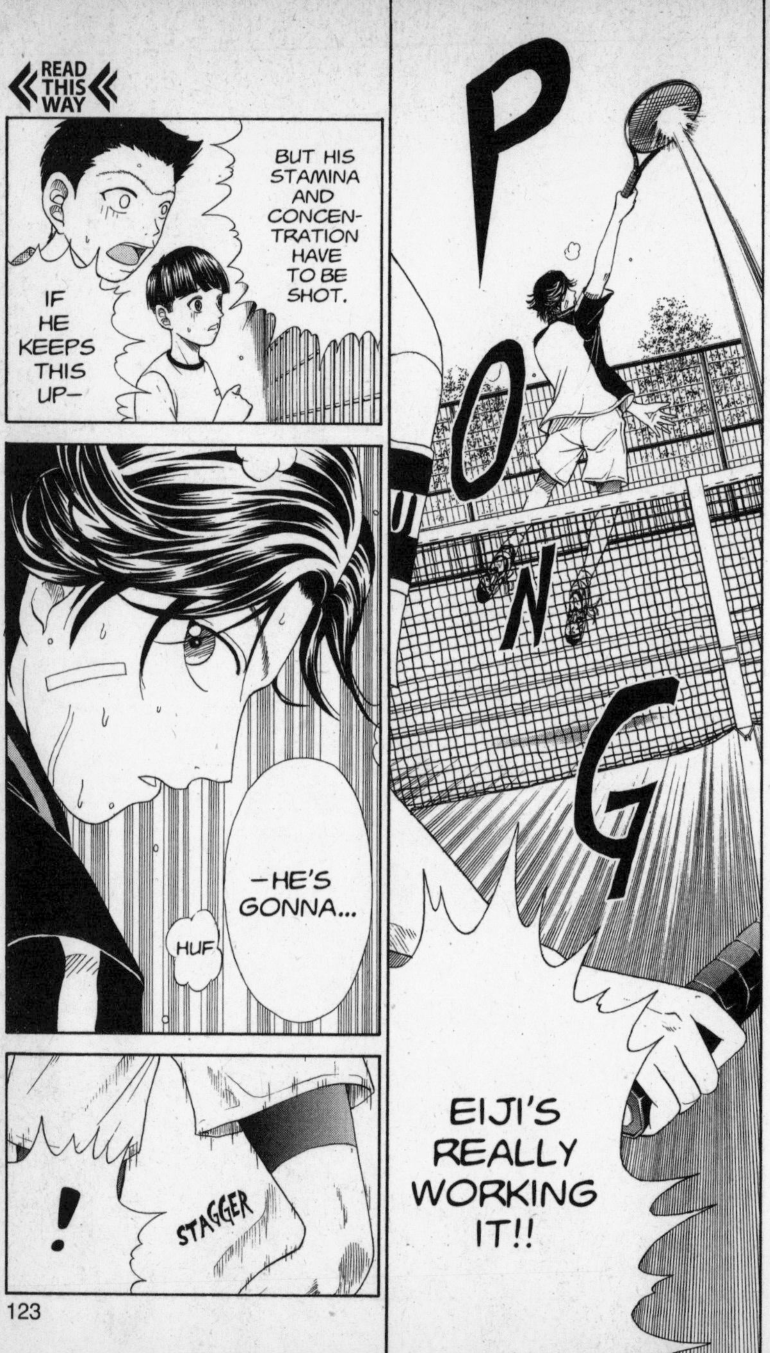

PONG
EIJI'S REALLY WORKING IT!!
BUT HIS STAMINA AND CONCENTRATION HAVE TO BE SHOT.
IF HE KEEPS THIS UP—
—HE'S GONNA...
HUF
!
STAGGER

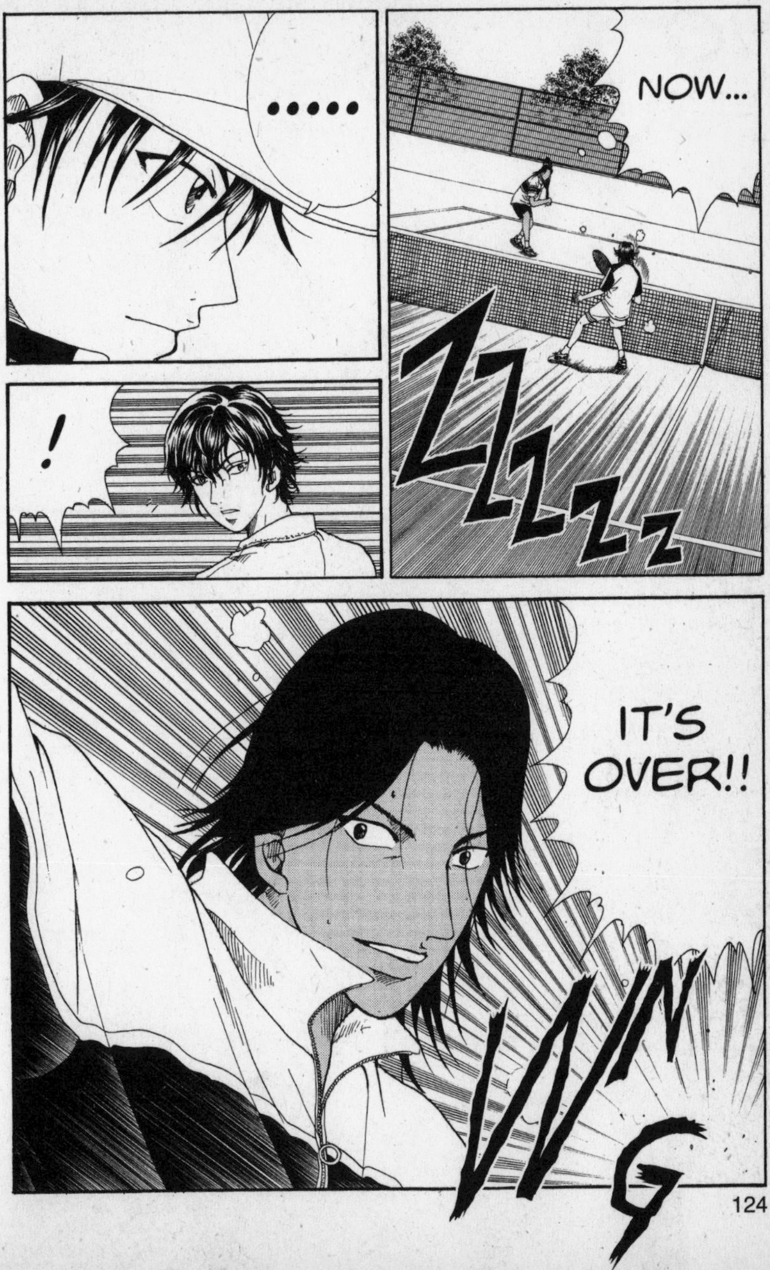
NOW...
ZZZZZ
.....
!
IT'S OVER!!

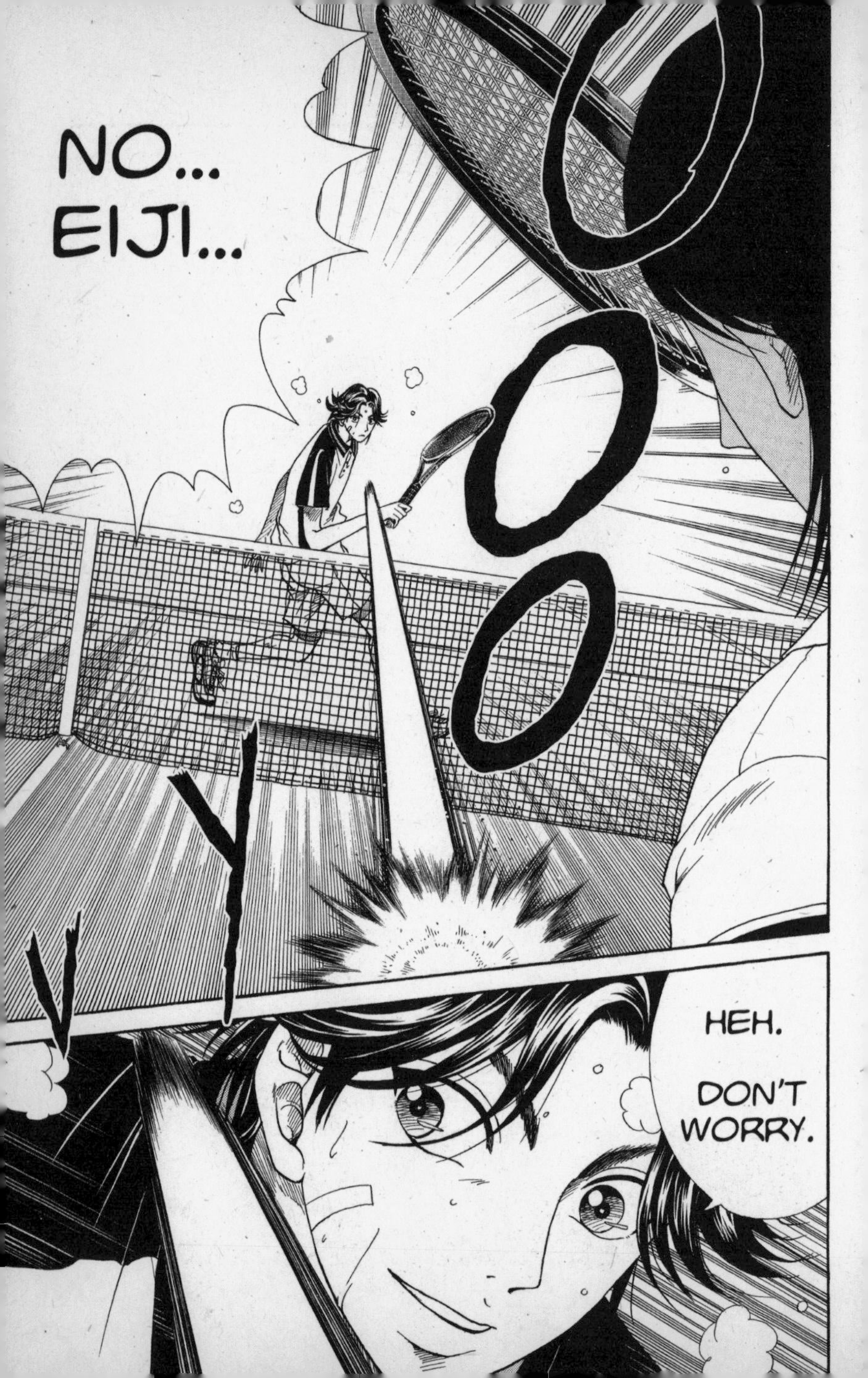
NO... EIJI...
HEH.
DON'T WORRY.

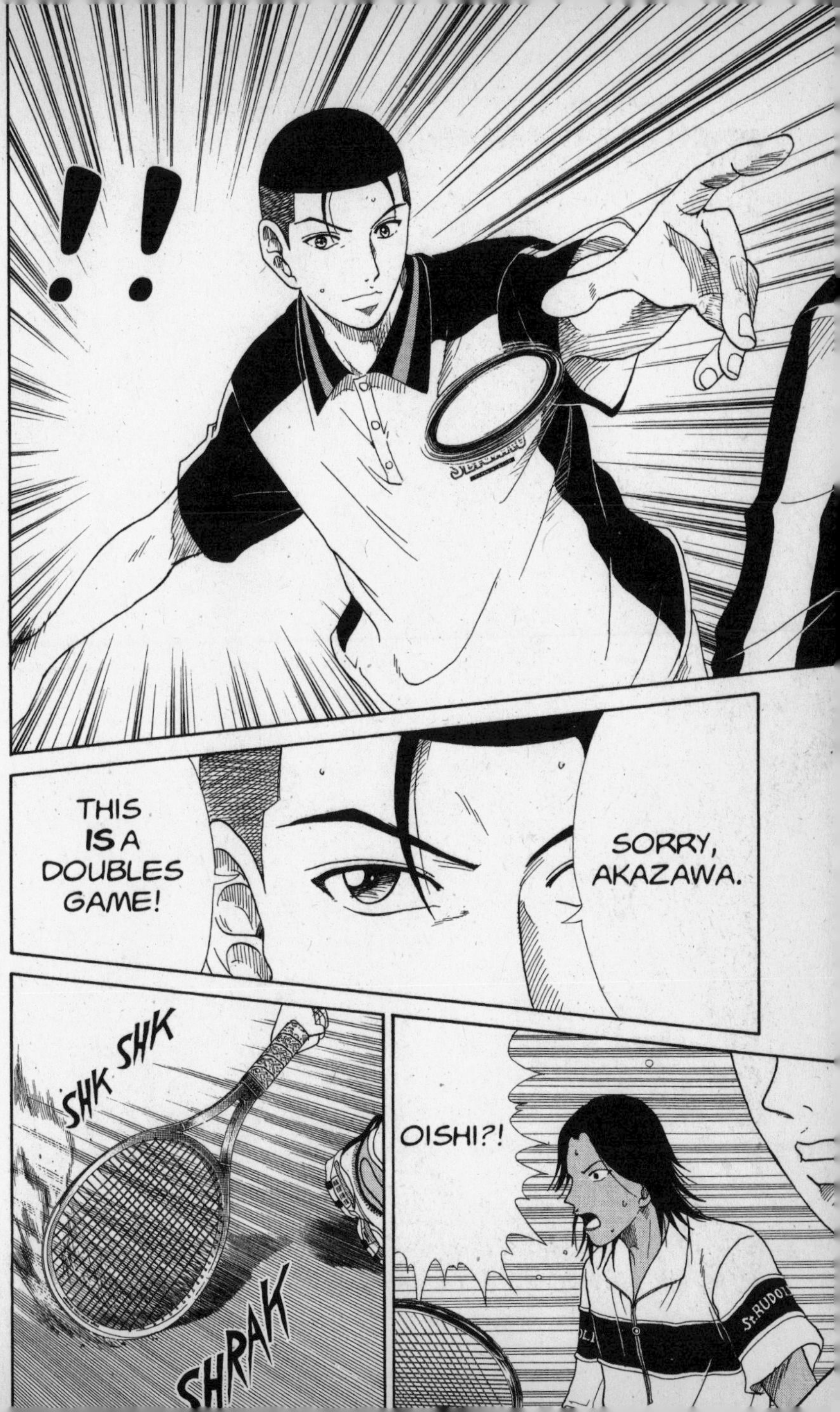
!!
SORRY, AKAZAWA.
THIS IS A DOUBLES GAME!
OISHI?!
SHK SHK
SHRAK

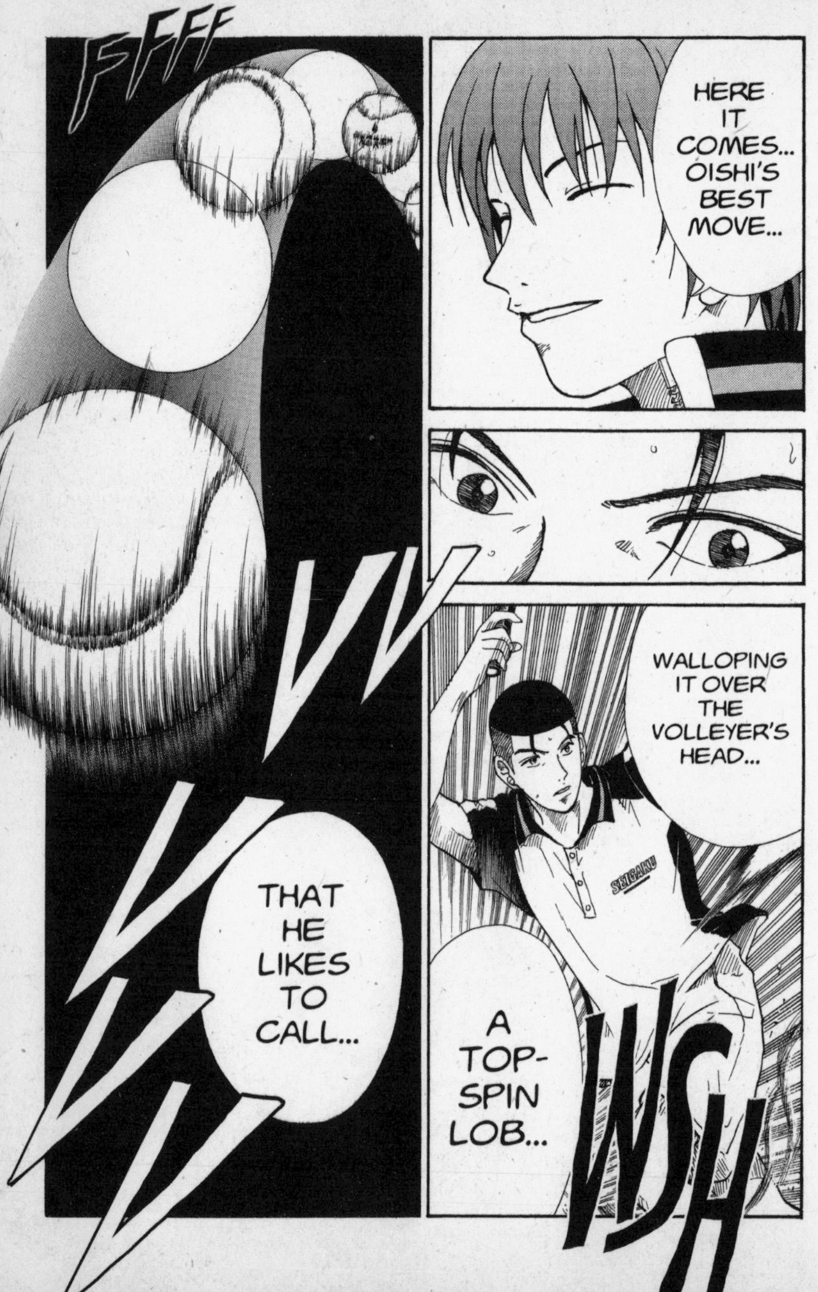
HERE IT COMES... OISHI'S BEST MOVE...
WALLOPING IT OVER THE VOLLEYER'S HEAD...
A TOP-SPIN LOB...
WSH
FFFF
THAT HE LIKES TO CALL...

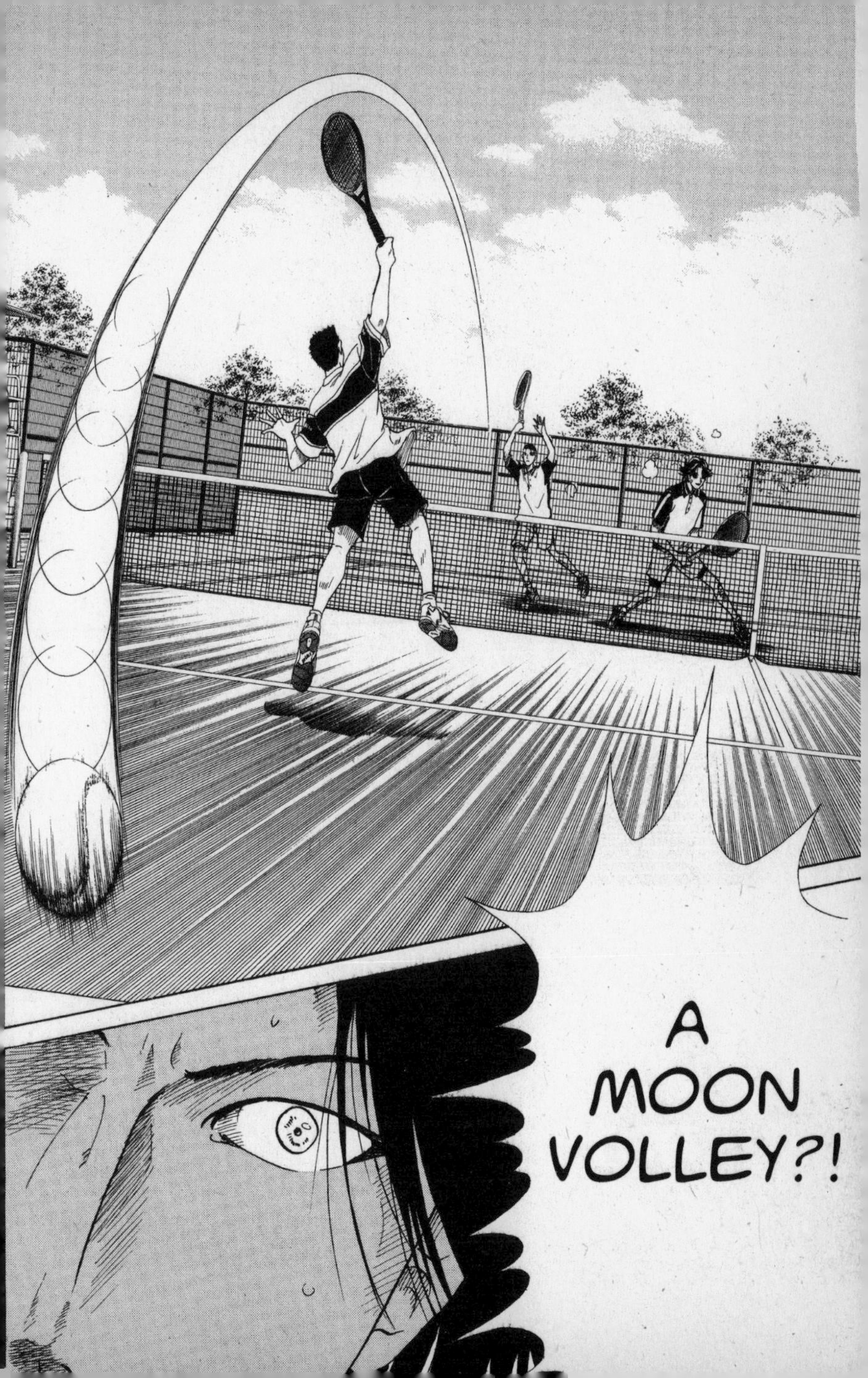
A MOON VOLLEY?!

READ THIS WAY

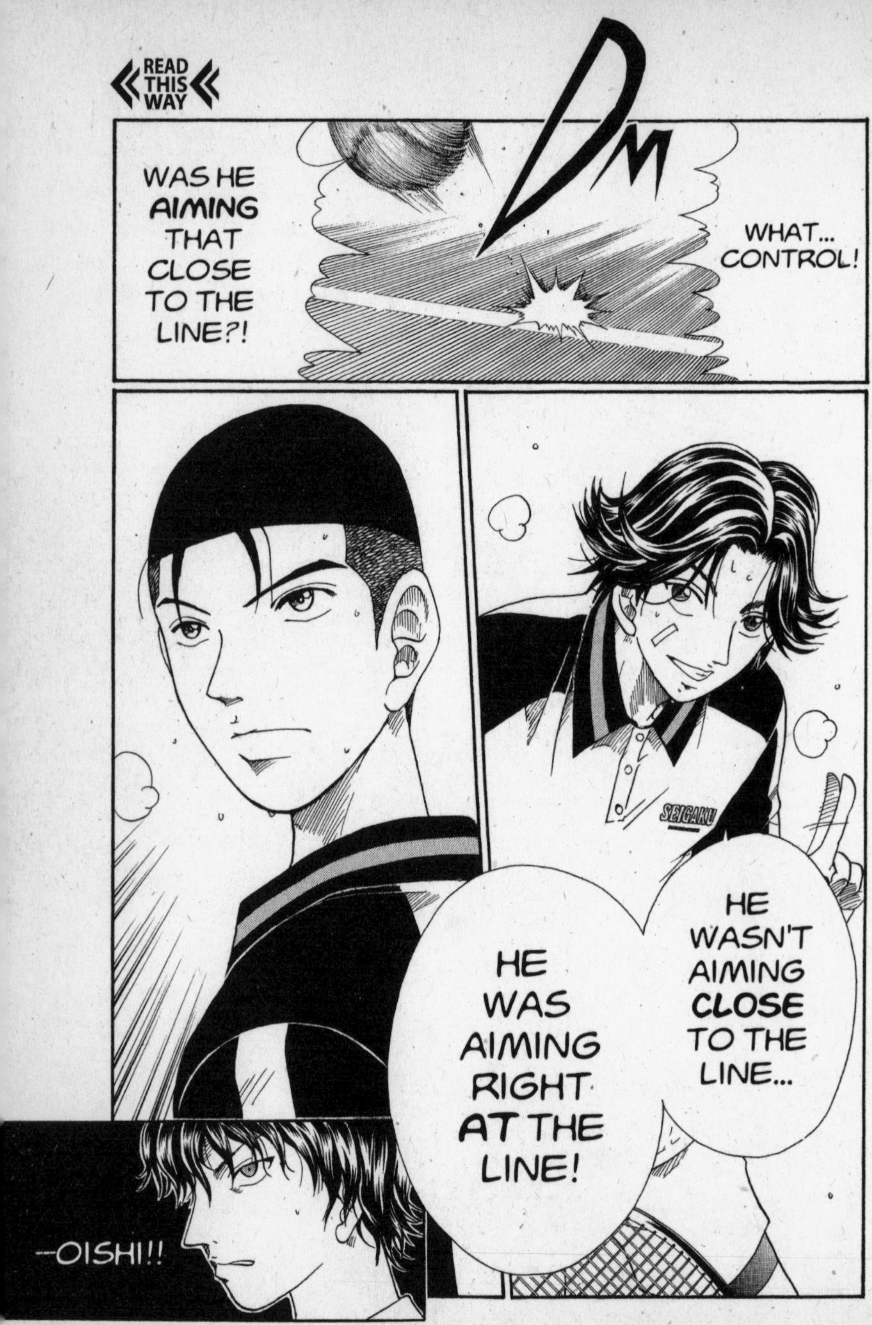
WHAT... CONTROL!
WAS HE AIMING THAT CLOSE TO THE LINE?!
HE WASN'T AIMING CLOSE TO THE LINE...
HE WAS AIMING RIGHT AT THE LINE!
--OISHI!!

GENIUS 58: BATTLE!

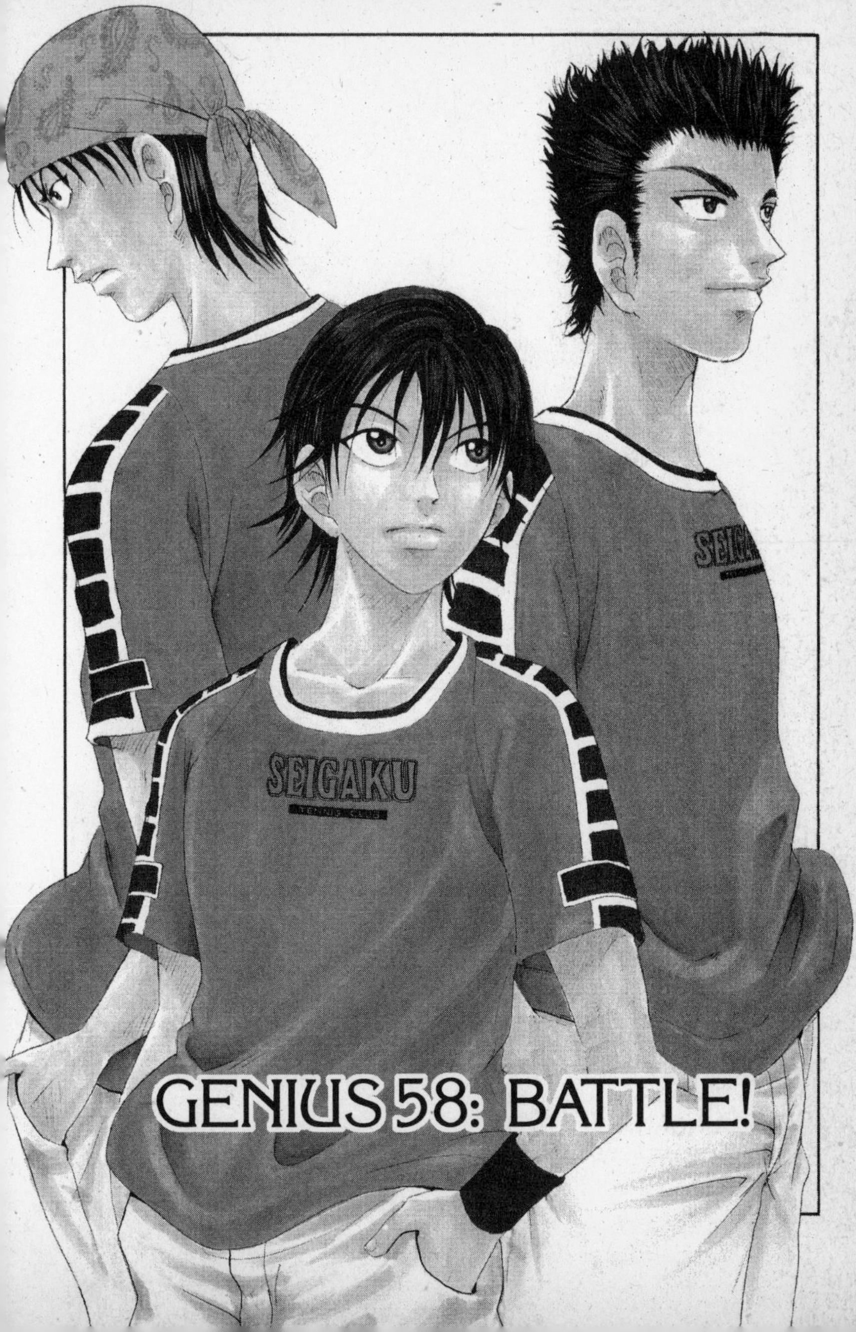
SEIGAKU

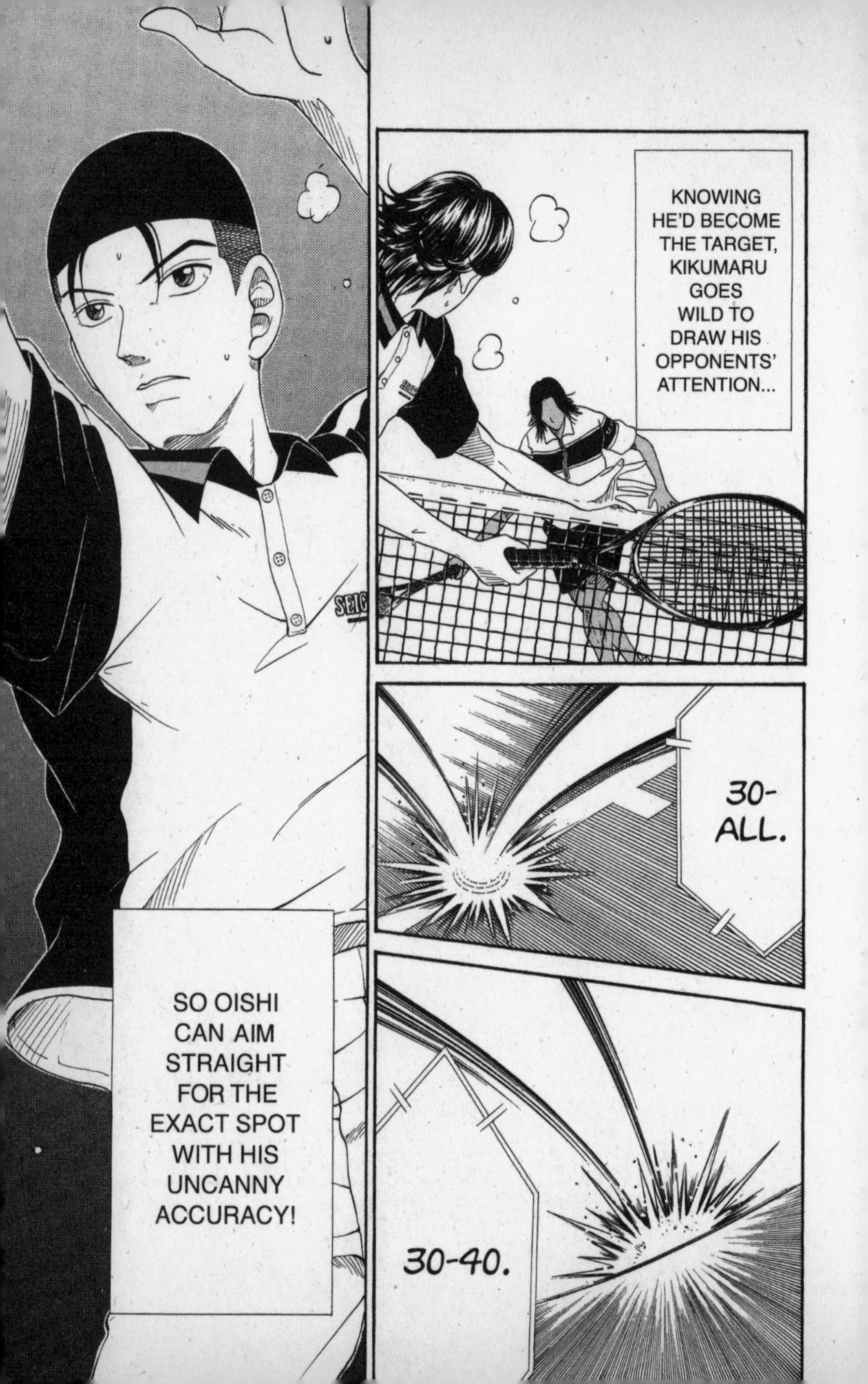
KNOWING HE'D BECOME THE TARGET, KIKUMARU GOES WILD TO DRAW HIS OPPONENTS' ATTENTION...
30-ALL.
30-40.
SO OISHI CAN AIM STRAIGHT FOR THE EXACT SPOT WITH HIS UNCANNY ACCURACY!

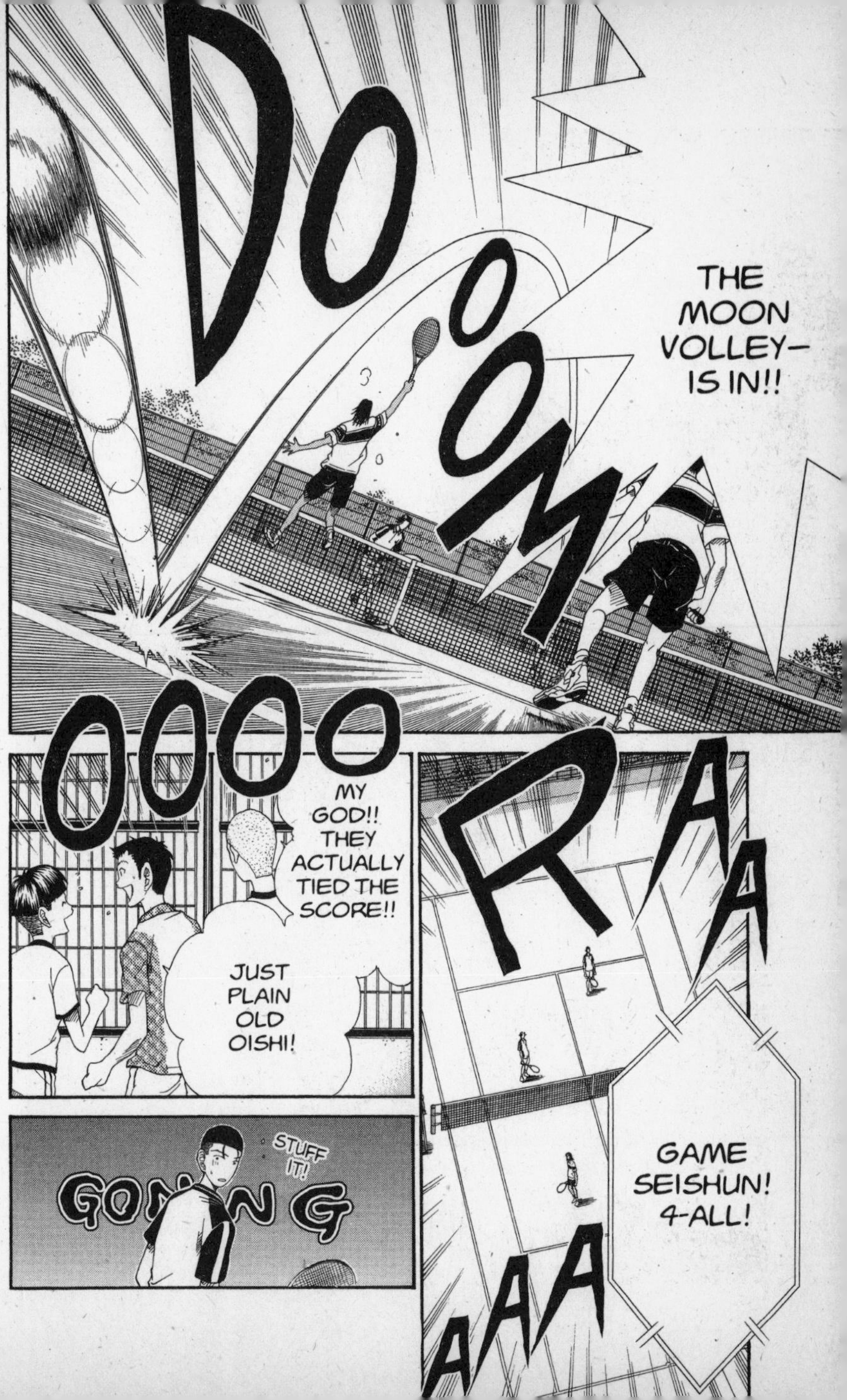
DOOOM
THE MOON VOLLEY— IS IN!!
OOOORAAAAAA
GAME SEISHUN! 4-ALL!
MY GOD!! THEY ACTUALLY TIED THE SCORE!!
JUST PLAIN OLD OISHI!
GONNG
STUFF IT!

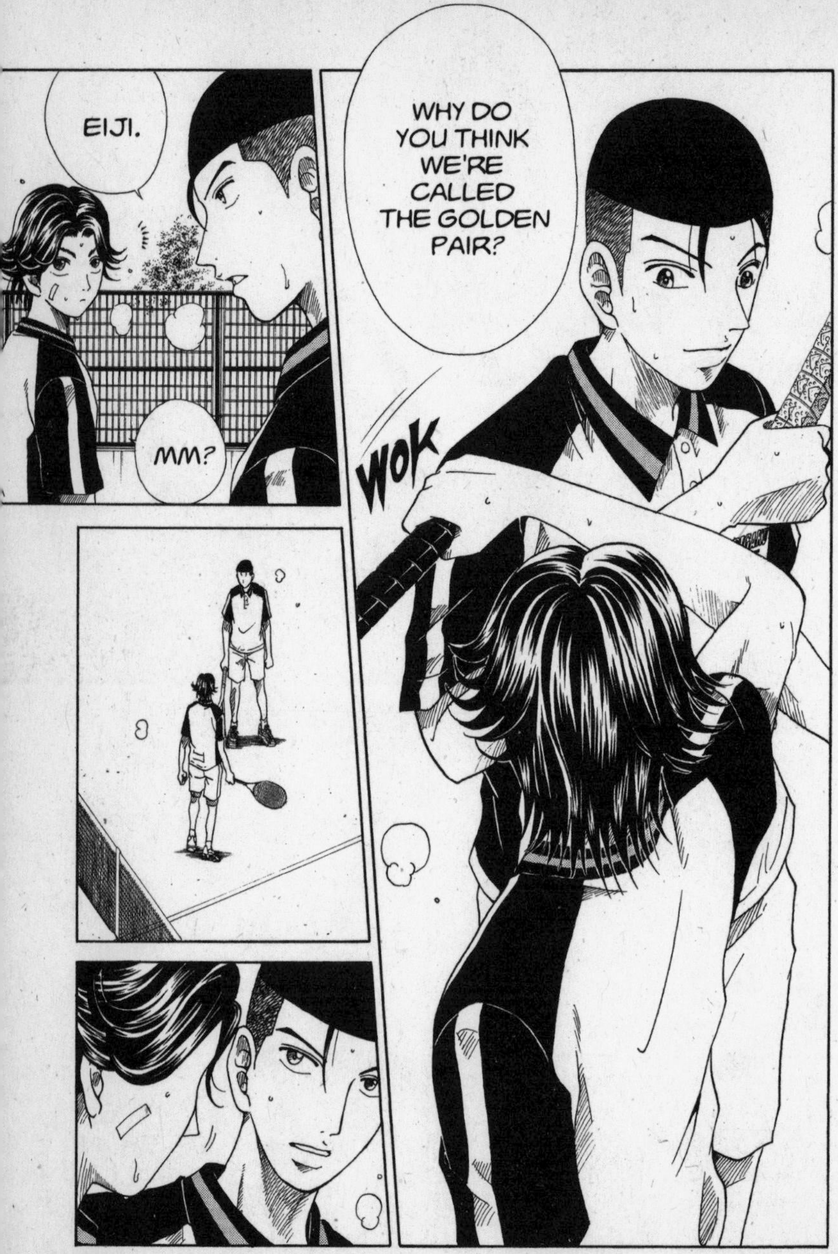
WHY DO YOU THINK WE'RE CALLED THE GOLDEN PAIR?
WOK
EIJI.
MM?

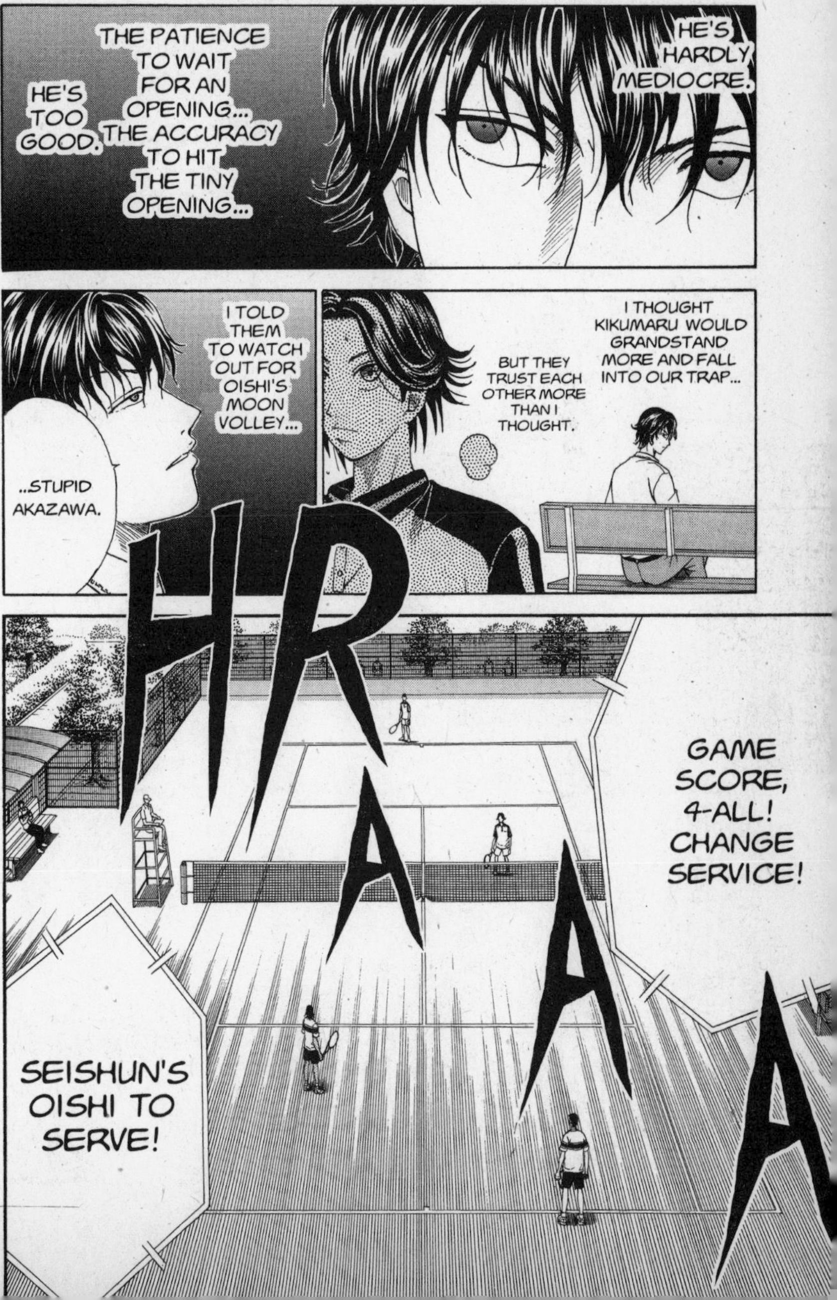
HE'S HARDLY MEDIOCRE.
THE PATIENCE TO WAIT FOR AN OPENING... THE ACCURACY TO HIT THE TINY OPENING...
HE'S TOO GOOD.
I THOUGHT KIKUMARU WOULD GRANDSTAND MORE AND FALL INTO OUR TRAP...
BUT THEY TRUST EACH OTHER MORE THAN I THOUGHT.
I TOLD THEM TO WATCH OUT FOR OISHI'S MOON VOLLEY...
...STUPID AKAZAWA.
HRAAA
GAME SCORE, 4-ALL! CHANGE SERVICE!
SEISHUN'S OISHI TO SERVE!

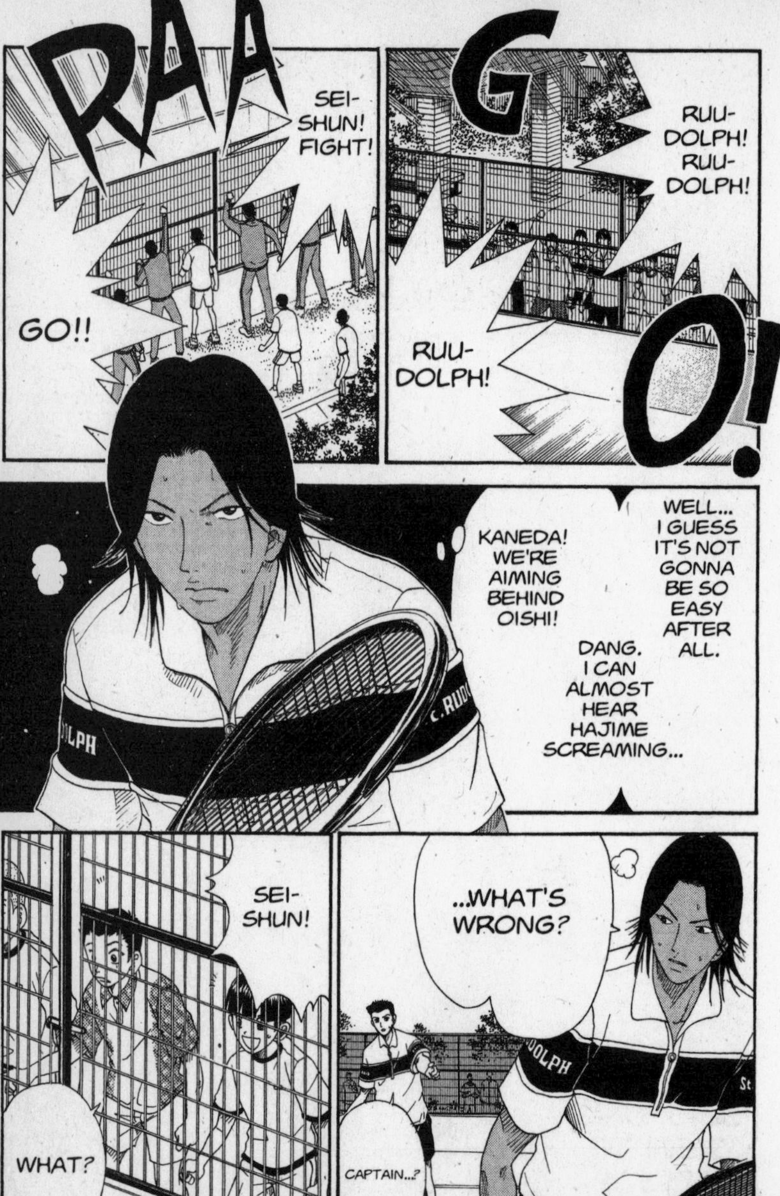
RUU-DOLPH! RUU-DOLPH!
RUU-DOLPH!
RAAGO!
SEI-SHUN! FIGHT!
GO!!
WELL... I GUESS IT'S NOT GONNA BE SO EASY AFTER ALL.
DANG. I CAN ALMOST HEAR HAJIME SCREAMING...
KANEDA! WE'RE AIMING BEHIND OISHI!
...WHAT'S WRONG?
CAPTAIN...?
SEI-SHUN!
WHAT?

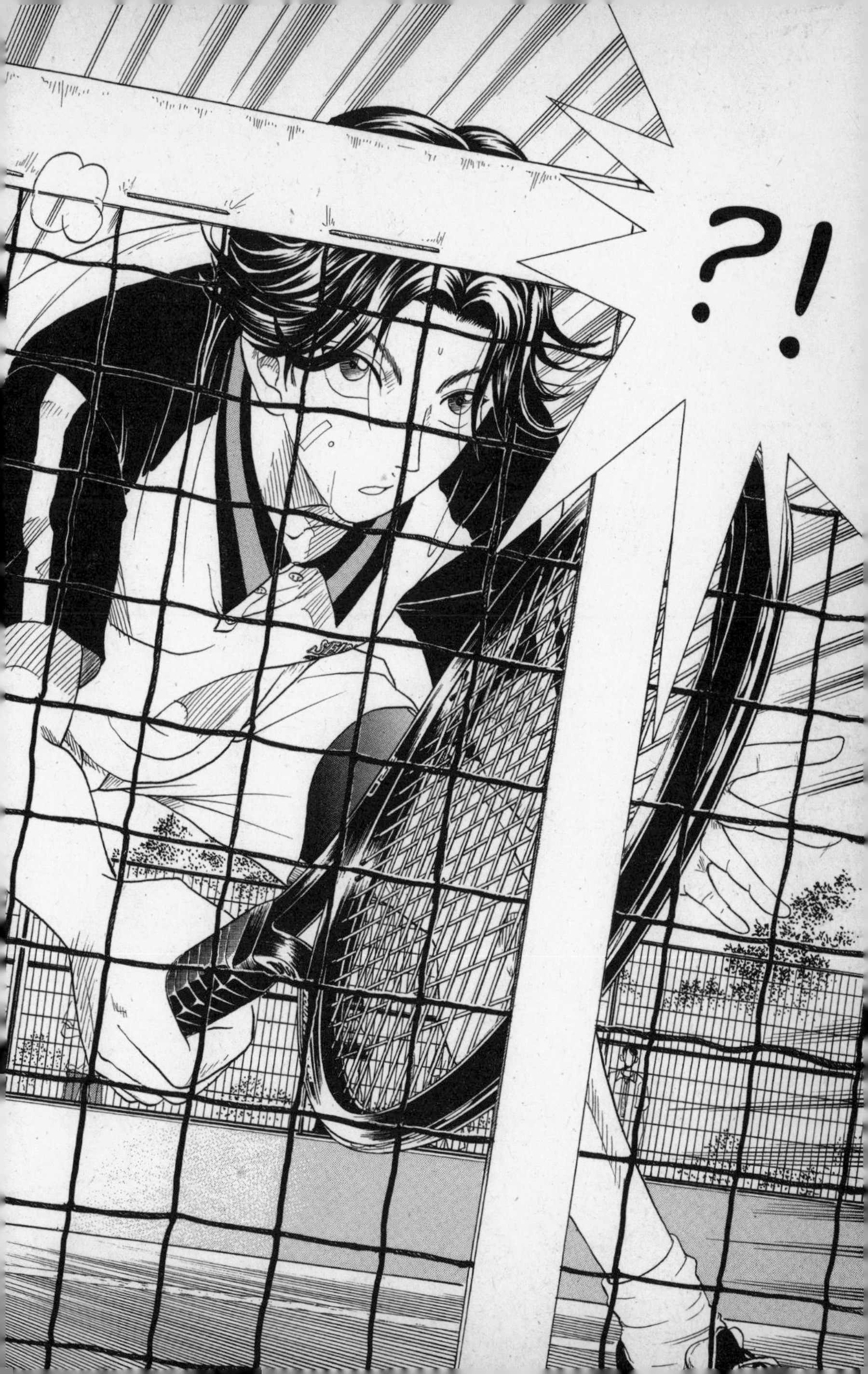
?!

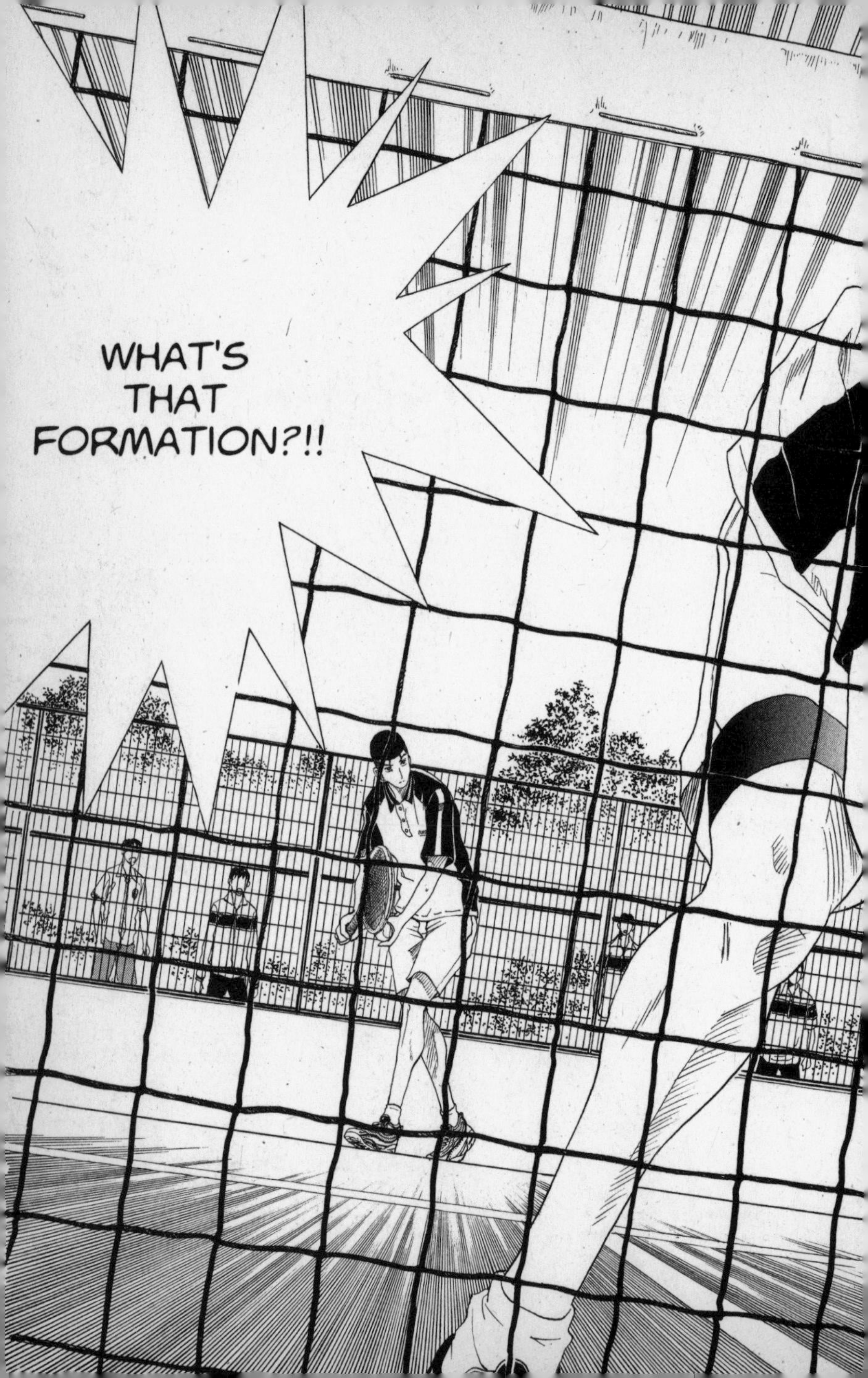
WHAT'S THAT FORMATION?!!

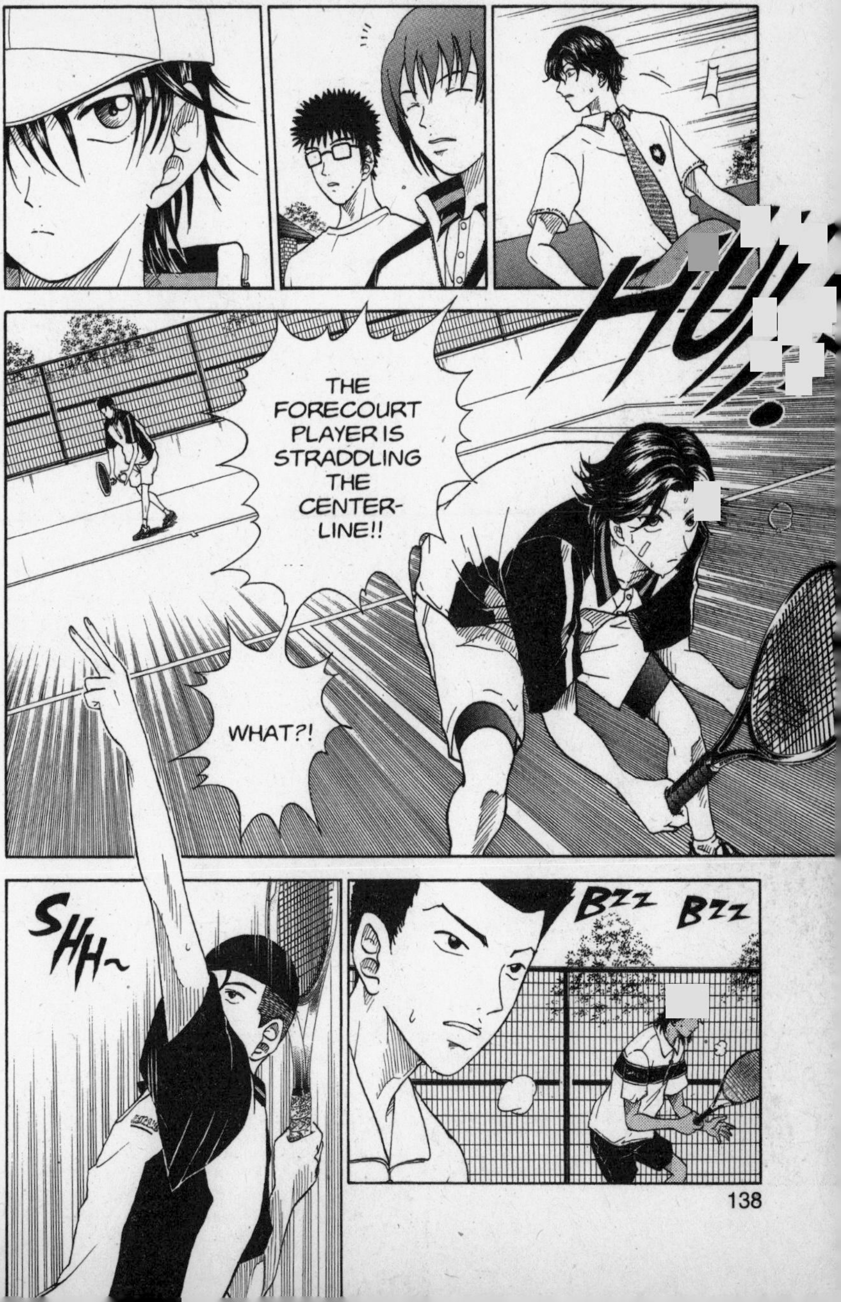
HU!
THE FORECOURT PLAYER IS STRADDLING THE CENTER-LINE!!
WHAT?!
BZZ BZZ
SHH~

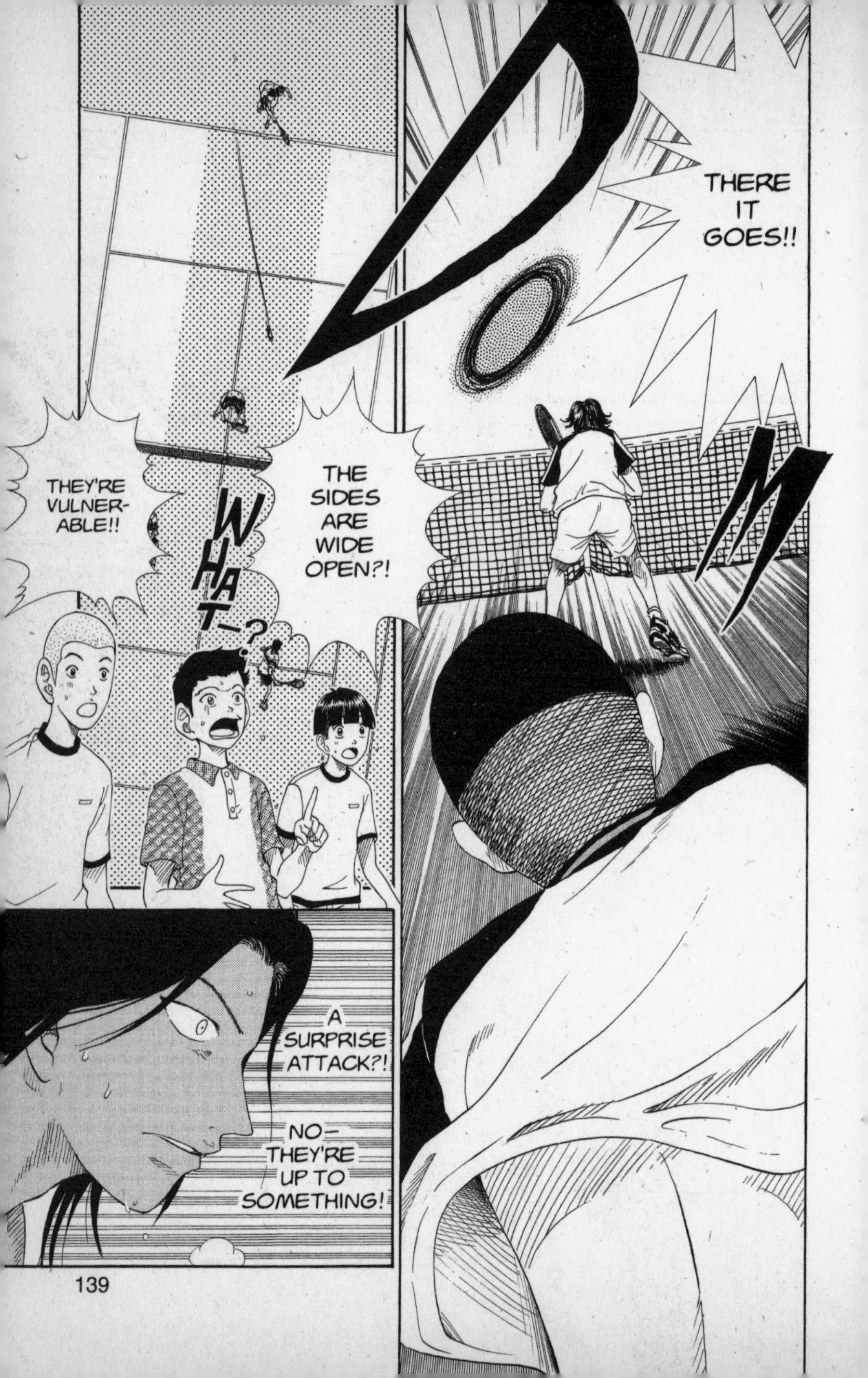
DOM
THERE IT GOES!!
THE SIDES ARE WIDE OPEN?!
THEY'RE VULNERABLE!!
WHAT—?
A SURPRISE ATTACK?!
NO— THEY'RE UP TO SOMETHING!

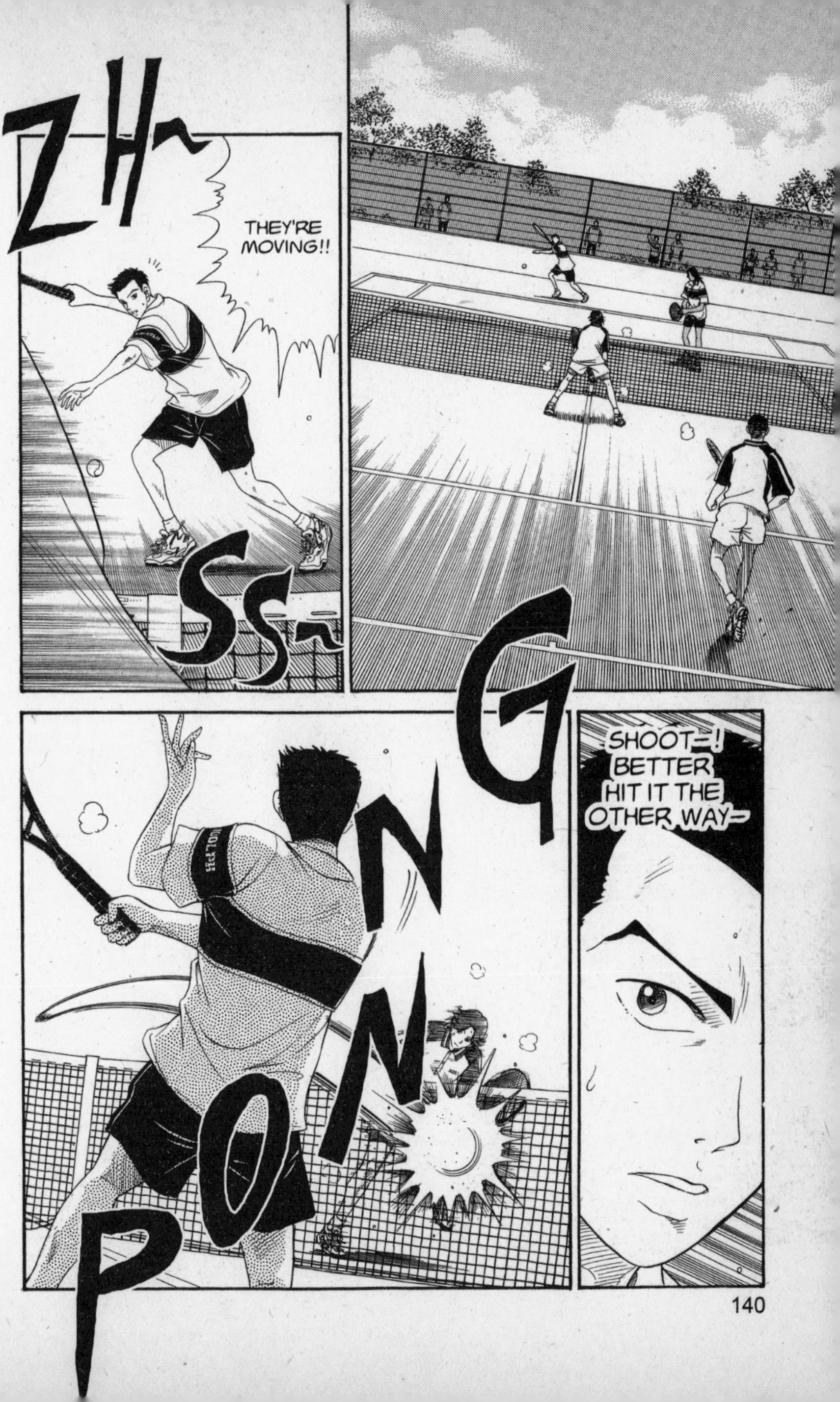
ZH~
THEY'RE MOVING!!
SS~
SHOOT—! BETTER HIT IT THE OTHER WAY—
PONNG

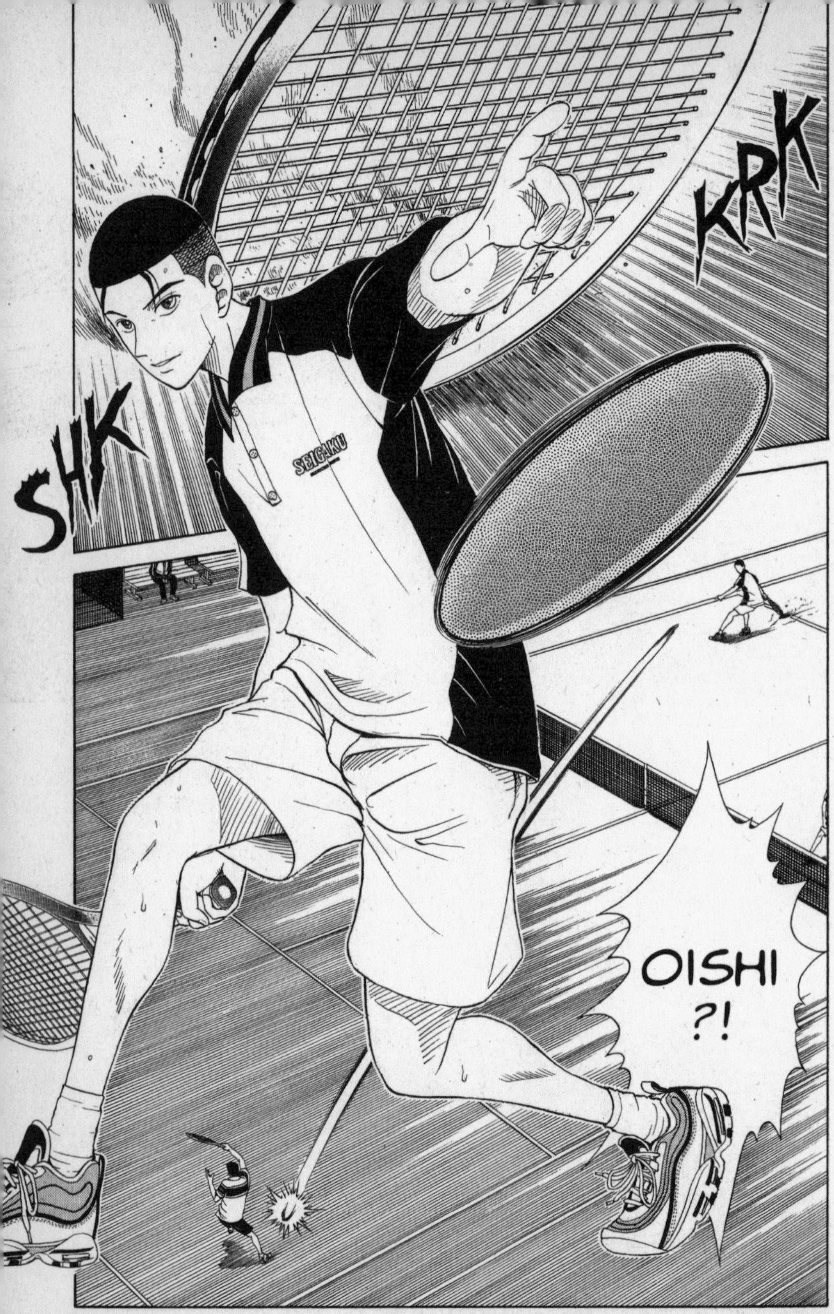
KRK
SHK
SEIGAKU
OISHI ?!

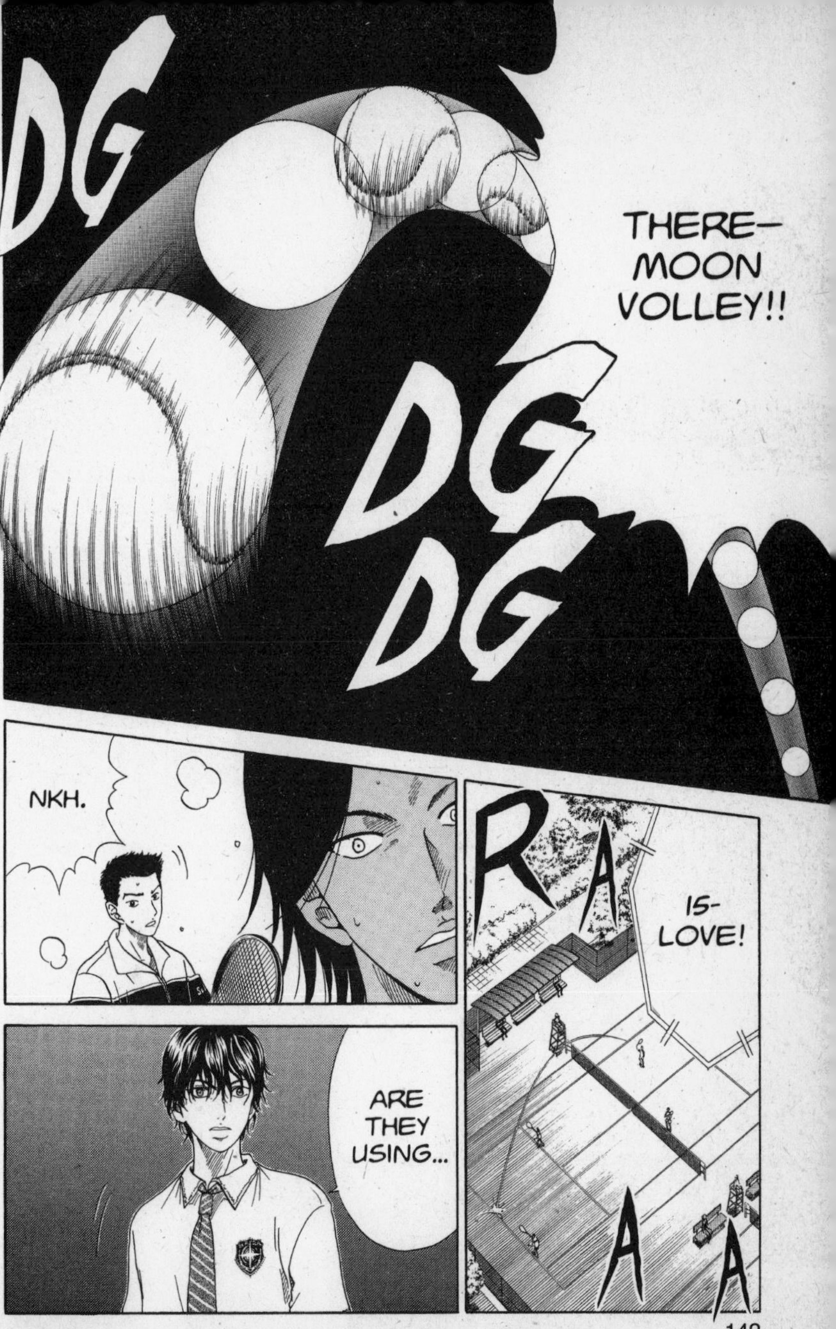
THERE—MOON VOLLEY!!
DG
DG
DG
DG
R A A A
15-LOVE!
NKH.
ARE THEY USING...

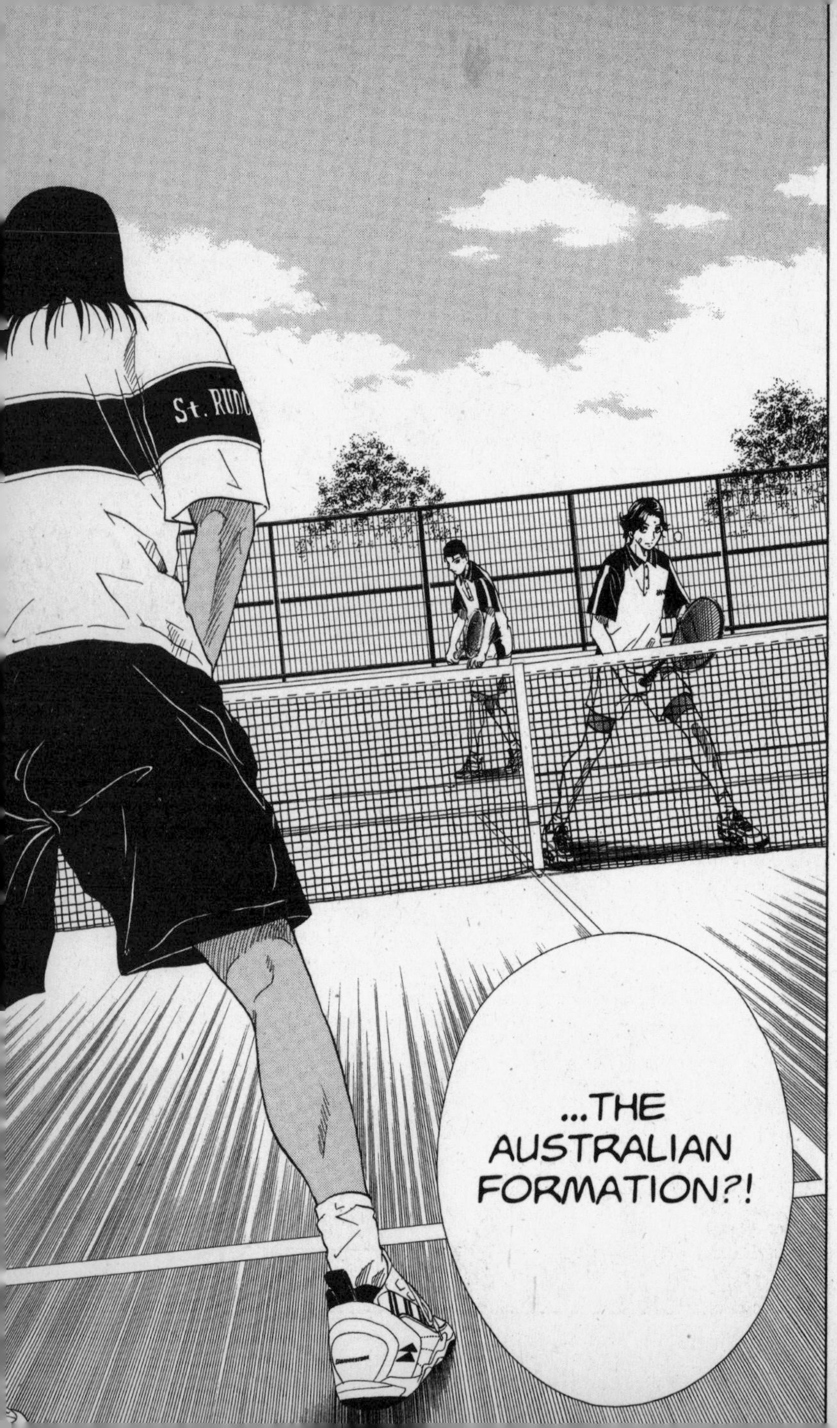
St. RUDO
...THE AUSTRALIAN FORMATION?!

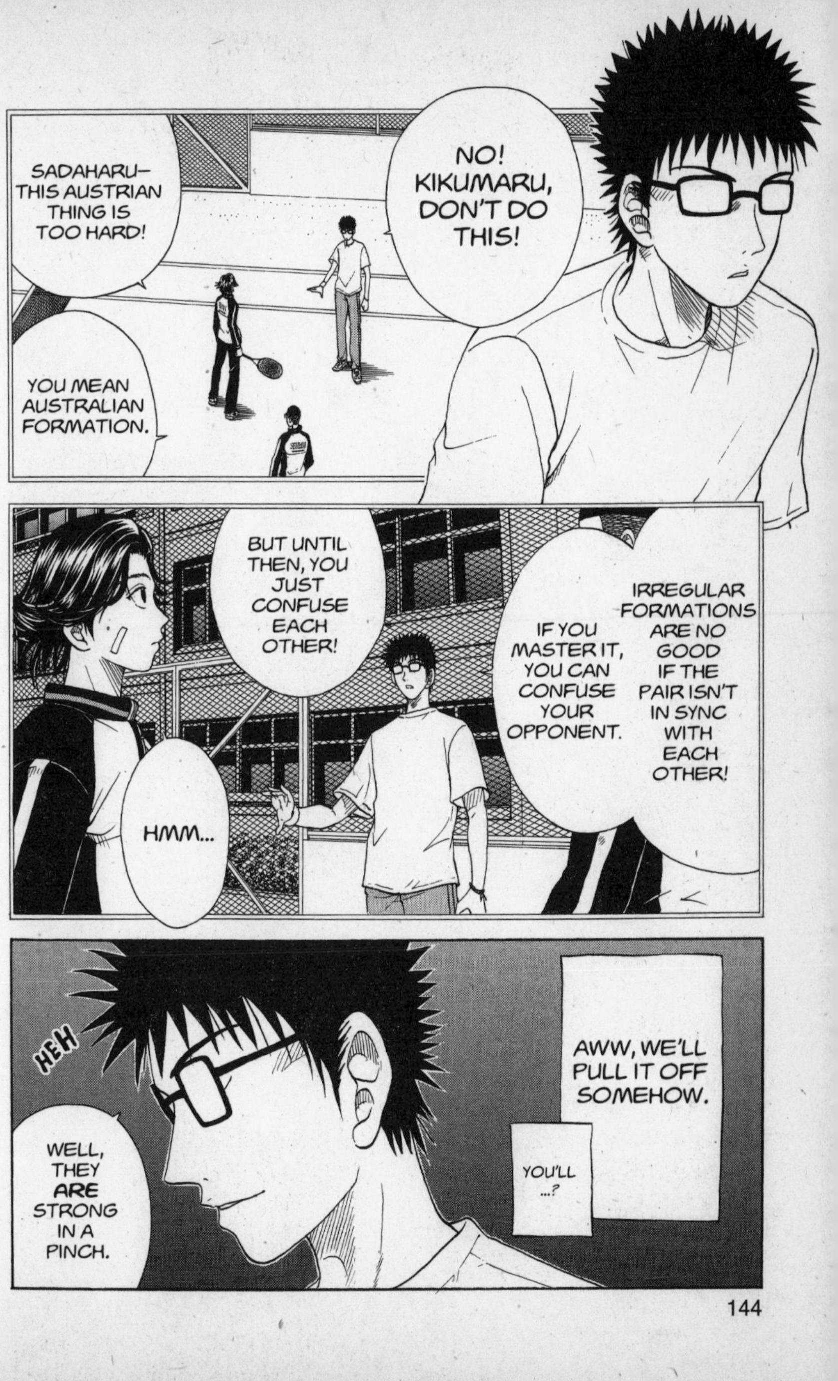
NO! KIKUMARU, DON'T DO THIS!
SADAHARU— THIS AUSTRIAN THING IS TOO HARD!
YOU MEAN AUSTRALIAN FORMATION.
IRREGULAR FORMATIONS ARE NO GOOD IF THE PAIR ISN'T IN SYNC WITH EACH OTHER!
IF YOU MASTER IT, YOU CAN CONFUSE YOUR OPPONENT.
BUT UNTIL THEN, YOU JUST CONFUSE EACH OTHER!
HMM...
AWW, WE'LL PULL IT OFF SOMEHOW.
YOU'LL ...?
HEH
WELL, THEY **ARE** STRONG IN A PINCH.

READ THIS WAY

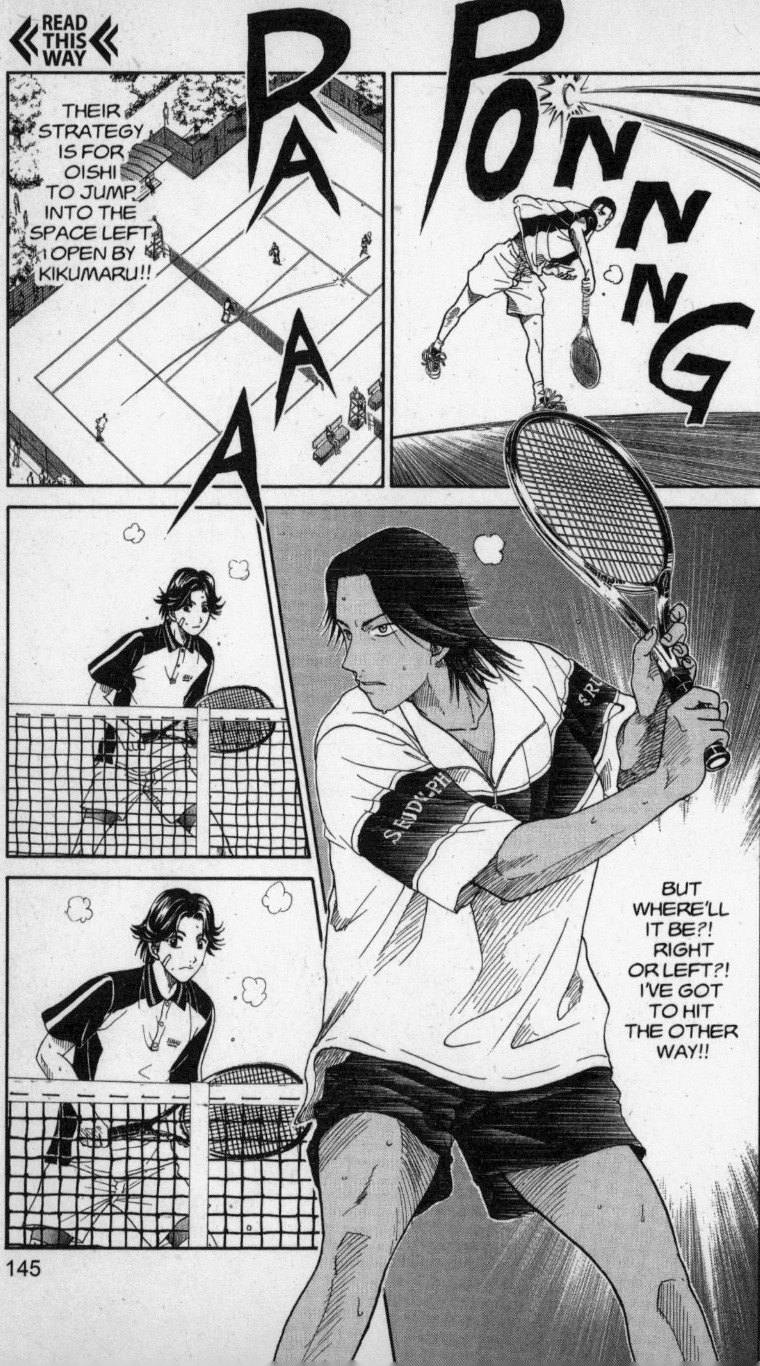

PONNNG
THEIR STRATEGY IS FOR OISHI TO JUMP INTO THE SPACE LEFT OPEN BY KIKUMARU!!
PAAAA
BUT WHERE'LL IT BE?! RIGHT OR LEFT?! I'VE GOT TO HIT THE OTHER WAY!!

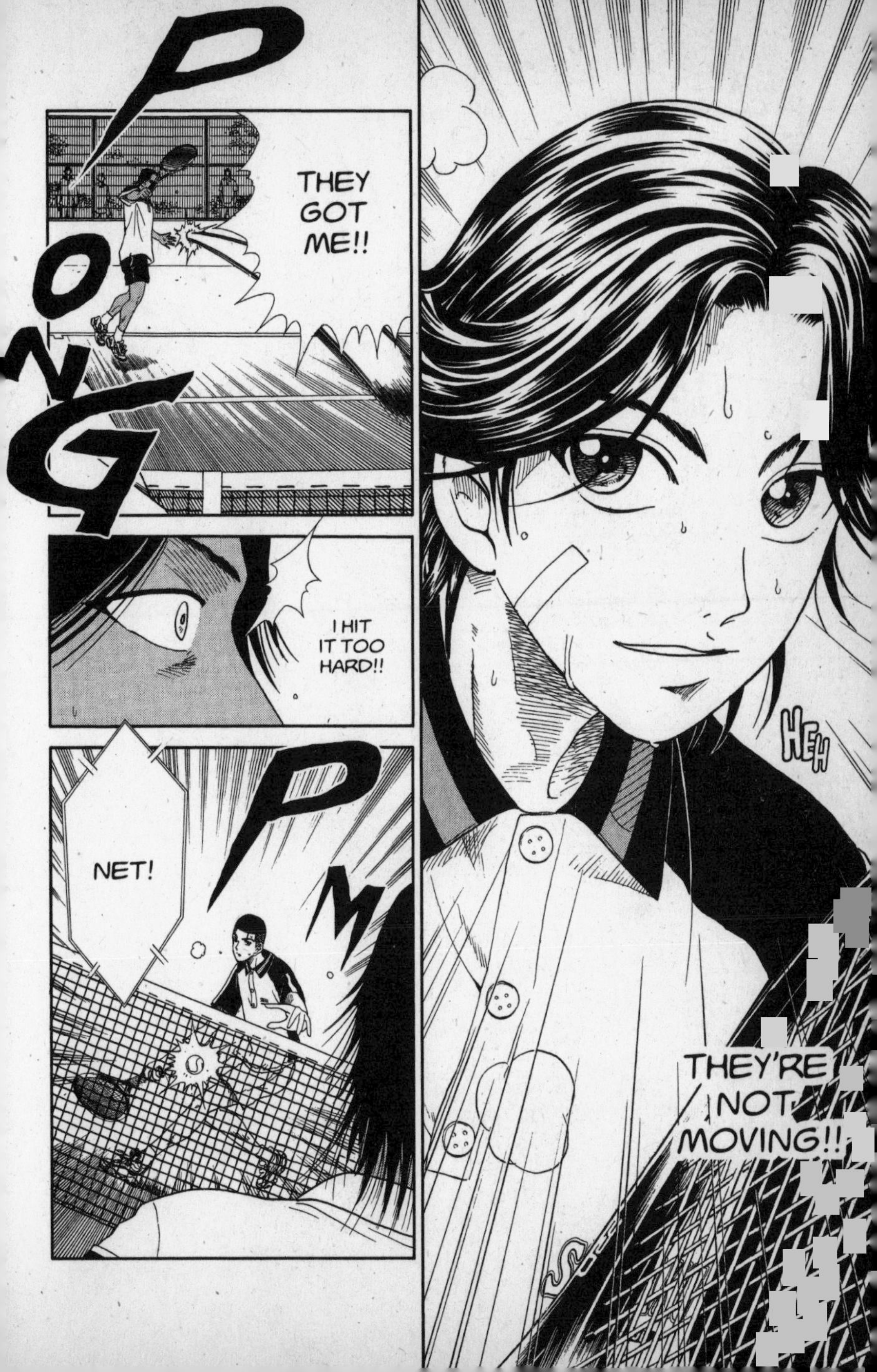
HEH
THEY'RE NOT MOVING!!
PONG
THEY GOT ME!!
I HIT IT TOO HARD!!
PM
NET!

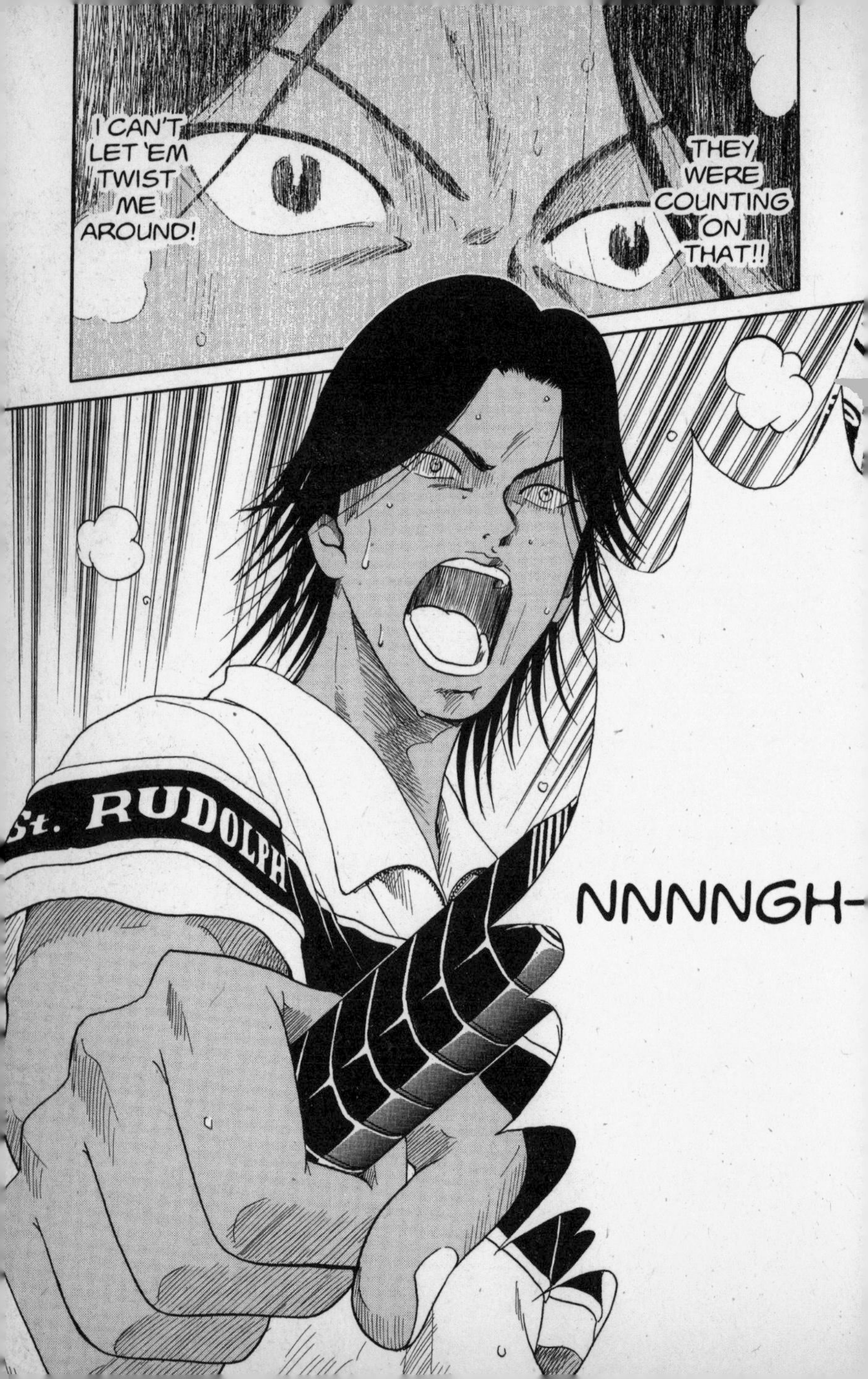
THEY WERE COUNTING ON THAT!!
I CAN'T LET 'EM TWIST ME AROUND!
NNNNGH-
St. RUDOLPH

テニスの王子様

THE PRINCE OF TENNIS™

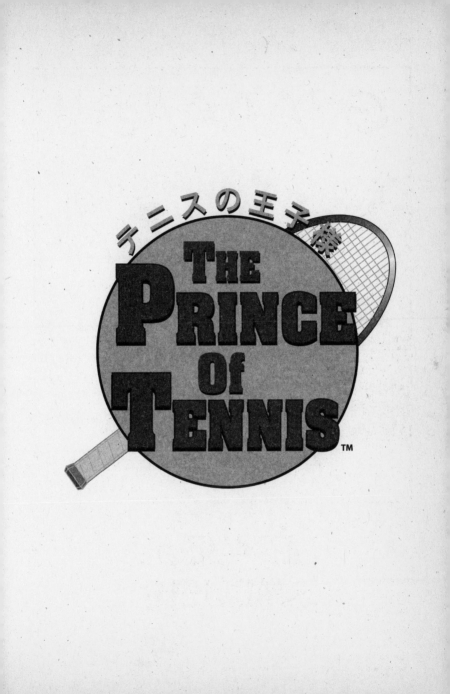

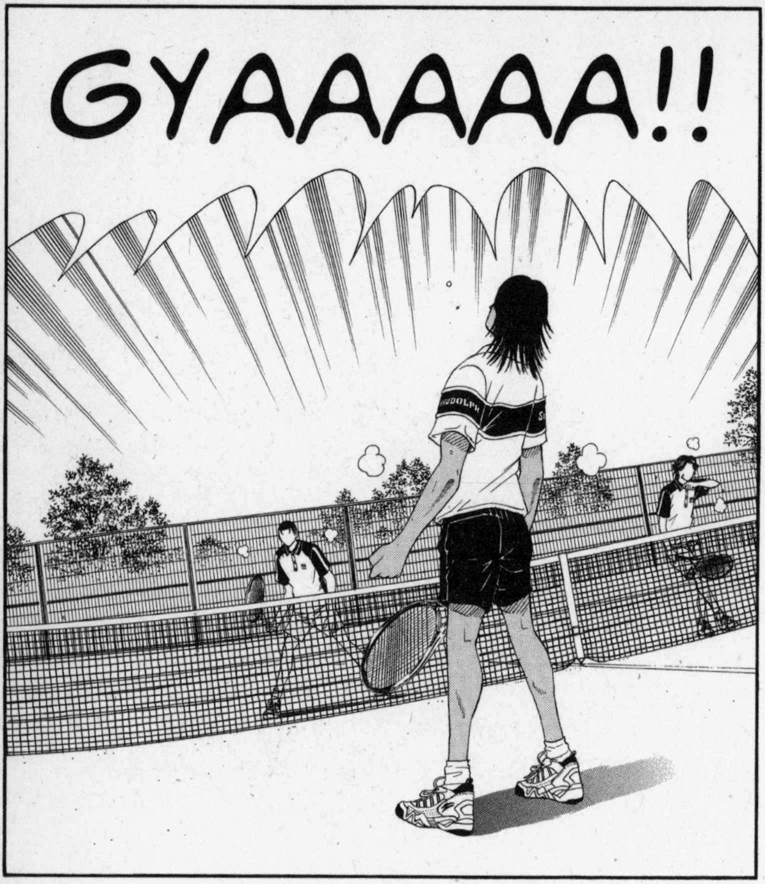
GYAAAAA!!
RUDOLPH

GENIUS 59: AMBUSH!

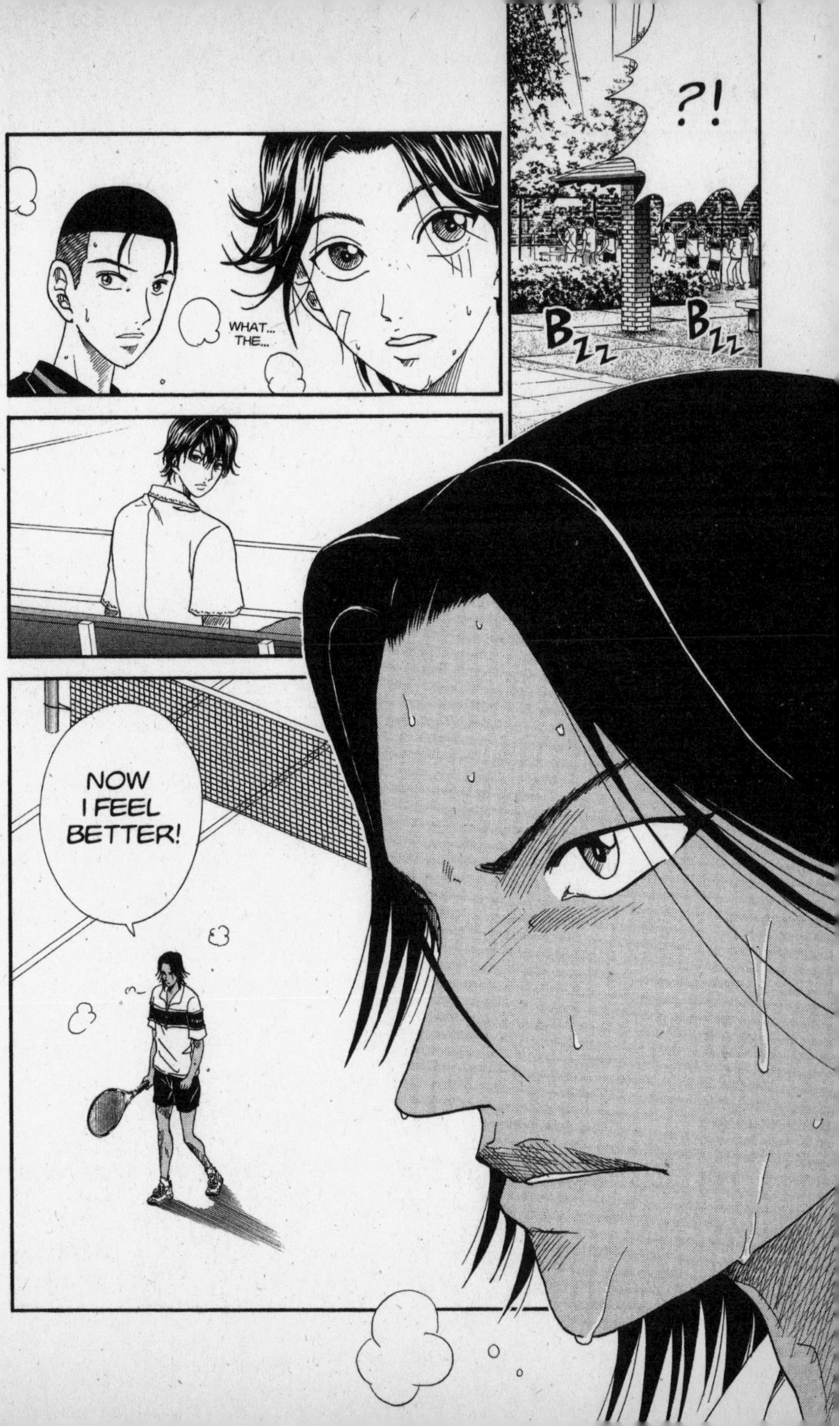
?!
Bzz
Bzz
WHAT... THE...
NOW I FEEL BETTER!

READ THIS WAY

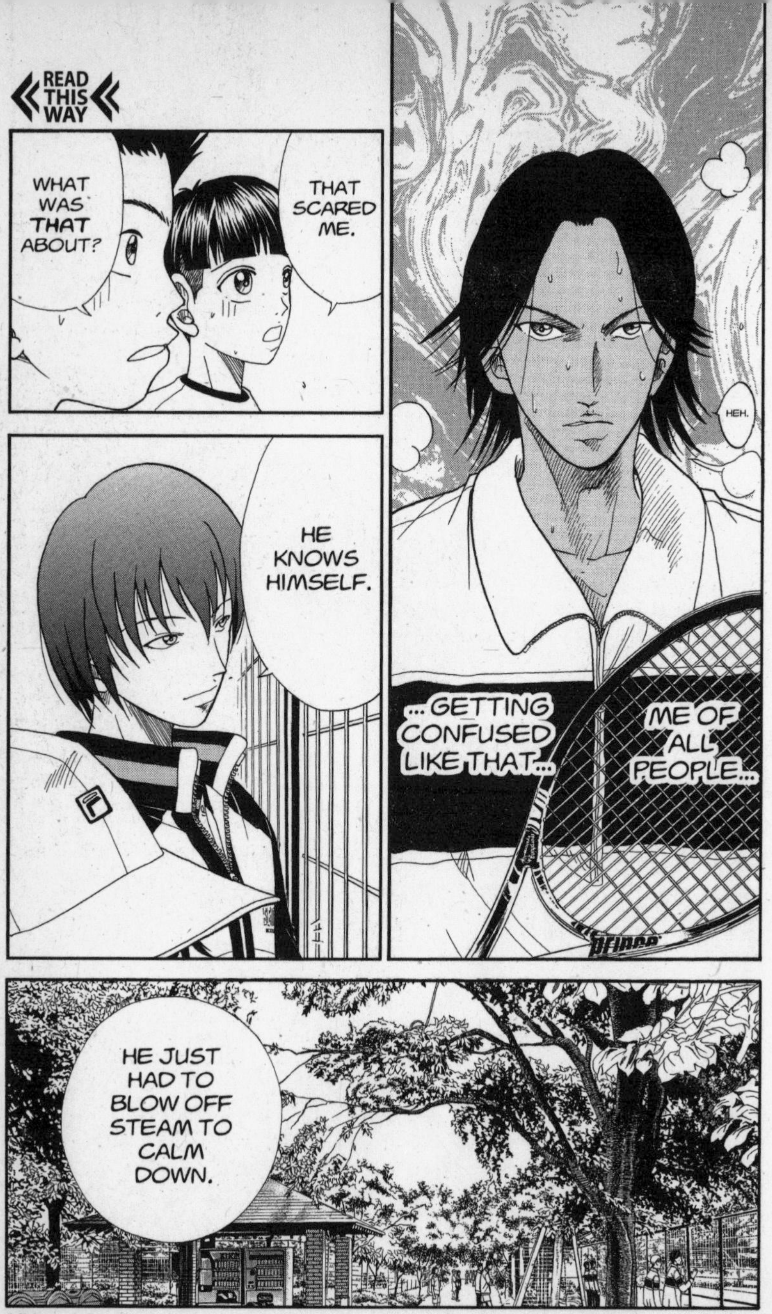
HEH.
ME OF ALL PEOPLE...
...GETTING CONFUSED LIKE THAT...
THAT SCARED ME.
WHAT WAS THAT ABOUT?
HE KNOWS HIMSELF.
HE JUST HAD TO BLOW OFF STEAM TO CALM DOWN.

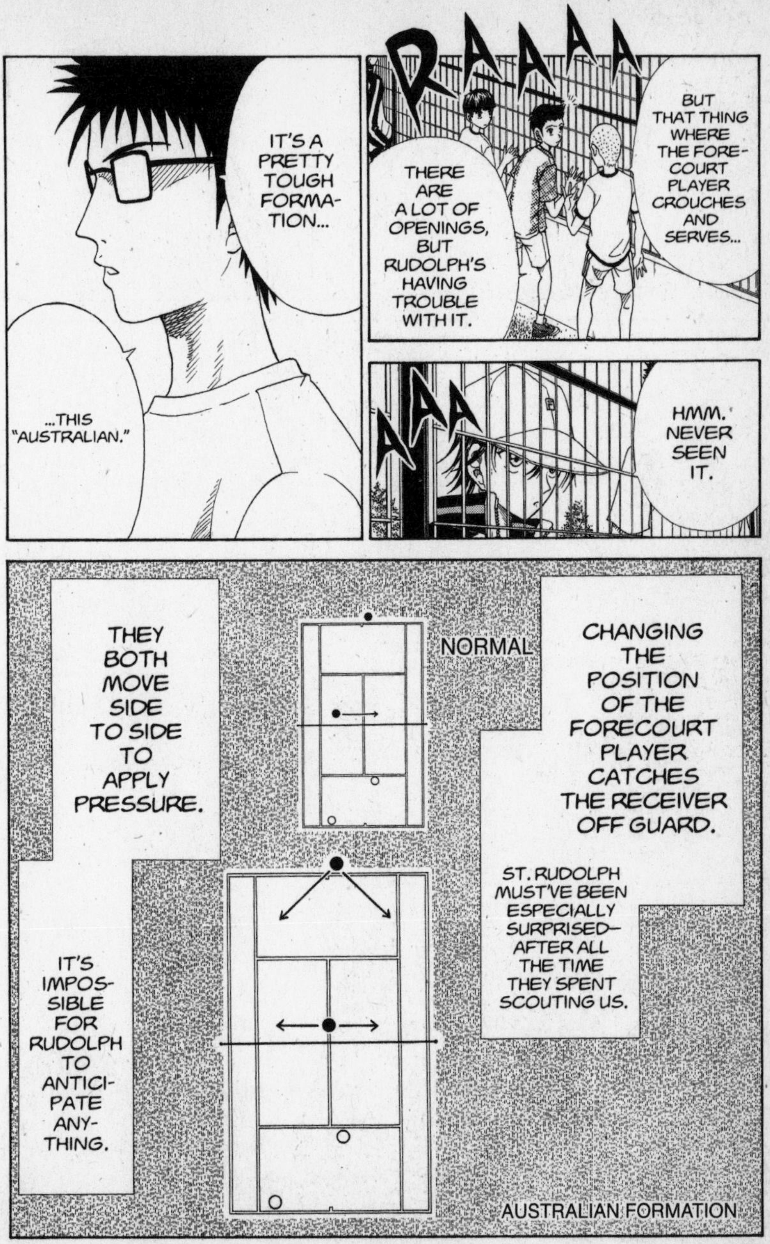
RAAAA
BUT THAT THING WHERE THE FORECOURT PLAYER CROUCHES AND SERVES...
THERE ARE A LOT OF OPENINGS, BUT RUDOLPH'S HAVING TROUBLE WITH IT.
AAA
HMM. NEVER SEEN IT.
IT'S A PRETTY TOUGH FORMATION...
...THIS "AUSTRALIAN."
CHANGING THE POSITION OF THE FORECOURT PLAYER CATCHES THE RECEIVER OFF GUARD.
ST. RUDOLPH MUST'VE BEEN ESPECIALLY SURPRISED—AFTER ALL THE TIME THEY SPENT SCOUTING US.
NORMAL
THEY BOTH MOVE SIDE TO SIDE TO APPLY PRESSURE.
IT'S IMPOSSIBLE FOR RUDOLPH TO ANTICIPATE ANYTHING.
AUSTRALIAN FORMATION

READ THIS WAY

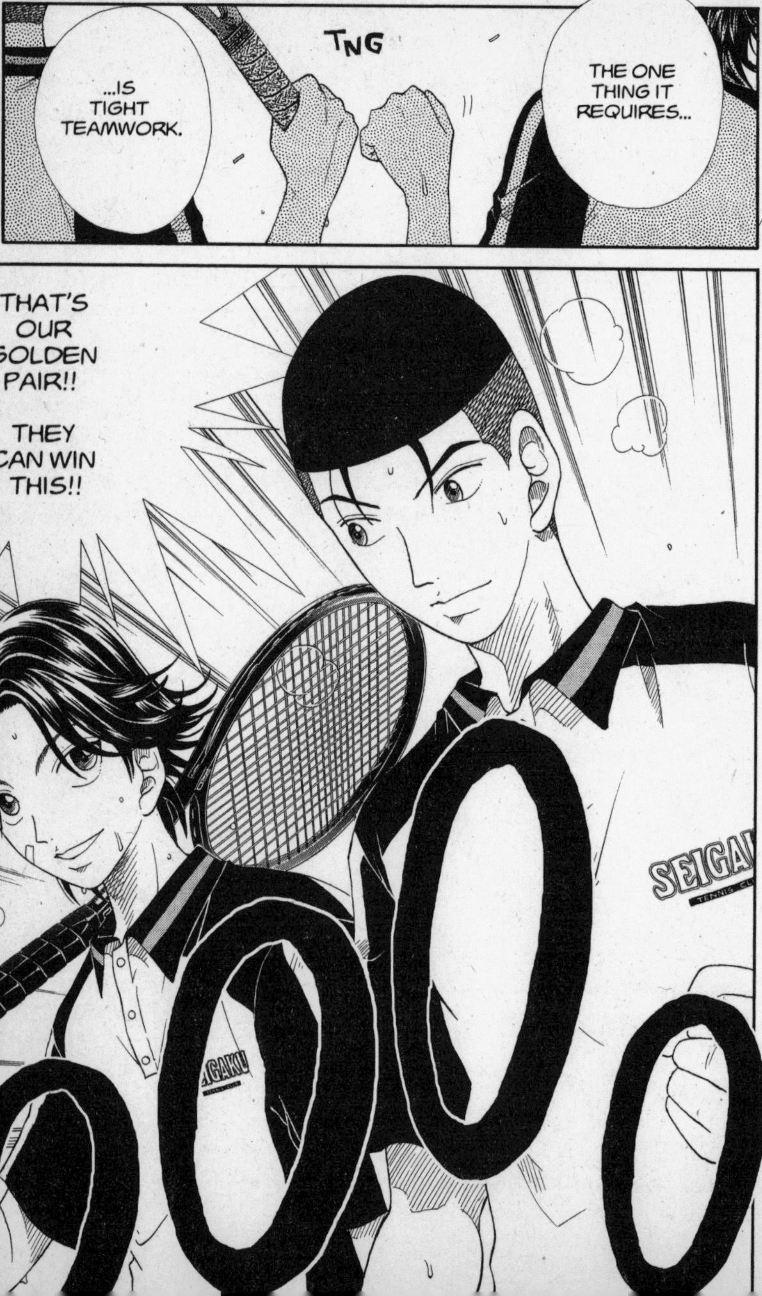
THE ONE THING IT REQUIRES...
TNG
...IS TIGHT TEAMWORK.
THAT'S OUR GOLDEN PAIR!!
THEY CAN WIN THIS!!
OOOO

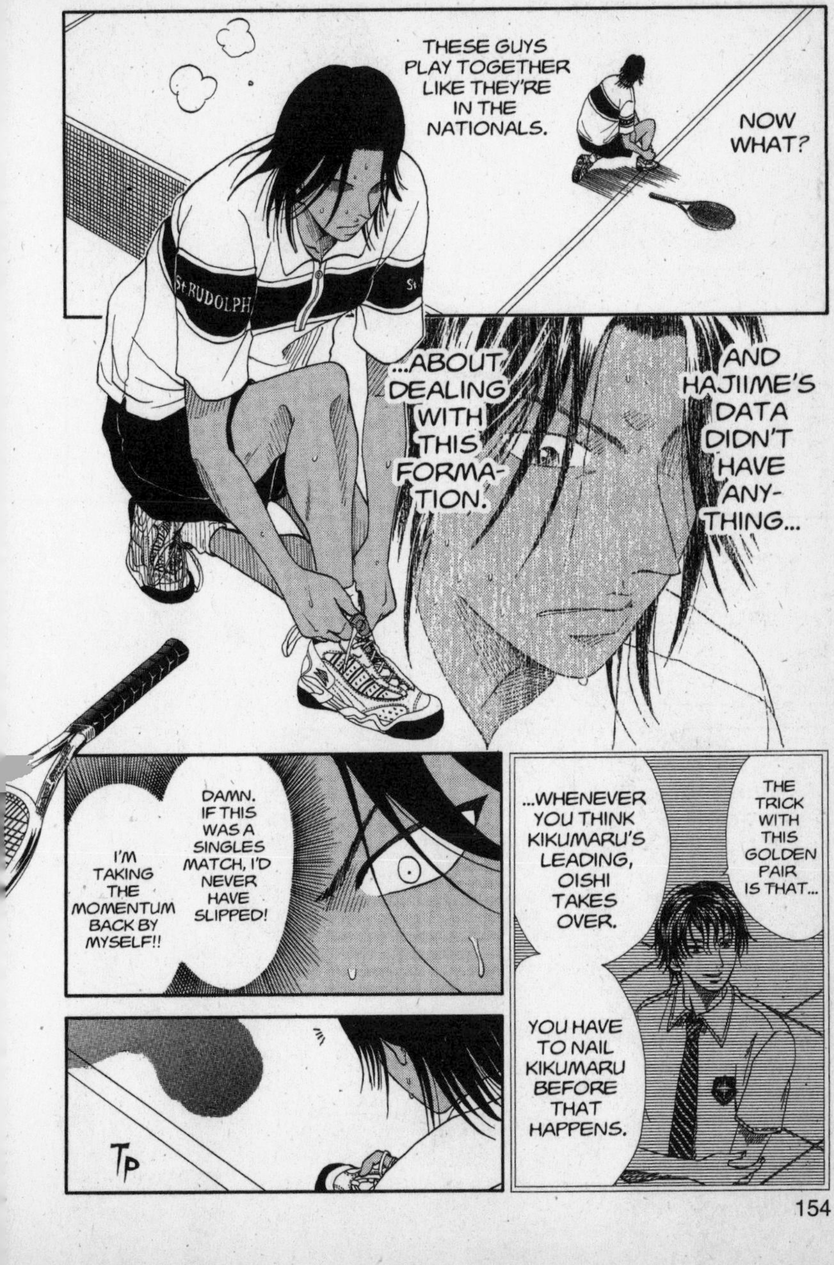
NOW WHAT?
THESE GUYS PLAY TOGETHER LIKE THEY'RE IN THE NATIONALS.
AND HAJIIME'S DATA DIDN'T HAVE ANYTHING...
...ABOUT DEALING WITH THIS FORMATION.
THE TRICK WITH THIS GOLDEN PAIR IS THAT...
...WHENEVER YOU THINK KIKUMARU'S LEADING, OISHI TAKES OVER.
YOU HAVE TO NAIL KIKUMARU BEFORE THAT HAPPENS.
DAMN. IF THIS WAS A SINGLES MATCH, I'D NEVER HAVE SLIPPED!
I'M TAKING THE MOMENTUM BACK BY MYSELF!!
TP

READ THIS WAY

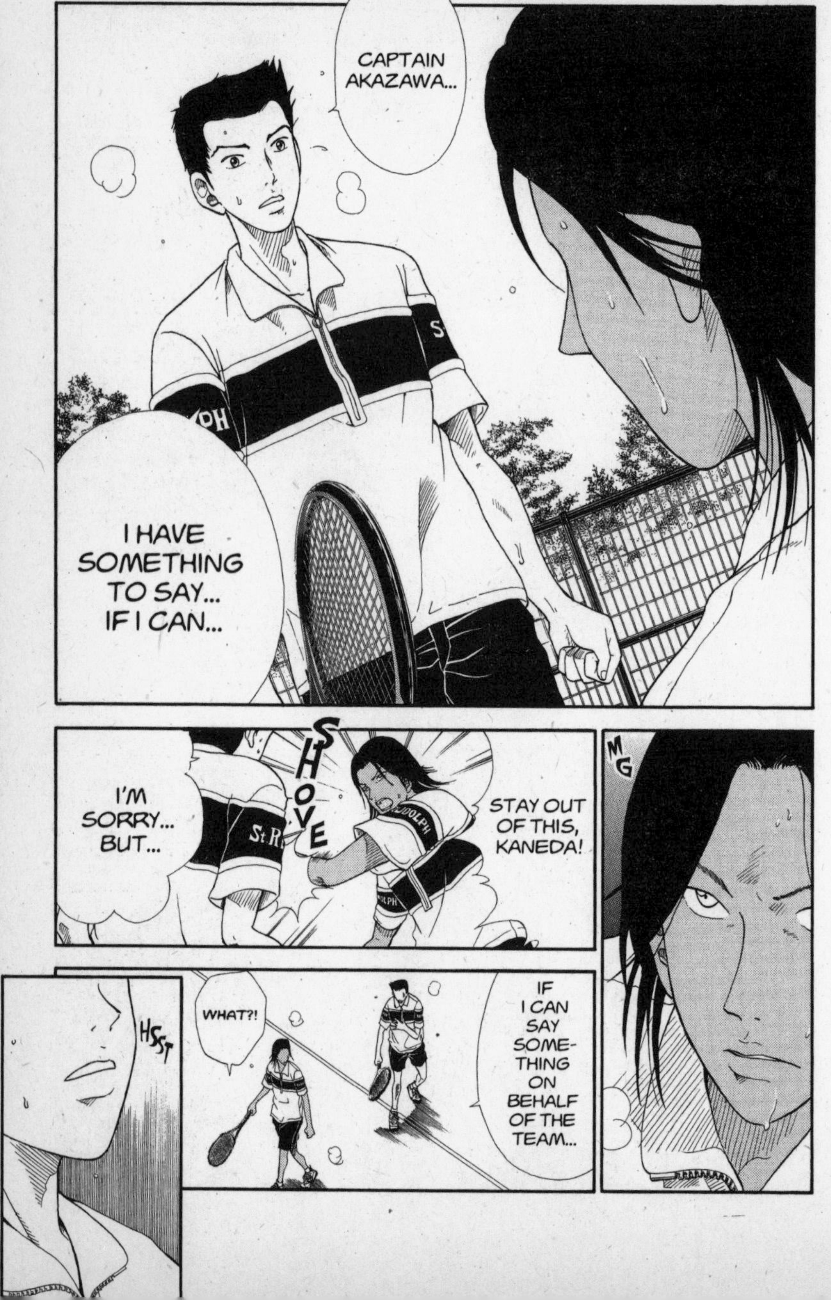
CAPTAIN AKAZAWA...
I HAVE SOMETHING TO SAY... IF I CAN...
MG
STAY OUT OF THIS, KANEDA!
SHOVE
I'M SORRY... BUT...
IF I CAN SAY SOME-THING ON BEHALF OF THE TEAM...
WHAT?!
HSST

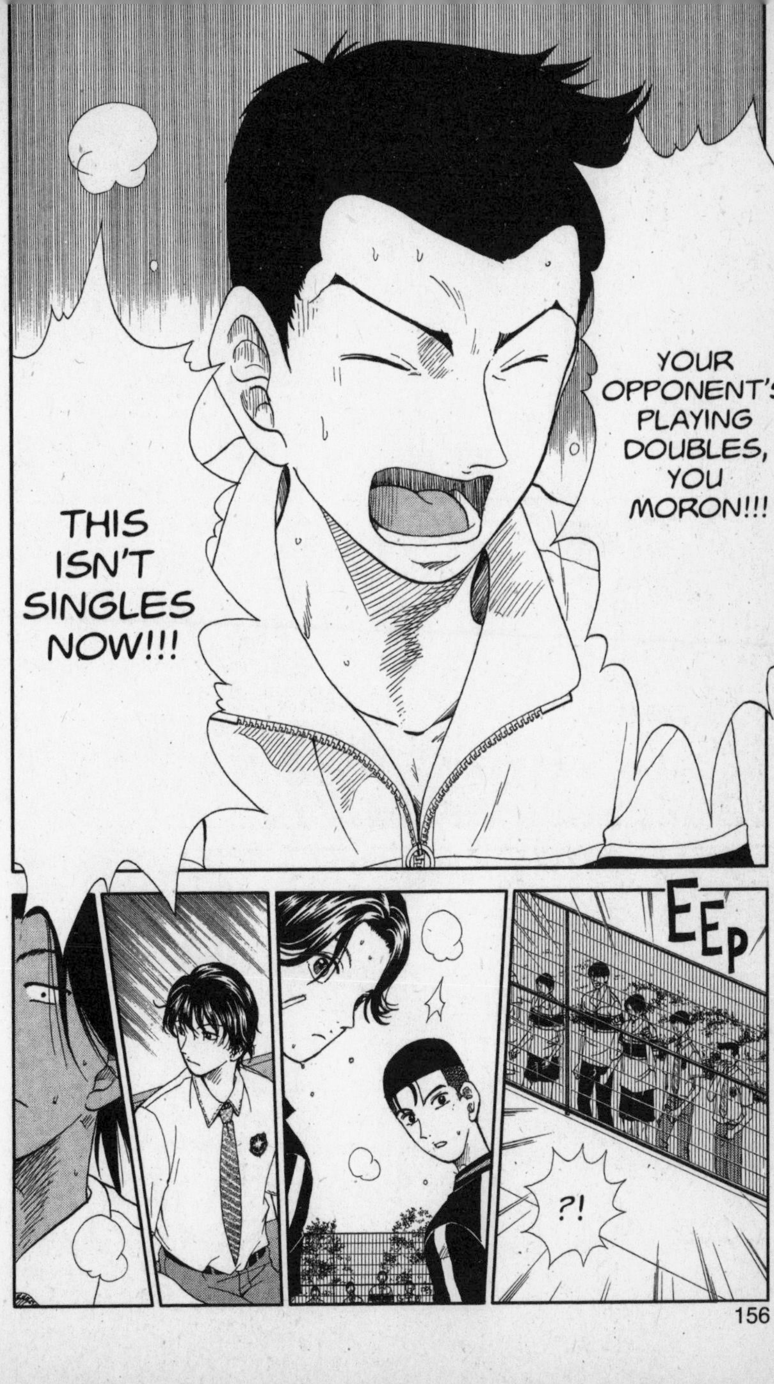
YOUR OPPONENT'S PLAYING DOUBLES, YOU MORON!!!
THIS ISN'T SINGLES NOW!!!
EEP
?!

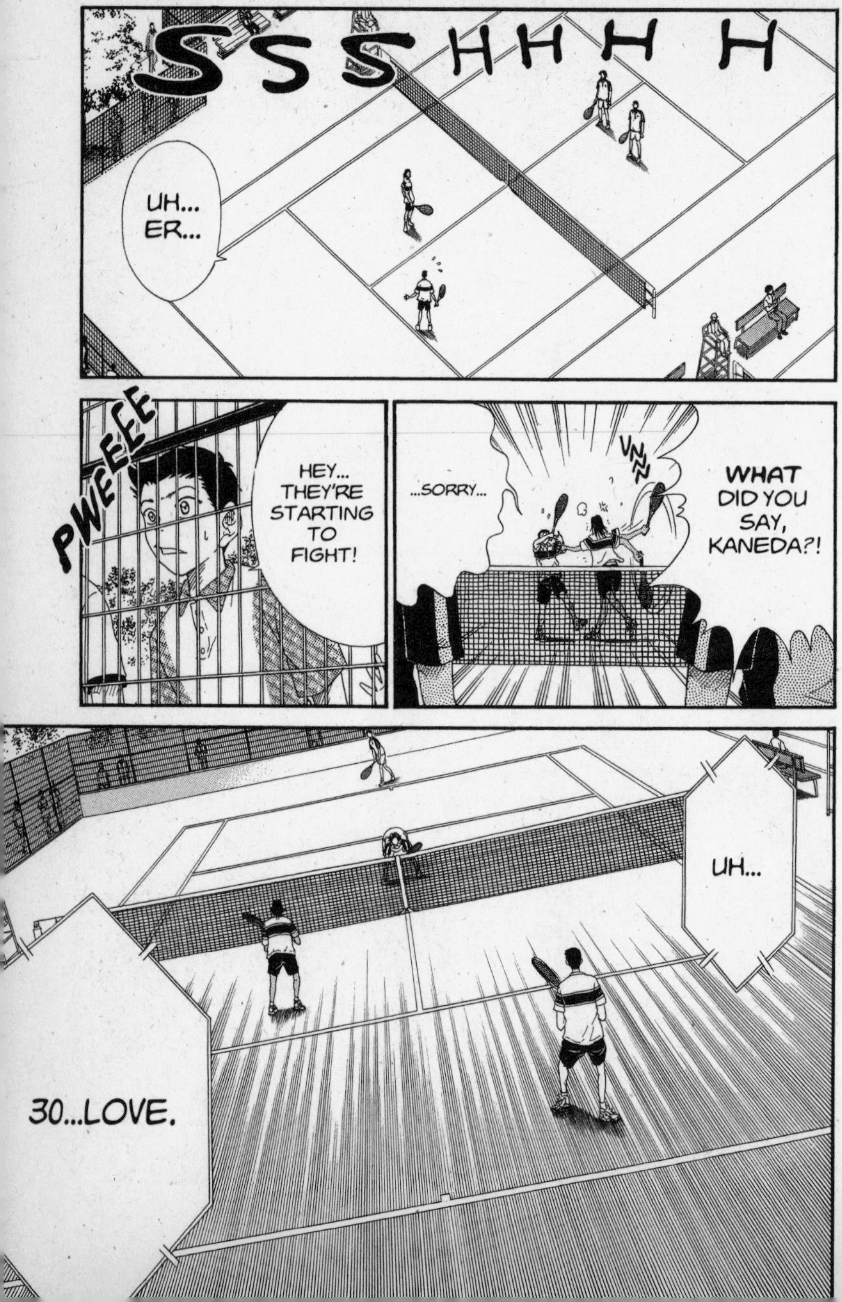
SSSHHHH
UH... ER...
WHAT DID YOU SAY, KANEDA?!
VNNN
...SORRY...
HEY... THEY'RE STARTING TO FIGHT!
PWEEEE
UH...
30...LOVE.

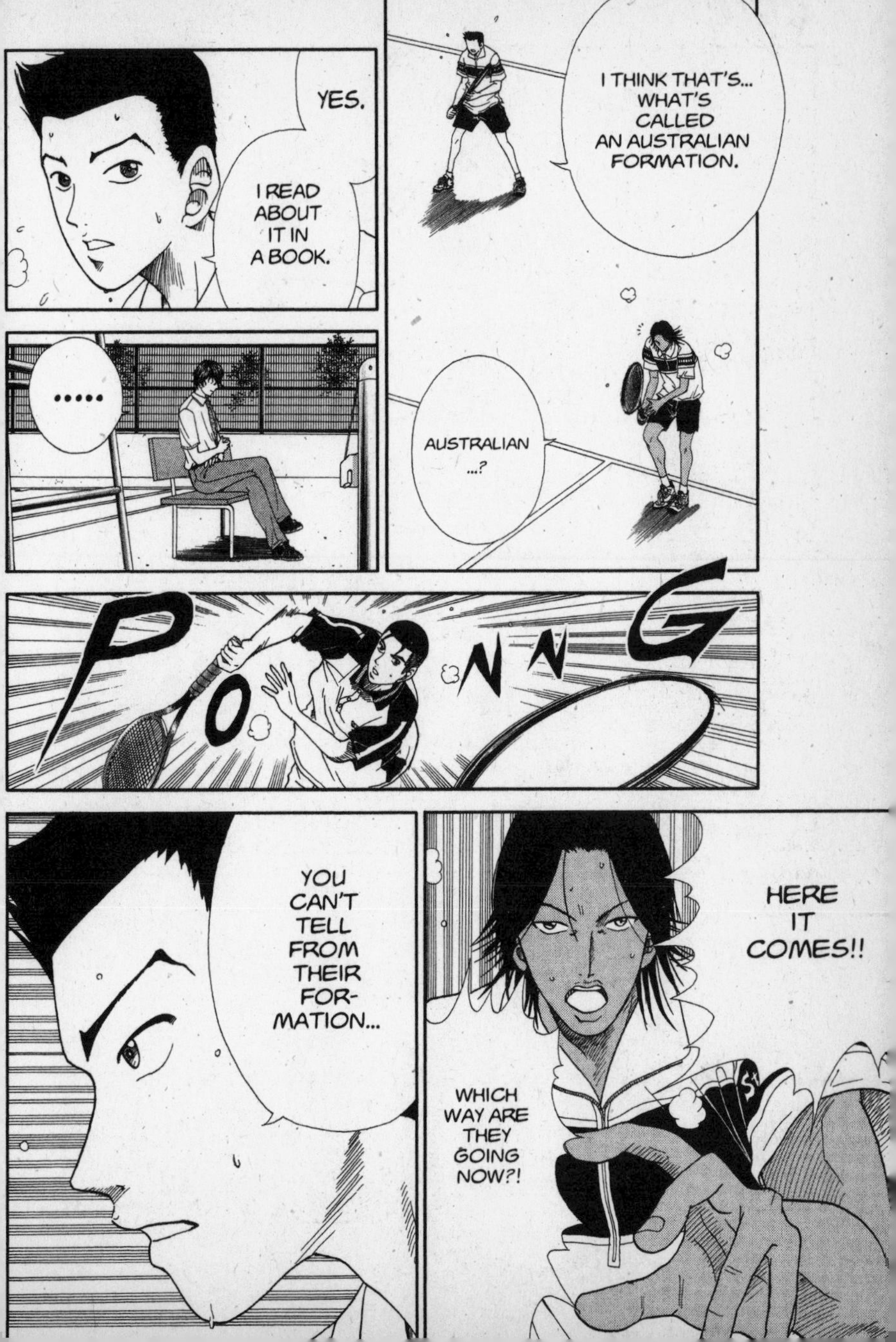
I THINK THAT'S... WHAT'S CALLED AN AUSTRALIAN FORMATION.
AUSTRALIAN ...?
YES.
I READ ABOUT IT IN A BOOK.
.....
PONNG
HERE IT COMES!!
WHICH WAY ARE THEY GOING NOW?!
YOU CAN'T TELL FROM THEIR FOR-MATION...

READ THIS WAY

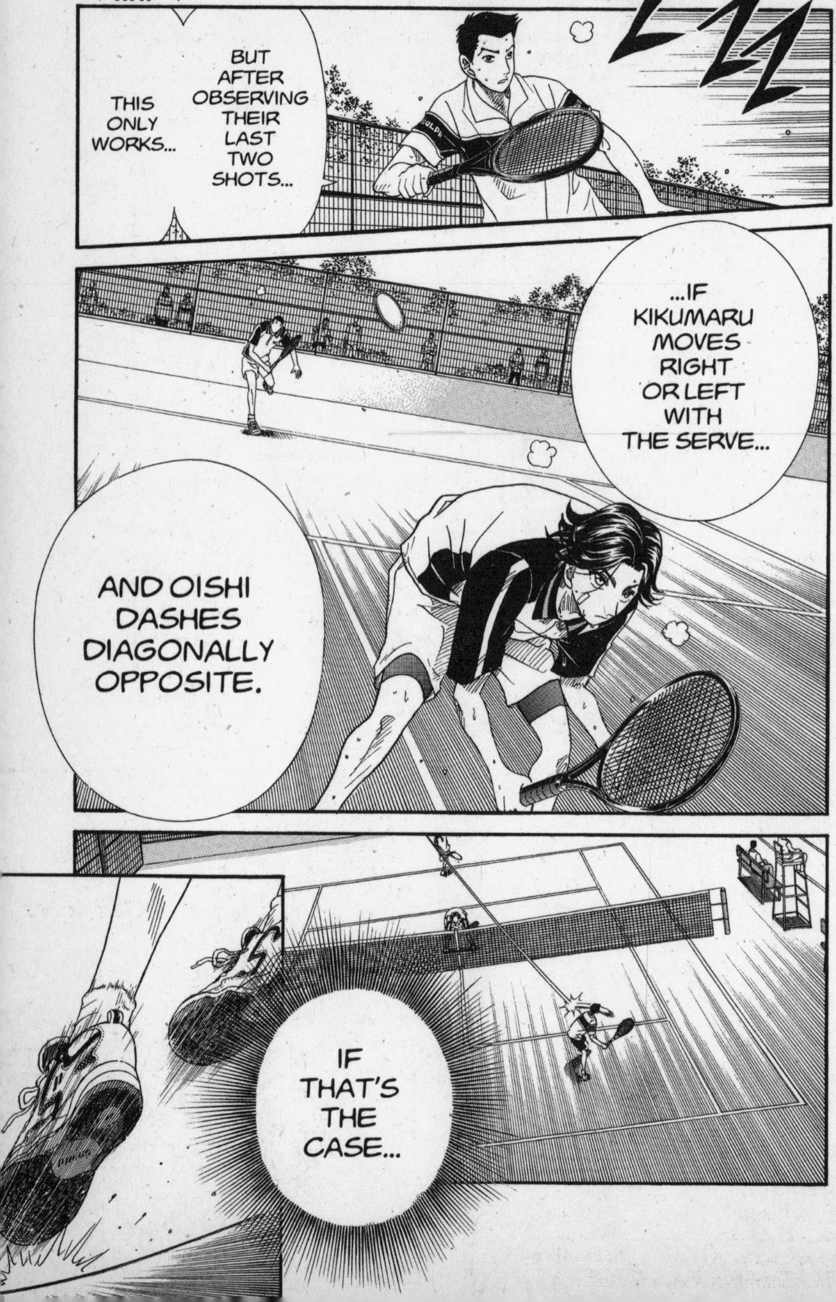

BUT AFTER OBSERVING THEIR LAST TWO SHOTS...
THIS ONLY WORKS...
...IF KIKUMARU MOVES RIGHT OR LEFT WITH THE SERVE...
AND OISHI DASHES DIAGONALLY OPPOSITE.
IF THAT'S THE CASE...

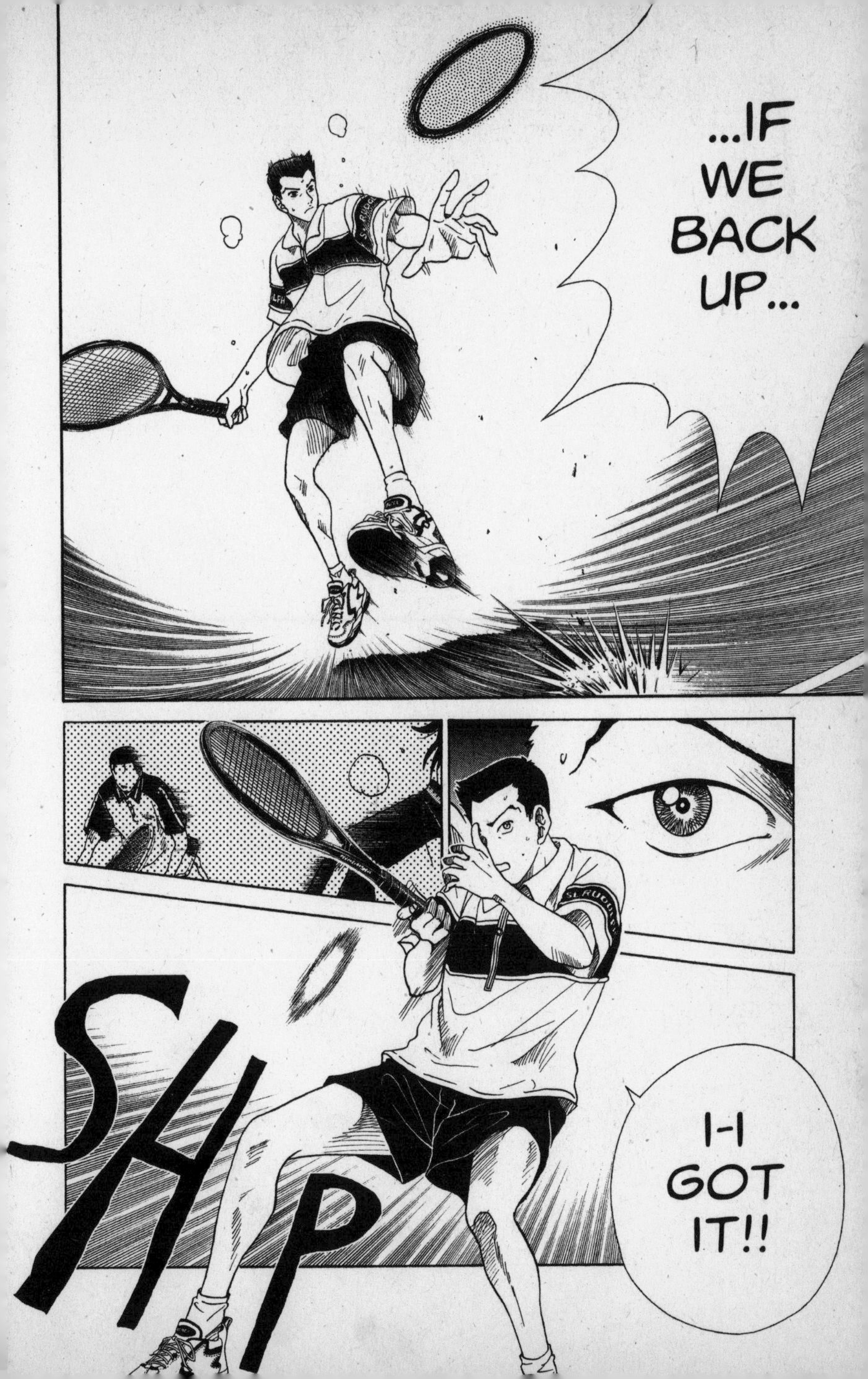
...IF WE BACK UP...
I-I GOT IT!!
SHP

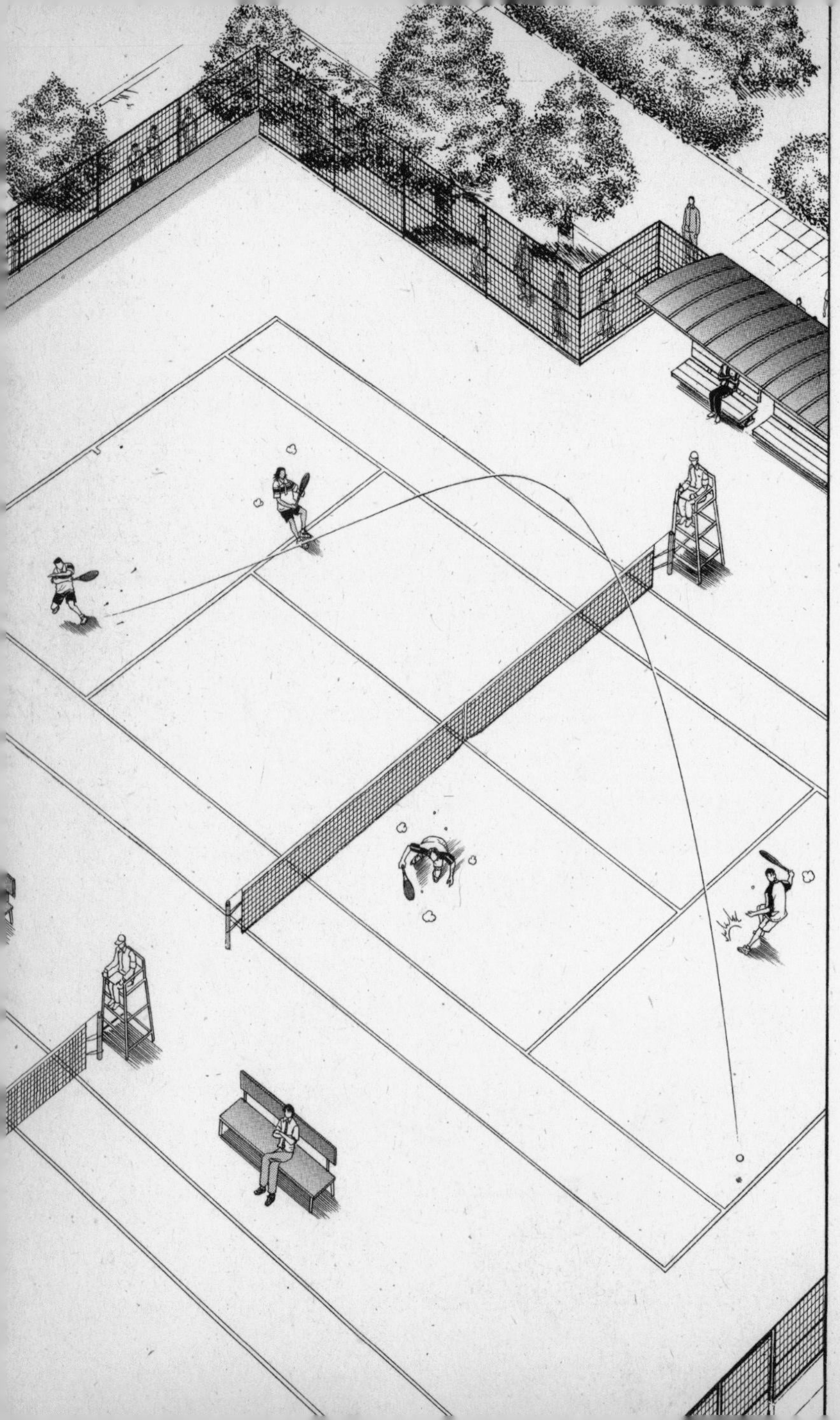

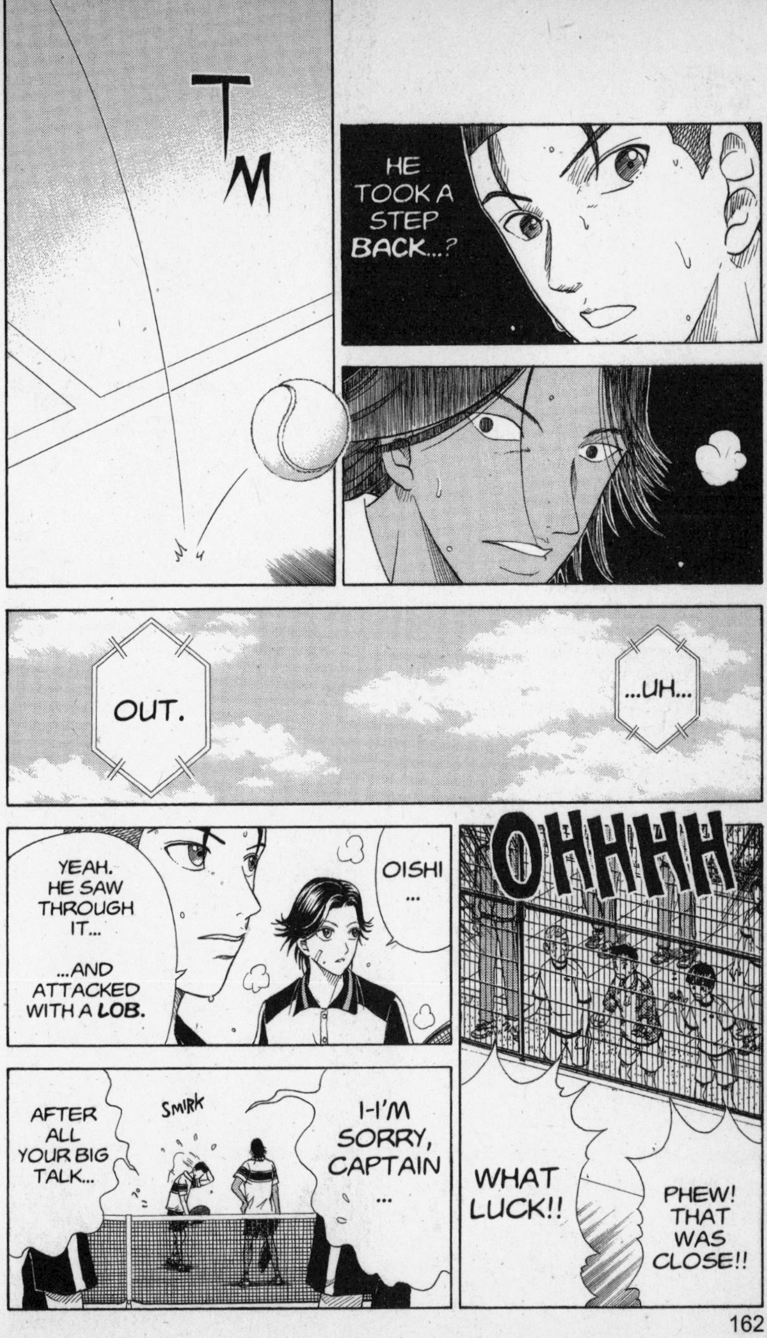
HE TOOK A STEP BACK...?
TM
...UH...
OUT.
OHHHH
PHEW! THAT WAS CLOSE!!
WHAT LUCK!!
OISHI ...
YEAH. HE SAW THROUGH IT...
...AND ATTACKED WITH A **LOB.**
I-I'M SORRY, CAPTAIN ...
SMIRK
AFTER ALL YOUR BIG TALK...

READ THIS WAY

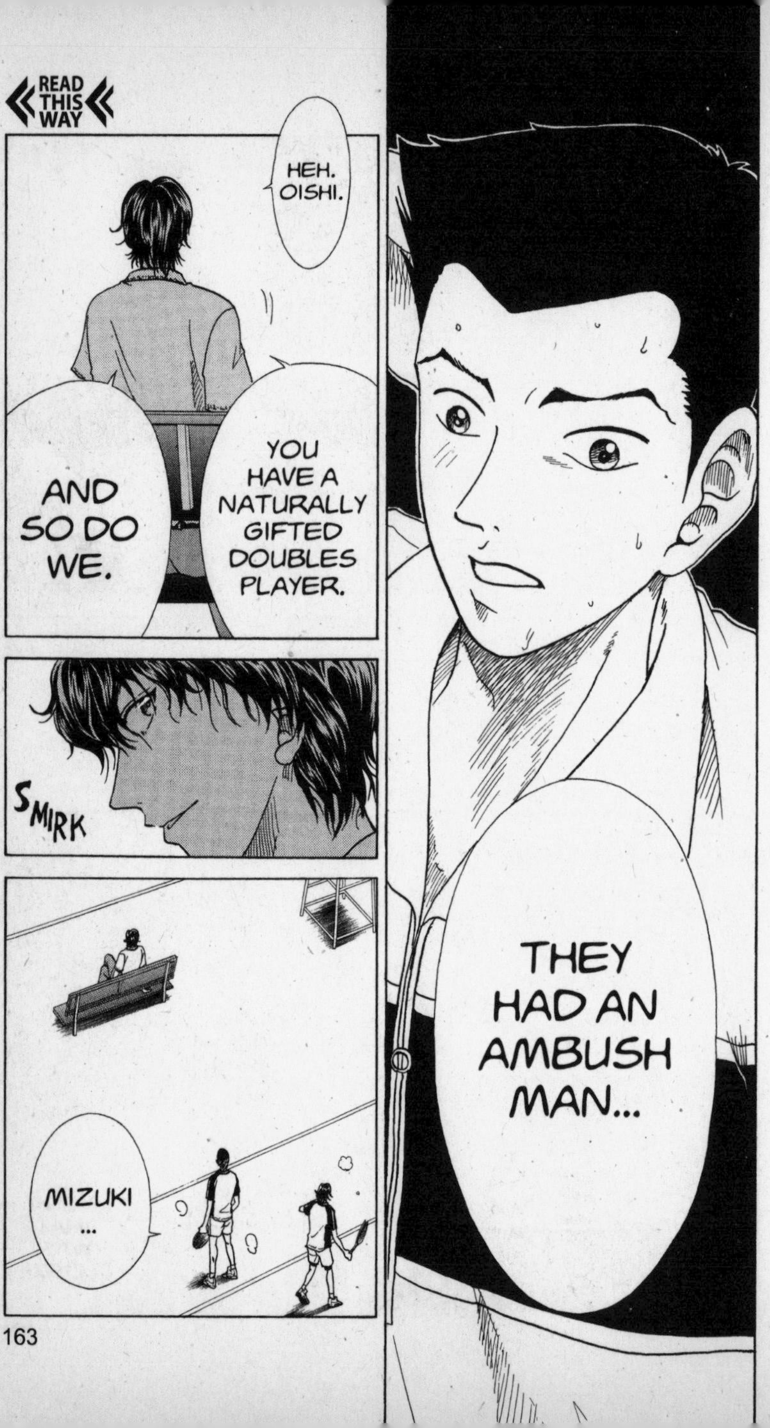
THEY HAD AN AMBUSH MAN...
HEH. OISHI.
YOU HAVE A NATURALLY GIFTED DOUBLES PLAYER.
AND SO DO WE.
SMIRK
MIZUKI ...

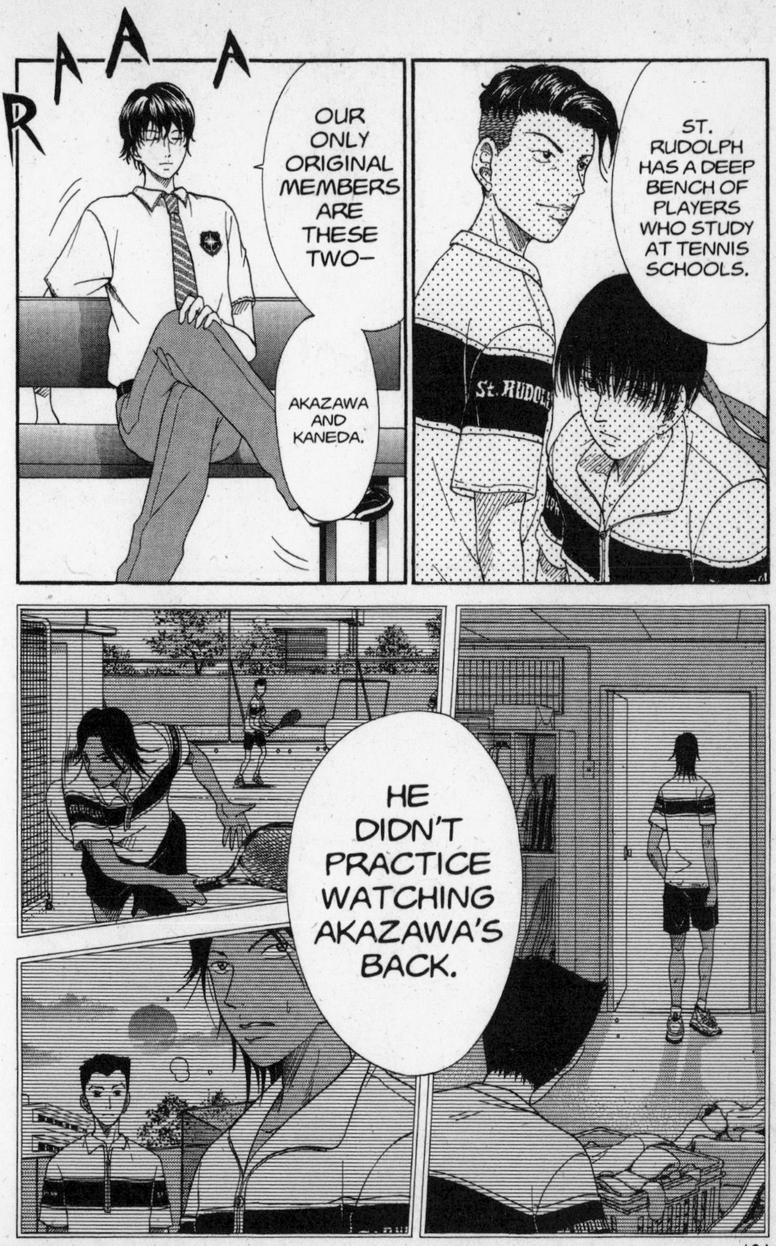
ST. RUDOLPH HAS A DEEP BENCH OF PLAYERS WHO STUDY AT TENNIS SCHOOLS.
RAAA A
OUR ONLY ORIGINAL MEMBERS ARE THESE TWO—
AKAZAWA AND KANEDA.
St. RUDOL
HE DIDN'T PRACTICE WATCHING AKAZAWA'S BACK.

READ THIS WAY

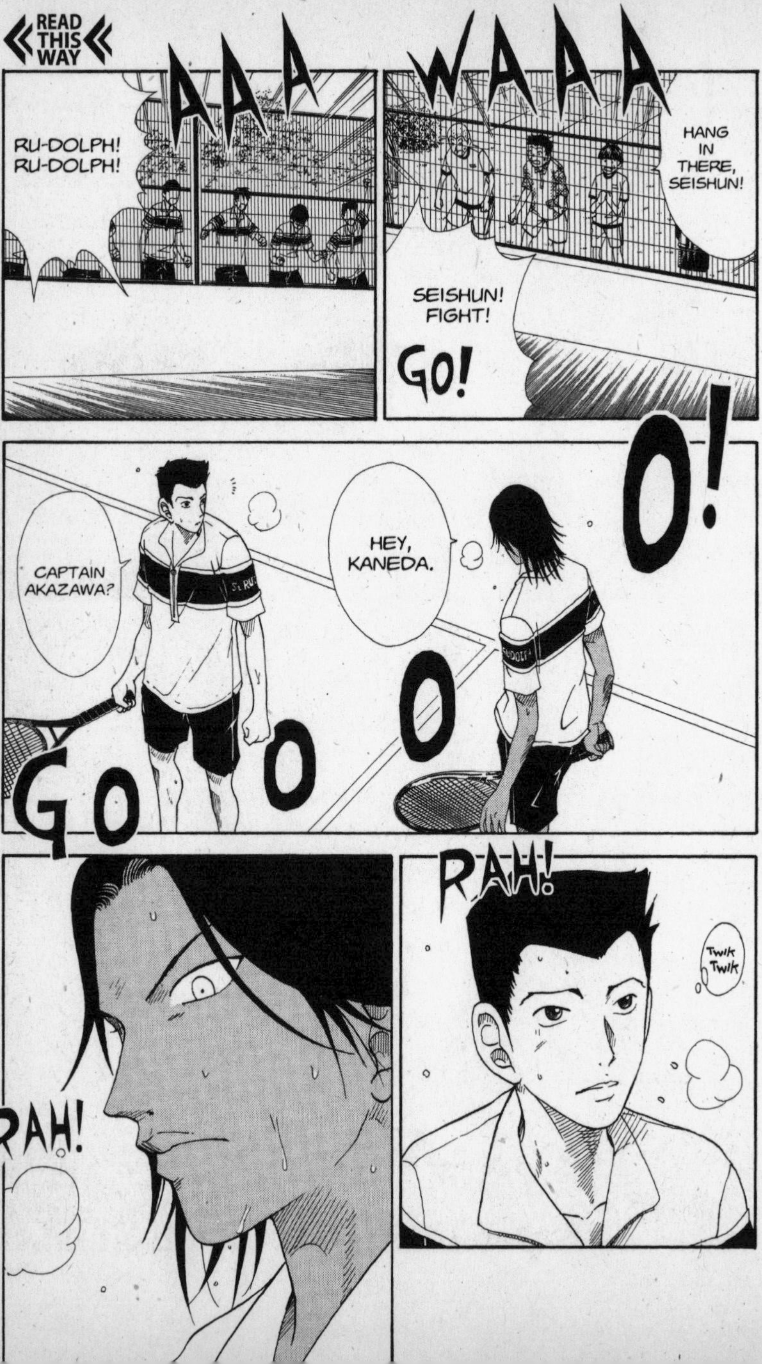
WAAA
HANG IN THERE, SEISHUN!
SEISHUN! FIGHT!
GO!
AAA
RU-DOLPH! RU-DOLPH!
HEY, KANEDA.
CAPTAIN AKAZAWA?
GOOOO!
RAH!
Twik Twik
RAH!

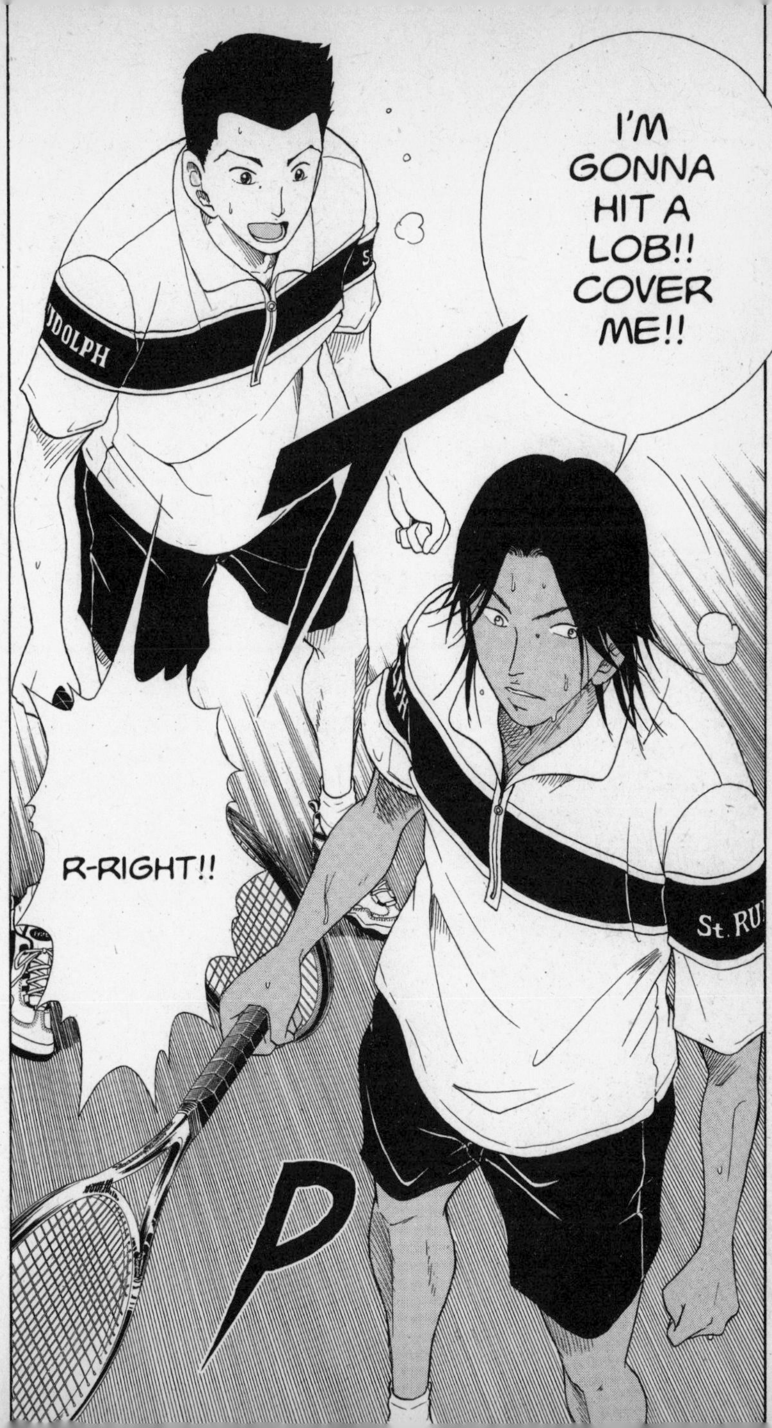
I'M GONNA HIT A LOB!! COVER ME!!
R-RIGHT!!

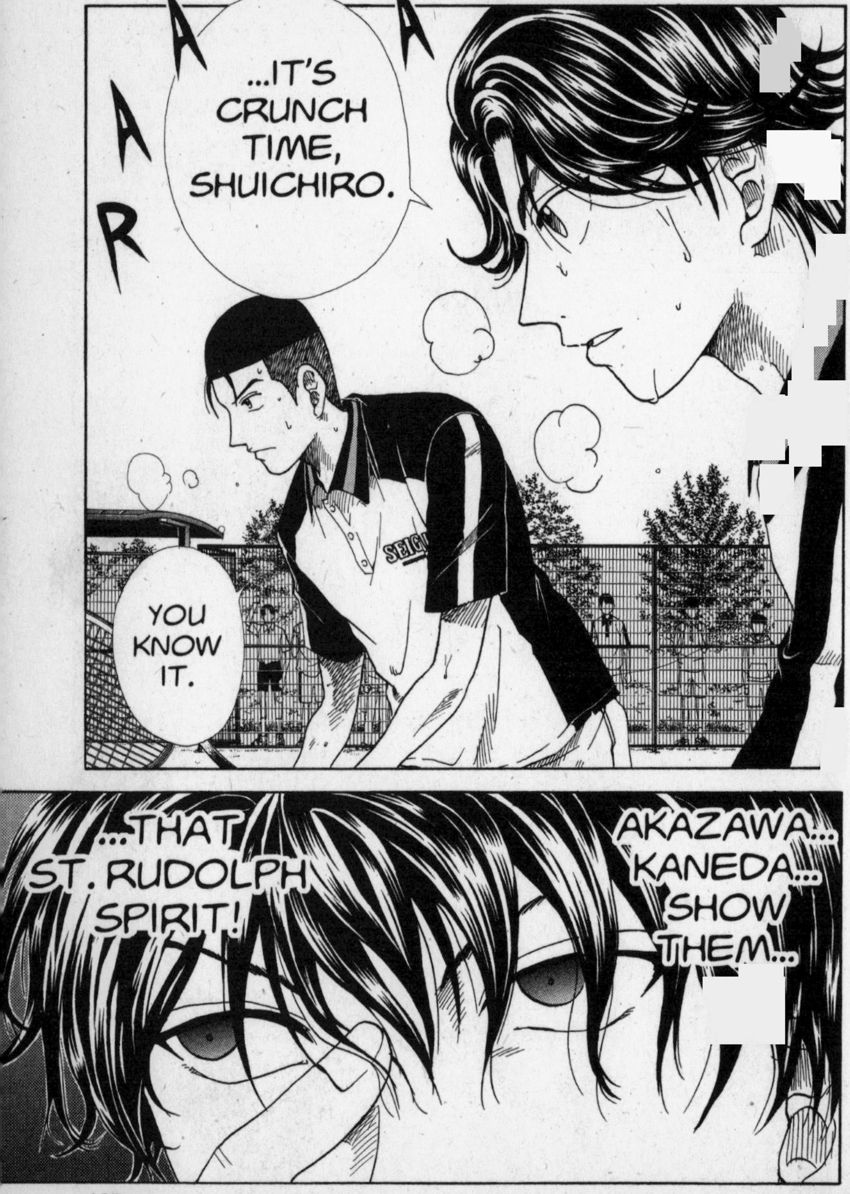
RAAA
...IT'S CRUNCH TIME, SHUICHIRO.
YOU KNOW IT.
AKAZAWA... KANEDA... SHOW THEM...
...THAT ST. RUDOLPH SPIRIT!

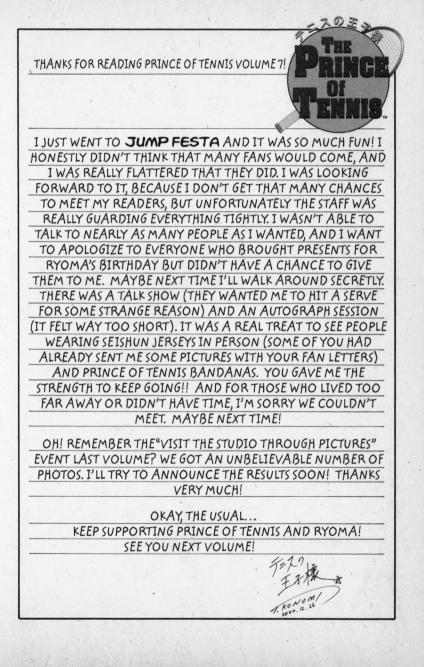

THANKS FOR READING PRINCE OF TENNIS VOLUME 7!

THE PRINCE OF TENNIS

I JUST WENT TO **JUMP FESTA** AND IT WAS SO MUCH FUN! I
HONESTLY DIDN'T THINK THAT MANY FANS WOULD COME, AND
I WAS REALLY FLATTERED THAT THEY DID. I WAS LOOKING
FORWARD TO IT, BECAUSE I DON'T GET THAT MANY CHANCES
TO MEET MY READERS, BUT UNFORTUNATELY THE STAFF WAS
REALLY GUARDING EVERYTHING TIGHTLY. I WASN'T ABLE TO
TALK TO NEARLY AS MANY PEOPLE AS I WANTED, AND I WANT
TO APOLOGIZE TO EVERYONE WHO BROUGHT PRESENTS FOR
RYOMA'S BIRTHDAY BUT DIDN'T HAVE A CHANCE TO GIVE
THEM TO ME. MAYBE NEXT TIME I'LL WALK AROUND SECRETLY.
THERE WAS A TALK SHOW (THEY WANTED ME TO HIT A SERVE
FOR SOME STRANGE REASON) AND AN AUTOGRAPH SESSION
(IT FELT WAY TOO SHORT). IT WAS A REAL TREAT TO SEE PEOPLE
WEARING SEISHUN JERSEYS IN PERSON (SOME OF YOU HAD
ALREADY SENT ME SOME PICTURES WITH YOUR FAN LETTERS)
AND PRINCE OF TENNIS BANDANAS. YOU GAVE ME THE
STRENGTH TO KEEP GOING!! AND FOR THOSE WHO LIVED TOO
FAR AWAY OR DIDN'T HAVE TIME, I'M SORRY WE COULDN'T
MEET. MAYBE NEXT TIME!

OH! REMEMBER THE "VISIT THE STUDIO THROUGH PICTURES"
EVENT LAST VOLUME? WE GOT AN UNBELIEVABLE NUMBER OF
PHOTOS. I'LL TRY TO ANNOUNCE THE RESULTS SOON! THANKS
VERY MUCH!

OKAY, THE USUAL...
KEEP SUPPORTING PRINCE OF TENNIS AND RYOMA!
SEE YOU NEXT VOLUME!

T. KONOMI
2000. 12. 26

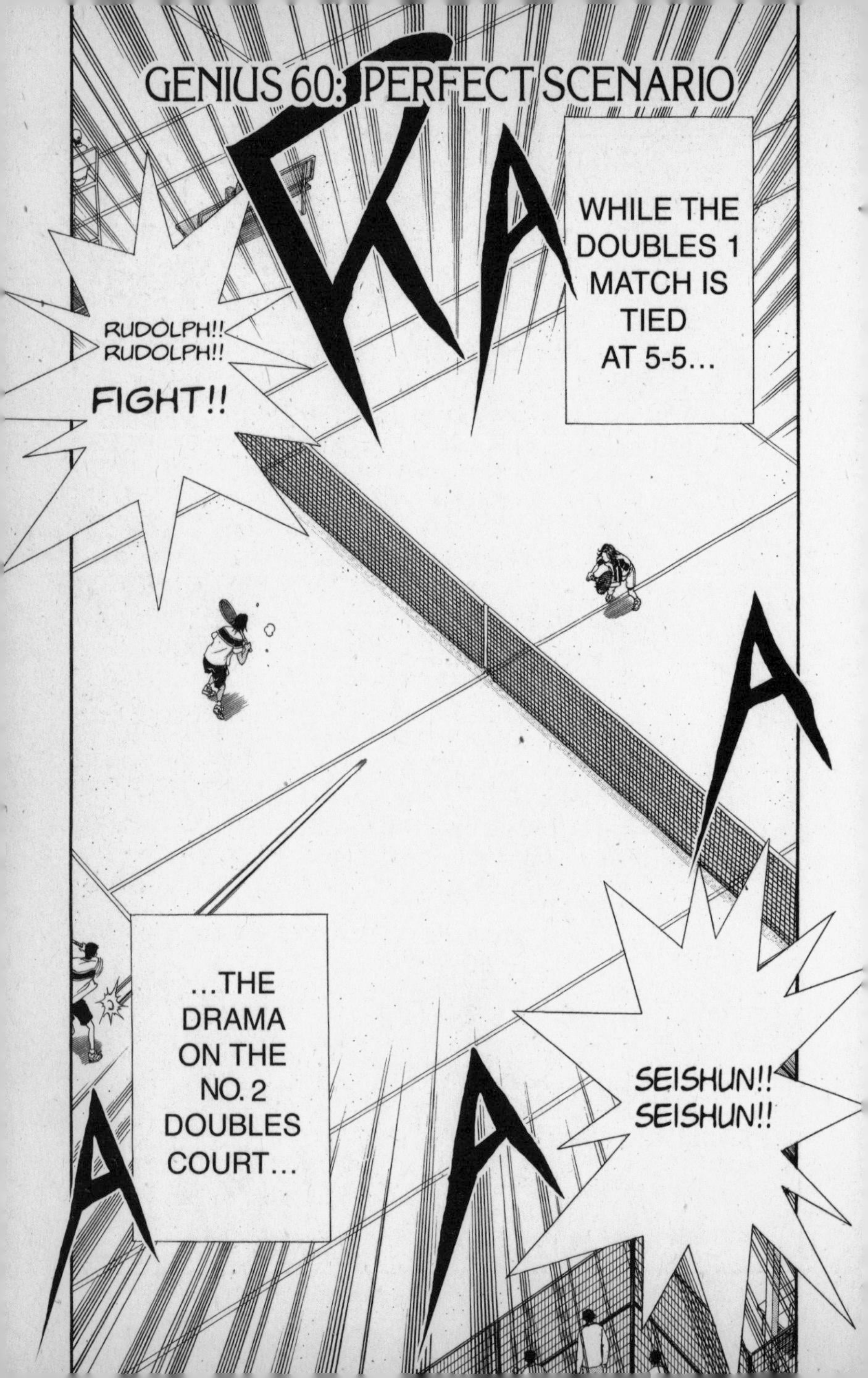
GENIUS 60: PERFECT SCENARIO
WHILE THE DOUBLES 1 MATCH IS TIED AT 5-5…
KAAA
RUDOLPH!! RUDOLPH!!
FIGHT!!
SEISHUN!! SEISHUN!!
…THE DRAMA ON THE NO. 2 DOUBLES COURT…

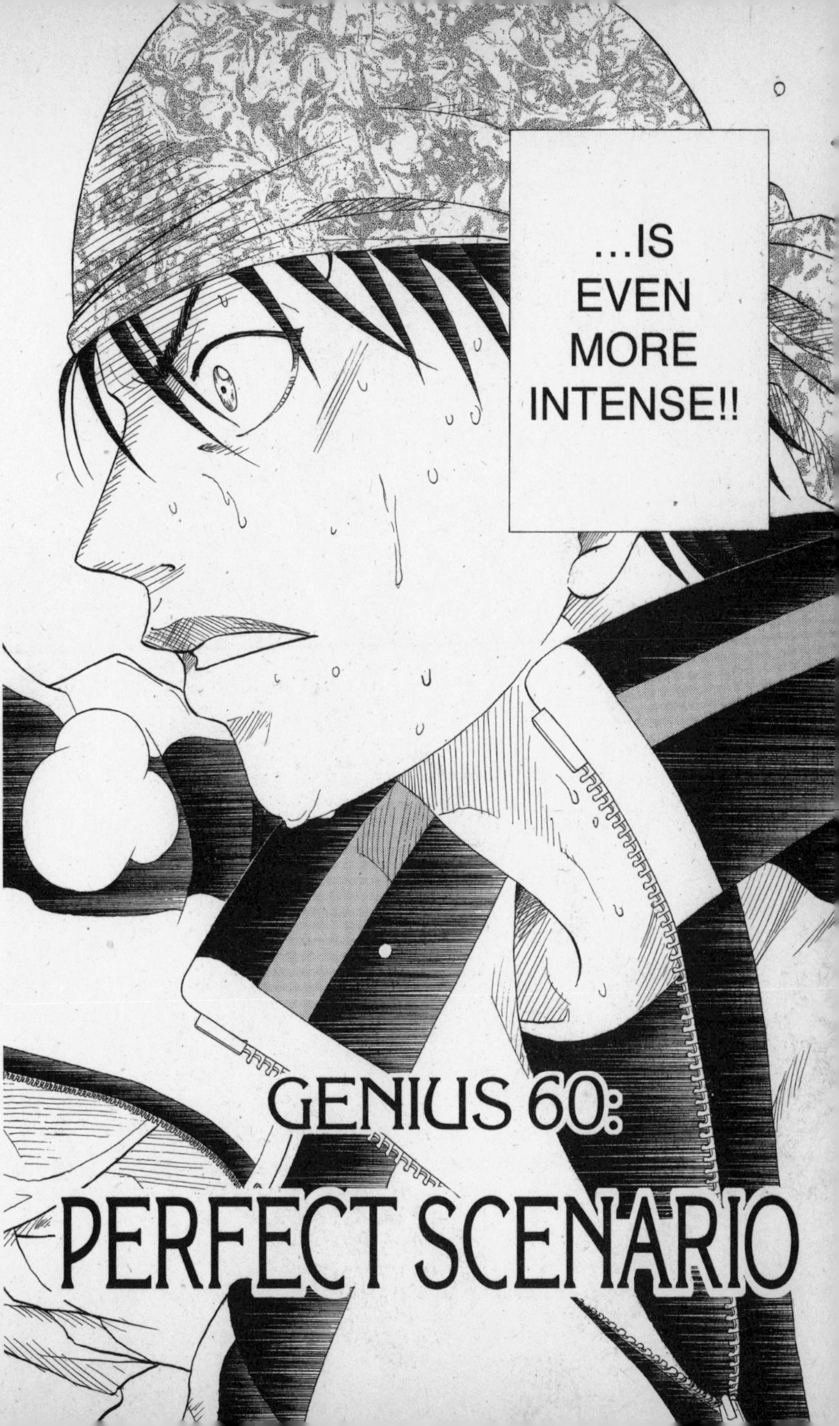
...IS EVEN MORE INTENSE!!
GENIUS 60:
PERFECT SCENARIO

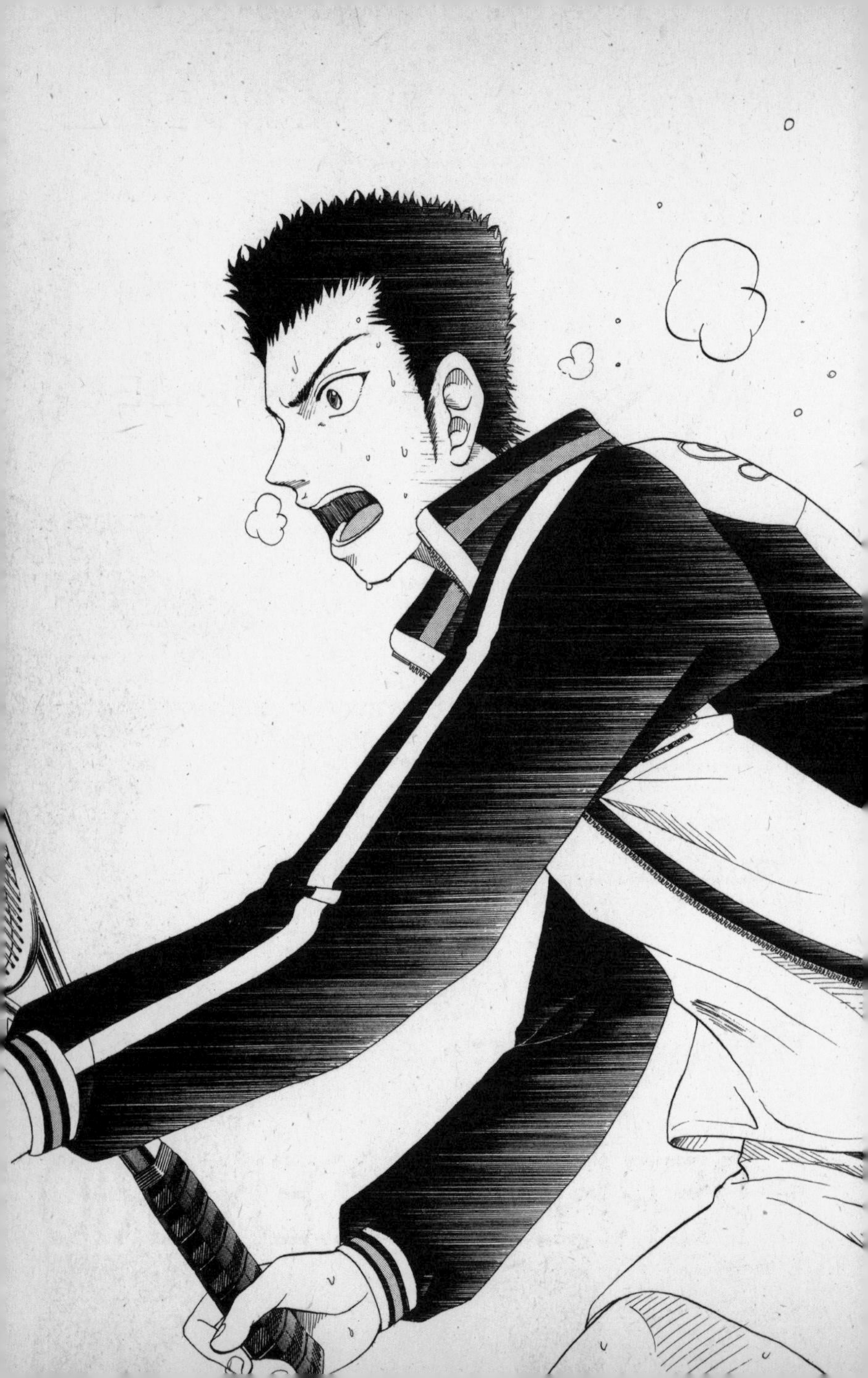

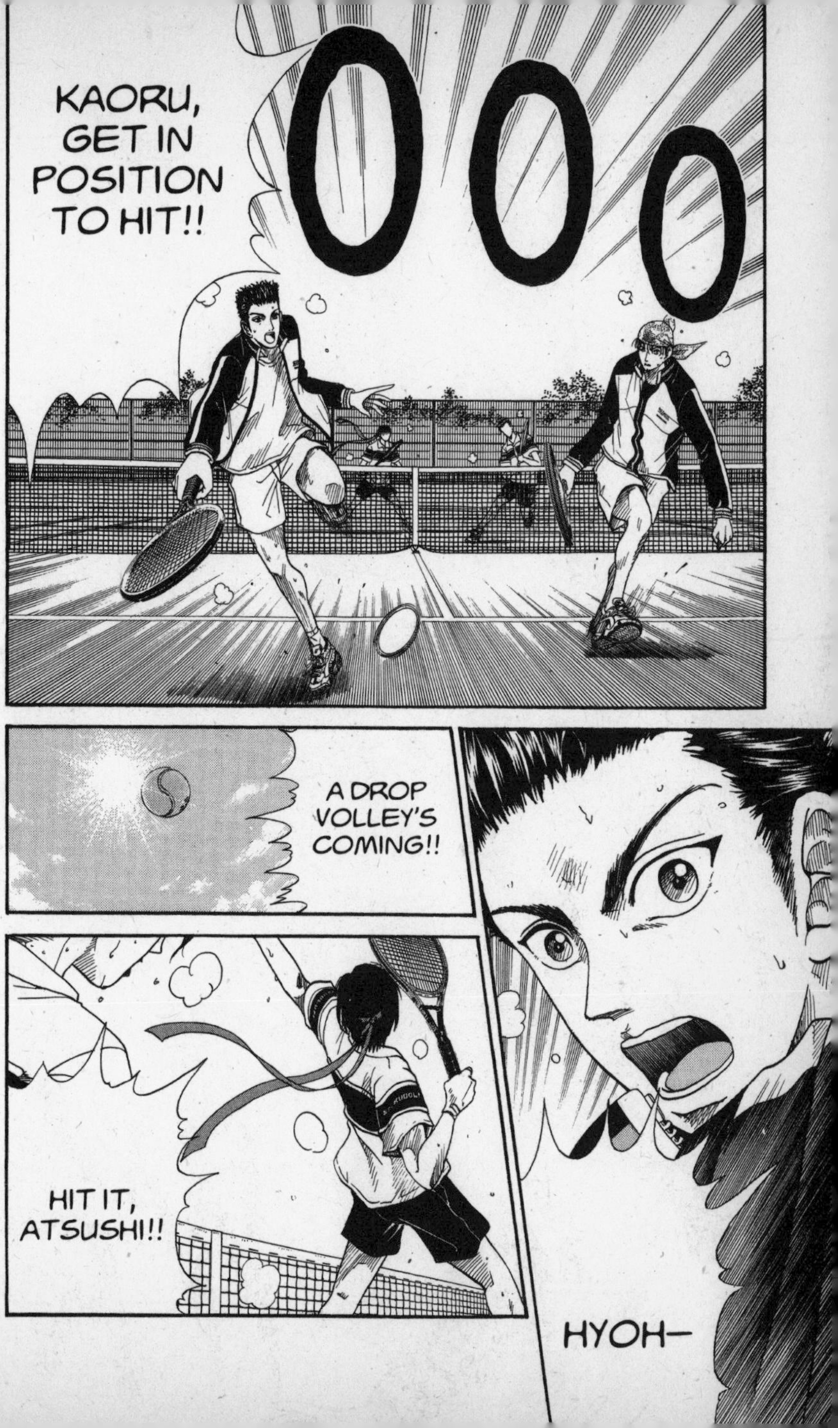
OOO
KAORU, GET IN POSITION TO HIT!!
HYOH—
A DROP VOLLEY'S COMING!!
HIT IT, ATSUSHI!!

READ THIS WAY

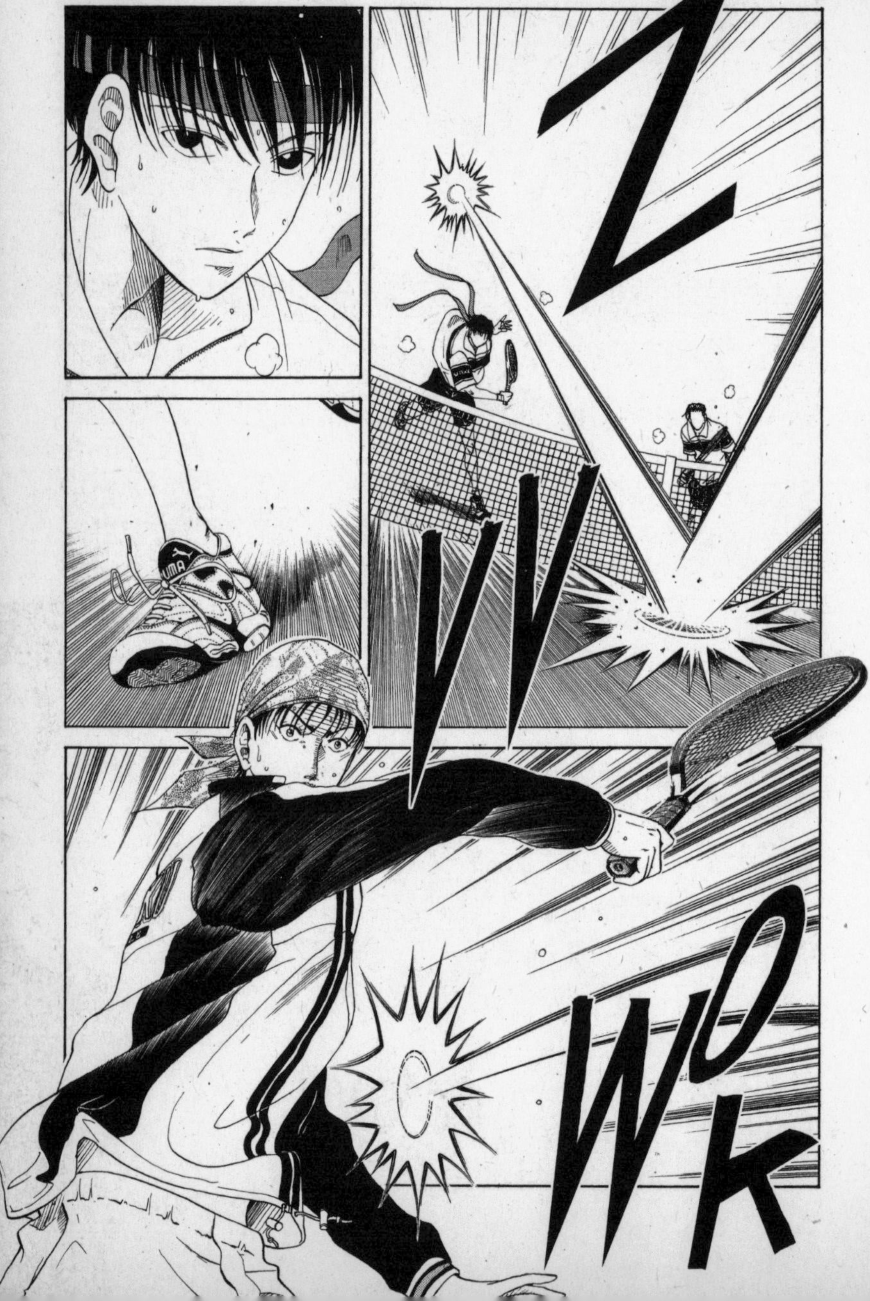

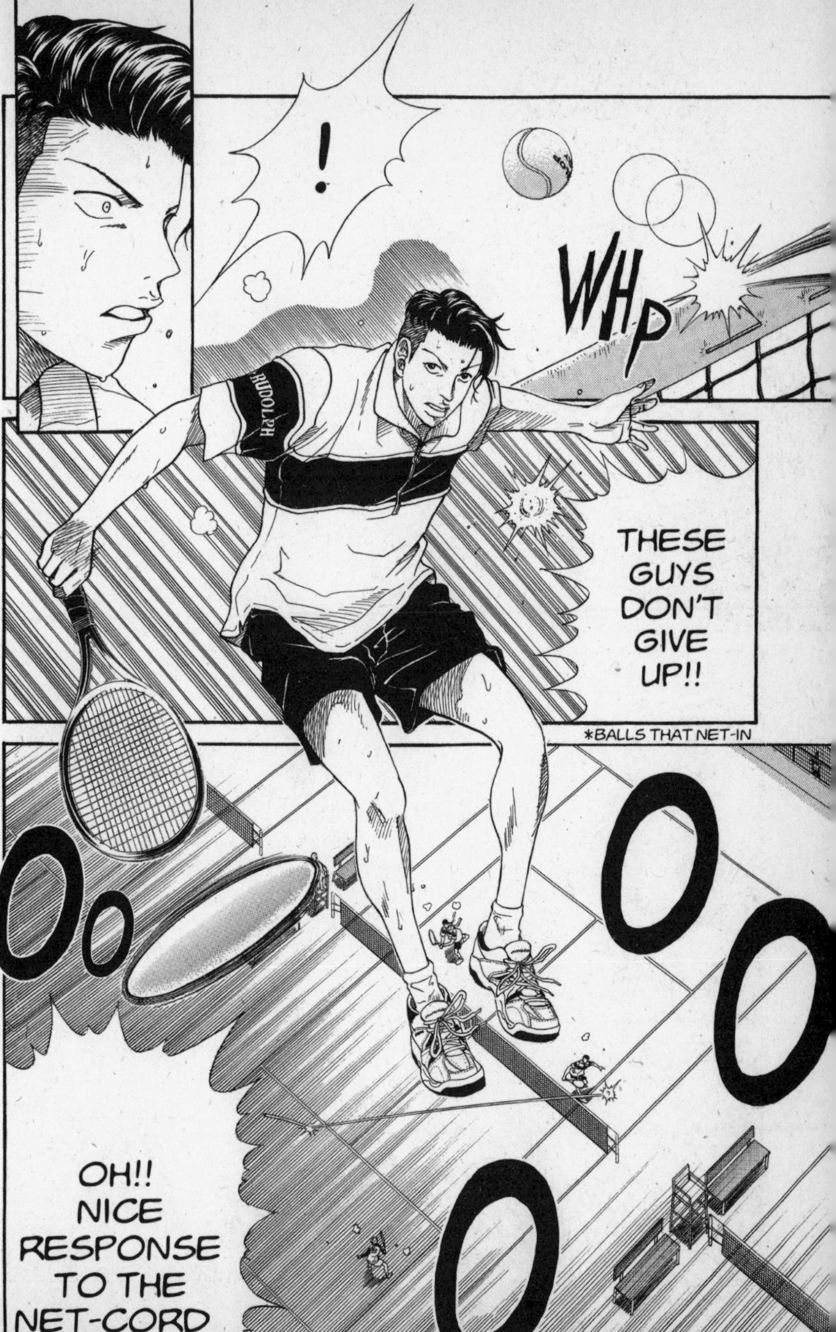
WHP
!
THESE GUYS DON'T GIVE UP!!
OH!! NICE RESPONSE TO THE NET-CORD BALL*!!
OOOOO
RUDOLPH

*BALLS THAT NET-IN

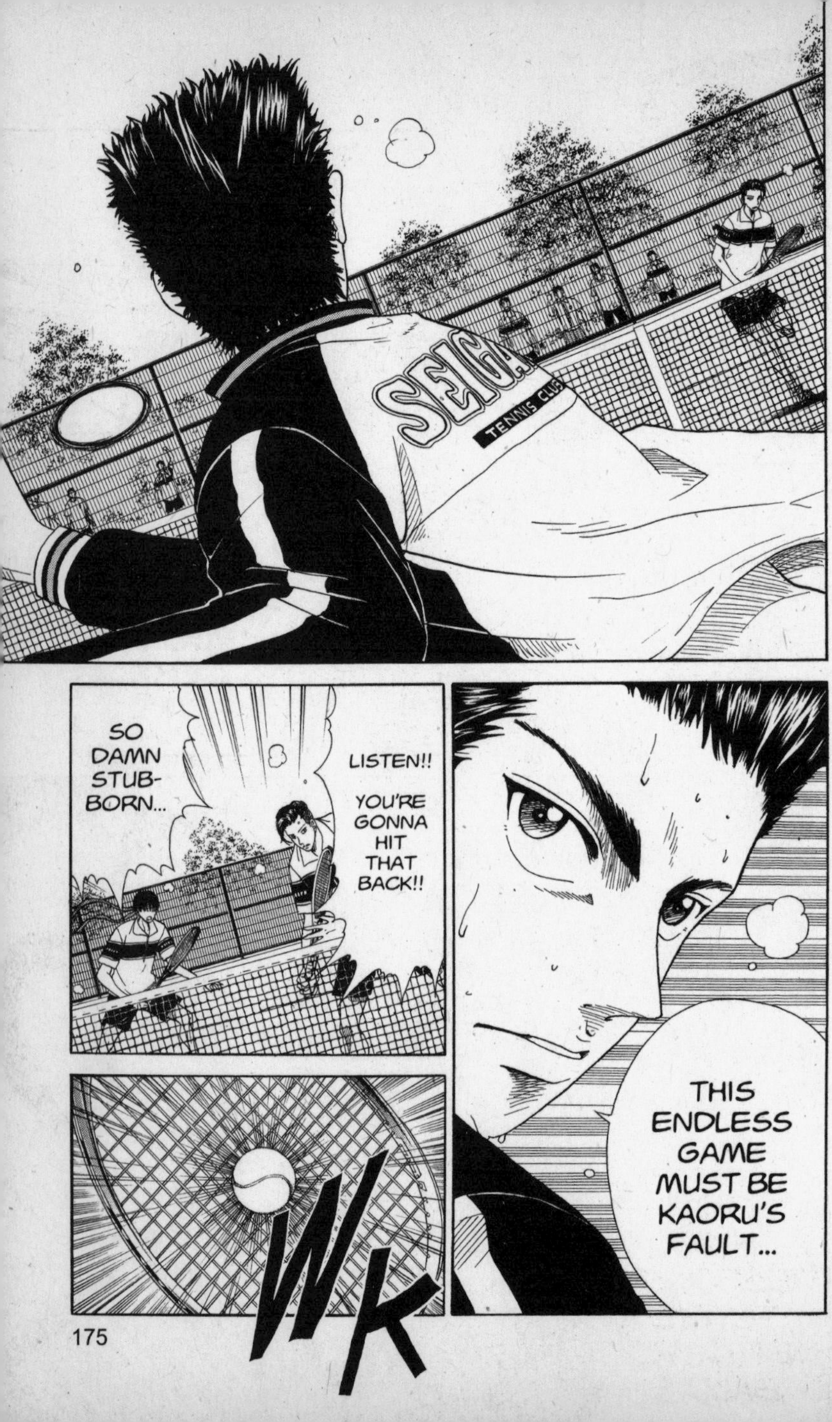
THIS ENDLESS GAME MUST BE KAORU'S FAULT...
LISTEN!! YOU'RE GONNA HIT THAT BACK!!
SO DAMN STUB-BORN...
WK

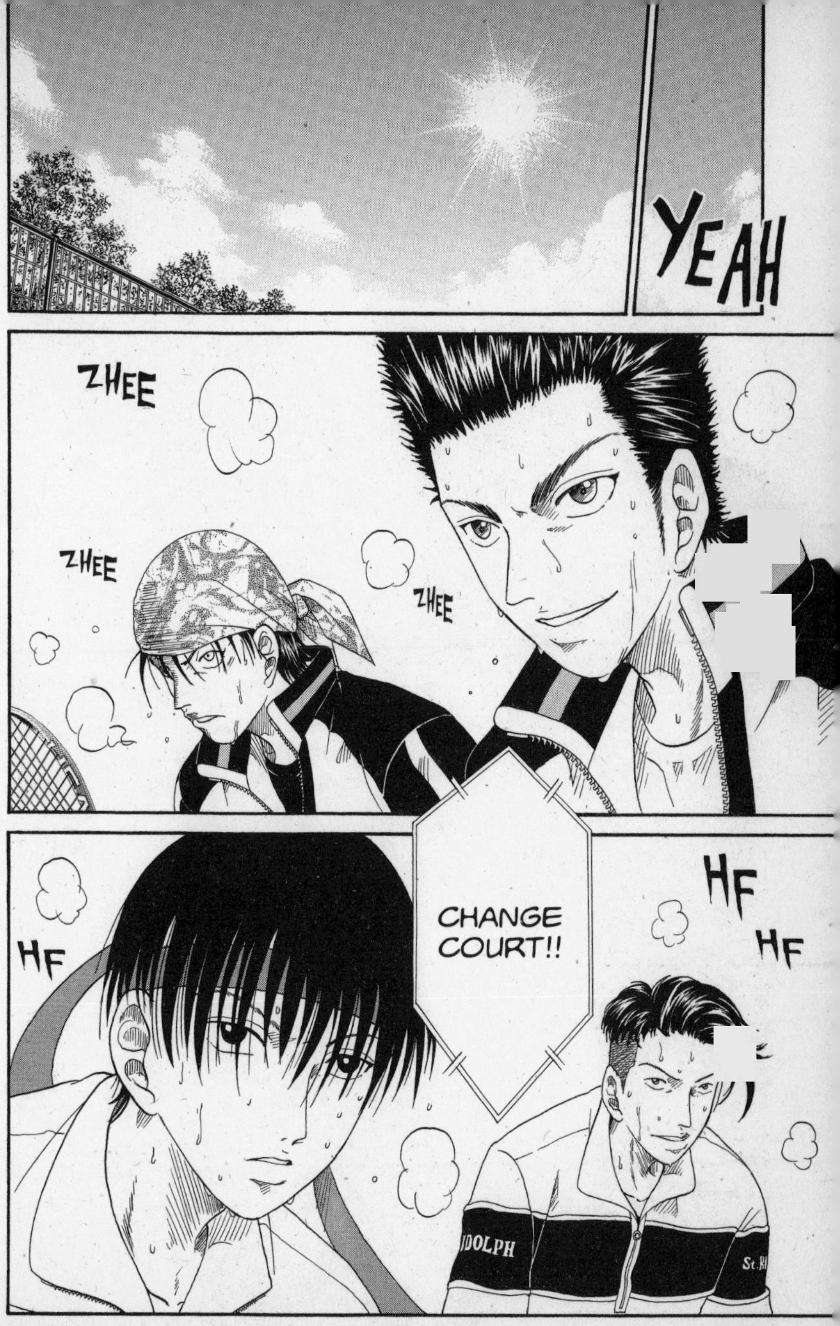
YEAH
ZHEE
ZHEE
ZHEE
HF
HF
CHANGE COURT!!
HF
DOLPH
St.R

READ THIS WAY

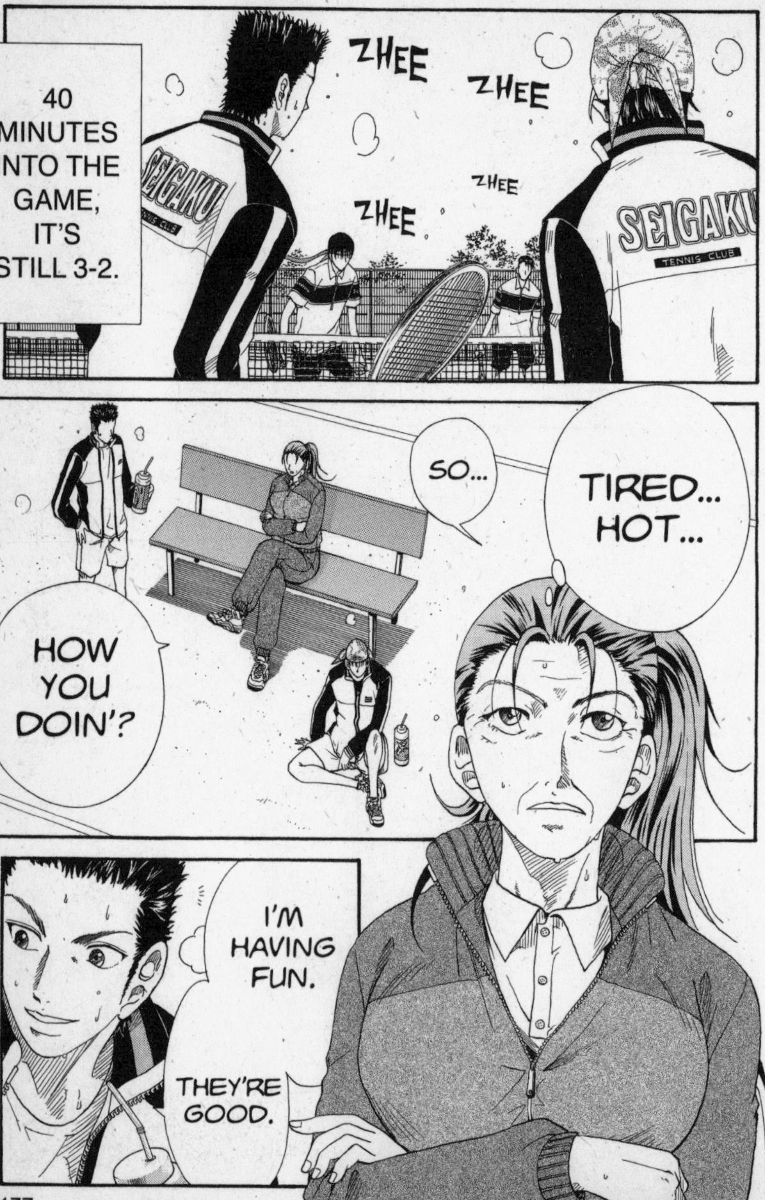
40 MINUTES INTO THE GAME, IT'S STILL 3-2.
ZHEE
ZHEE
ZHEE
ZHEE
SEIGAKU
TENNIS CLUB
SEIGAKU
TIRED... HOT...
SO...
HOW YOU DOIN'?
I'M HAVING FUN.
THEY'RE GOOD.

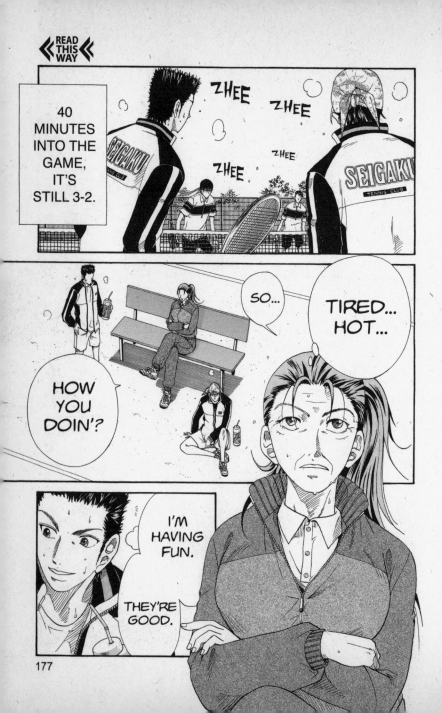

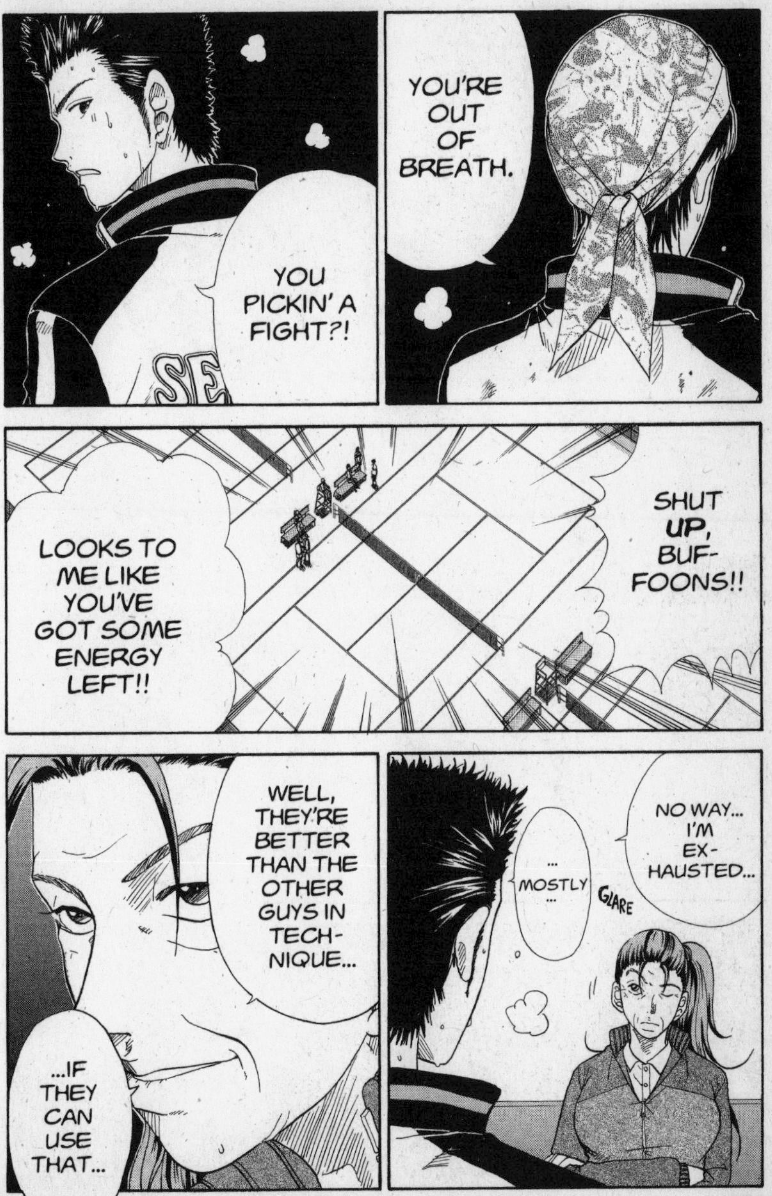
YOU'RE OUT OF BREATH.
YOU PICKIN' A FIGHT?!
SHUT UP, BUFFOONS!!
LOOKS TO ME LIKE YOU'VE GOT SOME ENERGY LEFT!!
NO WAY... I'M EXHAUSTED...
... MOSTLY ...
GLARE
WELL, THEY'RE BETTER THAN THE OTHER GUYS IN TECHNIQUE...
...IF THEY CAN USE THAT...

READ THIS WAY

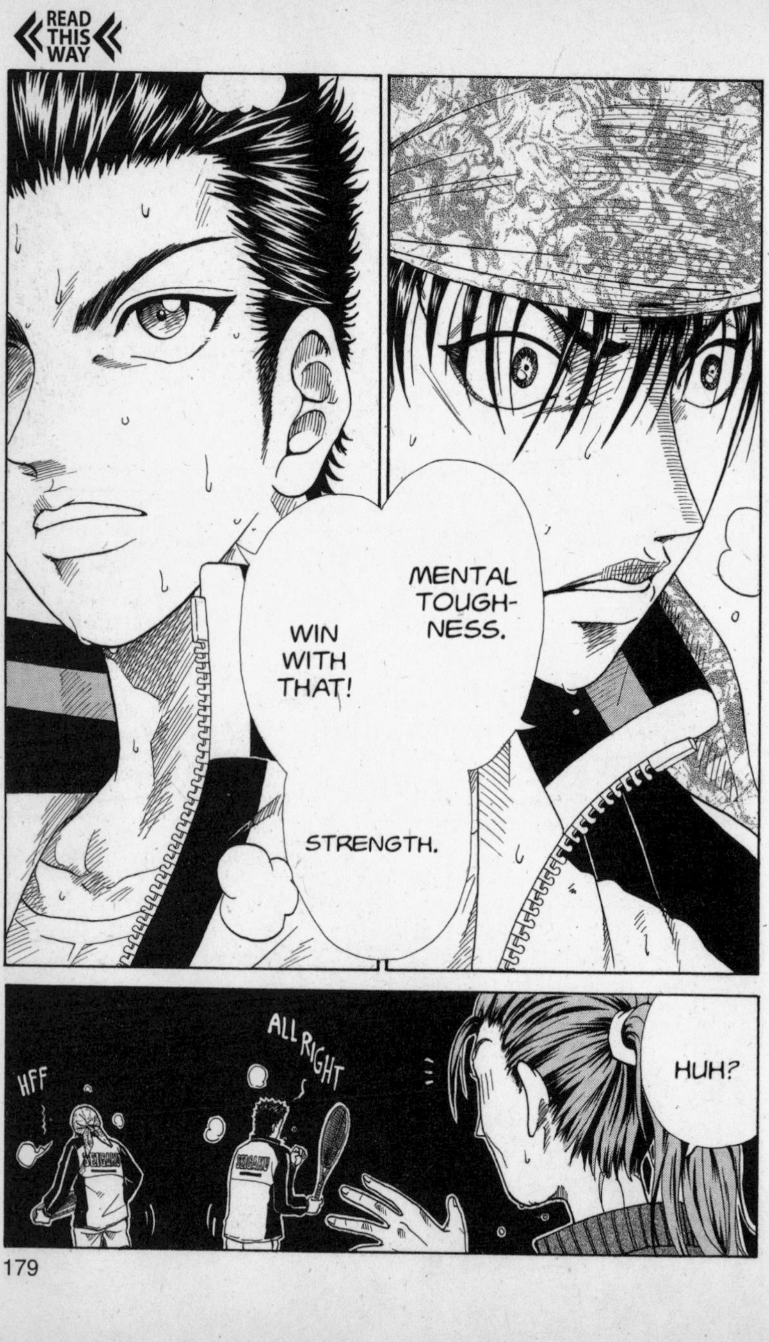
MENTAL TOUGH-NESS.
WIN WITH THAT!
STRENGTH.
HUH?
ALL RIGHT
HFF

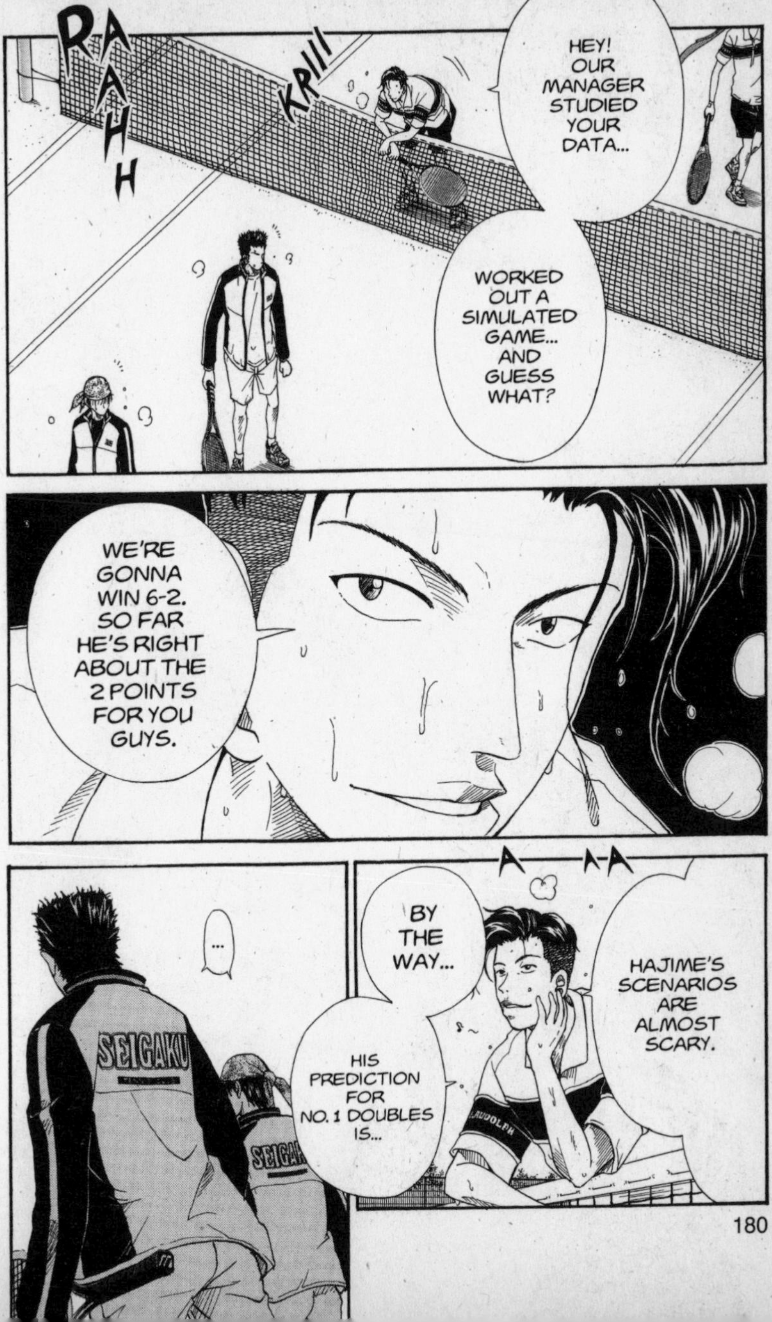
RAAHH
KRIII
HEY! OUR MANAGER STUDIED YOUR DATA...
WORKED OUT A SIMULATED GAME... AND GUESS WHAT?
WE'RE GONNA WIN 6-2. SO FAR HE'S RIGHT ABOUT THE 2 POINTS FOR YOU GUYS.
A AA
HAJIME'S SCENARIOS ARE ALMOST SCARY.
BY THE WAY...
HIS PREDICTION FOR NO. 1 DOUBLES IS...
...
SEIGAKU
SEIGAKU

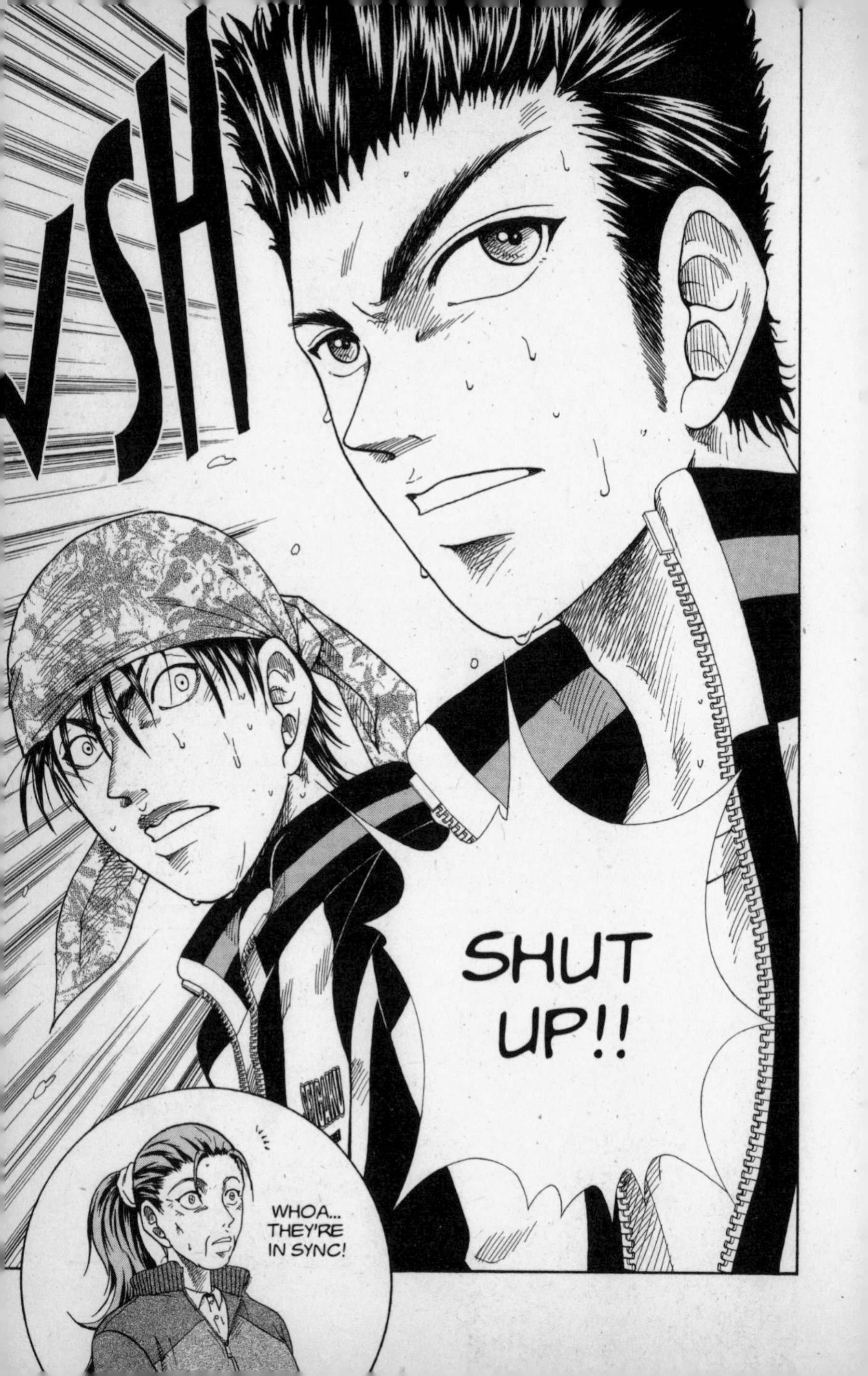
SHUT UP!!
WHOA... THEY'RE IN SYNC!

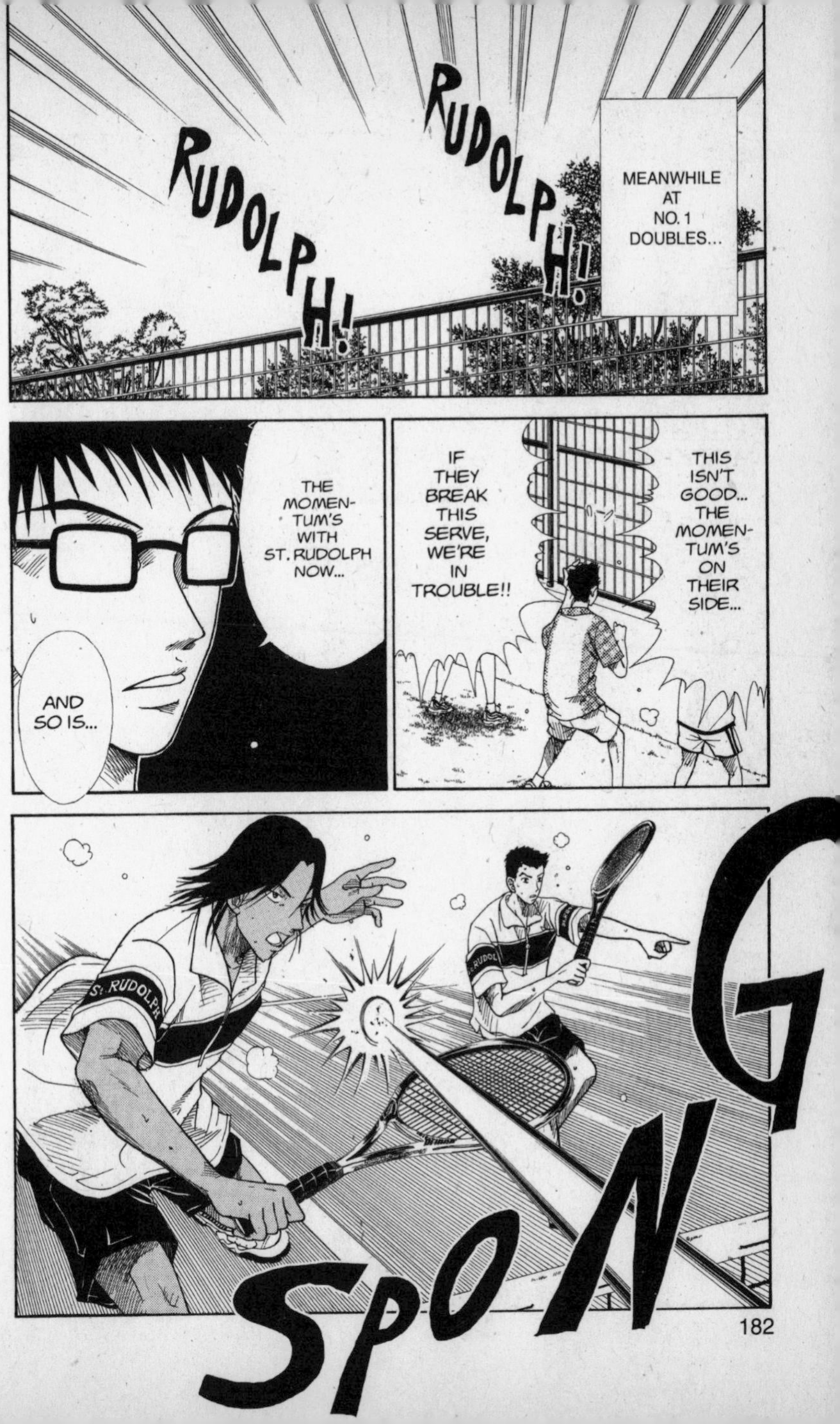
MEANWHILE AT NO. 1 DOUBLES...
RUDOLPH!
RUDOLPH!
THIS ISN'T GOOD... THE MOMEN-TUM'S ON THEIR SIDE...
IF THEY BREAK THIS SERVE, WE'RE IN TROUBLE!!
THE MOMEN-TUM'S WITH ST. RUDOLPH NOW...
AND SO IS...
ST. RUDOLPH
SPONG

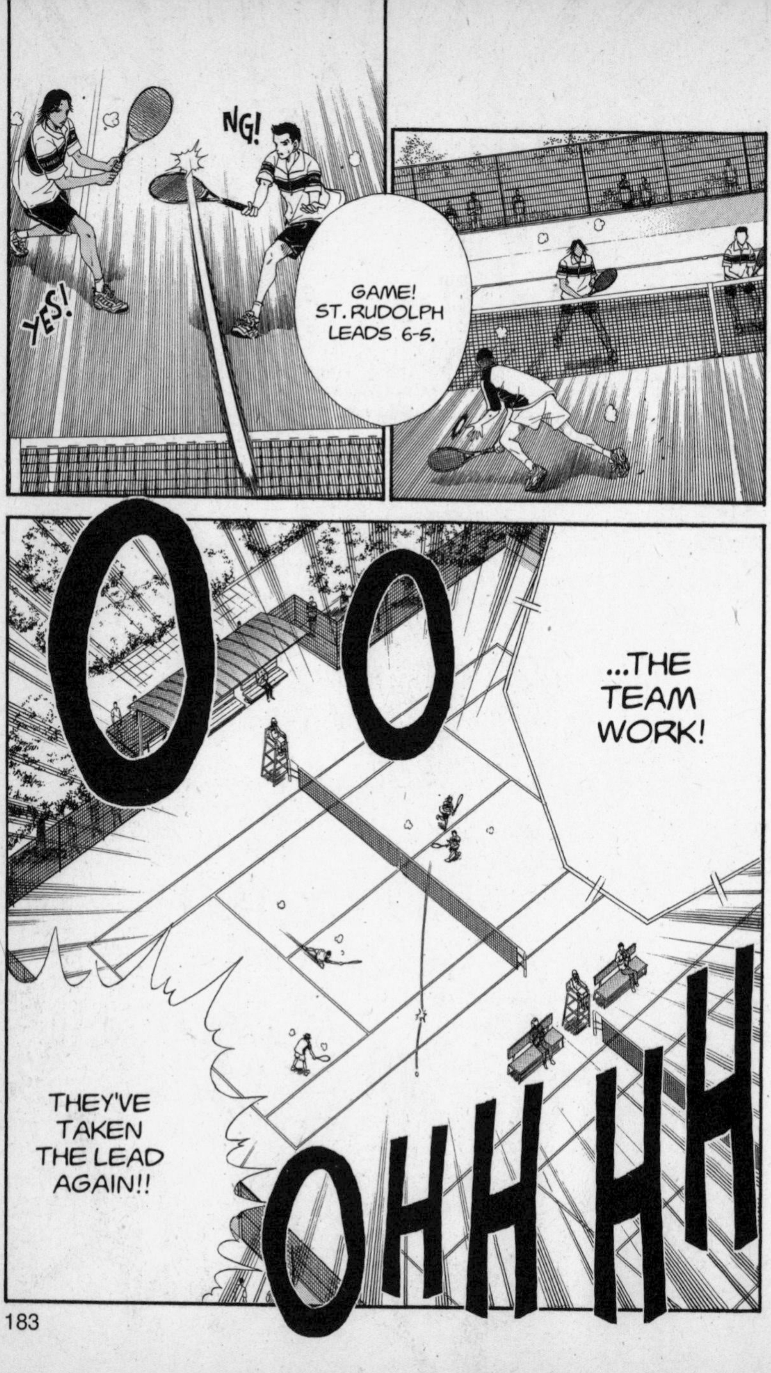
NG!
GAME! ST. RUDOLPH LEADS 6-5.
YES!
...THE TEAM WORK!
OO
THEY'VE TAKEN THE LEAD AGAIN!!
OHHHH

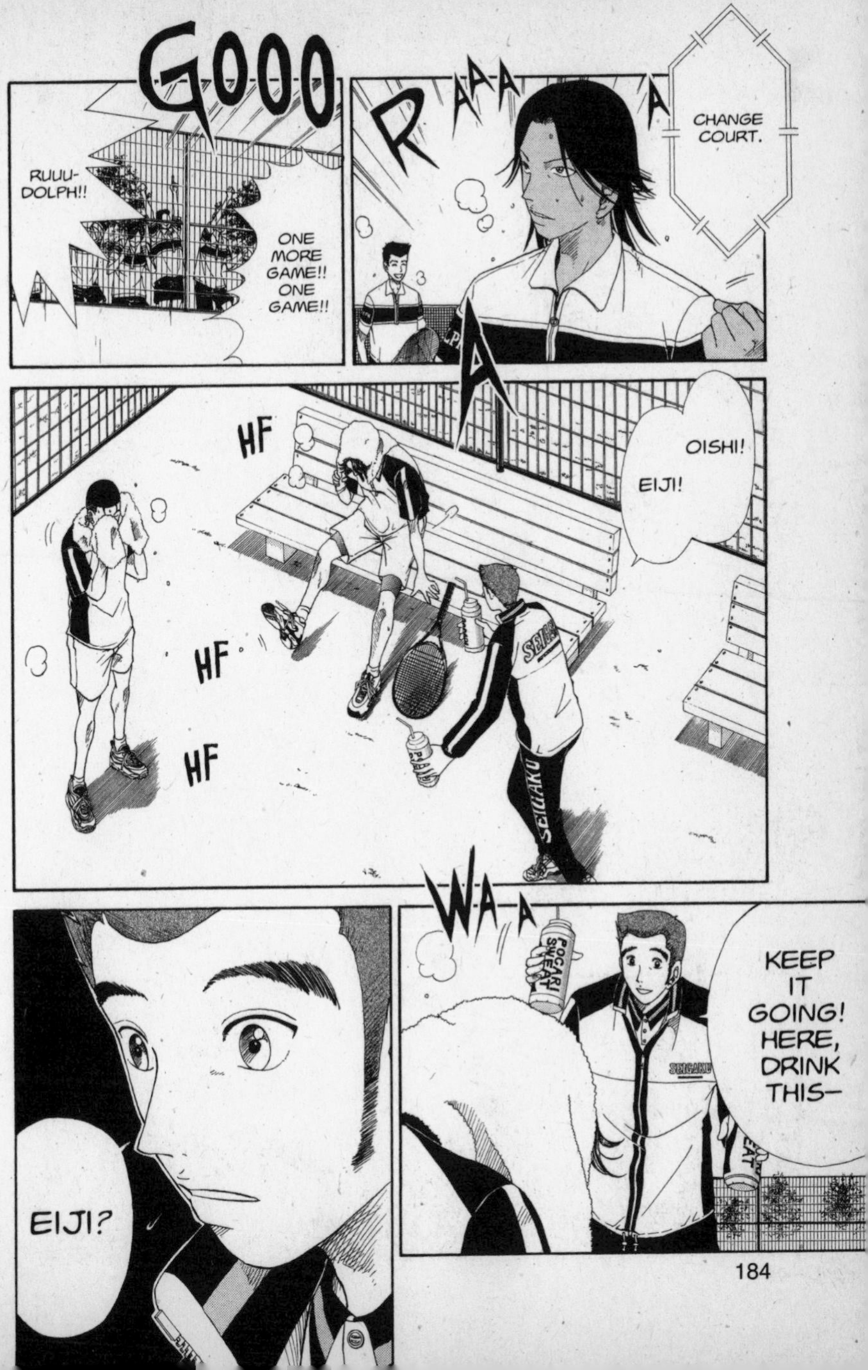

GOOO
RAAA A
CHANGE COURT.
RUUU-DOLPH!!
ONE MORE GAME!! ONE GAME!!
OISHI!
EIJI!
HF
HF
HF
WAA
KEEP IT GOING! HERE, DRINK THIS—
POCARI SWEAT
EIJI?

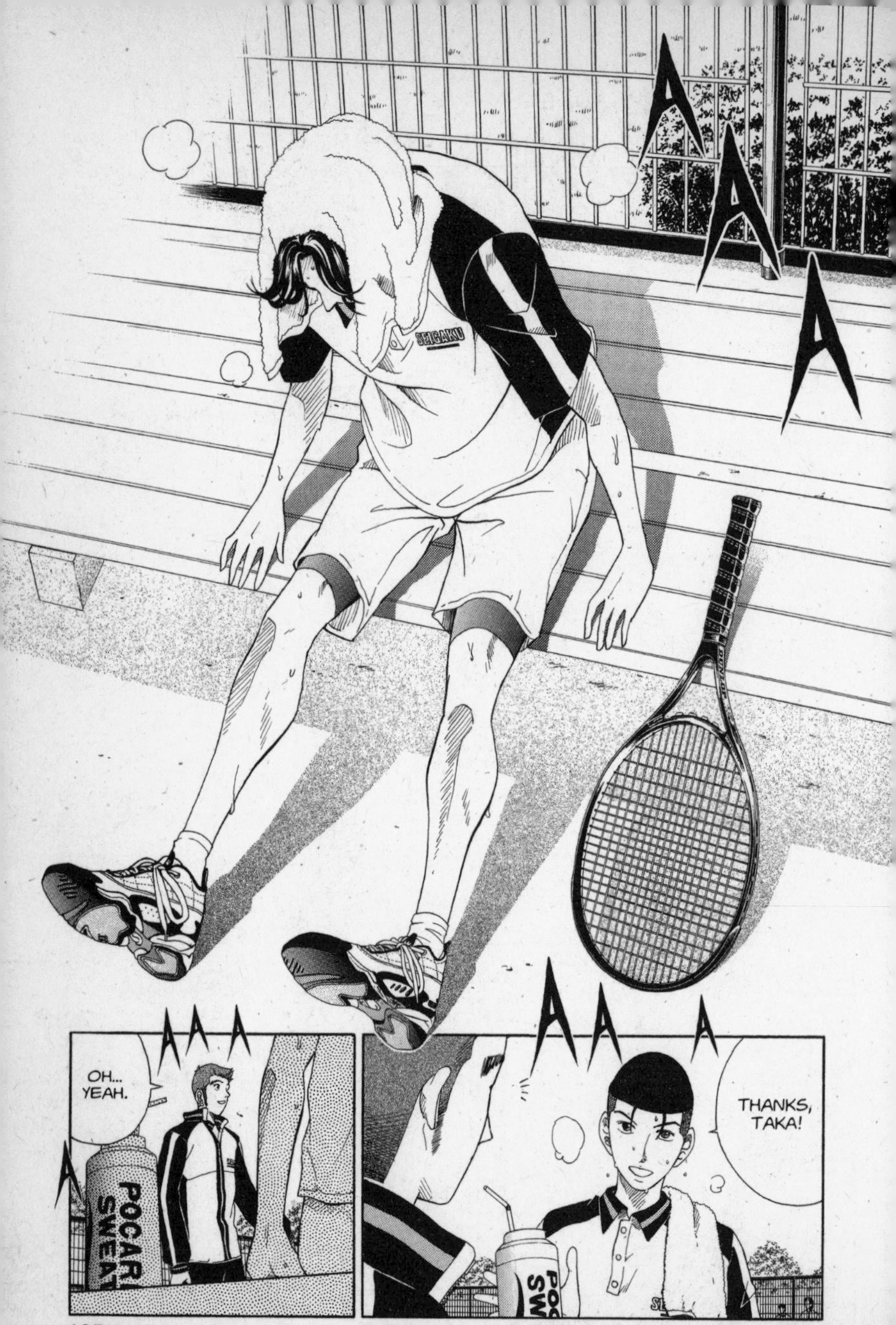

A A A A
SEIGAKU
A A A
THANKS, TAKA!
A A A A
OH... YEAH.
POCARI SWEAT

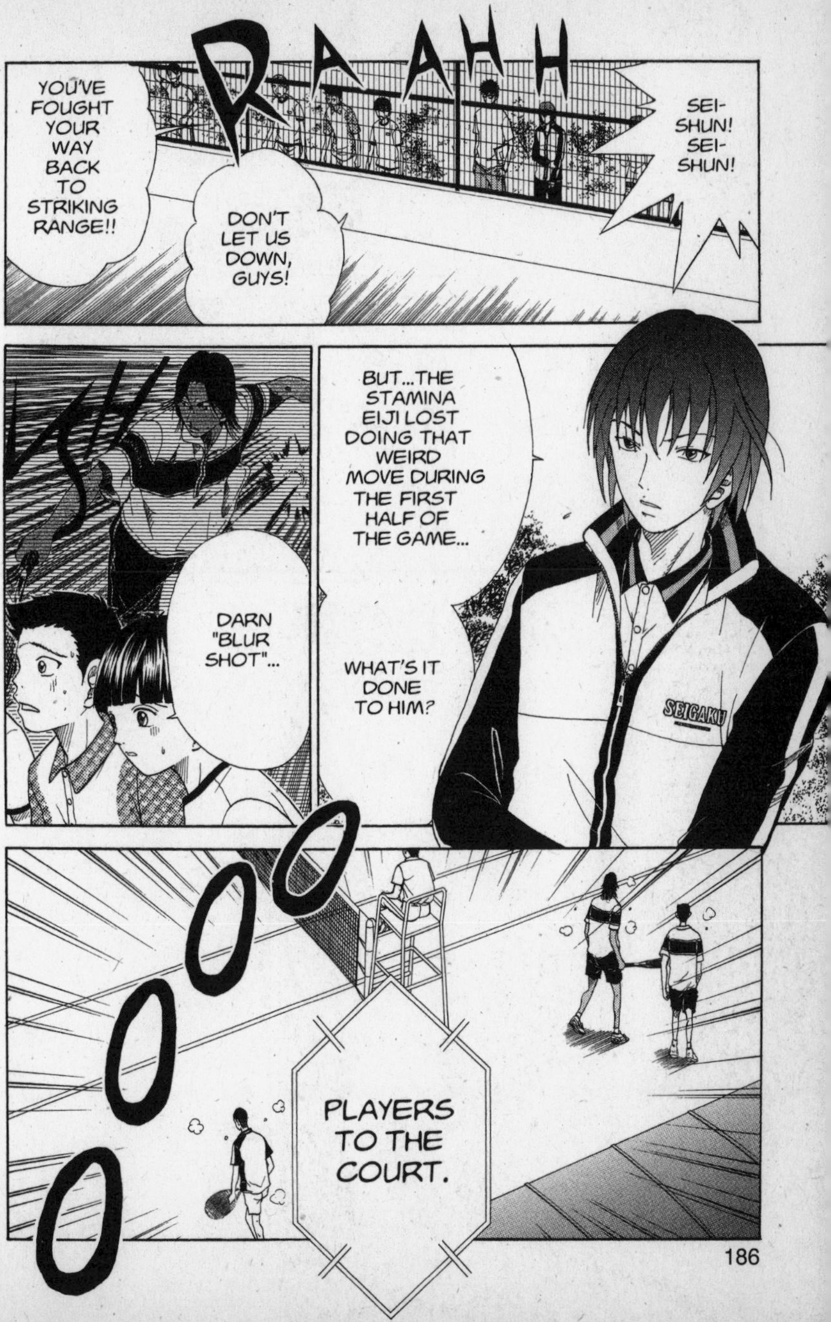
SEI-SHUN! SEI-SHUN!
RAAHH
DON'T LET US DOWN, GUYS!
YOU'VE FOUGHT YOUR WAY BACK TO STRIKING RANGE!!
BUT...THE STAMINA EIJI LOST DOING THAT WEIRD MOVE DURING THE FIRST HALF OF THE GAME...
WHAT'S IT DONE TO HIM?
DARN "BLUR SHOT"...
PLAYERS TO THE COURT.
OOOOOO

READ THIS WAY

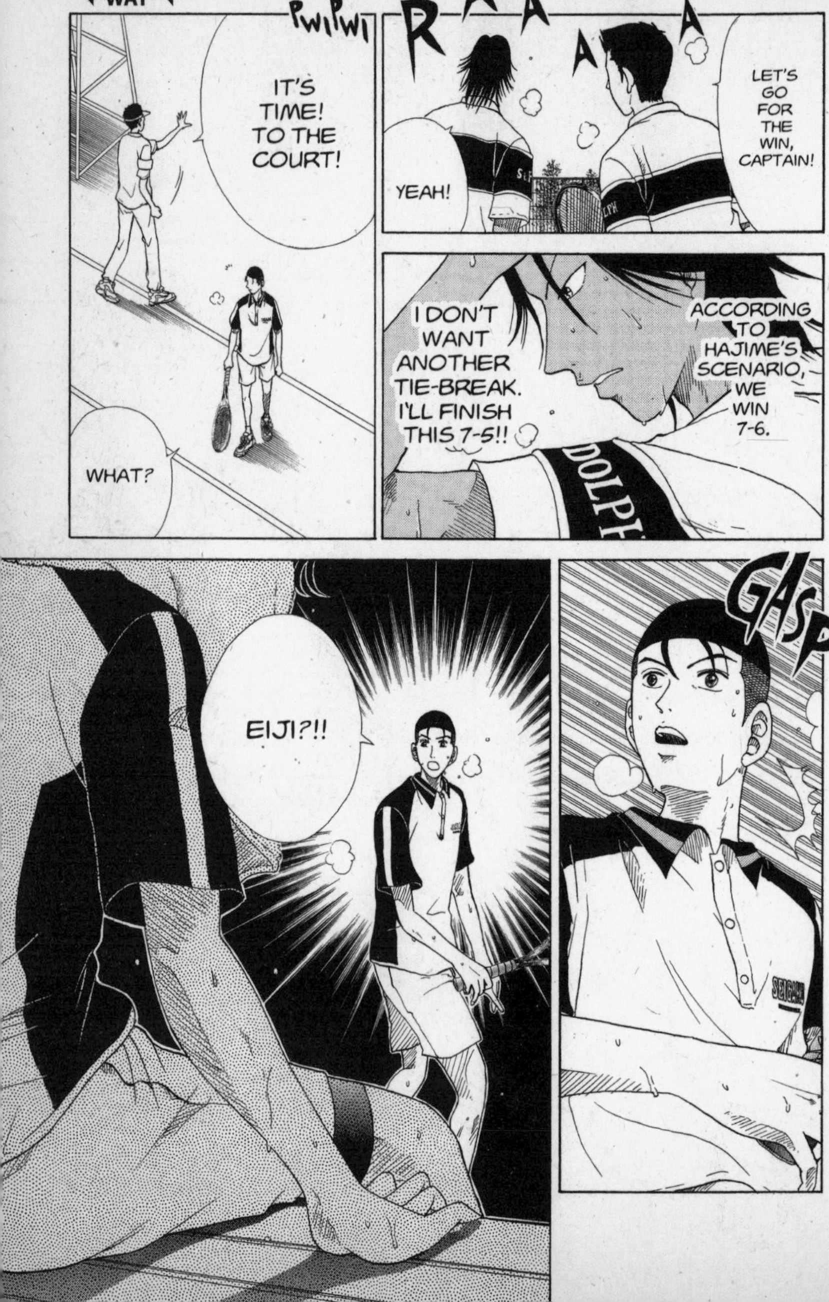

LET'S GO FOR THE WIN, CAPTAIN!
RAAAAA
YEAH!
ACCORDING TO HAJIME'S SCENARIO, WE WIN 7-6.
I DON'T WANT ANOTHER TIE-BREAK. I'LL FINISH THIS 7-5!!
PWIPWI
IT'S TIME! TO THE COURT!
WHAT?
GASP
EIJI?!!

THE PRINCE OF TENNIS

PRINCE OF TENNIS
SPECIAL EDITION

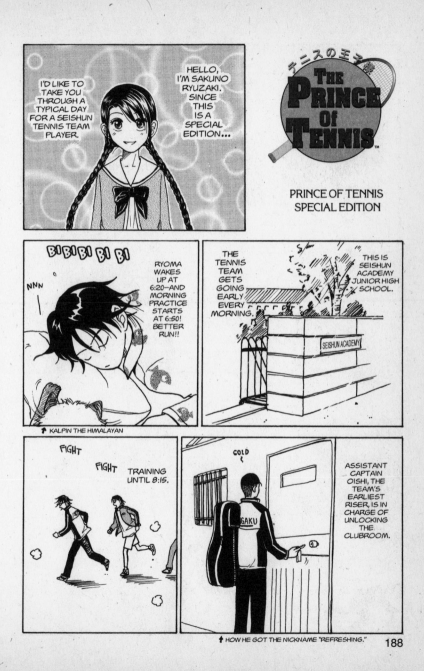

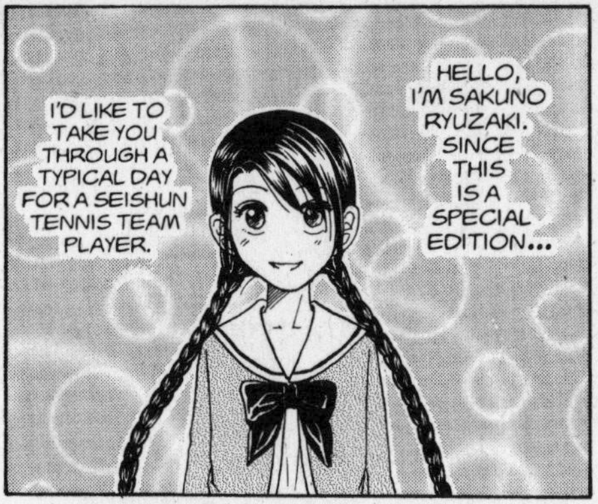
HELLO, I'M SAKUNO RYUZAKI. SINCE THIS IS A SPECIAL EDITION...
I'D LIKE TO TAKE YOU THROUGH A TYPICAL DAY FOR A SEISHUN TENNIS TEAM PLAYER.

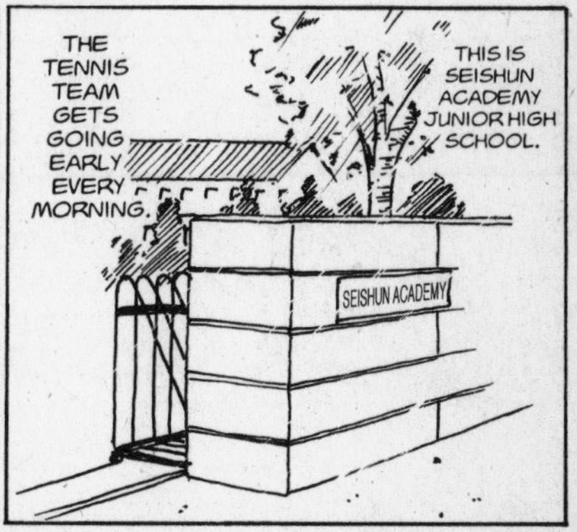
THIS IS SEISHUN ACADEMY JUNIOR HIGH SCHOOL.
THE TENNIS TEAM GETS GOING EARLY EVERY MORNING.
SEISHUN ACADEMY

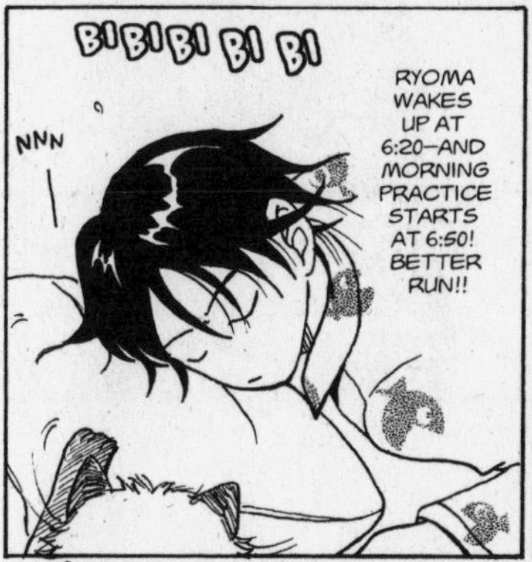
BI BI BI BI BI
RYOMA WAKES UP AT 6:20—AND MORNING PRACTICE STARTS AT 6:50! BETTER RUN!!
NNN

↑ KALPIN THE HIMALAYAN

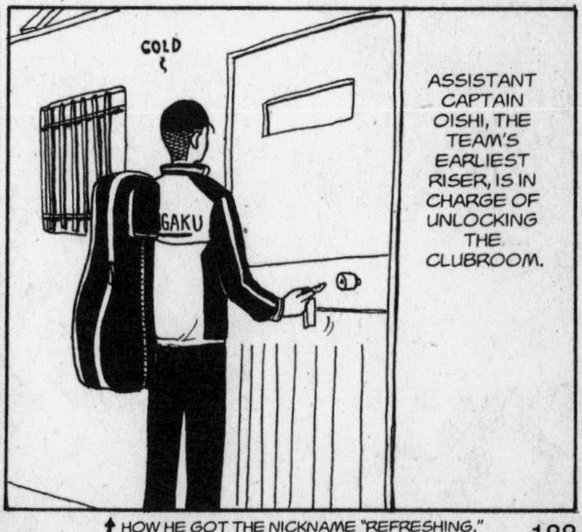
ASSISTANT CAPTAIN OISHI, THE TEAM'S EARLIEST RISER, IS IN CHARGE OF UNLOCKING THE CLUBROOM.
COLD
GAKU

↑ HOW HE GOT THE NICKNAME "REFRESHING."

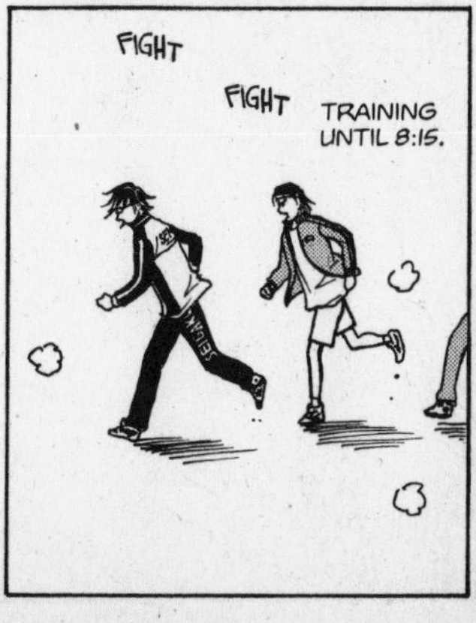
TRAINING UNTIL 8:15.
FIGHT
FIGHT
SEIGAKU

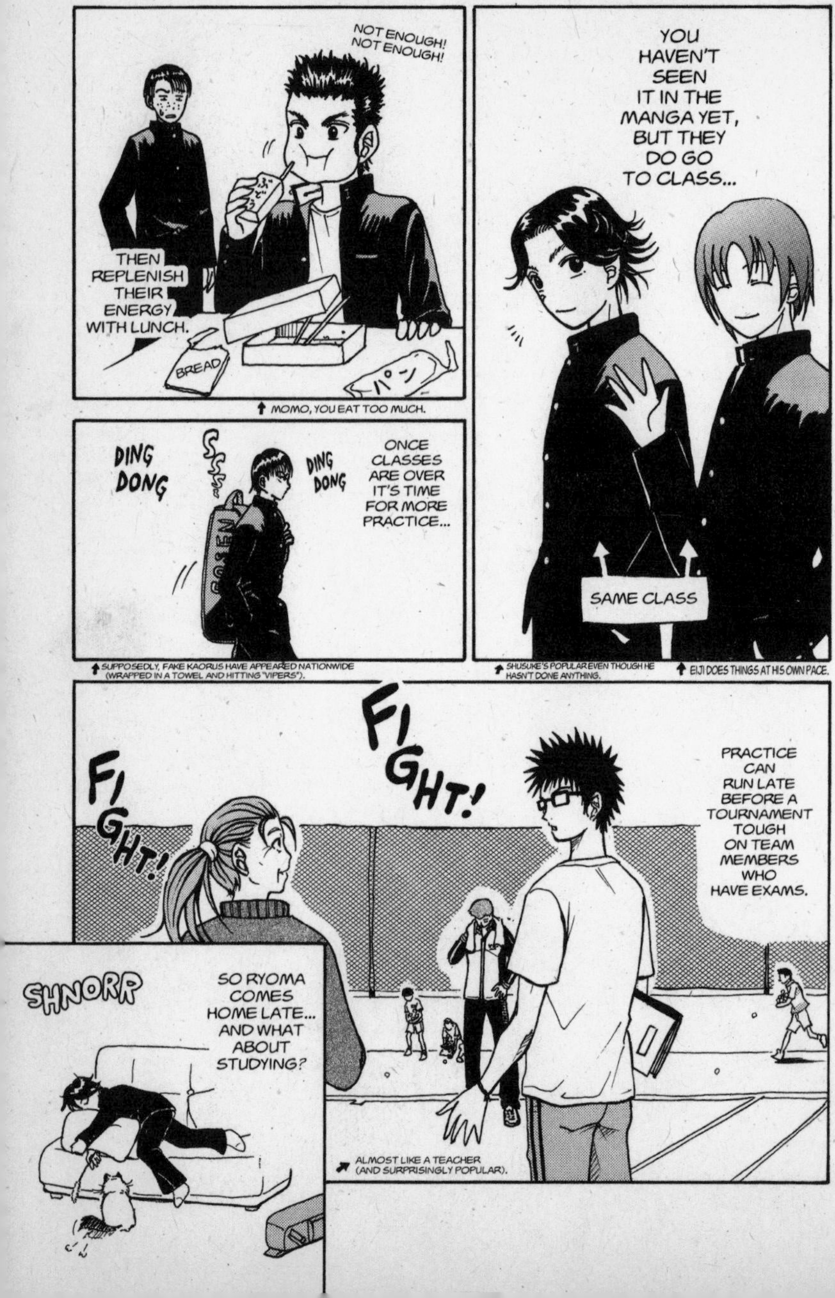
YOU HAVEN'T SEEN IT IN THE MANGA YET, BUT THEY DO GO TO CLASS...
SAME CLASS
SHUSUKE'S POPULAR EVEN THOUGH HE HASN'T DONE ANYTHING.
EIJI DOES THINGS AT HIS OWN PACE.
NOT ENOUGH! NOT ENOUGH!
THEN REPLENISH THEIR ENERGY WITH LUNCH.
BREAD
MOMO, YOU EAT TOO MUCH.
ONCE CLASSES ARE OVER IT'S TIME FOR MORE PRACTICE...
DING DONG
DING DONG
SUPPOSEDLY, FAKE KAORUS HAVE APPEARED NATIONWIDE (WRAPPED IN A TOWEL AND HITTING "VIPERS").
FIGHT!
FIGHT!
PRACTICE CAN RUN LATE BEFORE A TOURNAMENT TOUGH ON TEAM MEMBERS WHO HAVE EXAMS.
ALMOST LIKE A TEACHER (AND SURPRISINGLY POPULAR).
SO RYOMA COMES HOME LATE... AND WHAT ABOUT STUDYING?
SHNORR

In the Next Volume...

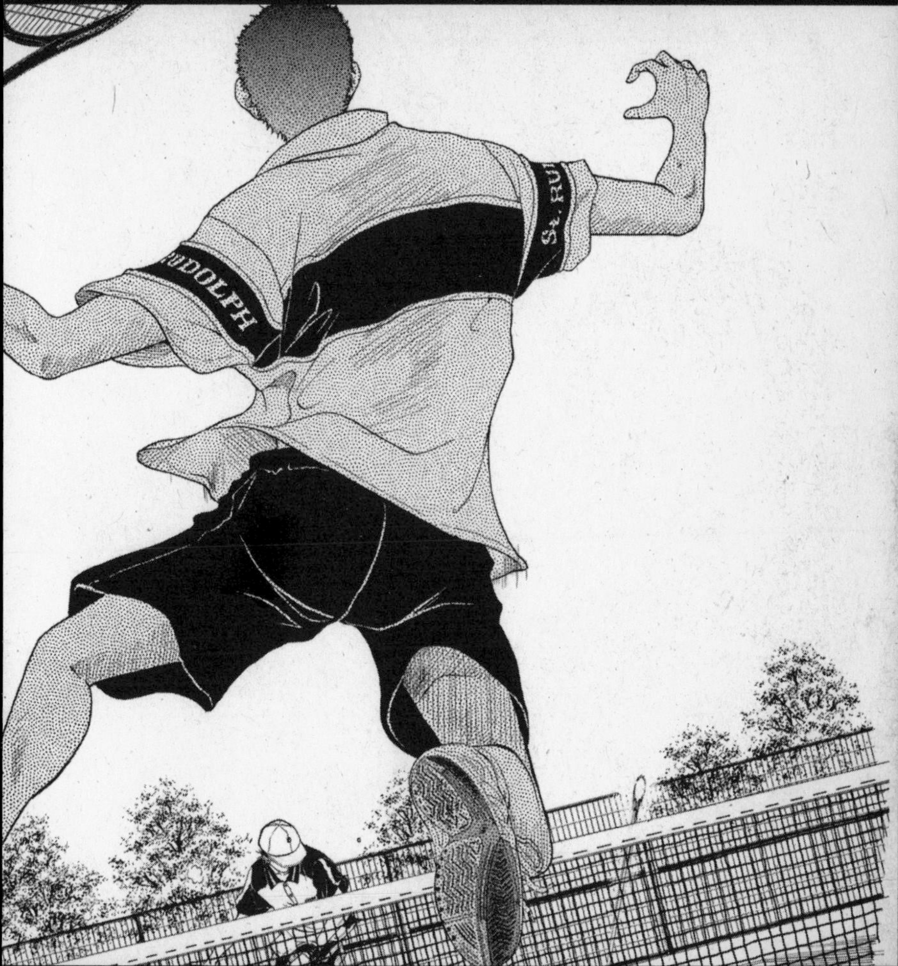

RUDOLPH
St. RU

With Eiji—Shuichiro's doubles partner—too exhausted to even step on the court, the fate of Seishun Academy rests on the shoulders of the other powerhouse doubles tandem of Momo and Kaoru. But danger lurks at every corner, for The Prince of Tennis Ryoma Echizen encounters trouble against St. Rudolph's lefty killer Yuta as well. After all, it's not everyday that Ryoma faces a player specifically trained to demolish lefties...

Available in July 2005

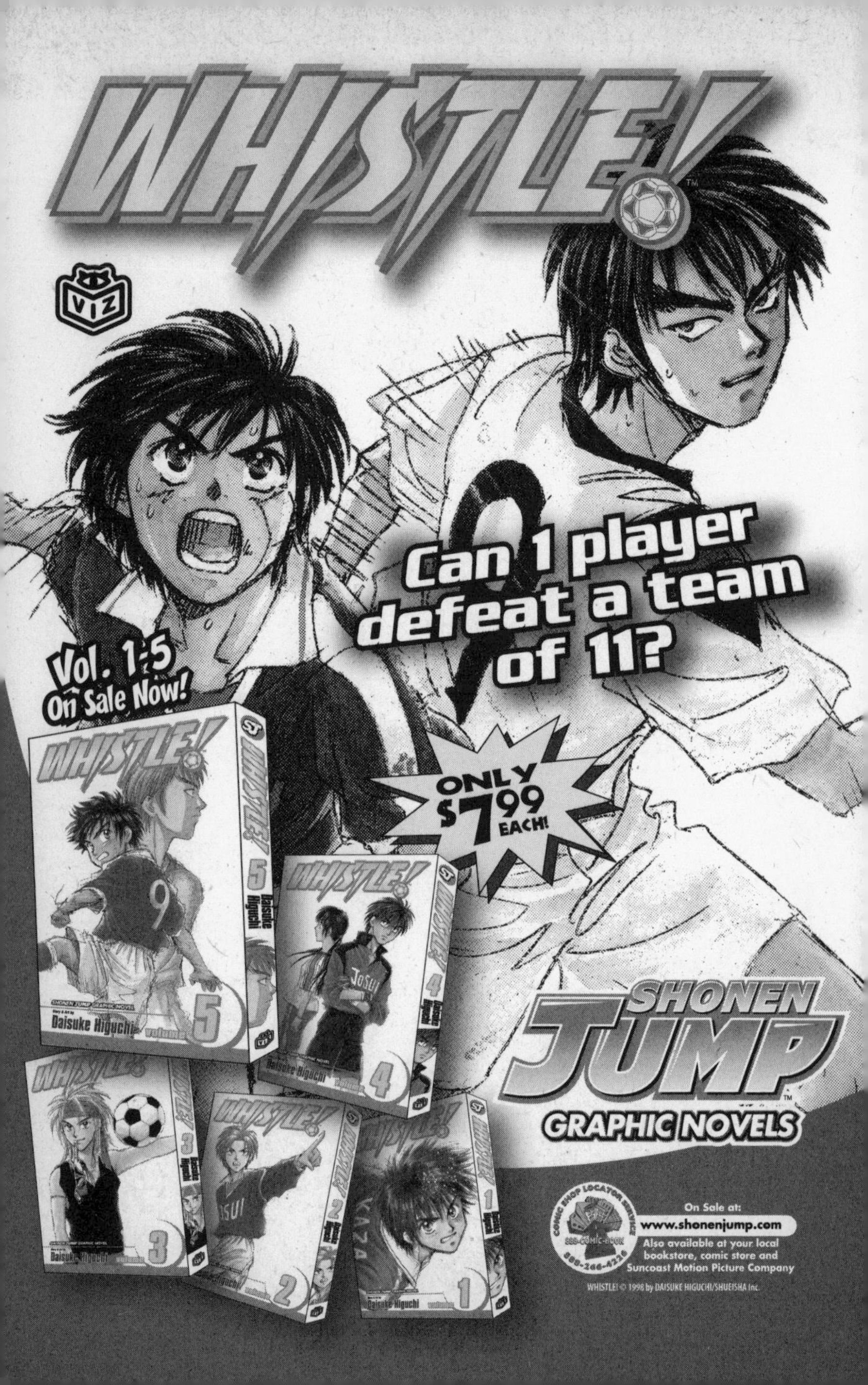
WHISTLE!
Can 1 player defeat a team of 11?
Vol. 1-5 On Sale Now!
ONLY $7.99 EACH!
SHONEN JUMP
GRAPHIC NOVELS
COMIC SHOP LOCATOR SERVICE
888-COMIC-BOOK
888-266-4226
On Sale at:
www.shonenjump.com
Also available at your local bookstore, comic store and Suncoast Motion Picture Company
WHISTLE! © 1998 by DAISUKE HIGUCHI/SHUEISHA Inc.

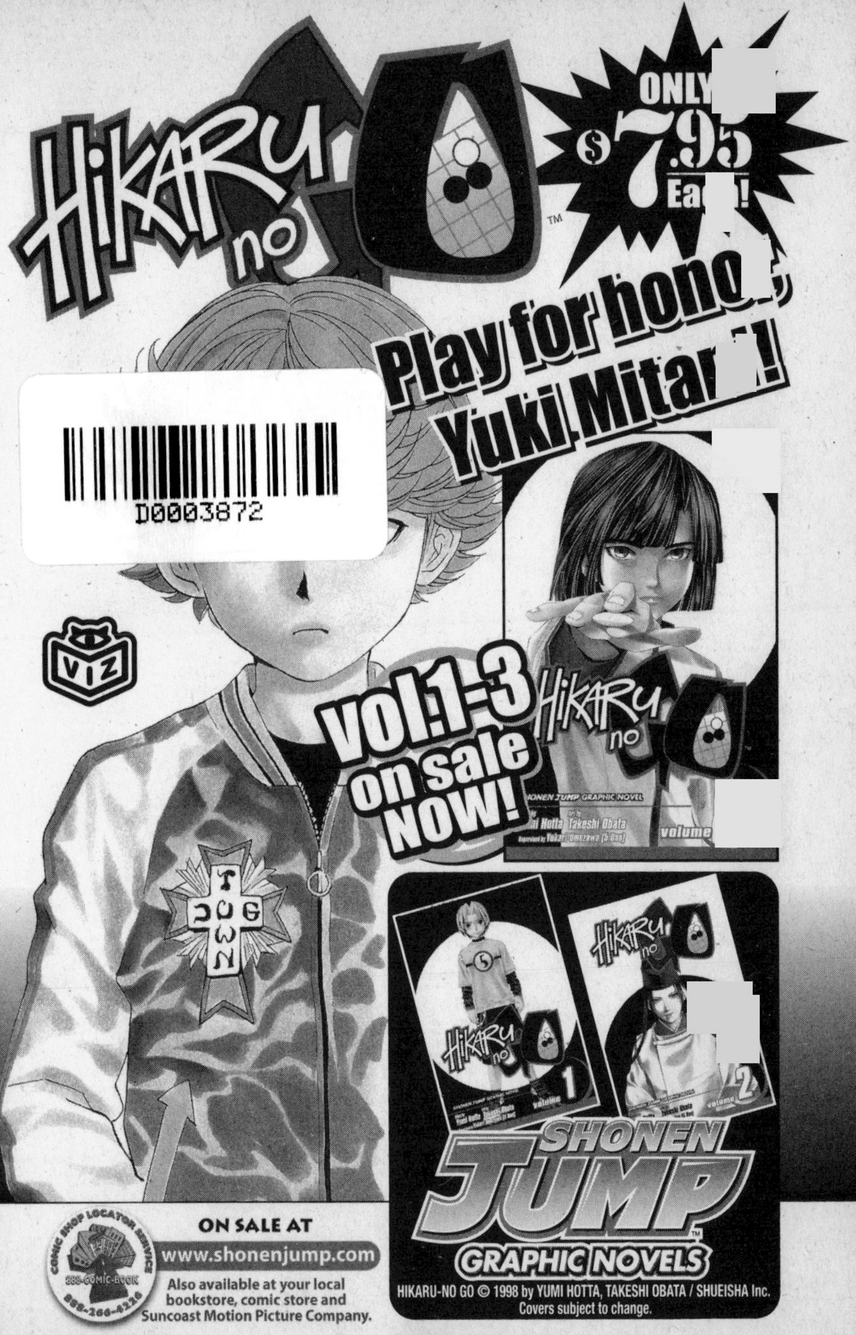

HiKARU no
ONLY
$7.95
Ea !
Play for hono
Yuki Mita !
D0003872
vol.1-3 on sale NOW!
HiKARU no
HiKARU no
HiKARU no
SHONEN JUMP GRAPHIC NOVELS
ON SALE AT
www.shonenjump.com
Also available at your local bookstore, comic store and Suncoast Motion Picture Company.
COMIC SHOP LOCATOR SERVICE
888-COMIC-BOOK
888-266-4226
HIKARU-NO GO © 1998 by YUMI HOTTA, TAKESHI OBATA / SHUEISHA Inc.
Covers subject to change.